## DATE DUE

DEMCO, INC. 38-2931

# BEHAVIORAL COUNSELING IN MEDICINE

# BEHAVIORAL COUNSELING IN MEDICINE

## Strategies for Modifying At-Risk Behavior

Michael L. Russell, Ph.D.

New York   Oxford
OXFORD UNIVERSITY PRESS
1986

Oxford University Press

Oxford   New York   Toronto
Delhi   Bombay   Calcutta   Madras   Karachi
Petaling Jaya   Singapore   Hong Kong   Tokyo
Nairobi   Dar es Salaam   Cape Town
Melbourne   Auckland

and associated companies in
Beirut   Berlin   Ibadan   Nicosia

APR 1 4 1987.

Copyright © 1986 by Oxford University Press, Inc.

Published by Oxford University Press, Inc.,
200 Madison Avenue, New York, New York 10016

Oxford is a registered trademark of Oxford University Press

Library of Congress Cataloging-in-Publication Data

Russell, Michael L.
  Behavioral counseling in medicine.

  Includes bibliographies and index.
  1. Behavior therapy.   2. Counseling.   3. Medical
personnel and patient.   4. Allied health personnel and
patient.   I. Title.   [DNLM: 1. Behavior Therapy—
methods.   2. Counseling—methods.   WM 425 R965b]
RC489.B4R87   1986        616.89'142        85-29668
ISBN 0-19-503990-4

Printing (last digit):   9 8 7 6 5 4 3 2 1

Printed in the United States of America
on acid-free paper

# Contents

# BEHAVIORAL COUNSELING IN MEDICINE

# 1. Introduction

## Health Behaviors in Medicine

During the twentieth century clinical medicine has experienced a major shift in emphasis due to a marked decline in the occurrence of the acute infectious diseases. Diseases such as influenza, measles, mumps, pneumonia, polio, smallpox, and tuberculosis no longer threaten us as they once did. Advances in pharmacology and public health practices have controlled or eliminated the diseases that were the major causes of mortality and morbidity prior to this century.

Increasingly, the physician's clinical work is devoted to managing chronic conditions that persist and slowly progress despite medical treatment. Currently, chronic diseases comprise the principal diagnosis for 16 of the top 20 conditions for office visits to internists (see Table 1). These include cardiovascular, endocrine, gastrointestinal, immunological, neoplastic, and pulmonary diseases.

Accompanying this shift in emphasis has been a major change in the clinician's role. The acute illnesses demand immediate intensive treatment of the patient over a relatively brief period of time with the goal of curing the disease. The clinician's role is to diagnose the illness and select an appropriate treatment for the patient. The patient is only minimally involved in this process, providing specific information about symptoms when requested. It is anticipated that if the diagnosis is accurate, then the treatment will be successful and the patient will return to a normal level of functioning upon recovery.

In contrast, the chronic diseases require continuing, often palliative treatment, frequently with little expectation of cure. The goal of treatment is to halt or slow the disease's progression, while recognizing that eventually the patient may suffer disability or death from it. Unlike the patient with an acute illness, the patient with a chronic disease becomes more actively involved in his own care. He is expected to return for periodic follow-up office visits so that the

Table 1. 20 most frequent principal diagnoses for office visits to internists, 1980–1981*

| Principal diagnosis | Percent distribution |
|---|---|
| 1. Essential hypertension | 12.5 |
| 2. Diabetes mellitus | 4.9 |
| 3. Other forms of chronic ischemic heart disease | 3.9 |
| 4. Osteoarthritis and allied disorders | 2.3 |
| 5. Acute upper respiratory infections at multiple or unspecified sites | 2.1 |
| 6. Rheumatoid arthritis and other inflammatory polyarthropathies | 2.1 |
| 7. Allergic rhinitis (including hay fever) | 1.4 |
| 8. Obesity and other hyperalimentation | 1.2 |
| 9. Hypertensive heart disease | 1.1 |
| 10. Bronchitis, not specified as acute or chronic | 1.1 |
| 11. Symptoms involving respiratory system and other chest symptoms | 1.1 |
| 12. Cardiac dysrhythmias | 1.1 |
| 13. Asthma | 1.1 |
| 14. Angina pectoris | 1.0 |
| 15. Other disorders of soft tissues | |
| 16. Functional digestive disorders, not elsewhere classified | 0.9 |
| 17. Chronic airway obstruction, not elsewhere classified | 0.9 |
| 18. Malignant neoplasm of female breast | 0.9 |
| 19. Acute pharyngitis | 0.9 |
| 20. Peripheral enthesopathies and allied syndromes | 0.9 |

*Listing excludes the following diagnoses: general medical examination, general symptoms, and neurotic disorders.

Adapted from National Center for Health Statistics, B.K. Cypress: Patterns of ambulatory care in internal medicine. The National Ambulatory Medical Care Survey, United States, January 1980–December 1981. *Vital and Health Statistics*, Series 13, No. 80. DHHS publication No. (PHS) 84-1741. Washington, DC, Public Health Service, 1984.

clinician can monitor his progress, to follow his prescribed medication regimen, and to make specific changes in health-related behaviors.

The effect of changes in health-related behavior for the prevention, moderation or deceleration of a chronic disease is a promising adjunct to traditional treatment. Undesired behaviors such as cigarette smoking, certain dietary patterns (e.g., high sodium, high saturated fat, low fiber), and a low level of physical activity appear to influence many chronic diseases. For example, it has been reported that approximately 30% of type II diabetes (i.e., adult onset) can be controlled without medication if the patient can achieve and maintain a weight

Table 2. Matrix of health behavior changes frequently recommended for secondary prevention in common chronic diseases

| Disease or condition | Health behaviors frequently recommended | | | | | |
|---|---|---|---|---|---|---|
| | Drug adherence | Weight loss | Diet adherence | Physical activity | Smoking cessation | Stress reduction |
| Cardiovascular | | | | | | |
| Hypertension | X | X | X | X | X | X |
| Post–myocardial infarction | X | X | X | X | X | X |
| Coronary heart disease | X | X | X | X | X | X |
| Endocrine | | | | | | |
| Diabetes | X | X | X | X | | X |
| Gastrointestinal | | | | | | |
| Constipation | | | X | X | | |
| Dyspepsia | | | X | | | |
| Irritable bowel syndrome | X | | X | | | |
| Peptic ulcer | X | | X | | X | X |
| Ulcerative colitis | X | | X | | | |
| Genito urinary | | | | | | |
| Sexual dysfunction | | | | | | X |
| Immunological | | | | | | |
| Asthma | X | | | | X | X |
| Rheumatoid arthritis | X | X | | | | X |
| Rhinitis | X | | | X | | |
| Systemic lupus erythematosis | X | | | | | X |
| Neurological | | | | | | |
| Epilepsy | X | | | | | |
| Oncological | | | | | | |
| Colon | X | | X | | | |
| Lung | X | | | | X | |
| Mouth | X | | | | X | |
| Pain | | | | | | |
| Low back | X | X | | | | X |
| Tension headache | X | | | | | X |
| Pulmonary | | | | | | |
| Chronic bronchitis | X | X | | X | X | |
| Emphysema | X | X | | X | X | |
| Renal | | | | | | |
| Chronic renal disease | X | | X | | | |
| Surgery | X | X | X | X | | X |

Developed, in part, from Stein JH (ed): *Internal Medicine.* Boston, Little, Brown, 1983.

close to the ideal for his age and height. Many patients with hypertension may substantially reduce their blood pressure through a combination of a modest weight loss and a reduction of dietary sodium. Pain patients may enjoy a substantial reduction in discomfort by controlling their stress reactions. Table 2 indicates the widespread effect that the changes in health-related behavior discussed in this book can have on common chronic diseases. If patients can achieve and maintain changes in these different kinds of behavior, they may be able to influence their disease, its symptoms, and the level or type of medication needed to control it.

The term health-related behavior is used in this book to stress the potential contribution of these changes in this behavior in promoting health as well to control chronic disease. The term emphasizes that this behavior not only affects the symptoms of the chronic disease, but in many cases may lead to an improved general health status. If they are achieved and maintained, health-related behaviors may influence the quality of patients' lives and possibly longevity.

## Problems in Achieving Health Behavior Change

Most clinicians in practice recognize the potential effects of their patients' health-related behaviors on their medical condition. When a patient with a chronic disease exhibits behavior that places him at risk, the clinician should recommend lifestyle changes to complement the medical treatment. Fortunately, many patients are able to achieve and maintain the suggested changes.

Unfortunately, there are a substantial number of patients who are not able to achieve these changes. When this occurs, the clinician usually assumes that either the patient lacks essential information about the lifestyle change program or the motivation to make the changes. If the patient seems to lack information, the clinician might review the program with him to ensure that he understands the specific steps he must take. If the patient seems to have the information, but cannot get a program started, the clinician might review the importance of achieving the desired behavioral change to control the disease. If the patient seems to continue to have difficulty, the clinician might recommend that he join a formal program that would provide both needed information and motivation (e.g., attend a weight loss class, group exercise program, smoking cessation clinic). Having exhausted these possibilities, however, the clinician has had little else to offer. If the patient continues to be unsuccessful, many clinicians may eventually grow tired of attempting to persuade the patient to make these changes. Some fear that if they continue, the patient may become annoyed, resent the clinician's continued efforts, and not return for needed follow-up visits. As a result, their efforts cease and the patient's habits remain unchanged.

## Health Behavior Counseling

Health-related behavioral counseling offers the clinician a new method for helping patients achieve desired lifestyle changes. It is designed specifically for use by the clinician in a medical clinic and provides a systematic approach to problem solving based on fundamental principles of learning and guided by empirical data. Using this counseling the clinician seeks to develop an understanding of the patient's behavior problem by identifying those factors that tend either to promote or to suppress it. This functional analysis leads to a series of interventions designed to discourage the problem behavior and to encourage an alternative desired behavior. It is a pragmatic approach to solving the behavioral problem that uses observable data to determine whether or not the counseling is successful. Throughout the counseling, both the clinician and the patient are able to judge the degree of success that is occurring.

Although the counseling steps are designed to enable the clinician to aid many patients, it also helps those patients whose problems are not resolved entirely. It does this by increasing the patient's understanding of his health-related behavior and the factors that appear to affect it. If the patient is later referred for specialized treatment by a therapist, this understanding becomes the foundation upon which additional tests and interventions will be built. In this respect the counseling approach parallels other activities in the primary care setting that constitute the initial steps in assessment and intervention. If the problem is determined to be complex or unresponsive to these initial efforts, the information that is collected during the counseling process contributes to the eventual understanding and solution of the problem.

### The Goal Is Behavior Change

The goal of behavioral counseling in a medical setting is for the patient to achieve a specific change in a health-related behavior. To achieve this change, the patient must acquire new cognitive or behavioral skills. The purpose of the individual counseling sessions is to work with the patient to understand the current undesired habit, and guide him to develop and use specific skills that will promote and sustain a desired alternative behavior. In other words, the clinician makes the assumption that by learning new skills the patient can exert control over his health-related behaviors.

This approach sets health-related behavior counseling apart from many other counseling approaches. It identifies a specific behavior as the object of the counseling and involves other aspects of the patient's life only insofar as they affect the targeted behavior. Little or no time is devoted to attempting to discover why a particular long-standing behavior began. Rather it is assumed that regardless of how a behavior initially got started, it continues to exist for the patient because of factors that are currently influencing him. To change the behavior the clinician must identify these factors, select an intervention to reduce or eliminate them, and develop a method to promote the desired alternative behavior.

*Exclusion Versus Inclusion Approach to Diagnosis*

Behavioral counseling differs considerably from medical practice in its approach to diagnosis. In medicine, the physician uses a diagnostic approach that is exclusive in nature. He strives to obtain accurate information about the patient's condition, using laboratory tests, information from a physical examination, historical data, and observation. Initially the physician identifies the general disease area and several potential diagnoses. Using additional laboratory tests and observations, the clinician then systematically excludes (i.e., "rules out") diagnoses that do not correspond with the data available. This approach to diagnosis is based on the fact that the characteristics of many diseases are known and distinct. Each disease is, in turn, associated with a specific recommended treatment.

In health-related behavioral counseling, the clinician uses an approach to diagnosis that is inclusive in nature. Because no classification of behavioral problems with specific recommended treatments currently exists, the clinician adopts a different diagnostic style. The clinician uses self-observations by the patient, historical data, and his own observations of the patient to develop a basic understanding of the patient's problem. A treatment is then implemented based on this understanding of the problem. As new information becomes available, this understanding becomes more specific and detailed. The development of the behavioral diagnosis is one of adding to the initial description of the behavior to make it more complete and accurate, rather than excluding competing diagnoses.

This difference in diagnostic style can be uncomfortable for clinicians initially because, unlike in medicine, there are only general guidelines for understanding the problem behavior and selecting a treatment. The clinician is never quite sure that a treatment will work for a patient. He can only be certain of his behavioral diagnosis after a treatment, based on the diagnosis, is successful.

*A New Relationship with the Patient*

As a result of the focus on specific voluntary behaviors in the patient, and the inclusive approach to diagnosis, behavior counseling for health problems requires a different type of interaction with the patient than traditional medical care. The clinician must collaborate with the patient throughout the counseling relationship. The clinician cannot present himself as an expert with the best solution to the problem. In most cases, the patient has far more information than the clinician about his daily activities, his interactions with those people around him, and the factors that may be affecting the health behavior of concern. As a result, the clinician must establish a partnership with the patient to develop an understanding of the problem, to select an intervention strategy, to tailor it to the patient's lifestyle, and to assess its effects. The patient is an integral part of the counseling because the goal of the counseling is the patient's acquisition of new self-control skills. To be successful, the patient must understand these skills, expend the effort to acquire them, and apply them appropriately on his own.

## New Role for the Allied Health Professional

An important aspect of behavioral counseling in medicine is that it can be conducted by an allied health professional. Although a physician's knowledge of a patient's background and medical status are persuasive reasons why a physician might wish to conduct counseling with his patients, it is important to realize that the skills can be mastered and applied effectively by a nurse, physician assistant, or dietitian. In many clinics these individuals take primary responsibility for the patient's lifestyle change program while the physician retains primary responsibility for the patient's medical care. Together they collaborate in the total management of the patient's care. Both are aware of the specific medical and behavioral problems, and the treatments that are being implemented with the patient.

The allied health professional as counselor has several practical advantages for the practicing physician. One is that an allied health professional often can see a patient for counseling upon immediate referral while the physician continues to see other patients for medical problems. This keeps the clinic schedule flowing smoothly, as planned. Another advantage is that because the allied health professional's time is less expensive than the physician's, the clinic is making good use of its available resources. The physician's skills are used with those patients most in need of his expertise. Finally, the allied health professional usually is the individual who has more flexible time than the physician to conduct the follow-up telephone calls or appointments that are needed when patients have difficult problems. This is an important aspect of successful counseling for health-related behavior change.

## Origins of Health-Related Behavior Counseling

Health-related behavior counseling has its origins in behavioral counseling, developed in the field of educational psychology in the mid to late 1960s.[1-4] Behavioral counseling arose as an educationally based approach to help individuals ". . . learn how to solve certain interpersonal, emotional, and decision problems."[5] Behavioral counseling emphasizes teaching the client specific skills that will enable him to resolve the presenting problem as well as similar problems in the future. The aim is for the client to achieve and maintain specific changes in behavior in order to achieve desired goals. For example behavioral counseling has been used to help individuals resolve marital problems, improve social skills, decide upon career choices, and overcome fears and anxieties. Health-related behavioral counseling builds upon the behavioral counseling approach, extending it to the management of health-related behavior of individuals with chronic disease who are being treated in the outpatient medical clinic.

Behavioral counseling for health problems should not be confused with *behavior therapy*. In the former the patient is approached as a rational individual with the capacity to learn. The patient's problem is that he has been unable to acquire a new health-related behavior. It is assumed that he is psychologically and emotionally stable. This approach contrasts with behavior therapy which is used with an individual who has a serious emotional, interpersonal, or behavioral problem which causes distress. Behavior therapy is the treatment of choice for many patients with psychiatric diagnoses.

Health-related behavioral counseling is part of a broader movement in medicine termed *health psychology*. Health psychology has been defined by Matarazzo as follows:

> Health psychology is the aggregate of the specific educational, scientific, and professional contributions of the discipline of psychology to the promotion and maintenance of health, the prevention and treatment of illness, the identification of etiologic and diagnostic correlates of health, illness, and related dysfunction, and the analysis and improvement of the health care system and health policy formation.[6]

This definition emphasizes the attention of the clinician to the individual's total physical and psychological well-being. It recognizes the need for the integration of psychology and medicine, with each making contributions to the patient's care. Health-related behavioral counseling represents an important aspect of health psychology, providing a specific method for achieving these goals.

## Practical Considerations

Although behavioral counseling is an effective approach to certain kinds of health problems, the clinician must be aware of both its potential costs and possible benefits in clinical practice.

### Costs

There are definite costs associated with offering behavioral counseling for health problems. The clinician must spend valuable time acquiring a sufficient level of skill in counseling to be helpful to the patient. This is time not spent seeing other patients. Methods for accomplishing this efficiently are discussed later in this chapter.

The clinician who begins counseling patients to change health-related behavior will also find that his use of clinical time changes. He will spend increasing amounts of time with the patient during the first few visits to understand the patient problem and to develop a treatment program. When the program is successful, the time spent in follow-up visits decreases to about the same amount that is spent for routine monitoring. This contrasts with the usual care of patients who do not receive behavioral counseling. The clinician spends relatively less time initially with these patients, concerning himself mainly with offering continued encouragement, education, and support. However, because those patients receiving routine care often continue to have problems, the clinician may actually spend a good deal of time with them to resolve their problems because of the greater number of sessions needed.

The major question regarding the costs of behavioral counseling is whether or not time spent counseling is covered by the patient's medical insurance coverage. If the physician provides the counseling, the costs usually can be included as part of a routine follow-up office visit. If, however, the physician desires a nurse or physician's assistant to assume the role of counselor, the situation becomes less clear. Some companies cover this expense of counseling if it is considered patient education, while others do not. In most cases health insurance companies simply have not had sufficient experience with the long-term benefits associated with permanent lifestyle changes to include counseling in their policies. Hopefully this will be changing in the near future.

*Benefits*

The benefits of successful behavioral counseling to the patient's medical status are discussed in detail in the chapters that follow. In addition, however, there are several, less obvious, non-medical benefits that accrue to the clinician.

Clinicians who provide their patients with effective behavioral counseling demonstrate that they have a genuine interest in helping the patient live as healthy a life as possible; they are not merely interested in resolving or controlling the patient's current medical problem. With a greater sense of the clinician's concern about his well-being, the patient may develop a greater trust in the physician.

As the clinician counsels the patient, he learns more about his personal life. This information can be very helpful when the clinician must make a judgment regarding the best course of treatment for the patient. It also is useful when tailoring the recommended treatment to the patient's lifestyle. The more the clinician knows about the patient, the greater the sense of rapport that develops between them. The patient feels more at ease with the clinician, and will be more likely to discuss sensitive medical problems or concerns. This open communication can, in turn, help the physician better understand the patient's medical problems.

Increased rapport also tends to decrease the possibility of the patient feeling misunderstood or ignored. If problems do occur in future treatment, a basic understanding developed over time will help to resolve them before they become legal disputes. This rapport should also help the clinician feel less of a need to practice defensive medicine. If he does not need to worry about defending in court why he did not use a particular medical test or procedure, the clinician may be able to reduce the costs of treatment. Tests or procedures may be omitted that would be used only to rule out diagnoses with low probabilities of occurrence. If the patient trusts the clinician, and the clinician knows his patient, these tests become an unnecessary expense. As a result, the clinician may become more competitive and offer better care than other individuals who do not have good rapport with their patients.

Rapport with the clinician naturally leads to enhanced patient satisfaction with the medical care provided. If the patient is satisfied, he is likely to return to the clinician for continued medical care. Moreover, it is often the case that a satisfied patient is the best referral source a clinician could have. Other patients, dissatisfied with the lack of concern and the defensive approach of other clinicians, will be attracted to the clinician who exhibits genuine concern and interest in helping his patients.

As with any treatment that increases the clinician's efficiency, behavioral counseling helps the clinician do a better job in less time. If the clinician has decided to recommend health-related behavioral changes to patients, he must decide how to manage those patients who are not successful. Ignoring these patients is efficient but irresponsible. Other methods of helping the patient may require less time (e.g., motivational talks, more patient education), but are less likely to succeed for most patients. Behavioral counseling may require more time initially, but after a few visits, many patients have been helped, and the others may be appropriate for referral to a specialist. In either case, the clinician will not be spending his time in vain.

Finally, patients may eventually be more willing to pay personally for behavioral counseling. Several life insurance companies are currently offering discounts on their life insurance policies for individuals who adopt certain health-related behavior. People who do not drink, do not smoke cigarettes, and exercise regularly can some times receive a 10 to 15% reduction in their policy premium. This reduction may more than pay for the cost of the counseling sessions required.

## This Book

This book is written for the practicing physician or allied health professional who desires to learn how to conduct health-related behavioral counseling with medical patients. The first half of this book aims to provide a basic understanding of this counseling process. The remaining chapters present staged applications of behavioral counseling to specific health-related behavioral problems. In order to make the book useful to as many clinicians as possible, no assumptions are made about the clinician's current skills. All skills needed to successfully apply behavioral counseling for health problems are included.

Chapters 2 through 5 provide the foundation for conducting counseling. Chapter 2, "Counseling for Health Behavior Change," offers a basic model for understanding behavioral problems. It reviews the common difficulties in achieving changes in self-care behavior and how behavioral counseling can help to resolve these problems. Chapter 3, "Basic Interviewing," presents the need for and use of 14 fundamental interviewing skills. These skills are the basic tools for collecting information from the patient. Chapter 4, "Behavioral Counseling," presents a set of 13 fundamental counseling skills necessary to implement behavioral counseling. These skills include the specific actions the clinician would use in a counseling session. Chapter 5, "Maintaining Health Behavior Change," reviews the difficulties patients frequently encounter in following their behavioral change programs. The chapter also includes a model for understanding these problems, as well as three common types of maintenance problems and their treatment.

Chapters 6 through 11 describe how behavioral counseling is used in the most common behavioral change programs. These programs include adherence to a medication regimen, adherence to a therapeutic diet, achievement of weight loss, initiation of a physical fitness program, cessation of cigarette smoking, and reduction of stress reactions. These health-related behaviors were selected because of their frequent occurrence and their widespread effects on the common chronic diseases encountered in the outpatient medical clinic. Control of these health behaviors can have a substantial effect on a patient's prognosis.

All the chapters discussing the application of counseling to a specific health-related behavior follow the same format. Each chapter begins with a brief discussion of the prevalence of the behavior followed by a discussion of why the behavior is difficult to change. The latter offers a basic model for understanding the behavior. Throughout the book, however, theory is presented only insofar as it helps the reader understand the rationale for a specific step. Detailed descriptions of the research studies supporting the recommendations made in each chapter have not been included.

Each chapter presents three major staged programs for managing the health behavior of concern. These programs represent a synthesis of effective methods for managing the behavior. Appropriate cautions regarding their use also are included. The programs described in each chapter offer a basic structure for resolving the presenting problem, independent of the specific intervention techniques used. As such, the skills are generic to the problem area and not dependent upon the use of a specific intervention strategy (e.g., cues, contracts, muscle relaxation). In this way the programs are sufficiently flexible to incorporate new intervention techniques which may be developed in the future, without altering their basic structure.

The first major program described in each chapter is the one that the clinician should use initially with all patients. The basic program discusses each of the steps for selecting a behavioral change program and presenting it to the patient. Included is the basic information the patient needs to get started. Because many patients are able to achieve the desired change on their own, the basic programs are designed to provide patients with the necessary information with minimal investment of time by the clinician.

In all chapters, the basic program provides guidance for implementing a behavioral change program regardless of the type of program recommended. For example, the chapter on weight loss does not include a specific weight loss diet. The chapter on therapeutic diets does not include a specific diet for reducing dietary sodium. Each chapter refers the reader to several sources that describe how the specific goals can be obtained.

The second major program in each chapter comprises a series of steps to help a patient who is struggling to begin the behavioral change program. This program requires more time than the initial one, and is used only with those patients who have not been successful. Also included common problems that clinicians might encounter, and solutions that have proven to be effective.

The third major program in each chapter is designed to help patients who have unique problems that require intensive counseling. These patients' problems arise from specific lifestyle circumstances which require detailed analysis in order to develop an accurate understanding and a successful intervention. This program requires the most time and expertise of the clinician.

Finally, each chapter closes with a detailed case illustration that presents how a clinician would use each of the three major programs with a patient in the clinic. The case illustration is based on a composite of clinical patients typically treated in the outpatient medical clinic. The clinician can follow the logical sequence of applying the behavioral counseling process in the clinic. Each case includes examples of clinical forms completed by the patient and the clinician at each step in counseling. Blank copies of each of these forms are included in the Appendix for use by the clinician.

Because it is anticipated that a certain percentage of patients will require more advanced assessment or treatment than the clinician can offer, the final chapter of the book discusses how to refer the patient to a therapist specializing in difficult health-related behavioral change problems. The chapter includes a discussion of the typical problems requiring referral, what to say to the patient, and what to communicate to the therapist. It also includes a description of what the therapist might do, and some of the more common skills training programs that a therapist may use with a patient. The chapter closes with a discussion of how to select a therapist, and how to set appropriate expectations for continuing contact.

## Suggestions for Acquiring the Clinical Skills

Although the clinical skills described in the following chapters are not difficult to understand, their appropriate use requires some practice. It is suggested that the clinician plan a self-instructional program to acquire these skills before counseling patients. This program should provide an opportunity for the clinician to practice using these skills and then a review of whether the skills were used appropriately. The self-instructional program can be divided into four basic parts.

The first part should be to develop a basic understanding of the purpose and steps in behavioral counseling in medicine. The clinician should review Chapters 2 to become thoroughly familiar with each of the 11 steps of this counseling and the typical approach for resolving maintenance problems. These steps are the basis for all the counseling discussed throughout the book. The clinician should learn the rationale for each step, how each step is related to others, and how each step is applied in clinical practice.

The second part should concentrate on the acquisition of the interviewing skills. Chapter 3 should be carefully reviewed until the clinician is thoroughly familiar with each of the skills. He should be able to listen to a conversation and rapidly provide an example of each of the interviewing skills at any point. A good exercise is to use a televised interview to practice using the interview skills. When the interviewee has responded to a question from the interviewer, the clinician should select an interview skill, and use it appropriately in response to what the interviewee has just said. Once comfortable with this, the next step is to use the interviewing skills as part of the routine interactions with patients in the clinic. This does not require counseling of the patient. Rather, as part of the usual medical interview or discussions, try to use each of the interviewing skills. This should continue until the use of each of the interviewing skills is natural and comfortable.

The next part is to learn the basic counseling skills, Chapter 4. These can be difficult to learn because they are used in a clinician's dialogue with the patient and depend upon the patient's specific responses. Usually these skills are acquired through practice with another clinician or a staff member who is willing to take the role of a patient with a specific problem. The clinician interviews the simulated patient and uses the counseling skills to help him resolve the problem. It is extremely helpful to tape-record these practice sessions so that the clinician can critique his performance. It is very difficult to remain involved in a counseling interaction while attempting to self-critique at the same time.

The last part of the self-instruction program is the integration of the behavioral counseling skills, the maintenance skills, the basic counseling skills, and the basic interviewing skills into a single unified program (i.e., Chapter 5). The integrated skills are then applied to a specific health-related behavioral problem. In the beginning most clinicians feel more comfortable choosing a behavioral problem with which they already are very familiar. In this way the content of the change program (i.e., the specific therapeutic diet, drug regimen, weight loss diet) is known to the clinician and attention can be devoted to the counseling process. It is suggested that the integration of these skills be practiced with a colleague simulating a patient, and the session tape-recorded. The clinician can review his performance and evaluate his use of each skill.

## References

1. Krumboltz JD: Behavioral counseling: rationale and research. *Personnel and Guidance Journal* 1965; 44:383–387.
2. Krumboltz JD: Behavioral goals for counseling. *Journal of Counseling Psychology* 1966; 13:153–159.
3. Krumboltz JD (ed): *Revolution in Counseling: Implications of Behavioral Science.* Boston, Houghton Mifflin, 1966.
4. Krumboltz JD, Thoresen CE: *Behavioral Counseling: Cases and Techniques.* New York, Holt, Rinehart and Winston, 1969.
5. Krumboltz JD, Thoresen CE: *Counseling Methods.* New York, Holt, Rinehart and Winston, 1976.
6. Matarazzo JD: Behavioral health's challenge to academic, scientific and professional psychology. *Am Psychol* 1982; 37:1–14.

# 2. Counseling for Health Behavior Change

## Health Behaviors

Most patients seek medical care for the improvement of their health status. They expect that the clinician will resolve their medical problems effectively and efficiently while minimizing costs and their physical discomfort. To accomplish these goals, the clinician focuses attention on the patient's symptoms, physical findings and laboratory analyses in order to arrive at a diagnosis, select appropriate treatment, and form a reasonable prognosis.

Regardless of the clinician's skill, however, the accurate diagnosis and selection of appropriate treatment does not automatically resolve the patient's medical problem. Optimum treatment often requires that the patient becomes directly involved in the treatment process. The clinician may recommend that the patient adopt health behaviors that support the prescribed therapy. For acute illnesses, these behaviors facilitate the patient's rapid recovery and minimize the likelihood of complications. Usually they are temporary modifications of the patient's daily activities with the expectation that the patient will discontinue the behaviors when the illness has been cured. A patient with a bacterial infection, for example, might be instructed to follow a specific regimen of antibiotic medication, to engage in hygienic routines, and to limit physical activity.

For the chronic diseases and risk factors, however, optimum medical care is usually directed toward controlling the problem rather than curing it, relieving its symptoms, and stopping its progress. The physician may prescribe a combination of medications for symptomatic relief, a regimen of health behaviors, and the elimination of behaviors that place the patient at risk of continuing medical problems. For example, a patient with diabetes may be prescribed insulin, a carbohydrate-controlled diet, and a hygienic routine for foot care. Similarly, a patient with cardiovascular disease may be prescribed an anticoagulant drug and a program of graded physical activity program. In addition both of these patients might be encouraged to stop cigarette smoking.

This book discusses health behaviors that are actions or activities performed by the patient that contribute to the treatment of a disease or injury, to the maintenance of current health status, or to a reduction in the likelihood of future medical problems. Some health behaviors are new activities for the patient that would be desirable as part of his daily routine. Examples include adherence to a medication regimen, performance of a physical exercise routine, and adoption of a specialized diet. Other health behaviors are actions that function as replacements for current, undesirable behaviors which are increasing the patient's risk of continued medical problems. Examples of these behaviors include the cessation of cigarette smoking, the reduction of high levels of stress, and the attainment of an ideal weight.

The definition of a health behavior emphasizes that it is the patient who has responsibility for its performance. It is this feature that distinguishes a health behavior from other medical procedures that may effect the patient's medical status but are performed by others. For example, a diabetic patient's adherence to a self-administered regimen of insulin injections would be considered a health behavior, while receiving an antibiotic injection from a physician would be considered a medical procedure. Thus, it is not the nature of the activity (i.e., the injection) that defines an activity as a health behavior, rather it is whether the patient has been identified as having the responsibility for performing the action.

Unfortunately, many patients experience difficulty adopting the health behaviors recommended for their treatment. However, the clinician can aid the patient in the adoption of needed health activities. To do so effectively the clinician must acquire new skills to interact with the patient in a manner that is fundamentally different from the clinician-patient interaction typical of medical practice. In addition, the clinician must possess a thorough understanding of the basic principles that guide human behavior.

## Functional Relationships Among Behaviors

Patient health behaviors function very much like any other behavior over which the patient has direct control. The fact that these health behaviors are associated with medical care does not set them apart from other behaviors. Health behaviors have the same orderly patterns of action and interaction with other activities as do all other behaviors. To understand their continued presence or absence requires an understanding of how new behaviors are learned and maintained.

Humans exist in a state of continuing activity. We are constantly acting or interacting with the environment around us, seeking and responding to the stimuli with which we come in contact. If a video-camera were to observe an individual for a day, the recording would reveal a constant stream of behaviors, one seemingly flowing into the next with no apparent beginning or end. Upon completion, one behavior becomes the foundation upon which the following behavior rests, which, in turn, supports the succeeding behavior, and so on.

As an aid to understanding this continuing activity, psychologists describe a set of related activities linked by the concept of a *behavior*. Behavior is a relative term that can be used to describe any set of conceptually related activities. Once the behavior is operationally defined, it is then treated as a unit, as if the set of activities was a single action. The concept that links these activities together provides guidance as to when the behavior begins and when it ends. For example, "taking a single dose of medication" is often referred to as a behavior. However, direct observation would reveal that the set of activities comprising this behavior might include: filling a glass with water, opening a pill bottle, extracting two capsules, placing the capsules in the mouth, and swallowing the capsules with the water. Even though each of these activities (e.g., opening the pill bottle) might be further defined by a sub-series of actions (e.g., locating the pill bottle, pushing down on the cap, twisting the cap counterclockwise), when performed in sequence they compose the behavior of "taking a dose of medication." The behavior begins with filling a glass with water and ends with swallowing the capsules.

Grouping related activities into a single behavior and observing the behavior as a unit can be extremely useful in clinical medicine. It enables clinicians to seek factors that appear to be influencing a particular set of activities. Regardless of how the behavior is operationally defined, it remains the smallest unit of analysis. This approach is similar to a biochemist's consistent grouping of hydrogen and oxygen elements together in the molecule $H_2O$ and then labeling it "water." Subsequent studies are then conducted to identify the unique properties of water and its interaction with other molecules.

The clinician's analysis of a behavior proceeds in a similar manner to the biochemist's analysis of a molecule. The clinician assumes that lawful relationships exist between the behavior and those activities and events that are surrounding it. It is assumed that human behavior is no more arbitrary than any other biological phenomenon. A behavior occurs and continues to reoccur as a result of identifiable causal factors. Although the logical connections between the behavior and the events that are affecting it may be complex and obscure, nevertheless they exist. With behaviors that carry health risks, the clinician's task is to determine what these factors are, under which conditions they exist, and how they operate to promote and/or suppress the behavior.

Usually the clinician can identify events or activities in the patient's environment that have a direct effect on the behavior of concern (Figure 1). Some stimuli will be discovered routinely to precede the behavior. In a sense, the occurrence of the behavior is being controlled by these stimuli. For example, the behavior of "smoking a cigarette" is often linked to the antecedent event of

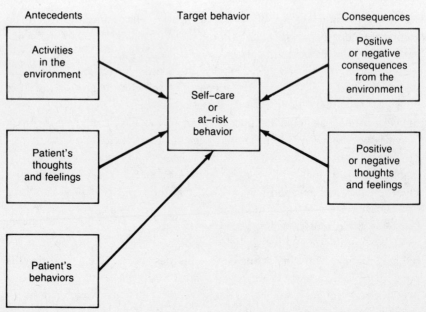

Figure 1. Interaction of multiple factors affecting a patient's self-care or at-risk behavior.

"drinking a cup of coffee." The coffee drinking usually precipitates smoking a cigarette.

The antecedents become linked to the behavior through those events that usually follow the behavior. The nature and frequency of consequences can have a dramatic effect on a behavior. Positive consequences (i.e., pleasurable events) tend to increase the likelihood of the behavior recurring in a similar situation in the future, while negative consequences (i.e., aversive events) tend to decrease this possibility. As a result, the antecedents that are linked to the situation when the behavior occurs are functioning as cues to identify those specific situations when known consequences will occur. For the cigarette smoker, the antecedent of "drinking a cup of coffee" is followed by the behavior of "smoking," which is followed by the consequences of a pleasurable taste and a relaxed feeling. It is important to note that the linkage of antecedent-behavior-consequence involves the person's perceptions of the current environment and experience with the consequences in similar situations in the past. In other words, a person performs actions in the present situation based on the results of behaviors performed in the past.

The person's behavior also is influenced by his current thoughts and feelings. Cognitive behaviors, or "cognitions," can function as antecedents and consequences for overt behaviors, influencing the person's actions in a manner similar to environmental events. For example, the overt behavior of watching a

television commercial may provoke thoughts of spending one's time more pro-
ductively and lead to participation in a physical activity such as bicycling or
jogging. If the sequence of observable activities were all that was known, it would
appear that because the two behaviors were conceptually unrelated (i.e., watching television and bicycling), the participation in the physical activity occurred
"spontaneously" without a related antecedent.

Just as an overt behavior can lead to other observable behaviors, a thought,
image or feeling can lead to another cognition. That is, these covert activities
(i.e., thoughts and feelings) occur in logical sequence with the preceding and
succeeding cognitions bringing about current ones. A thought or image or feeling can lead to a series of thoughts, each related to the prior one in the sequence. These sets of cognitions are considered behaviors, although private ones.
The major difference is that the patient is the only one who is able to observe
these mental activities. Regardless, cognitive events influence each other in
the same manner as overt behaviors. The same principles of learning seem to
apply.

Although the concepts of antecedents and consequences influencing a patient's behavior are straightforward, when working in combination, their influence on human behavior can be subtle and complex. The exact linkage of
antecedent-behavior-consequence can be difficult for the clinician to determine. Even the patient often is not aware of consistent relationships among
behaviors. Sometimes simple observations of the patient's activities (e.g., a daily
log of activities) will reveal an association between actions that typically precede
a behavior and reinforcing events that routinely follow it. For example, it might
be observed that a hypertensive patient consistently eats tasty low-sodium meals
at home that are prepared by his wife who is supportive of his efforts to maintain a sodium-restricted diet. In other situations, however, he engages in undesirable behaviors by selecting foods that are high in sodium at lunch with
friends in the cafeteria at work yet no observable negative consequences appear
to be present. It is only revealed later through discussions with the clinician
that he does not wish his co-workers to know that he has high blood pressure
and believe that he is ill. The avoidance of an aversive situation (i.e., the co-
workers finding out about the patient's high blood pressure) is the motivation
that is supporting the undesirable behavior. In these cases, the clinician must
rely on the patient to provide information that will identify the relationships
between the behavior of concern and the events surrounding its occurrence.

The goal of behavioral counseling is to alter either the antecedents or consequences of the current undesirable behavior to such a degree that the alternative health behavior is elicited and supported instead. Unfortunately, most
health behaviors have patterns that make them extremely difficult to initiate.
Conversely, behaviors that place the patient at risk for further disease or illness
have enduring patterns that are difficult to change. Consider the behaviors of

Table 1. Comparison of positive and aversive consequences for a patient
who wishes to replace an at-risk behavior with a self-care behavior

| | Immediate consequences | | Long-term consequences | |
| --- | --- | --- | --- | --- |
| | Positive | Aversive | Positive | Aversive |
| Current at-risk behaviors | Many | Few | Few | Many |
| Desired self-care behaviors | Few | Many | Many | Few |

proper diet, sufficient physical activity, or adherence to a drug regimen for glaucoma. From the perspective of the patient who does not currently possess these behaviors, the changes required to achieve them have a consistent pattern. The desired behavior is usually accompanied by immediate consequences that are, at best, mildly unpleasant (Table 1). It is only the long-term (and possibly only theoretical) effects that are positive. For example, medication for glaucoma can result in mild to moderately unpleasant side effects. Further, the regimen requires that the patient insert a new behavior into the daily routine, which can be mildly disruptive. It is only the long-term effects of reducing intraocular pressure and avoiding deterioration in vision that benefits the patient.

The situation is almost exactly reversed when the clinician is faced with the problem of eliminating an undesirable behavior. The current behavior (e.g., the at-risk behavior) is almost always followed by immediate positive consequences, while the immediate aversive consequences are minimal. For the smoker, cigarette smoking produces several immediate reactions. The sensation of smoking is agreeable, the uncomfortable symptoms of withdrawal from nicotine are eliminated, the physical handling of the cigarette is satisfying and the mental images associated with smoking are pleasurable. The immediate aversive effects may include such minor irritations as coughing, stained fingers, and the cost of purchasing more cigarettes. It is only the long-term effects of cigarette smoking that are overwhelmingly aversive (e.g., loss of cardiovascular fitness, increased risk of developing lung cancer, emphysema or heart disease). As a result the act of smoking a cigarette is strongly supported and only mildly inhibited.

The situation changes dramatically for the cigarette smoker who stops smoking. The immediate consequences are aversive (e.g., increased physical discomfort, the absence of familiar routine which may have a calming effect in stressful situations), while the positive consequences only occur in the future (e.g., sharpened sense of taste, increased stamina, decreased risk of developing diseases). Thus the act of stopping smoking is immediately punished, and the positive consequences are delayed.

This pattern of immediate predominantly positive consequences for the at-risk behaviors and immediate predominantly aversive consequences for the desired health behavior is commonly observed in patients who possess at-risk behaviors. It is because this pattern is so difficult to alter that many patients have problems reaching their goals. For those patients who do succeed in achieving their goal, there are few naturally occurring incentives other than the long-term positive consequences to maintain the self-imposed routine. As a result, many patients return to their at-risk behaviors.

### Difficulties Making Changes in Behavior

In general, many patients are able to follow the treatment program that has been prescribed for them. For these patients, a simple statement from the clinician of what health behaviors they need to adopt, together with the rationale for these changes, is sufficient. The clinician need not be concerned about these "good" patients.

Other patients experience real difficulty trying to adopt a health behavior or eliminate an undesirable behavior. These patients have problems that fall in one or more of the following categories: (1) insufficient knowledge of the disease or its treatment, (2) rejection of the medical diagnosis, (3) rejection of the medical prescription, (4) lack of self-management skills to establish the new health behavior as a habit, or (5) intermittent self-debate due to conflict with other priorities (Table 2). A patient may have any of these problems at virtually any point in treatment, and also may have more than one of these problems at the same time.

The clinician's first step is to determine the nature of the patient's problem in order to intervene appropriately. As illustrated in Table 2, the clinician must first determine that the patient has sufficient knowledge of the disease, the prescribed medical treatment and the recommended health behaviors. Further, the patient has made the decision to follow the recommended program. Once these conditions have been met, then behavioral counseling may be appropriate for problems involving the patient's lack of skills to establish the health behavior as a habit, or to resolve recurrent self-debates that the patient may be having regarding the prescribed regimens.

### Patient Education

Most patients require at least some education concerning their chronic disease, its prognosis, and the relationship between the treatments that have been prescribed and the disease. The goal of patient education is to transmit this infor-

Table 2. Major categories of patient problems and appropriate clinical approach

| Patient problem | Clinical approach |
| --- | --- |
| Patient lacks knowledge of the disease or its treatment | Patient education |
| Patient rejects the medical diagnosis | Patient education |
| Patient rejects the prescribed medication | Patient education |
| Patient lacks needed skills required to establish the self-care regimen as a habit | Behavioral counseling |
| Patient engages in frequent self-debate as to whether or not to follow the prescribed self-care regimen | Behavioral counseling |

mation in such a manner that the patient is able to understand it, relate it to the disease and its treatment, and recall the information when needed in the future.

This process usually involves the transmission of two different types of knowledge to the patient: (1) what the disease is and the details of its treatment, and (2) why the treatment is necessary. First, the patient is taught about the disease, including how the condition was acquired, and how it may affect others who are close. The specifics of treatment are explained so that patients know what can be expected from their physicians, and what they must do for themselves. For the diabetic patient this information would include: (1) a discussion of the production and function of insulin in the body, (2) the probable cause of insufficient insulin production, (3) the procedures of a self-managed insulin regimen, and (4) the details of recommended health programs for diet and hygiene.

The second type of information provided to the patient concerns the medical implications of treatment and non-treatment of the disease. This gives the patient reasons for following the prescribed treatments. The patient learns about the natural course or progression of the disease if left untreated. The patient also learns the positive consequences that can be anticipated if the treatment regimen is followed, and the negative consequences that are likely if the regimen is ignored or only partially observed. The patient's illness and treatment are discussed in terms of what is likely to happen in the future. The diabetic patient would learn: (1) the long term damage that occurs in the cardiovascular system when diabetes is left uncontrolled, (2) the likely progress of the diabetes if controlled using drug therapy, and (3) the positive influence of diet to aid in the control of the disease. Following this instruction, the patient should have a good understanding of the rationale for the prescribed treatment and a clear plan of action in mind.

## The Patient's Decision

Upon learning about their disease and the recommended regimens for medications and new health behaviors, some patients decide that they do not wish to participate in part or any of the treatment program. This is not an uncommon decision among older patients with chronic conditions such as arthritis, cancer, cardiovascular disease, or kidney failure. In many cases, these patients are symptom free (or at least symptom-controlled) and have accommodated to their current lifestyle. They may be aware of the potential increased risk of future disease or illness by not adopting the health behaviors, but they have chosen not to follow the recommended treatment program because the anticipated side effects are too unpleasant. Often patients accurately perceive that their quality of life would be adversely affected. Others reject as too uncomfortable the idea of modifying lifelong habit patterns, particularly in light of the few years of life they believe they may have remaining.

A similar attitude is sometimes encountered in adolescent and young adult patients who may be symptom-free. For them the control of a current disease by adopting health behaviors brings unpleasant side effects and disrupts normal daily activities. Limitations and restrictions may be rejected because the long-term rewards are too far in the future. These young patients may ignore, deny, or rationalize the health behaviors as not being significant. This is often the case with the young patient who has hypertension or diabetes, or who ignores preventive programs of smoking cessation, weight loss, and participation in regular vigorous physical exercise.

In these situations, the clinician is wise not to introduce a formal program to initiate a health behavior or eliminate an undesirable behavior. Instead, one should probe the patient's reasons for adopting this attitude. Does he lack information regarding the disease or the proposed treatment program? Does the patient have unfounded fears regarding the treatment program or recommended health behaviors? Does he hold unrealistic views of what is expected? The start of a behavior change program should await the answers to these questions as well as the patient's clear expression of a desire to follow the recommended treatment program.

Ultimately, the clinician must accept the informed patient's decision regarding acceptance or rejection of the recommended treatment. The difficulty for the clinician, of course, is how to determine whether or not the patient has made a truly informed decision. Professional ethics requires that clinicians be satisfied in their own minds that patients fully understand the medical consequences of non-treatment of the disease or condition they have. Every effort should have been made to provide information in a manner that patients can understand so that they are fully aware of the likely consequences. Clinicians also must be convinced that patients' rejection of a health behavior routine is not simply a rationalization which is masking their inability to carry out the prescribed regimens. These are difficult decisions for clinicians which call for an in-depth understanding of a patient's knowledge, beliefs and attitudes. They require deft use of interviewing and counseling skills, coupled with insightful clinical judgment.

## Self-Management Skills for Habit Acquisition

Although the knowledge that the absence of certain behaviors will increase the risk of disease may convince a person of the need for change, many who possess this knowledge still are not able to make the permanent changes in their lifestyle. Haynes et al. (1979), for example, have reported that at best only 60% of all patients who have been prescribed a regimen of antihypertensive drugs are taking sufficient medication to control their high blood pressure. The remaining 40% either do not take the medication or take their medication at infrequent intervals. The National Center for Health Services Research (1979) reports that among patients who currently smoke cigarettes, 64.7% have tried to stop smoking but have not succeeded.

These patients lack important skills in self-management needed either to establish a health behavior as a habit or to eliminate a behavior that is detrimental to their health status. They need to learn how to arrange their environment to contain the necessary antecedent conditions to stimulate the occurrence of the desired behavior, and to provide the positive consequences to encourage its reoccurrence. In the end, the patient needs to know how to make the desired changes in a way that will be the most effective, least uncomfortable, require the least amount of effort, and have the greatest chance of resulting in a permanent change in lifestyle. These are skills that the clinician trained in behavioral counseling for health behavior change can provide.

## Self-Debate

Other patients are able only intermittently to follow a recommended medical and behavior change program. These patients usually possess all of the knowledge and self-management skills necessary to make the changes; however, they do not achieve a consistent pattern of adherence. Their problem often is that they have recurrent debates with themselves as to whether they should adhere to the program on that particular day.

The observed fluctuation in the patient's adherence results from changes in the delicate belance among the many positive and negative factors associated with the prescribed regimen. The patient weighs the strength of these factors and decides whether or not to follow the regimen from day to day. As the number and nature of these consequences change, the relative desirability of the new behavior is re-evaluated against the positive and negative consequences of competing or alternative behaviors. Sometimes the self-debate is resolved in favor of the regimen, and sometimes it is not. For example, a patient may frequently self-debate when a medication has been prescribed that has adverse side effects. The patient may consider the positive factors of controlling the progress of the disease, the elimination of other restrictions on lifestyle when the disease is controlled, and feelings of enhanced self-esteem for following a difficult medication regimen. However, these positive factors are mitigated by the presence of negative factors that encourage the patient not to follow the regimen. The negative factors, however, might include a high level of stress, sleepiness, the apathetic attitude of his family, or a busy schedule.

Many of the influences that affect a patient's decision to follow a medication or health regimen are relatively stable. These include the patient's knowledge of the disease, its progression, and its consequences. If only these stable factors were operating, the patient would make a decision that would be unchanging. But other, fluid factors change on a frequent basis and can have a strong effect on the patient's decision. These include the patient's current emotional, psychological, and physiological state. As these fluid factors become stronger or weaker, the patient's decision may alternate. The clinician's adroit use of health behavioral counseling may help these patients who self-debate to reduce the influence of the negative factors, and to establish or strengthen the influence of positive factors. As a result of the clinician's intervention, the patient's self-debate may become increasingly resolved in favor of following the prescribed treatment regimen.

It is recommended that the clinician repeatedly review in detail the patient's knowledge, attitudes and behaviors during the course of treatment. Initially, the clinician should determine if the patient has received sufficient accurate information about the disease, the rationale for its treatment, and the details of how to implement the prescribed regimen. The clinician also should determine if the patient has made a firm decision to attempt the prescribed program. If so, and the patient experiences difficulties, he may benefit from behavioral counseling focused on instructing the patient in self-management skills to make the desired changes. If the patient possesses these skills, then the clinician should examine whether the patient is engaging in repeated self-debates regarding the benefits of following the recommended program versus engaging in competing, undesirable behaviors. In either case, behavioral counseling appropriately conducted can be of benefit to the patient.

## Behavioral Counseling

Behavioral counseling is a specialized type of counseling designed to help patients acquire health behaviors and eliminate behaviors that place them at risk

Table 3. Eleven-step behavioral counseling process

*Step* 1: *Identify the problem.*
    Clinician and patient define the patient's problem behavior.

*Step* 2: *Select goals for counseling.*
    Clinician and patient agree on the specific health behaviors that the patient would
    like to acquire.

*Step* 3: *Collect information.*
    Clinician systematically reviews patient's risk behavior patterns with patient.

*Step* 4: *Develop behavioral diagnosis.*
    Clinician and patient agree on the behavioral patterns that appear to be supporting
    the problem behaviors and the patterns that appear to be preventing or inhibiting
    the desired health behaviors.

*Step* 5: *Generate intervention program.*
    Clinician and patient develop and tailor an intervention program to effect both the
    desired health behavior and eliminate the problem behavior.

*Step* 6: *Intervene.*
    Patient uses the intervention program in his/her home environment.

*Step* 7: *Review program's progress.*
    Clinician and patient review the behavioral diagnosis and modify it based on the
    results of the initial intervention program.

*Step* 8: *Generate revised intervention program.*
    Clinician and patient modify the intervention program based on the revised behav-
    ioral diagnosis.

*Step* 9: *Intervene.*
    Patient uses the revised intervention program in his/her home environment.

*Step* 10: *Generate maintenance strategies.*
    When intervention program is successful, it is gradually withdrawn and maintenance
    strategies introduced. It is anticipated that the natural environment should eventu-
    ally support the new, desired health behavior.

*Step* 11: *Review behavior change process.*
    Clinician reviews with patient the health behavior change process so that the patient
    can anticipate the development of potential problems with the new health behavior
    patterns and avoid or resolve them before they become major difficulties.

for continuing medical problems. The clinician follows a logical sequence of steps to analyze and diagnose the problem, and to prescribe and manage a behavior change program (Table 3). These steps guide the clinician's efforts throughout the counseling process.

Behavioral counseling provides a systematic method for working with patients to develop an understanding of the behavioral patterns that are preventing a health behavior from becoming established or are maintaining an at-risk behavior. Specific strategies are then introduced that are designed to promote the desired behavior. The success of these strategies is carefully monitored and adjustments are made as needed. When appropriately applied, behavioral counseling maximizes the likelihood that the patient will be able to achieve the desired health behavior changes and maintain them over time.

Behavioral counseling is most effective with patients who have made a conscious decision to attempt to follow the treatment program recommended for them. The patient has made a commitment to take the steps necessary to modify daily habits of diet, smoking, exercise, and so on. However, the patient is unable to achieve these changes alone and is seeking the clinician's aid. The patient needs a specific plan for making these changes, a plan that will have the maximum chance of success, in the shortest time, and as effortlessly as possible.

The patient should be cautioned that the clinician cannot promise a quick resolution of his behavioral problems. Neither can the clinician guarantee that a permanent change in his health behaviors will necessarily be achieved. Rather, the clinician can offer to help the patient develop a behavior change program that will have a good chance of resulting in steady improvement in the patient's behavioral problem. However, a successful change program requires considerable effort over time from the patient. The patient must possess an enduring commitment to change and a willingness to tolerate some discomfort. If so, then the behavioral counseling approach offers a reasonable way of confronting and resolving these difficult problems.

A major strength of behavioral counseling is its focus on the patient's observable actions, feelings, and thoughts associated with the behaviors targeted for change. The clinician evaluates the patient's progress by measuring changes in the observable behavior. As described earlier, these are examined in terms of their consistent patterns and their function within the patient's daily activities. The focus on observable behaviors offers several advantages in the context of health care activities. Unlike the treatment of medical diseases or psychological dysfunctions, the behavioral problem is easily recognized by the patient and its treatment is readily understandable. Both clinician and patient are able to assess the effects of the intervention strategy and adjust the strategy as needed. As a result, the patient usually gains a clear understanding of the rationale for the behavioral interventions.

Behavioral counseling has the further advantage that it can be conducted within a limited number of sessions. If the patient's problem is one of not being aware of the best methods for initiating and maintaining health behaviors, then there should be evidence of change in the desired direction occurring within the first few days of the intervention. If no progress is observed after a revised strategy is attempted, then a significantly more detailed analysis of the at-risk behavioral patterns, an increased investment of time and effort by the patient, and a set of counseling sessions over some period of time may be required. In these cases, the most reasonable course may be referral to a behavioral psychologist for intensive counseling to resolve the behavior problems.

Behavioral counseling is extremely flexible. Although the steps in the counseling process to analyze and intervene, to re-analyze and re-intervene, are not changed from patient to patient, the specific strategies to change the patient's at-risk behaviors vary considerably. New methods to initiate behavioral changes are developed and old methods are discarded as less effective. Techniques from any source can be assimilated into the health behavioral counseling model.

Behavioral counseling is a positive approach to the patient with at-risk health behaviors. The problem facing the clinician and the patient is to develop a strategy that will accomplish the necessary changes in the patient's behavioral patterns. If a behavior change program is not successful the assumption made is that either the behavioral diagnosis was inaccurate or the treatment was ineffective. In neither case is the patient considered "deficient." Rather, the patient's behavior is viewed as the logical result of the current combination of factors associated with the behavior. It is not assumed that the current behavior is a permanent, enduring part of the patient's lifestyle.

Because the patient's behavioral patterns are considered the problem, counseling focuses on changing them, not changing the patient's personality. The clinician does not take the role of psychotherapist and attempt to help the patient resolve personal or psychological problems. If a program to resolve a behavior problem does not succeed initially, it should not be considered as symptomatic of a psychological problem. A straightforward explanation of this philosophy usually puts the patient at ease and maintains his motivation to continue trying to change a difficult behavioral pattern.

Nonetheless, when successful, behavioral counseling achieves more than a change in the patient's healthy at-risk behaviors. Because patients are collaborators in the behavioral counseling process, they acquire some understanding of the behavioral patterns and of the factors that appear to have the most influence on them. They learn how to evaluate their own behavior patterns, and what to do to alter them. Through counseling, patients become aware of their own behavioral patterns and how they interact. As a result, they can continue to observe the targeted health behavior, evaluate its status and re-institute a behavior change program if necessary. This long-term preventive capability serves to maintain the new desired health behaviors even when a person is confronted with unanticipated new difficulties in maintaining the new routines.

Although behavioral psychological principles structure the health behavioral counseling process, it is not the counseling process itself that leads to the patient's adoption of health behaviors. That is, the patient does not achieve new health behaviors as a result of something that the clinician does to him. Rather, changes arise from a collaboration between the patient and the clinician. The counselor and patient develop a specific intervention based on behavioral principles that will support the health behavior or eliminate the undesirable at-risk behavior. Although the nature of the intervention varies depending on the target behavior and the patient's lifestyle, the same steps in the counseling are followed with each patient.

## Role of the Clinician

Behavioral counseling requires the clinician to function in a somewhat different role with the patient than in the treatment of illnesses. There is a shift from the data collection, diagnosis, and treatment of a medical entity to the data collection, diagnosis, and treatment of a behavioral problem. Because resolving health behavioral problems is a fundamentally different process than that used in resolving medical problems, the clinician must deliberately alter the nature of the interaction with the patient. In contrast to medical treatment in which the clinician is the "expert" who possesses knowledge and has access to treatments outside the patient's experience, in behavioral counseling the clinician becomes a collaborator with the patient throughout the counseling process. The clinician is a guide or facilitator who works with the patient to eliminate the at-risk behaviors. The success of the counseling is equally dependent upon the participation of both the clinician and the patient in the treatment.

The collaborative nature of the behavioral counseling relationship does not mean that the clinician and the patient are assumed to have equal knowledge or experience with health behavior change programs. The clinician clearly has experience and clinical judgment regarding the potential treatment programs and the behavioral diagnosis that the patient does not have. However, the patient has detailed knowledge about his or her own daily activities, lifestyle, potential problems, and family relationships of which the clinician can, at best, only become partially aware through discussions during their interviews. These differences must be recognized and put to use, because the patient's and clinician's spheres of knowledge complement each other in the collaborative counseling relationship.

It should be emphasized, however, that given the time-limited nature of the counseling process, and the sequence of steps necessary in each behavior change program, the clinician remains ultimately in control of the counseling process. Behavioral counseling is neither a non-directed nor a patient-directed activity. It has a clear progression with easily recognizable steps. It is the clinician's responsibility to monitor the counseling progress and re-direct the interviews as appropriate.

The role of the behavioral counselor is a new, expanded role for the clinician. Just as the primary care clinician is the initial contact with the patient who needs treatment for a pressing medical problem, the same clinician also is the appropriate first contact with the patient who wants to resolve a behavioral problem.

The role has developed partly from the increasing attention paid to the association between certain risk factors and subsequent diseases. Contributing to its development has been the recognition of the serious difficulties that patients often experience in attempting to make major lifestyle changes recommended by their physicians. Clinicians have a responsibility to their patients that if a major lifestyle change is recommended to reduce or eliminate an at-risk behavior, it should be prescribed with a carefully defined "dosage" and "regimen." Given the large number of patients who are unsuccessful in making the desired changes on their own, and the resulting frustration, disappointment, and potential loss of self-esteem, the clinician should approach recommending behavioral changes in a manner similar to prescribing a medication. Recommended behavioral change programs should be carefully thought through with a weighing of the consequences, probable success, potential side effects and potential effects on the at-risk behavior. Friendly advice to a patient to "lose weight" or "get some exercise" or "stop smoking" without reviewing with the patient how to achieve these desirable goals is unwise.

To be an effective health behavior counselor, physicians and allied health professionals do not need to have had formal training in counseling, clinical psychology, or psychiatry. The methods of behavioral counseling have been successfully acquired by dietitians, physician assistants, nurses, and physicians. With practice and critical self-evaluation, clinicians can acquire proficiency in the use of interviewing and counseling skills that will enable them to help many patients achieve significant changes in at-risk behaviors. Once mastered, these skills can be used in relatively brief clinic visits, with the understanding that if serious difficulties are encountered the patient may benefit from referral to a behavioral psychologist.

To conduct behavioral counseling effectively, however, the clinician must have a firm grasp of the principles and rationale for the approach. Moreover, the clinician must master a combination of specific skills in interviewing, problem identification and analysis, and behavioral counseling. These skills are defined and illustrated in Chapters 3, 4, and 5. Later chapters describe how the process is applied to a variety of commonly recommended health behaviors.

### Limitations

Earlier in this chapter several general types of problems were identified that prevent patients from adhering to prescribed health programs. All of these problems are at least potentially amenable to counseling. Others, however, are not.

Patients who may have to be referred for other treatment and who should be identified early include those with serious psychological or behavioral problems. Although their medical status would benefit from the health behaviors recommended, they are at high risk for failure. Moreover, the treatment of their psychological problems should take precedence. The patient should be encouraged to seek other, appropriate treatment. Chapter 12, "Referring Patients for Psychological Counseling," discusses this in detail.

Among the patients who require individual and detailed assessment before the decision is made to refer them elsewhere or to begin behavioral counseling are:

1. Patients with alcohol or other drug dependencies.
2. Patients who are clinically depressed.
3. Patients who are currently experiencing major crises or who have serious turmoil in their personal lives (e.g., recent bereavement, divorce, marital problems, unemployment).
4. Patients who have failed several times previously in their attempts to change at-risk behaviors.
5. Patients who have chronically irregular or erratic daily schedules.

Of course, each patient must be carefully evaluated as to the individual circumstances surrounding his or her current lifestyle and problem. In some cases, the clinician may decide that although the risk of failure is high, the patient may still benefit. Further, the health behavior change may have a direct positive effect on the other areas of the patient's life. For example, initiating a physical fitness program tends to lead to increased alertness, increased energy, lifting of depression, and ability to handle stress more easily. However, the clinician must remember that behavioral counseling incurs costs for the patient and for the clinician. Time, effort, money, and the potential psychological effect of failure must be carefully considered in relation to the anticipated benefits. This can be a difficult clinical decision.

## Implications

Behavioral counseling expands the clinician's role in the management of medical illnesses and injuries. It provides the clinician with tools to help the patient change behaviors that could otherwise compromise the effective treatment of the patient's medical problem. If adherence to behavioral regimens can be achieved, the clinician can accurately evaluate the specific effects of the prescribed regimen and "fine-tune" the patient's medical care to achieve optimum results. With medication, for example, the type of drug can be changed, the dosage adjusted, and the schedule modified. The results one aims for is for the patient to receive the most effective medication in the best possible regimen with the fewest side effects.

The patient's adherence to recommended health programs also can have a dramatic effect on the patient's medical status. Health behaviors can promote the healing process and restore compromised abilities. The elimination of at-risk behaviors can provide the patient with an improved long-term prognosis.

As a result, the illness or injury is treated in the most effective and efficient manner.

The patient's adoption of the prescribed drug or health regimens also can have a substantial effect on the cost of medical care. Swift, effective medical care reduces the patient's symptoms and speeds control or cure of the disease or illness. Fewer office visits may be required to find an effective treatment and complications may be avoided or reduced. As a result, the patient can be more rapidly shifted to a follow-up program of intermittent visits. This has the effect of reducing the cost of medical care to the patient. With the maintenance of health programs, the risk of future illnesses is also reduced, and future health care costs also may be avoided.

The benefits of behavioral counseling are not achieved without some costs, however. The clinician must spend additional time with the patient to explore the patient's difficulties following the prescribed medication and health treatment programs. Behavioral counseling depends upon face-to-face contact with the clinician. In addition, the patient may be required to return for one or more follow-up visits at the clinic to monitor and adjust the behavior change program. The clinician, the patient, and the medical insurance carrier must accept the rationale of investing a few minutes more during the initial treatment of a chronic disease with the promise of reduced long-term medical costs.

The most important implication of behavioral counseling is that health professionals must acquire new skills for use in the clinical setting. Although the ability to effectively counsel a patient for behavior change is not difficult, it does require a specific set of skills that are not obtained from experience. The clinician must learn these skills and their appropriate application through training and practice. These skills can be acquired through continuing education programs, formal coursework, or, as indicated in later chapters, self-instruction.

The clinician also should identify professionals in the community to whom patients with serious psychological or behavioral problems can be referred. Psychologists or social workers with expertise in behavioral counseling can work with the clinician in resolving the patient's health-related behavioral problems, and accept patients into treatment who have serious or difficult problems. With the rapid growth of the field of behavioral medicine, an increasing number of trained individuals are available to help the medical patient cope with a disease or illness. Similarly, training in interviewing and behavioral counseling is becoming a part of the curriculum for dietitians, physician assistants, and nurses. This expertise should be drawn upon to aid the patient with behavioral problems.

The following three chapters provide a detailed discussion of each of the fundamental skills in interviewing, problem identification and analysis, and behavioral counseling that would be needed by the clinician working with medical patients. These skills have been successfully acquired by practicing physicians, physician assistants, nurses, dietitians, physician assistants, and other medical professionals. These skills are considered basic to effective behavioral counseling. It is highly recommended that each skill is mastered prior to initiating a behavioral counseling program with a patient.

## References

1. Haynes RB, Taylor DW, Sackett DL: *Compliance in Health Care*. Baltimore, Johns Hopkins Press, 1979.
2. Bonham GS: Use habits of cigarettes, coffee, aspirin, and sleeping pills, United States, 1976. *Vital and Health Statistics: Series 10, Data from the National Health Survey; no. 131*. DHEW publication No. (PHS) 80-1559.

# 3. Basic Interviewing

The aim of behavioral counseling is to help the patient initiate and maintain significant changes in daily activities that currently are inhibiting the treatment or prevention of a medical disease or condition. These changes involve the modification of established habits such as poor diet, lack of physical exercise, cigarette smoking, and stress reactions. The focus of counseling is on the patients' current problem health behaviors, and their thoughts and feelings about them.

Behavioral counseling involves the clinician in a different interaction with the patient than that which typically occurs when the patient is seeking treatment of a medical problem. In the treatment of a disease, the physician commonly assumes the role of "expert," with both patient and physician acknowledging the physician's specialized medical knowledge and skills. In this role the physician has primary responsibility for the accurate diagnosis and treatment of the illness. As a result the physician is usually active and directive in seeking specific information from the patient regarding the presence and nature of particular symptoms of the disease. In this relationship the patient's role is usually one of cooperation and dependence. The patient is expected to provide accurate information in response to the physician's questions, and to submit to physical examination procedures and tests, as necessary. The physician then synthesizes a diagnosis of the problem using the patient's objective descriptions of the presenting symptoms together with other information independently obtained by the physician from the physical examination and from laboratory tests. Once the diagnosis has been determined, an appropriate medical treatment is prescribed for the patient. The patient is expected to accept the physician's medical diagnosis, and follow the prescribed regimen, as instructed, to resolve the presenting medical problem.

Compare this with the clinician-patient relationship developed in counseling for health behavior change. The clinician follows the same analytic process (i.e., data collection, diagnosis, selection of the intervention, examination of the effects of the intervention, and modification of the intervention, if necessary), but interacts directly with the patient in the development of a behavioral diagnosis, as well as in the design and implementation of all interventions. Discussions with the patient regarding the selection of the goals of counseling, the analysis of the factors contributing to the problem behavior, and the collection of pertinent information, are crucial aspects of the counseling process. The clinician relies considerably more on the patient's active participation during counseling for behavior change than is usually the case when the physician is treating a patient's medical problem.

The nature of the intervention selected to resolve the health behavior problem also differs from the treatment of a medical problem. Usually, to change health-related behavior, the patient is required to make significant changes in daily routines and habits. In most cases the patient is the only one who has knowledge of, and continuing control over, the activities and factors which are supporting or exacerbating the health behavior problem. As a result the clinician must involve the patient directly in the diagnosis and in the selection of the intervention if the problem behavior is to be resolved successfully.

Good rapport between the clinician and the patient is essential to the behavioral counseling process. Behavioral counseling depends upon the patient's willingness to collaborate with the clinician and to be active in the behavior change program. From the moment of initial contact, the clinician strives to develop an open, positive relationship with the patient in which the patient senses that he is understood and accepted by the clinician. The patient must be willing to relate intimate details of his lifestyle freely to the clinician as they affect the problem behavior.

Although rapport between the clinician and the patient often appears to occur spontaneously, it is usually the result of the timely use of a variety of interviewing skills (Table 1). The clinician demonstrates a genuine interest in helping to resolve the patient's problems, and is willing to work with the patient in resolving these difficulties. In doing so, a respect for the patient's personal values is manifest, in which the patient's lifestyle is accepted. In working to resolve the health behavior problems, the clinician does not express disapproval of a patient's values or seek to change them. Rather, the clinician seeks to help the patient achieve the new health behaviors in a way that is compatible with the patient's values.

The clinician is continually reviewing the patient's statements to ensure that rapport with the patient, once established, is not lost. The clinician examines the patient's responses to questions to determine the degree of detail, the relative risk the patient has taken to describe the problem and associated activities of concern, and the presence and depth of feelings expressed by the patient. The clinician also examines the patient's non-verbal behavior for signs of rapport. Body movement and gestures are observed for indications that the patient is relaxed, comfortable, and at ease with the discussion. For example, a patient

Table 1. Inventory of interviewing skills

1. *Relaxed.*
   Throughout the interview, maintain a relaxed, comfortable, confident manner.

2. *Interested.*
   Communicate both verbally and nonverbally an interest in the patient's problems and a personal willingness to help.

3. *Nonjudgmental.*
   Demonstrate your ability to regard the patient's lifestyle and personal characteristics in a nonjudgmental way.

4. *Nonsuggestive.*
   Avoid phrasing questions with implied answers while you gather new information.

5. *Open-ended.*
   Use open-ended questions in the initial stage of exploring a problem area.

6. *Progression.*
   As the discussion of a problem progresses, gradually direct more specific inquiries to the patient.

7. *Closure.*
   Avoid prematurely closing the discussion about a problem behavior or related topic.

8. *Non-interruption.*
   Avoid interrupting the patient.

9. *Probing.*
   Avoid high-pressure, probing questions.

10. *Listening.*
    Demonstrate active listening by using a combination of attentive silence, verbal and nonverbal encouragement, requests for clarification, paraphrase, reflection of feelings, restatement, and direct questions.

11. *Empathy.*
    Express empathy for the patient whose problems have not been alleviated.

12. *Opportunity.*
    After initial problems have been discussed, allow the patient the opportunity to discuss other problems or issues.

13. *Questions.*
    Ask the patient if he has any questions regarding the intervention plan.

14. *Restatement.*
    Before the patient leaves,
    a. Ask the patient to restate his understanding of the new intervention plan
       or
    b. Restate the new intervention plan, and if there were no changes made in a recent strategy, restate it and obtain the patient's agreement to the details of the plan.

who is seated comfortably (e.g., not leaning backward, or in a stiff upright position), who makes and retains eye contact, and who maintains a relatively open posture (e.g., arms not crossed, hands relaxed) is communicating an open, positive attitude to the clinician. In general, the more willing the patient is to offer a detailed description of the specific problem behavior and related thoughts and feelings, and the more at ease the patient appears to be, the greater the degree of rapport the patient feels with the clinician.

## Interviewing Skills

### Open-ended Questions

The use of open-ended questions during the interview is a particularly effective interviewing method that has been applied in a variety of counseling settings including psychiatric, medical, and dental clinics. This approach directly solicits the patient's perceptions, attitudes, and understanding of the problem health behavior. Using a variety of specific interviewing skills, the open-ended interviewing style promotes rapport with the patient, and elicits accurate descriptive information regarding the influence the problem behavior on the patient's daily activities, and vice versa.

The open-ended interviewing approach is based on the observation that the patient's spontaneous reporting of information to the clinician will most rapidly provide the clinician with an understanding of the patient's feelings and attitudes regarding the problem behavior, and place the behavior within the context of other significant activities. When the discussion begins, the patient is offered an uninterrupted opportunity to describe and discuss the problematic health behavior and associated issues. The clinician uses an open-ended question or statement to suggest that the patient describe the problem without indicating specifically what the patient should discuss. The initial open-ended question or statement is deliberately phrased to elicit discussion by the patient. If properly phrased, an open-ended question cannot be answered by a simple yes or no. For example the clinician could initiate the discussion of a problem health behavior by using one of the following open-ended questions:

"You mentioned that you have had some difficulty taking all of the medication. Would you describe what the problems have been?"

"I'd like to learn more about the type of physical exercise you get during a typical week."

Broad, open-ended questions and statements communicate the clinician's concern and interest in learning about the patient's problems, yet afford the patient the opportunity to discuss any aspect of the problem behavior. The patient is not being directed as to which information should be discussed, rather the clinician is seeking to know which aspects of the problem behavior are the most prominent for the patient. In this way the clinician is able to learn the patient's perceptions, attitudes, and feelings about the problem behavior, information which is extremely difficult to ask for directly. At the same time, the patient is also providing needed objective information which can be used later in developing the behavioral diagnosis and treatment.

Properly phrased, an open-ended question does not communicate the clinician's biases to the patient. The nature and order of the clinician's questions about the patient's experience can influence the patient's reporting of these experiences. Some patients will attempt to read into the questions what the clinician expects to hear. For these patients, either a question which suggests an answer, or a series of questions dwelling on a particular aspect of a problem that are asked before the patient has had an opportunity to discuss the problem, can direct the patient's attention to minor aspects of the problem or treatment with the expectation that they are significant. For example, the question, "Mrs. Stevens, have you experienced any change in your bowel habits since you have been on the medication?" might be an appropriate question after Mrs. Stevens has had an opportunity to offer her perception regarding the difficulties in taking her prescribed medication; however, if the question were asked initially in the interview the clinician might be communicating to Mrs. Stevens that disturbances in bowel habits are expected or of concern. Mrs. Stevens might then focus on her bowel habits rather than discussing other areas which have greater importance in terms of Mrs. Stevens' difficulties in taking the medication. Subsequently, she might become overly vigilant with regard to her bowel habits and unnecessarily concerned about fluctuations in routine.

Perhaps one of the most important advantages of the open-ended interviewing style is its demonstration of the clinician's desire to hear about the patient's concerns and problems. The clinician is implicitly saying to the patient, "I am interested in what you have to say, and what your experiences have been. Please tell me what has been troubling you." This statement directly communicates to the patient that the clinician is willing to work with him to resolve the presenting problems. From the initial inquiry the clinician is attempting to establish rapport with the patient and to develop a collaborative relationship.

When offered an open-ended opportunity to discuss problems or concerns, most patients will first discuss those which are most important to them (i.e., creating the most disruption or discomfort), and then discuss the less significant ones as the interview progresses. Often, this order will reveal the patient's priorities in terms of the problems. However, the clinician also should be aware that problems which the patient feels uncomfortable discussing due to embarrassment, shame, or guilt may not be revealed initially. Usually these problems will only be revealed if the patient feels sufficient trust and confidence in the clinician, or if the patient is directly asked about them.

While the initial use of open-ended questions or statements is appropriate with most patients, the clinician also must be aware that it is not necessarily the best approach for all patients, particularly those who are extremely verbal and eager to relate details of their problems. In this case, open-ended questions will generate a diffuse unfocused discussion, with too much time spent on extraneous information. The clinician must be prepared to shift rapidly to a more directive style, using interviewing techniques that increase the clinician's control over the direction and pace of the interview.

As the interview continues, the clinician uses other interviewing skills that encourage the patient to describe in his own way the problem behavior and its

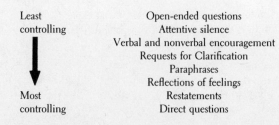

|  | Open-ended questions |
| Least | Attentive silence |
| controlling | Verbal and nonverbal encouragement |
|  | Requests for Clarification |
|  | Paraphrases |
|  | Reflections of feelings |
| Most | Restatements |
| controlling | Direct questions |

Figure 1. Sequence of interviewing skills, from least controlling to most controlling.

surrounding circumstances. These include: (1) non-verbal encouragements, (2) verbal encouragements, (3) attentive silence, (4) requests for clarification, (5) paraphrases, (6) reflection of feelings, and (7) restatements. As indicated in Figure 1, these skills vary in the degree to which they tend to elicit explicit information from the patient.

Usually, as the discussion of a particular topic continues, the clinician will progress from using the less controlling skills to using the more controlling skills. In this way the discussion moves from a discussion of the aspects of the problem which are most prominent for the patient to details the clinician needs to develop a behavioral analysis of the problem. The skills listed above are used to guide the discussion of a topic or to expand and clarify specific aspects of the discussion. They give the clinician the flexibility to cover a wide range of topics, and to direct the discussion as needed to explore a particular subject in detail.

*Attentive Silence*

Throughout the interview the clinician communicates a genuine interest in helping the patient develop a program to achieve the desired health behavior change. The clinician demonstrates a willingness to listen and a desire to understand the patient's problems as the patient perceives them. The clinician can communicate this attitude most effectively by adopting a relaxed, attentive posture and remaining silent while the patient is describing a problem area.

Though silent, the clinician is not passive but rather is attempting to conceptualize and understand the patient's problems. Thus the clinician should not appear to be uninterested, bored, or inattentive (e.g., scanning the patient's chart while either one is talking).

The clinician's silence reflects a desire to have the patient fully express himself in order to understand his perceptions of the problem. The highest value is placed on hearing the patient's explanations, thoughts, or feelings, particularly as they occur to the patient during the course of the discussion. Therefore, the clinician is careful to listen to the patient, even if the patient attempts to

Table 2. Examples of phrases, facial expressions,
and gestures that encourage a patient to continue
the discussion

---

*Phrases*
Yes
I understand.
Okay.
Uh-huh.
Go on.

*Facial expressions*
Attentive
Continued eye contact

*Gestures*
Head nodding
Open body posture (e.g., arms uncrossed, body facing the
    patient, hands open)

---

interrupt the clinician, and to avoid interrupting the patient when he is speaking. In general, it is more important to hear the patient's comments than to interject with one's own thoughts since, in most cases, the patient will be absorbed in his own thoughts and will not fully attend to the clinician's question or statement

Occasionally during the discussion the patient will pause before continuing with the narration. Often during these moments the patient is choosing the proper word to convey his thoughts or feelings, formulating a thought, or deciding whether to discuss an aspect of the problem with the clinician. The clinician's proper response is to continue to express an attentive, relaxed attitude and remain silent. Since this silence interrupts the pace of the dialogue, it can be uncomfortable for the clinician. Desiring to pursue the resolution of the problem and feeling pressures from the limited interview time usually available, the clinician may be tempted to continue the interview by suggesting what the patient might be trying to express, or completing the patient's sentence, or asking a question. However, those aspects of a problem that are the most difficult for the patient to describe or discuss are frequently the most critical for the clinician to understand. When these situations occur, the clinician should remain silent and allow the patient time to formulate his thoughts and feelings.

## Encouragement

Once the patient begins describing a topic, the clinician uses a combination of phrases, facial expressions, and gestures which indicate to the patient that the clinician is listening to his narrative, understanding what is being described, and wants to hear more (Table 2). These responses by the clinician encourage

Table 3. Examples of phrases, facial expressions, and gestures that indicate that the clinician is seeking clarification of what the patient has previously stated

---

*Phrases*
I'm sorry.
I didn't follow you.
Humm?
I don't understand.

*Facial expressions*
Puzzlement
Raised eyebrow

*Gestures*
Head shake, "no"
Movement of the head or body toward the patient
Tilting of the head

---

the patient to continue with the description of the topic without communicating the clinician's reaction to the patient's statements. Usually the clinician uses these techniques while the patient is speaking.

The timing of such encouragement is critical to its effectiveness. It is essential to avoid interrupting or interfering with the patient's account. Further, the clinician must also be careful to use the techniques of encouragement intermittently. Continual use will result in the patient eventually ignoring the intended message. Rapid use of these techniques can be taken as an indication that the clinician wishes the patient to condense the discussion and move on to other topics. Thus, not only will the patient be discouraged from giving further information but rapport can also suffer due to his perception of a lack of interest on the clinician's part.

## Requests for Clarification

As the discussion continues, the patient may make a statement which the clinician does not understand. A request for clarification can be made directly and also communicated in facial expressions and gestures (Table 3).

The clinician is careful to phrase the request for clarification so that it does not imply disapproval (i.e., seeking to know "why" the patient performed a particular behavior). Rather, he is asking the patient to repeat or rephrase what was previously stated (i.e., seeking to know "what" the patient said or did). This not only allows the clinician to get more accurate information, but also communicates interest to the patient.

Table 4. Examples of the clinician's use of paraphrase, reflection of feelings, and restatement in response to the patient's statements

| Patient's statement | Alternative clinician responses |
| --- | --- |
| Over the past two months it has been very difficult for me to stay on my weight loss diet. Right now, I'm spending more time working late at the office than ever before. When I finally do get home, I'm usually so hungry that I won't give much thought to preparing dinner. I'll just reheat some left-overs, or a frozen dinner. Other times I'll just stop in a fast-food restaurant on the way home. I know that I shouldn't, but sometimes I just don't have the energy to prepare dinner when I have worked hard all day. | *Paraphrase*<br>As I understand it, when you have been working late at the office you often are very tired and, as a result, are less likely to make the effort to prepare a low-calorie meal for yourself.<br><br>*Reflection of feeling*<br>You sound frustrated that you haven't been able to stay on your diet and a bit guilty about being too tired in the evenings.<br><br>*Restatement*<br>Working late . . . ?<br>Fast-food restaurant . . . ?<br>You said you don't have the energy to prepare dinner when you have worked hard all day . . . ?<br><br>*Direct questions*<br>How often do you work late at the office?<br>What time do you usually arrive home?<br>Do you anticipate having to work late very often over the next two months? |

## Paraphrase

A paraphrase is an explicit statement by the clinician that summarizes a longer account by the patient. The clinician offers a paraphrase to ensure that he has correctly understood what the patient has said, and given the patient the opportunity to agree with or modify the clinician's perception. The dialogue presented in Table 4 illustrates the clinician's appropriate use of a paraphrase.

Notice that the paraphrase used in Table 4 is a brief statement containing what the clinician selects as the essence of the patient's previous statement. When used skillfully, a paraphrase is not only a method for summarizing the patient's statements, but also an explicit demonstration of the clinician's desire to clearly understand what the patient has described. In this way the clinician's use of paraphrases contributes to the development of rapport with the patient.

## Reflections of Feelings

Throughout the interview session, the clinician is seeking to identify and understand the patient's feelings about the topic(s) or problem(s) under discussion. This information aids the clinician in identifying the important facets of the problem and in developing a specific intervention. The clinician must be confident that the patient's feelings associated with the problem behavior have been revealed.

Occasionally, therefore, after the patient has described a particular aspect of the problem, the clinician may choose to direct attention to the apparent affective responses displayed by the patient during the description. The clinician's reflection of a patient's feelings is an inferential statement based on the patient's facial expressions or gestures, or the emotional tone of the patient's statements. Through careful observation of the patient, the clinician usually has obtained some evidence that the patient is experiencing a particular emotion. The clinician is not guessing or projecting his own feelings onto the patient, nor is he suggesting how the patient ought to feel. The dialogue presented in Table 4 illustrates the clinician's appropriate reflection of a patient's feeling.

In this dialogue the clinician chose to ignore for the moment the information the patient was presenting and instead focused attention on the patient's feelings of frustration and guilt. Later in the interview the clinician will re-direct the interview to a discussion of the information content. As the example illustrates, the patient may be experiencing several feelings at the same time (e.g., anger and frustration, guilt and hopelessness). The clinician should refer to each of these feelings, and offer a brief yet accurate reflection to the patient. The patient's response to the clinician's statement usually will indicate the extent and nature of each of the feelings mentioned. The patient's response will indicate whether the clinician's perception is accurate, whether the patient acknowledges the apparent feelings, and to what degree the feelings are an important aspect of the problem.

Some patients have considerable difficulty identifying or expressing the feelings they have about themselves and their problems. It is important that the clinician be able to elicit these feelings in a gentle way, without confrontation or accusation. The clinician's use of reflection of a feeling should be perceived by the patient as part of the clinician's continuing attempt to understand the patient's problem and its effect on the patient.

Through the course of the health behavior change program, the patient may experience some discomfort and failure in making the desired behavioral changes. To maintain support, it is important for the clinician to show that he recognizes and has an empathic understanding of the patient's difficulties. Empathic statements usually are relatively brief (Table 5). Note in the examples that the clinician is not *sympathizing* with the patient by expressing agreement or support for the patient's feelings. By empathizing with the problems the clinician is recognizing the depth of the emotional reactions expressed by the patient without condoning or supporting their continued presence. These fears or anxieties will often become a target of a health behavior change program as it progresses.

Table 5. Examples of empathy versus sympathy as expressed by the clinician

| Empathy | Sympathy |
| --- | --- |
| From what you have said about your irregular schedule while you are traveling on business trips, I can see how difficult it was for you to remain on your jogging program. | It is a real shame that you weren't able to stay on your jogging program while you were traveling. |
| Your craving for a cigarette must have caused you considerable discomfort. | I am very sorry you are having such a tough time stopping because of your craving for a smoke. |

## Restatement

As the patient discusses the targeted health behavior and activities associated with it, the clinician must be able to sift through the information and direct the discussion toward describing more fully a particular issue raised by the patient. In open-ended interviewing, the clinician encourages the patient to expand the description of a particular topic but avoids asking direct questions or specifying which aspect of the topic the patient should discuss. In this way, the clinician is asking for more information on a topic but the patient is free to determine which aspects to present.

A restatement is simply a repetition of a word or phrase used in the immediately preceding discussion. Often the restatement is given the inflection of a question. However, the restatement is not presented as a challenge to the patient. The clinician should not be questioning the validity of what the patient has said, but rather seeking a more complete description. The dialogue in Table 4 offers several examples of the appropriate use of restatement.

## Direct Questions

A direct question is a narrowly focused question designed to obtain specific information from the patient. The direct question is used to elicit additional information which was not reported spontaneously. After the patient has been given the initial opportunity to describe a problem or issue, the clinician follows-up in a non-directive way (i.e., with encouragements, paraphrases, restatements, and reflections of feelings) to obtain additional information. However, the patient may not describe spontaneously all aspects of the problem behavior in sufficient detail for the clinician to understand it adequately. The clinician can then use direct questions to obtain additional specific information.

The direct question is a relatively narrowly focused question which requests information about a circumscribed aspect of a topic. Examples are presented in Table 4. Usually, these questions inquire who, what, where, when or how.

These questions ask for a report of the circumstances surrounding a behavior, and for details of activities or events as they occurred in the past. Open-ended questions are used to ask the patient to consider a problem area, select those aspects of the problem that are most prominent for the patient, and report the patient's perceptions of the issues. In contrast, direct questions ask for an objective reporting of the facts.

Direct questions should be phrased neutrally. That is, the direct questions do not contain implied answers such as "You haven't stopped taking your medication at anytime during the last three months, have you?" Better phrasings would be: "Did you stop your medication at anytime in the last three months?"; Have you cut down on your cigarette smoking?" Similarly, properly phrased direct questions do not contain several answers for the patient to consider (i.e., multiple choice questions), such as, "Did you start smoking again because you felt under more pressure at work lately, or because the side effects from withdrawal were too great for you?" Rather the clinician should allow the patient to answer the question without prejudice. In this case, for example: "What do you believe was the major factor that led you to resume smoking?"

When open-ended questions and statements give away to direct questioning of the patient, the nature of the dialogue shifts from a patient-directed narrative to clinician-directed reporting by the patient. The control of the interview clearly shifts to the clinician and the patient provides the information requested. Recognizing that direct questions must be used at times, the clinician should strive to use them only when necessary.

The clinician must be particularly careful to avoid using a series of direct questions. This high-pressure probing can lead the patient to believe erroneously that it is only done to provide the clinician with information, while the clinician's role is to diagnose the problem and to select the appropriate intervention. In particular, if the patient responds affirmatively to a direct question, the clinician should revert to an open-ended inquiry so that the patient can more fully explain the response.

## Interviews in the Brief Clinic Visit

The open-ended interviewing style is most productive when the clinician has sufficient time to fully explore each topic that arises in the discussion. Unfortunately, many clinicians are limited in the clinic setting to an abbreviated interview with the patient who is seeking counseling for health behavior change. Therefore, the clinician should be able to conduct an interview using modified open-ended interviewing style.

Before attempting to modify the open-ended interviewing style one should possess sufficient experience in using each of the previously described interviewing skills without time constraints. The clinician should have fully inte-

grated these interviewing skills into his own style and be able to conduct a behavior counseling sessions without undue attention to the interviewing skills which
are being used.

The most effective method of compressing the behavioral counseling process
is to collect, as efficiently as possible, the information necessary to develop the
behavioral diagnosis. To do so, the clinician must be aware of the information
that is essential to the counseling process and of that which is desirable but of
secondary importance. The type of information is discussed in detail in Chapter 4.

During the interview the efficiency of information collection can be increased in several ways. First, the clinician should avoid initiating discussion
of any topic that is not directly related to the problem behavior. Even in the
initial phase of the interview, the clinician should seek to establish rapport through
the use of questions that will reveal information about the patient's lifestyle rather
than irrelevant "social conversation." In this way the clinician opens the interview with an exchange that communicates concern about the patient's opinions, attitudes, and lifestyle while collecting information which could be used
later in the design of a behavior change intervention.

Second, the clinician should familiarize himself with the details of any past
discussions of the problem behavior, as indicated on the patient's chart. Before
the interview begins the clinician should know what information is available,
and what information is needed.

Third, the clinician should carefully consider whether each question asked
during the interview will contribute directly to the information needed to understand the problem behavior. The clinician should pause, rather than ask a
question that does not contribute to the fund of information that is needed. He
should be comfortable in reflecting for a minute before asking the next questions, rather than simply asking a series of questions to "keep the interview going."
Further, the clinician should pursue a focused line of questioning rather than
skipping around from topic to topic during the discussion. If necessary he should
indicate that the discussion can return later in the interview to a new topic or
sub-topic introduced by the patient. This will help the clinician understand the
problems in one area at a time, and will also help ensure that the patient offers
a complete description of a topic without omitting important details (a hazard
when the discussion skips from one topic to another).

Fourth, properly designed written questionnaires can be particularly helpful
in reducing the amount of time needed for the behavioral counseling interview. These questionnaires can be developed to provide a current description
of the patient's attitudes, behavior, and problems. The clinician can rapidly scan
the questionnaire before the interview, identify continuing problems, and avoid
exploring areas of lesser concern for the patient. Similarly, records which the

patient maintains at home between clinic visits can be extremely valuable in providing a rapid summary of detailed changes in the patient's behavior. These give the clinician a view of the patient's health behavior change program that would be very time-consuming to obtain during the interview, even if the patient could recall the details over time at all. Examples of these questionnaires and patient-maintained records for specific health behaviors are presented in the following chapters.

While the clinician should pursue every method to improve the efficiency of data collection, this must not compromise his efforts to discuss the patient's attitudes and beliefs regarding the target behavior and the proposed treatment plan. The clinician must seek the patient's opinions, feelings, and reactions in addition to the factual information about the targeted behavior. Since the patient is the one who implements the treatment plan, it is most important for the patient to believe that an appropriate behavioral diagnosis has been made, and that a promising intervention has been developed. The best intervention strategy obviously will not succeed if the patient fails to implement it.

**Practical Exercise**

While the interviewing skills discussed in this chapter are relatively straightforward in theory, most clinicians find that their application in the actual clinical setting requires some practice and review. The following exercises are recommended for the clinician who wishes to develop these skills.

The most effective method of rapidly developing interviewing skills is to tape-record an interview and then carefully review the use of each interviewing skill during the discussion. Initially these interviews should be conducted without making any attempts to modify your current interviewing style. The purpose of recording the interview is to obtain a valid record of your current skills in order to identify those skills which you currently possess, those skills which you will need to practice, and those skills which you do not possess. Review the audiotape using the inventory of interviewing skills presented in Table 1 and determine whether you feel each was adequately demonstrated. Remember, the goal of this training is to be able to use each of the skills in a clinical interview comfortably and naturally. Eventually you should be able to use a blend of skills without having to devote much attention to their use.

Repeated practice in formulating each of the interviewing skills in response to a patient's statement will improve your flexibility in their use. It is recommended that you review a tape-recording of an interview which you have conducted with a patient and stop the tape after each statement by the patient. Then, as rapidly as possible, formulate an appropriate statement using each of the seven interviewing skills. Repeated practice of this exercise will rapidly develop your ability to select and formulate a response during an interview in the office or clinic setting without having to pause and reflect on the proper wording.

Another useful exercise is to observe an interview conducted by an experienced colleague with a patient. As a non-participant in the interview you will be able to identify how your colleague uses each of the interviewing skills. Particular attention should be focused on the way in which the clinician phrases the open-ended questions, paraphrases, restatements, reflections, etc., and the sequence of their usage.

# 4. Behavioral Counseling

## The Patient's Decision

The goal of behavioral counseling is the permanent modification of a patient's health behavior. However, it is the patient who either rejects or accepts the physician's recommendation regarding the specific health behavior to be changed. The first step in the behavioral counseling process is a careful examination by the clinician and the patient of the decision to initiate the health behavior change program at this time. The clinician must review with the patient the factors that have entered into the decision, and the strength of each factor. Why has the patient decided to make a change in the health-related behavior? What prompted the decision? How strong is the desire for change?

If the patient is seeking to change a long-standing behavior, the clinician should determine why the patient has decided to make a change at this point. What are the reasons that contributed to the patient's decision, and in particular, what has occurred recently that prompted the patient to take action? Behavior of long standing requires considerable investment of time and effort for successful change. The patient must be prepared to accept some disruption of the normal daily routine, perhaps physical discomfort, and the gradual achievement of the desired changes. Once achieved, the patient must be aware that the change will require continued effort to be maintained. It may be several months before the patient has adapted to the new routines necessary to support the desired behavior. Therefore, the patient should be encouraged to give due consideration to the nature of the program before entering into it. If the patient has not clearly made this decision, or is not willing to invest the time and effort required, the clinician should encourage the patient to carefully re-consider the decision before beginning the health behavior change program.

In exploring the factors that contributed to the patient's decision to change, the clinician should seek the patient's perceptions of the positive and negative aspects of the desired health behavior. If, for example, the patient is interested in stopping cigarette smoking, the clinician should determine what the patient believes will occur if success is achieved. What are the major positive effects? What are the secondary positive effects? Does the patient anticipate any major or secondary negative effects? Does the patient have realistic expectations of the consequences of the change? If these expectations are unrealistic (e.g., that the patient will have a more active social life after stopping smoking), then even if the behavior change program is initially successful, the long-term maintenance of the change is unlikely. When the expected major positive effects of the behavior change program do not occur, it is unlikely that the patient will continue to invest time and effort in the program.

Programs that do not succeed in maintaining the desired health behaviors over time are not only disappointing for the patient and clinician, they can also undermine the patient's confidence in ever changing a health-related behavior. Unsuccessful programs tend to promote the patient's erroneous belief that the problem behavior is a permanent part of his personality. The patient begins to accept himself as a fat person, or a smoker, or non-athletic, or heart-attack prone, or possessing a "type A" personality. Once fixed, these negative self-images reduce the likelihood that the patient will decide in the future to change the behavior.

Clues to the degree to which patients have negative attitudes toward themselves will emerge from an analysis of past efforts to change health behaviors (Table 1). The clinician should examine the history of a patient's health behavior change programs including when they were initiated, why the patient embarked on the programs, what the patient's goals were, what methods were used, how successful the patient was in achieving the goals, how successful the patient was in maintaining the behavioral changes, and what the patient's thoughts were about the success or failure of the programs. The patient's answers to these questions will provide the clinician with valuable information for assessing the patient's current decision to change a health-related behavior. They also will indicate the patient's current capability for initiating and maintaining significant changes in lifestyle. This information will be extremely useful in designing a program with a greater probability of success.

### Identifying Troublesome Health-Related Behaviors

The clinician should recognize that many patients will not readily volunteer to discuss a particular troublesome aspect of their lifestyle. They may need to be offered an opportunity to bring it up. The clinician should explicitly ask if the patient has other problems of concern before beginning a detailed discussion of any particular behavior. In this way a discussion of a behavior of secondary concern is not inadvertently prolonged.

When several problem health behaviors are identified, the clinician should investigate each one to gain an understanding of the nature of the problem, the extent of the time and effort that would be required to change the behaviors

Table 1. Inventory of behavioral counseling skills used to resolve problem health behaviors

---

1. *Daily routine.*
Clinician obtains the details of patient's daily routine at home during the week.

2. *Weekend routine.*
Clinician obtains details of patient's routine at home on weekends.

3. *Travel routine.*
Clinician obtains details of patient's daily routine when away from home.

4. *Problems.*
Clinician specifically identifies all health behavior problems of concern to patient.

5. *Behavior profile.*
Clinician obtains specific information regarding frequency, duration, and intensity of the behavior.

6. *Behavior analysis.*
Clinician obtains specific information regarding the antecedents and consequences of the behavior.

7. *Patient's thoughts.*
Clinician obtains information to develop an analysis of patient's thoughts about the particular problem (i.e., antecedents and consequences).

8. *Summarization.*
Before offering a strategy to resolve a particular problem, clinician summarizes his understanding of the problem.

9. *Intermediate goals.*
Clinician collaborates with the patient in the selection of changes in behavior as intermediate goals on the way to the final, desired health behavior.

10. *Treatment development.*
Before offering a treatment to resolve a problem, clinician provides patient with opportunity to develop the treatment. Later, clinician provides patient with an opportunity to modify treatment plan to be used.

11. *Reaction.*
Clinician obtains patient's explicit support for the strategy designed to resolve the problem.

12. *Data.*
Clinician designs an appropriate data collection system for recording changes in patient's behavior as a result of the implementation of the strategy designed to resolve the problem.

---

and the degree to which the patient desires to change. This exploration will place each problem behavior in perspective with regard to other problem behaviors, and indicate still others that may be affecting the targeted behavior, or may be affected by the intervention program. In either case the clinician is alerted to the need to assess periodically the current status of certain behaviors.

## Selecting Goals

Once the behavior has been identified for the initial behavior change program, the next step in the counseling process is to achieve a clear definition of the goals of the program. The patient and the clinician must agree on these goals at the outset. The desired behavior should be operationally defined in terms of activities which the patient can readily observe and identify. For example "stopping smoking" could be defined variously as "a complete abstinence of smoking any tobacco product," or "a complete abstinence of smoking cigarettes" (i.e., a pipe or cigar are permitted). The patient and the clinician must agree on the goal of the program to avoid misunderstandings in interpreting and assessing subsequent progress. The patient should always have the responsibility of selecting the goals of the behavior change program.

### Analyzing the Patient's Problem Behaviors

All behavior change programs are designed to alter the behavioral patterns in which the patient's problems are enmeshed. The clinician, therefore, must obtain an accurate description of the behavior the patient wishes to change, and identify the interrelationships between this targeted behavior and other, associated behaviors in the patient's daily activities. For example, beginning a program of walking may affect the patient's morning routine (including time of awakening), or his evening quiet time, or his usual lunch hour habits. Once these behavioral patterns are identified, a specific program can be developed that will take them into account. The identification of these interrelated behavioral patterns is probably the most difficult and crucial task to be accomplished during the interviews with the patient.

All behaviors can be seen as interrelated, each element stimulated by preceding behavior and, in turn, leading to subsequent behavior. An individual's behavior may thus be viewed as a continuous chain. Embedded in this chain are the clusters of behaviors that influence the targeted behavior. The clinician attempts to identify the patterns of interrelated behavior that are associated with the targeted behavior and repeatedly occur over time.

The events that typically precede a targeted problem behavior (e.g., overeating, smoking) are carefully examined. Activities that are routinely observed to occur before the behavior may be provoking it. The answers to questions of who, when, and where are sought. These precipitating activities, or *antecedent behaviors*, can be any activity, physical location, social interaction, thoughts, feelings, or the passage of time that can be perceived by the patient. For example, if the problem is excessive calorie intake resulting in overweight, a behavioral analysis might reveal that the patient is eating nutritionally balanced meals that provide an appropriate calorie intake, but is also periodically consuming excessive calories from snack-type foods when feeling anxious. The analysis would explore the exact relationship between the patient's feelings of anxiety and eating. When does the eating occur? What is the patient doing? Who is present? (Table 2).

Some problem behaviors (e.g., smoking, eating) may be provoked by physi-

Table 2. Example of a functional analysis of a problem behavior (excessive calorie consumption leading to overweight)

| Antecedents | Problem behavior | Consequences |
|---|---|---|
| *When*. For approximately 24 hours prior to a stressful activity.<br><br>*Activities*. Patient is either at home watching television in the evening or taking a break from work.<br><br>*People*. Patient is with family in the evening, with two co-workers during breaks.<br><br>*Thoughts*. Patient reports thinking about how important making a good presentation is to his/her career.<br><br>*Feelings*. Patient reports being in a state of constant anxiety before having to make a public presentation; reports also feeling constantly hungry. | Problem behavior consists of the patient eating large quantities of sweet snack foods, including ice cream, cookies, various pastries. | Patient reports feeling satisfied and less anxious after having eaten. Reports occasionally receiving disapproving comments from spouse about snacking, which are ignored. Sometimes, to spite spouse, patient will have additional food. Also states that co-workers have never commented on these eating habits. |

cal locations (e.g., watching a movie, attending a sports event, going to a party). Others may be triggered by social interactions, such as family problems or job concerns. While still others, such as sleep disturbances, can be elicited by such private events as anxious thoughts or feelings. Smoking and eating are often stimulated by the simple passage of time (e.g. length of time since the last cigarette or the last meal). While temporal proximity does not always indicate that an antecedent event is provoking the problem behavior, observation of its repeated presence usually indicates that the event plays a role in stimulating that behavior.

These antecedent events or activities need not provoke a strong emotional reaction in the patient to have a significant effect on the patient's behavior. The antecedents of a problem behavior may be subtle to the point that the patient is not aware of their effect. That is, the patient may be reacting to an event, feelings, or physical location in a routine manner without being conscious of doing so. These subtle habitual daily routines may have a prominent role in stimulating problem behaviors. For example, the activities and events that stimulate cigarette smoking can be as unobtrusive as leaving a building, finishing a telephone call, driving on a freeway, or thinking about an upcoming vacation. It is possible that these activities may have been associated with an emotional response in the past which was then followed by the problem health behavior. Over time the emotional response may be diminished, and the antecedent event currently stimulates only the problem behavior. It is also possible that the current antecedent event may never have played a role in initiating the problem behavior, but is similar enough to the original antecedent events to continue to stimulate the problem behavior. In either case a careful review of the events, activities, and behavior that precede the problem behavior is essential to understand the behavioral pattern.

The events that typically occur following a targeted problem behavior also should be investigated. These events may be functioning as direct *consequences* of the behavior and either supporting or inhibiting its recurrence in the future. Positive consequences following the problem behavior tend to increase the likelihood that the patient will engage in the same act in a similar situation in the future, while adverse or negative consequences following the problem behavior tend to decrease the likelihood that it will be performed again in the future. The consequences of the problem behavior are defined in terms of the patient's perception of their existence and effect. That is, a positive consequence is positive only because the patient perceives it as positive. Similarly, a negative consequence is negative only insofar as the patient perceives it as aversive.

The consequences that influence a problem behavior can be exerted by any activity, social interaction, or private event. Positive consequences can include pleasant sensations, pleasing thoughts, social status, praise from others, the acquisition of desired items, or participation in a pleasurable event (Table 2). Negative consequences can involve either the inability to experience, acquire, or achieve desired positive consequences (e.g., being ignored by others, exclusion from pleasurable activities, absence of positive self-thoughts) or the experience of punishing events (e.g., criticism from others, derogatory thoughts about oneself, loss of social status). The patient interprets each of these activities or events as either positive or negative, and also determines their strength and value.

The clinician seeks this information directly from the patient who is the only one who can identify the presence, nature, and intensity of the consequences that are affecting the problem behavior. However, an accurate recall of the chain of events that preceded and followed the behavior will not always reveal the actual consequences. Often a patient's health-related behavior is being supported because it eliminates or avoids a negative consequence. The actual negative consequence may have occurred only a single time in the past, and the patient is determined not to allow it to recur. For example, some smokers avoid stopping smoking once they have experienced the effects of nicotine withdrawal, or have experienced a substantial increase in weight after they stopped smoking. The clinician should ask the patient what he perceives to be the positive and negative consequences of both the problem behavior and the new desired behavior.

## Analyzing the Effects of Starting a New Health Behavior

If, instead of attempting to eliminate or reduce a problem behavior, the patient is interested in initiating or increasing the occurrence of a new health behavior, such as an exercise program or taking medication, the clinician is still concerned with identifying the existing behavioral patterns. Since the new health behavior will be inserted into the patient's current daily routine, the behavior that will be disrupted or displaced by the new health behavior should be examined carefully.

Until demonstrated otherwise, it is best to assume that each of the patient's actions is (or has been) associated with desired consequences. Further, once established, the repeated performance of virtually any behavior will result in the behavior acquiring positive consequences. The behavior becomes expected, routine, comfortable, and eventually desired. As a result, the elimination of almost any habitual behavior will be, to some degree, uncomfortable, disorienting, and awkward. For example, if the patient desires to start a physical exercise program in the morning before breakfast, the clinician would examine the patient's current before breakfast routine. Of particular concern would be those activities that would be directly affected by the new program. Would the patient have to sacrifice sleep? or eat breakfast later? or stop reading the paper in the morning? What would be the consequences of such changes in the patient's normal morning routine?

## Examining Infrequent Desirable Behaviors

Some health behavior change programs are designed to increase the frequency of a currently existing health-related behavior. For example, the patient may be engaged in an active physical exercise, but doing so only two days each week. The goal of the program might be to help the individual determine how he could start a regular exercise program four or more times per week. In this case the clinician would review both the behavior patterns that typically occur during the times that the patient chooses to initiate the new exercise program, and also the behavior patterns that would occur when the patient did not engage in the exercise program. A detailed review of the antecedents and consequences for both the problem behavior (i.e., the activities that occur in place of the exercise program) and the desired behavior (i.e, the exercise program) would be needed since the behavioral change program will affect both.

## Regular and Irregular Schedules

Regardless of whether the target of the behavioral change program is to eliminate a currently existing problem, or to start a new health behavior, or to increase the frequency of a currently existing one, the clinician should examine the patient's typical routines throughout a day, a week, and a month. How regular are the patient's daily activities? How do they change on the week-end? How do they change from week to week as job demands fluctuate (e.g., shift work, monthly reports, travel). To what degree does the patient's behavior vary and are there patterns in the variations? The answers to these questions may indicate that the behavioral change program will need to have two or three different components, each directed at a particular behavioral pattern present during the week, on the weekend, or when the patient is traveling.

## The Behavioral Profile

Once the problem behavior has been identified and its relationship with other activities explored, a profile of this behavior should be developed that indicates its frequency, duration, and intensity. These three characteristics define the prominence of the behavior in the patient's daily activities. That is, how many, how often, and to what degree are the patient's daily activities affected by the problem behavior? Before starting a behavioral program it is important to obtain an accurate measurement of each of these characteristics so that changes in these measures can be used to evaluate progress.

The frequency of the targeted behavior is simply the incidence of that behavior over a given period of time. Usually the frequency is measured in number of times the behavior occurs per hour, day, or week. Typical frequency measurements are presented in Table 3.

The duration of a specific behavior is the length of time it lasts. Usually the duration is measured in minutes. Since duration tends to vary over time, its range should be obtained as well as its average. Programs to initiate a new be-

Table 3. Examples of frequency, duration, and intensity measurements for health behaviors

| Behavior | Frequency | Duration | Intensity |
|----------|-----------|----------|-----------|
| Diet | Mg cholesterol/day | NA | NA |
|  | Mg salt/day | NA | NA |
| Weight control | Calories/day | NA | NA |
| Exercise | Miles run/day | Total minutes | Effort |
|  | Laps of pool/day | Total minutes | Effort |
| Stress | Incidents/day or /week | Total minutes | 1–10 scale |
| Smoking | Cigarettes/hour or /day | Minutes/cigarette | Enjoyment |
| Medication | Doses/day | Total minutes | Side effects |

NA, not applicable.

havior, such as physical exercise, also usually aim to increase the duration of that behavior. Conversely, one of the goals of programs that attempt to eliminate or reduce a problem health behavior is to decrease the duration of the behavior (e.g., smoking, stress, sleep disturbances).

The intensity of a behavior is a subjective report of the patient's feelings about it. Usually intensity is conceptualized in terms of the degree of pleasant or unpleasant feelings. These include feelings of anxiety, pain, hunger, drowsiness, relaxation, enthusiasm, and contentment. The patient is asked to report the current intensity of the feeling on a scale of 1 to 10 (1 = none, 5 = moderate, 10 = extreme). While the patient's subjective reports regarding the intensity of a feeling associated with a behavior should not be used as a primary measure of the progress of a behavioral change program, they do represent a significant aspect of the patient's perceptions in the degree of success achieved.

## Collecting Information

People vary in their ability to recall their past activities accurately. Some people can describe their activities during one day a week ago in great detail, while others have great difficulty describing what they did yesterday. While part of the ability to remember one's own actions in the past is probably innate, the degree of difficulty in recalling daily activities is also related to the nature and number of an individual's activities during each day. The probability of remembering specific daily activities decreases with the total number of activities performed each day, the number of new activities performed each day, and the regularity of the daily schedule (i.e., whether the same activity is routinely performed at the same time each day). For example, it is considerably more likely that an office worker will recall his daily activities one week later if he has a steady, non-stressful, 9 a.m. to 5 p.m. routine that rarely varies. Each daily activity is expected and occurs in a definite, predictable sequence. Thus a new event is easily recognized because it stands out against the routine activities. However, the office worker who is under some stress to complete his assignments, and whose assignments vary daily, is much less likely to recall all of the events in a single day in the previous week. As a result, the patient may not be able to provide the clinician with sufficient detail regarding the problem behavior or the behavioral pattern surrounding it. The clinician needs additional information.

Often the patient is asked to collect information about the behavioral pattern that surrounds the problem behavior, or information regarding the behavioral profile. Information about the behavioral pattern is usually obtained in a daily record format (Table 4). This format provides room for the antecedents and consequences of the behavior of concern. Usually a patient is asked to describe "who," "where," "when," and any thoughts that preceded the behavior. Also,

Table 4. Example of daily log for identifying a behavioral pattern

| | | Antecedents | | | Consequences | | |
|---|---|---|---|---|---|---|---|
| | When | Who | Where | Positive | Negative | | Thoughts |
| 1. | ___ | ___ | ___ | ___ | ___ | | ___ |
| 2. | ___ | ___ | ___ | ___ | ___ | | ___ |
| 3. | ___ | ___ | ___ | ___ | ___ | | ___ |
| 4. | ___ | ___ | ___ | ___ | ___ | | ___ |

Behavior: _____

$3 \times 5$ inch index card will fit into shirt pocket or wallet.

the patient notes any prominent positive or negative consequences, thoughts, or feelings. Information regarding the behavior pattern is primarily useful when the problem health-related behavior is smoking, weight control, diet, stress reduction, sleep disturbance, or medication adherence difficulties.

In addition, the clinician may wish to obtain information about the behavior profile (e.g., frequency, duration, or intensity). While this information is not critical for determining the behavioral pattern or for selecting the intervention, it will be extremely valuable in assessing the effects of the intervention. It will be used as a benchmark against which future changes can be compared. Information regarding the behavior profile is usually obtained on a simple tally form (Table 5). This format requires the patient simply to enter a check mark for each occurrence, the duration (e.g., number of minutes), and a number indicating the intensity of the behavior (e.g., $1 =$ no stress, $5 =$ moderate stress, $10 =$ extreme stress). The behavior profile is useful for monitoring both the problem behavior being profiled and the new or altered behavior that is the goal of the program.

Collecting information about the problem behavior is an excellent "homework assignment" for the patient even if the clinician believes it and the associated behavioral pattern are fully understood. Collecting the information forces the patient to be continuously aware of the problem behavior for a given period of time. This self-awareness is often sufficient in itself to provoke a marked change in the problem behavior. This self-monitoring process brings the problem behavior into the patient's awareness on a daily basis, and, as a result, the patient gains a better understanding of the factors that are stimulating the behavior's occurrence and supporting its recurrence. At subsequent counseling sessions, the patient is able to provide accurate, current information about these factors. Further, with increased awareness, the patient is better able to predict the effects of the behavioral change program that is to be started soon.

Table 5. Example of form for recording frequency, duration (D), or intensity (I) of a behavior (behavior profile)

Behavior: _____

| Day 1 | Day 2 | Day 3 |
|-------|-------|-------|
| D: _____ | D: _____ | D: _____ |
| I: _____ | I: _____ | I: _____ |
| D: _____ | D: _____ | D: _____ |
| I: _____ | I: _____ | I: _____ |
| D: _____ | D: _____ | D: _____ |
| I: _____ | I: _____ | I: _____ |
| D: _____ | D: _____ | D: _____ |
| I: _____ | I: _____ | I: _____ |
| Tally only: _____ | Tally only: _____ | Tally only: _____ |

When used as the initial stage of the behavioral counseling process, self-monitoring also serves as a probe of the patient's self-management skills. How well can the patient consistently perform a simple task that is associated with the problem behavior? The patient's ability to collect information will be predictive of his ability to perform a similar, though more difficult task: implementing the behavioral change program. If the patient has difficulty collecting data, it is likely that he will also have difficulty consistently implementing the treatment. When these difficulties occur at an early stage, the clinician may wish to discuss them with the patient in order to avoid later difficulties with the behavioral change program. The design of the program may also be altered to maximize the likelihood of its implementation (perhaps at the expense of other features of the program). For example, if the objective is to initiate a physical exercise program, and the patient has demonstrated that he is not able to consistently keep a daily log of current physical activities, the clinician should discuss the details of the proposed exercise program with the patient in more detail than usual, and be sure to avoid selecting a time for the exercise program when other attractive activities are competing for the patient's attention. The clinician should also see that more frequent follow-up contacts with the patient are made during the first two weeks of the new exercise program than would ordinarily be necessary. The patient should be contacted every few days initially, then weekly, and then biweekly to ensure that he maintains the new program.

This extra care is necessary since the patient not only is starting a new activity (i.e., the exercise program) which is disruptive, and to some degree uncomfortable, but is also learning a new, self-management ability (i.e., keeping the daily records). The difficulties in learning both of these new behaviors simultaneously often make the first week or two of the program especially critical to its ultimate success.

### Principles of Behavioral Change

While many techniques are used in programs to change health-related behavior, the number of basic principles is small. These principles of behavior change are: (1) stimulus control, (2) shaping, (3) substitution of incompatible behavior, (4) positive reinforcement, (5) negative reinforcement, and (6) punishment. Each principle describes a particular effect that one behavior will have on another, if all other factors remain constant. These principles apply equally well to an individual's public behaviors (e.g., actions) or private behaviors (e.g., thoughts, feelings). While each principle will be described separately, it is rarely the case that these principles operate in isolation. Usually several are working in concert to produce the observed effect. This is true, of course, not only for the desired behavior but for the patient's current behavior. Difficulties in dealing with health-related behavioral problems usually do not arise from a lack of understanding of the basic principles (as these are relatively simple), but rather from problems in identifying the numerous principles that are usually involved and their complex interrelationships.

### *Stimulus Control*

The principle of *stimulus control* states that particular antecedent events, behaviors or physical objects will elicit a specific behavior, thought, or feeling from a patient. Through a repetition of this pattern over time (i.e., first the event, then the behavior), these events eventually control the performance of the behavior: when the individual perceives the stimuli, the behavior is performed routinely. Stimulus control is often present in behaviors related to the problems of smoking, stress, sleep disturbance, and overweight. For example, an overweight patient may respond to the sight of dessert-food in the refrigerator by eating; a patient who smokes may respond to the feeling of fullness after a meal by smoking a cigarette; the patient under stress may respond to constructive criticism with increased anxiety; a patient who has problems sleeping may respond to an initial delay in falling asleep by excessive worries of not sleeping and therefore not fall asleep.

The stimulus event which is prompting the problem behavior need not have a direct causal link to the patient's behavior. Stimulus events can acquire their influence through an association with the original cause of the behavior which is no longer present. The event, in these cases, is operating as a signal for an actual cause that does not exist. For the patient who is under stress, for example, a meeting with a supervisor who had previously criticized him can provoke extreme anxiety even though he knows that the topic of the meeting is non-threatening.

## Shaping

*Shaping* is the deliberate, gradual change in a behavior over time. The clinician uses this principle to help select with the patient a sequence of modest intermediate goals for the behavioral change program that will eventually lead to the new, desired behavior. Shaping is based on the observation that most patients are able to accommodate readily to small changes in behavior, while large changes in behavior tend to have too many aversive consequences to be tolerated. For example, a behavioral change program to stop smoking that incorporated the principle of shaping might require the patient to reduce by one the number of cigarettes smoked each day. Shaping is typically a component of physical exercise programs, in which the patient is encouraged to gradually increase the amount of time spent exercising, or the length of the run, or the number of repetitions of a particular activity.

Shaping is a very effective method for achieving dramatic changes in many health-related behaviors. However, it is important that the intermediate goals be selected with care so that the patient can achieve each goal without difficulty. Both the clinician and the patient should have confidence in the patient's ability to achieve each intermediate goal before an intervention is started. If there is doubt or hesitation on the patient's part, the goal should be reviewed, and, if necessary, modified. Behavioral change programs rarely fail as a result of slow gradual progress; however, they often fail as a result of overly ambitious intermediate goals and attempts to make too rapid progress. The patient should be eagerly anticipating the next goal rather than fearing it.

Once an intermediate goal has been achieved, the patient should remain at that level until it feels comfortable. That is, the patient should effectively accommodate to each intermediate level before progressing to the next goal. The time required for accommodation will vary from patient to patient and will depend upon the specific behavior being changed. The rate of accommodation may also vary depending upon the stage of the program. In achieving the initial goal in a behavioral change program, the patient is not only adopting a new behavior, but is also learning how to accommodate to these changes in the daily routine. Once these coping skills are learned, the patient should be able to accommodate to subsequent changes more rapidly. So, the patient who is beginning a new low salt diet may select as an initial goal simply removing the salt shaker from the table. A subsequent goal might be to purchase special foods and prepare salt-free meals. This later goal would require the patient to perform considerably more activities. If the patient has learned to cope with the initial disruption in his daily routine, he may be able to accommodate to several subsequent changes.

### Substitution of Incompatible Behavior

The substitution of incompatible behavior involves the performance of one behavior that effectively prevents an undesirable behavior from occurring. The behavior performed need not be the desired behavior itself; it may be a neutral one. That is, any acceptable behavior may be used that is effective in preventing the problem behavior from occurring. For example, patients who smoke often can substitute eating a small, light calorie food instead of smoking a cigarette. The act of eating temporarily blocks the urge to smoke and provides some degree of pleasure.

The principle of substituting an incompatible behavior is often applied when it is not feasible to gradually shape the new health-related behavior. In these situations, the desired behavior must be inserted into the patient's routine in its final form. For example, a patient who is feeling intense stress on the job needs an effective behavioral change program that will promptly reduce the anxiety. A gradual decrease in anxiety may not be tolerable or feasible. In this situation, the patient may learn and practice a stress reduction technique at home or elsewhere outside the workplace. When needed, he can then use the complete technique in the stressful job situation to prevent the stress from reaching uncomfortable levels. When the substitution of an incompatible behavior is used in this way, the clinician should consider whether the new incompatible behavior will be supported once introduced into the patient's daily activities. Will the patient perceive the consequences of the new behavior to be more positive and less aversive than the consequences of the old routine problem behavior? The new behavior will not survive for long if the problem behavior remains more desirable to the patient.

### Controlling Consequences

One of the most commonly used methods of changing a behavior is to alter the consequences that follow its occurrence. Most behavioral change programs are designed to ensure that positive consequences are consistently associated with the desired new behavior and do not follow the problem behavior. The weight of any consequences, however, is determined by the patient. That is, positive consequences are uniquely defined by each individual. For example, praise offered by the clinician to the patient who reports a three mile run may not be perceived as positive if the patient routinely runs five miles. While most people experience pleasurable feelings from many of the same events, the clinician should not assume that a particular consequence will be regarded as positive by a particular individual. The patient should describe which consequences he perceives as positive and which as negative or neutral. The behavioral principles of positive reinforcement, negative reinforcement, and punishment describe the expected effect on a behavior when different types of consequences routinely follow it.

Positive consequences following a behavior tend to increase the likelihood that the patient will perform the same behavior in the same situation in the future. A *positive reinforcement* can be any activity, thought, feeling, or behavior that the patient perceives as pleasurable. In the simplest cases, the positive consequence immediately follows the behavior. For example, immediate positive consequences support cigarette smoking (e.g., feelings of relaxation) or excessive eating (e.g., feelings of satisfaction). Often, however, the positive consequence is delayed. For instance, delayed positive consequences often support changes in diet (e.g., the consequence of a reduced risk of cardiovascular disease), weight reduction (e.g., the consequence of a more attractive figure), and physical exercise (e.g., the consequence of increased alertness and stamina). Family members, co-workers, friends, and one's own favorable self-evaluation are major sources of positive reinforcement.

The avoidance of unpleasant events, activities, thoughts, or feelings also serves as a positive consequence when it increases the likelihood that the patient will perform the same behavior in the same situation in the future to avoid the same unpleasant events. Usually this type of positive consequence is termed a *negative reinforcement*. Negative reinforcements are more difficult to observe than positive reinforcements. When a patient is performing a behavior to avoid an aversive consequence, the actual aversive consequence rarely occurs. The patient must identify what has been avoided. For example, one of the reasons offered by some smokers as to why they continue to smoke is that they do not wish to go through the withdrawal period when they stop smoking. This type of consequence is not evident from a simple review of the activities and events associated with a problem behavior. The patient must describe the imagined consequences of reducing or eliminating the current behavior.

*Punishment* occurs when a negative consequence follows a behavior and decreases the likelihood that the individual will perform the behavior in the same situation in the future or leads him to avoid the situation in which the behavior is punished. Like positive consequences, punishments can be any physical activity, social event, thought, or feeling experienced by the individual. Unfortunately many desirable changes in health-related behaviors guide immediate punishment. For example, physical exercise programs can result in unpleasant physical symptoms (e.g., sore muscles, disruption of normal routine); smoking cessation can result in increased anxiety or unpleasant physical symptoms due to nicotine withdrawal; changes in diet can result in an expenditure of more time, effort and money to obtain the allowable foods.

Another type of negative consequence following a behavior is the withdrawal of a positive event. This also reduces the likelihood that the person will perform the same behavior in the same situation in the future. It is usually the case with health-related behavior that this principle operates through the long-term consequences of problem behavior. For example, most people who smoke cigarettes are aware that the consequences of continued smoking sometimes include ill health and early death. The patient who is hypertensive and who skips taking his anti-hypertensive medication is forfeiting control of his blood pressure and is encouraging the development of cardiovascular disease.

Most often the clinician is confronted with multiple consequences for the problem behavior and for the desired new behavior. As described earlier in this chapter, the nature and degree of these consequences must be identified to understand the behavioral pattern that is supporting the problem behavior and that will affect efforts to change it.

With most health-related behavior that people want to change there is a general pattern: the individual perceives the immediate consequences as positive, but recognizes that the long-term consequences are or may be negative. For instance, the immediate consequences of smoking are pleasure and anxiety reduction, while the long-term consequence is an increased probability of developing cardiovascular disease, cancer, or chronic lung disease. Conversely, the immediate consequences of the new, desired behavior tend to be negative while the long-term consequences are positive. Smoking cessation produces short-term psychological and physical discomfort but has the positive consequences of improved stamina and lung capacity, and reduced risk of disease in the future.

With multiple positive and negative consequences affecting each behavior, the clinician is interested in developing a behavior change program that will shift the balance of these factors for both the problem behavior and the new desired health behavior. The behavioral change program usually will reduce or eliminate some of the negative effects of the new behavior and develop or increase positive effects for it. At the same time, the program will attempt to develop or increase negative effects of the problem behavior and decrease or eliminate its positive effects.

## Characteristics of Successful Behavioral Change Programs

Behavioral counseling is an empirically based approach to changing problem behaviors that emphasizes the necessity of tailoring the behavioral change program to the patient. The program used in behavioral counseling is not limited to a few techniques that are "behavioral." Any treatment program can be selected by the clinician and the patient so long as objective data are obtained that will verify whether the program is successful. For example, a patient can select any program in an effort to stop smoking, so long as the effects of the program are measured in terms of the number of cigarettes smoked. To the degree that it reduces the number of cigarettes smoked, the program is judged effective for that patient. If not, it should be modified or replaced regardless of other effects it might be having.

While the behavioral change program is being developed it should be kept in mind that the program is a temporary device for achieving the desired behavioral change. Once the new behavior is established, naturally occurring factors inherent in the new behavior or in the patient's environment are expected to maintain the new behavior over time. The patient should be aware that the behavioral change program will end as soon as is practical. For instance, if the patient is using a formal deep muscle relaxation procedure to reduce stress while at work, he should be aware that the practice sessions required to achieve a state of calm relaxed attentiveness will eventually be eliminated as the patient's feelings of stress are reduced. The goal of the stress reduction program is that the patient will be able to cope successfully with the stress encountered on the job without using the formal deep muscle relaxation procedures. Usually one of the explicit goals of subsequent sessions with the clinician is to develop a plan to withdraw the program.

When developing a behavioral change program, the clinician should consider whether the components and sequence of the program are as simple to follow as possible. The fewer the components of the program, the easier it will be for the patient to perform each one properly. The more flexible the sequence of the program's components, the easier it will be for the patient to implement the entire program. For example, a medication schedule that requires the patient to take tablets three times each day after meals is easier to follow than a medication schedule that requires the patient to mix powdered medication in water two times each day, one hour after breakfast and dinner. The simpler medication routine will also reduce the number of inadvertent errors made by the patient simply in attempting to fulfill all the components of the program.

A behavioral change program should be designed to blend with the person's routine daily activities. The easier it is for a person to incorporate the new program into his habitual activities, the more likely it is that the person will follow the program consistently. A low salt diet is easier to follow if there are several acceptable low salt dishes to choose from in a cafeteria than if one must place a special order for a low salt meal.

By the same token the degree to which a new behavioral change program disrupts the patient's normal routine must be considered. The greater the disruption of the patient's routine daily activities, the less likely it is that the program will be successful. An exercise program that is scheduled for the early morning may disrupt the breakfast schedule to the extent that the patient feels compelled to choose between breakfast or exercise. An alternative time should be identified when there is little chance that other activities will compete with the new program.

### Developing a Behavioral Change Program

Once the behavioral diagnosis has been determined, attention is directed toward the development of the behavioral change program. Most effective programs to change a health-related behavior combine several of the previously described behavioral principles into a program with several components that is tailored to the specific problem behavior and to the patient's lifestyle. Since there are multiple positive and negative factors affecting the problem behavior and the desired behavior, the details of the program must be carefully adjusted to each patient. There are no effective general-purpose behavioral change programs for specific problem behaviors. However, the clinician and the patient must select, adapt, and integrate these components into an individualized program for the patient.

Behavioral change programs work best when the patient has been encouraged to take an active role in the counseling process. If the patient has developed an understanding of the behavioral patterns surrounding the problem behavior, and shares a common understanding of the behavioral diagnosis with the clinician, then the patient can actively contribute to the development of the behavioral change program. Initially, then, the patient should be encouraged to suggest strategies for the program. This can be stated as a simple question to the patient, e.g., "So given the apparent pattern in your smoking, do you have any ideas how you might stop smoking?" Used early on, this question gives the patient the opportunity to guide the direction of the behavioral change program and may set the tone for the development and adjustment phase. In addition, the clinician learns whether the patient has already decided what would be the best method for resolving the problem. Some patients come into the clinic with a preconceived notion of exactly what they want in terms of treatment (e.g., medication, hypnosis, a specific popular weight loss program). These ideas should be elicited from the patient early in the development process and examined for their appropriateness.

Before developing a behavioral change program, the clinician should also ask the patient to review in detail any programs that the patient has attempted in the past. Past unsuccessful programs are good sources of information. The patient will often have labeled all the techniques used in these programs as ineffective. If an unsuccessful weight loss program included keeping a daily food record, for example, the patient may have a low opinion of the usefulness of keeping such a record when in fact, the failure was due to some other factor. The clinician should be prepared to explain carefully the purpose and differences between any components of the proposed program and similar components of an unsuccessful past program.

A review of past programs should also examine the degree to which they were successful. These programs may have been successful in changing the problem behavior in some situations but not in others. While the overall program may not have been effective, some components may be useful in the program that is about to be designed. For example, the patient may have participated consistently in a physical exercise group program offered several times each week in the summer, but stopped exercising in the fall when the program ended. In this case the pre-planned nature of the exercise sessions was a crucial component for the patient. For this patient, a carefully planned and structured physical exercise program is needed.

When a new behavioral change program is being developed, the clinician should resist presenting a detailed plan that he feels is "best" for the patient. The behavioral change program should be developed with the patient's participation. As appropriate, the clinician should suggest a general technique that may be helpful and ask the patient to develop a way of using the technique. The clinician might introduce the principle of stimulus control or cuing as a method to help the patient remember to perform the new behavior. With help from the clinician, the patient would then select a cue and determine how it would be used.

Once the behavioral change program has been planned, the clinician should ask the patient to review in detail each of its components. This review ensures that the patient understands each component, and increases the likelihood that he will implement each one. Some clinicians even write a "behavioral prescription" that summarizes all the components of the program agreed upon by the clinician and the patient (Figure 1). The written behavioral prescription itself acts as a cue to help the patient recall each of the components of the program.

After the review, the clinician should ask the patient if there are any questions about the plan. Any doubts or misunderstandings may then be resolved before problems occur. The clinician also should ask explicitly if the patient agrees to try the entire behavioral change program. Without the patient's complete support for the proposed program, it would be a mistake to go ahead. This does not mean that the patient necessarily feels that the program will be completely successful, just that he is willing to give the whole program a sincere effort. Thus, the clinician should further ask for the patient's reactions to the proposed program. That is, in the patient's opinion, will it be successful in reducing the problem behavior and/or acquiring the new health-related behavior? The clinician could use questions such as: "What is your reaction to this pro-

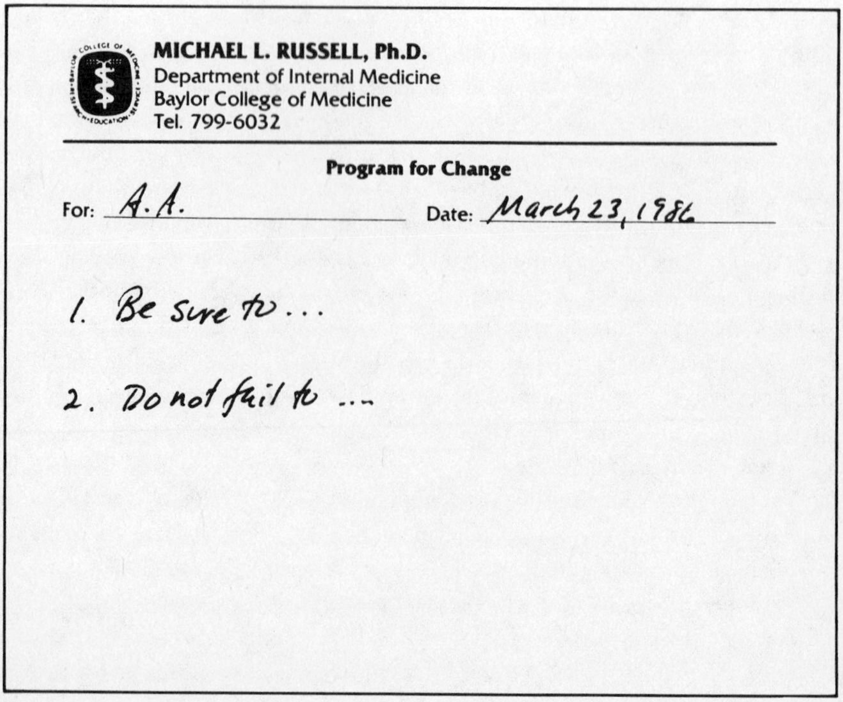

**MICHAEL L. RUSSELL, Ph.D.**
Department of Internal Medicine
Baylor College of Medicine
Tel. 799-6032

**Program for Change**

For: _A.A._                              Date: _March 23, 1986_

1. Be sure to ...

2. Do not fail to ...

Figure 1. Example of a behavioral prescription.

gram? How do you think this plan will work? What do you think is the likelihood that this plan will actually help you in changing this behavior?" Such questions function as probes to find out whether the patient is merely acquiescing to the clinician's guidance in developing the program or genuinely believes that it will be successful. For many patients, reservations regarding the proposed behavioral change program will not be volunteered unless specifically requested by the clinician. Properly phrased, the questions will communicate to the patient that the clinician is interested in his opinions and is willing to modify the behavioral change program as appropriate.

## Troubleshooting

Occasionally the patient will report after a week's trial of a new behavioral change program, that the program was unsuccessful. This should not automatically be considered a failure of the program. There are many reasons for such early reports of failure, and many initial failures can be remedied by minor adjustments in the program. The clinician's task is to diagnose the difficulty and appropriately modify the program.

The first step in troubleshooting an unsuccessful program is to determine what specifically the patient did to implement the program. The patient should describe in detail how each behavioral change strategy was used, and under what conditions. The clinician should examine whether the patient was actually carrying out the plan that was agreed upon, or whether only parts of the program were used in limited situations. If the program was only partially implemented, the clinician should determine whether the patient misunderstood the program or disagreed with the components that were not used.

If all the components of the program were implemented, the clinician should examine the effects of the program on the problem or new health behavior. Were there any situations where the program was effective? How did these situations differ from the situations in which the program was ineffective? What were the consequences that followed the successful and unsuccessful use of the program? Did the naturally occurring consequences for both the problem and desired new behavior occur as expected? The clinician should identify apparent differences between the successful and the unsuccessful use of the program and modify the program accordingly. In most cases of partial success, the initial behavioral change program can be readily adjusted based on the specific results of the program.

The clinician should also consider how often the program was successful. Some patients will expect 100% success in a behavioral change program within a brief period of time. Those with unrealistic expectations must be reminded that the problem behavior developed slowly over a long period of time and that one cannot hope to make and accommodate smoothly to a major change in lifestyle within one or two weeks. The acquisition of a new health-related behavior is a slow, gradual process and the patient should expect to experience continuing discomfort for several weeks.

If a patient is having difficulty with a behavioral change program, the clinician should be cautious in revising it. The immediate goal of the program should be reviewed, and, if appropriate, modified. Is the expected new behavior too large a step for the patient? Should a smaller step be selected? The clinician should feel that there is better than a 90% chance that the patient will be able to implement the revised program successfully.

The clinician should also develop a method to obtain data on the effects of the revised program. If a daily record describing the new behavioral change program has not been used previously, the patient should be instructed in the use of one. The daily record will provide the clinician with the details needed to make future adjustments in the program. The clinician should also consider contacting the patient within one week to determine whether the revised program is achieving success. This contact with the patient can be crucial since, if the revised program is also unsuccessful, the clinician should immediately make additional adjustments in the program or discontinue it. It is better for the clinician to remain in contact with the patient so they may make collaborative decisions about the program, than for the patient to be making unilateral decisions.

Whenever a program is unsuccessful the clinician must always make sure that the patient does not interpret the failure of the program as a personal failure, and does not resign himself to the attitude that the problem behavior cannot be resolved. An unsuccessful behavioral change program is simply a flawed play which should either be revised or terminated. New information will have been obtained from the effort, and the next program attempted should thus have a greater chance of success.

# 5. Maintaining Health Behavior Change

## The Problem

Achieving a routine of self-care behaviors or eliminating an undesirable at-risk behavior is a significant step for the patient. Often the desire to make these changes has preceded their accomplishment by days, weeks, or months, and their attainment is met with feelings of pride, relief, enthusiasm and congratulations from family and friends. Although the clinician should definitely recognize the patient's accomplishment, he should also be aware that the achievement of the initial goal of a health behavior change program is only the first step of a two-step program. To be truly successful, the patient's new self-care routine must become a permanent part of his daily activities.

Non-maintenance of a self-care regimen can have serious effects on the patient's medical care by compromising his medical treatment. If the patient is not following the self-care regimen, or only partially following it, he may not receive the full benefits of the treatment program. For example, the hypertensive patient who does not reduce the amount of sodium in his diet may negate the effects of a diuretic and drug he is taking. The diabetic patient who does not follow a carbohydrate controlled diet can effectively prevent his body's insulin from controlling the blood glucose levels.

Moreover, non-maintenance or intermittent maintenance can confound the interpretation of the medical data necessary to manage the patient's medical treatment. The clinician relies on physical and biochemical values to adjust the type and dosage of medication prescribed for the patient. If the patient only intermittently follows the medication regimen or other self-care routine, then the data may not accurately reflect the potential effectiveness of a specific treatment program, and the physician is left without a method for adjusting the treatment. In the worst case, the physician may assume that the patient is following the prescribed regimen, determine that the patient's disease is not controlled, and prescribe either stronger medications, increased dosages, or more complicated and costly diagnostic procedures.

73

Maintenance of a change in a self-care behavior is, in many ways, a more difficult challenge for the patient than the initial achievement of the behavior change. Once the desired change has been achieved, the patient may incorrectly believe that the new behavior will continue indefinitely, without further intervention. Sadly, this does not happen for many patients. Within months, the patient has returned to the previous routines.

The clinician must recognize that the maintenance phase of a health behavior change program requires planning and careful management if the patient is to continue to be successful. The clinician and the patient must continue to collaborate to ensure that the goals of the maintenance phase are met. These goals are (1) the gradual removal of the artificial aids that were introduced to help the patient achieve the desired changes, (2) the acquisition by the patient of the skills needed to respond effectively to new maintenance problems that may be encountered in the future, and (3) the establishment of the patient's independence from the clinician's continued maintenance. These goals clearly distinguish the maintenance phase from the initial achievement phase of counseling.

Maintenance of a self-care regimen is a problem due to the dynamic nature of the patient-environment interaction. Both the patient and the environment are continually changing. The patient acquires new knowledge, new attitudes, and new experiences over time, which can have substantial effects on his maintenance of a self-care program. The patient's environment is usually in a similar state of flux as the people, the activities, and even the physical surroundings that define it change.

The solution to the maintenance problem, therefore, is not to create a fixed, static program that will continue unchanged; such a program would fail eventually. Rather, the solution rests in anticipating the types of changes that might occur and providing the patient with a flexible program that will respond to these changes. To do this requires a clear understanding of the risks and problems involved with non-maintenance, the patient's problems in achieving the initial changes, and the selection and/or development of interventions tailored to the individual patient.

## The Magnitude of Non-maintenance

Patient non-maintenance is probably one of the most widespread and challenging problems faced in the clinical practice of medicine. It is a problem that can occur with almost any illness, type of treatment, or patient. Studies of patients' maintenance of their treatment regimens indicate that typically non-maintenance ranges from 20 to 80% of all patients. Unfortunately non-maintenance is not easy to detect and, for an individual patient, it may vary widely week to week. As a result, the clinician can never be certain of a patient's exact level of non-maintenance. Specific methods for estimating a patient's level of maintenance of a particular treatment regimen are discussed in the individual chapters to follow.

When the levels of patient maintenance of a long-term treatment regimen are plotted, the resulting curve is shaped like a "U" or a "J". Patients are typically classified by their position on this curve. Low adherers range between 0 and 40% adherence. Moderate adherers range between 40 and 80% adherence. High adherers follow their regimen greater than 80% of the time. Drop-outs or zero adherers are not following their regimens at all.

Although the patient's level of non-maintenance is not necessarily predictive of a particular type of problem, it is often associated with the number of problems the patient is experiencing, their extent, or complexity. In other words, the four different adherence categories do not contain distinctly different types of problems. Rather it appears that patients in all of the adherence groups experience similar problems, but some patients are able to cope more successfully with these problems than others.

**Predicting Non-maintenance**

One of the most frustrating aspects of patient non-maintenance is the absence of factors that may be predictive of a patient's non-maintenance of the treatment regimen. Most importantly, the clinician's judgment of whether or not a patient will maintain a regimen has been demonstrated repeatedly to be inaccurate. Clinical judgment is no better than chance in identifying the patient who will not maintain a treatment regimen. Moreover, none of the standard demographic characteristics are correlated with patient non-maintenance, including age, sex, socioeconomic status, marital status, education, religious preference, or race. Other factors appear to be necessary but not sufficient to guarantee maintenance of a regimen, including patient knowledge of the disease and its treatment, a positive attitude by the patient about the efficacy of the treatment, a positive working relationship between the clinician and the patient, and ease of access to the clinic with minimal waiting time in the clinic.

Only two variables have emerged as having a strong association with patient maintenance of a treatment regimen over time. The first is the structure of the treatment regimen that has been prescribed. Patients maintain regimens that require fewer administrations, involve fewer medications, have minimal side effects, and fit into the patient's daily routine. The second variable is the support of a family member. Patients who have supportive family members consistently have better long-term maintenance of their treatment regimens than those patients whose family members are not supportive. The incorporation of both of these variables into a treatment regimen is discussed in detail in subsequent sections, and in later chapters.

Given the difficulty of predicting a patient's maintenance from the observable characteristics of the patient, the disease, or the treatment, the clinician must rely on other methods to estimate the patient's maintenance of the regimen. Probably the most accurate source of information is the patient. If a patient is simply asked whether or not he intends to follow the prescribed treatment regimen, the patient's estimate will be the most accurate of all available methods. Therefore, it is strongly recommended that all patients be asked if they anticipate being able to follow the self-care regimen, and if they can foresee any problems that might occur which would prevent them from maintaining the program. However, the clinician always should bear in mind that any patient has the potential for non-maintenance. Maintenance of a treatment regimen should never be assumed until it has been demonstrated over time.

## General Strategies for Promoting Maintenance

Although long-term maintenance of a prescribed regimen can never be assured, the clinician can strongly influence the likelihood of its occurrence. These efforts begin with the design of the regimen itself. Usually the regimen can be structured so that the medical aspects of the problem are satisfied, and at the same time the likelihood of maintenance is optimized. Many of the techniques that promote the initial achievement of a self-care regimen also help to promote its maintenance. Other techniques are used more specifically to promote maintenance (Table 1).

### Step 1. Patient Education

Most patients desire to have at least a basic understanding of their disease, its prognosis, and the prescribed medical treatment. In fact, patients with acute illnesses usually only need to know the dosage and frequency of their education in order to ensure satisfactory treatment. It is often believed that other information, although perhaps of interest to the patient, has little effect on his progress. As a result, busy clinicians often do not provide any more information than is absolutely necessary for the patient to have a rudimentary understanding of his medical condition.

This situation changes substantially when the clinician recommends that the patient adopt specific long-term, self-care routines to aid the treatment or to prevent the recurrence of a medical problem. In these cases, the patient is being asked to make fundamental changes in his lifestyle, such as adopting a new diet, or physical activity, stopping smoking, or altering leisure activities. Because the patient must become intimately involved in the initiation of these programs, and because these programs affect other peoples as well, the clini-

Table 1. General counseling strategies for promoting maintenance

*Step 1: Educate patient.*
    Patient should have appropriate knowledge of the details of the recommended self-care
      routine including how, when, where, and to what degree it should be performed.

*Step 2: Suggest uncomplicated regimen.*
    Regimen should require few activities and be consistent from day to day.

*Step 3: Suggest compatible regimen.*
    Regimen should be tailored to the patient's usual schedule of daily activities.

*Step 4: Minimize side effects.*
    Regimen should involve activities that are the least aversive for the patient.

*Step 5: Specify behavior.*
    Regimen should have explicit, observable objectives.

*Step 6: Monitor progress.*
    Patient should have a simple method of monitoring progress toward the objectives of
      treatment.

*Step 7: Use the natural environment.*
    Regimen should incorporate the patient's natural social, physical, and occupational envi-
      ronment in supporting maintenance of the routine.

*Step 8: Continue contact with same clinician.*
    One clinician should be designated as having responsibility for managing the patient's
      maintenance of a prescribed self-care regimen, and the patient should always be sched-
      uled to see that clinician for follow-up visits.

---

cian needs to provide the patient with highly specific information about these self-care programs, and its relationship to the likely progress of the disease.

To decrease the chances of non-maintenance problems, the clinician should provide sufficient information so that the following questions can be answered.

1. The patient understands the specific self-care routine that is being recommended. What is to be done? To what degree is it to be advised? Under what conditions will it be supported?
2. The patient understands the interaction between the recommended self-care programs and the prescribed drug treatments. Is it required? Is it strongly advised? Is there no relationship?
3. The patient understands the relationship between the self-care routine and the progress of the disease condition. What effects are likely? When would these effects be noticed?

This information enables the patient to understand why the self-care program is being recommended, and exactly what he is expected to do. Understanding the answers to "What? Why? and Who?" may avoid non-maintenance problems if the patient encounters difficulties in the future.

*Step 2: Uncomplicated Regimen*

The regimen should involve a simple set of activities that are few in number, and do not change from day to day throughout the week. Patients are more likely to remember to perform each activity in the desired sequence if the regimen is simple. For example, a medication regimen should have all medications taken together at the same approximate times each day and in the same relation to meals (e.g., medications are taken twice each day after breakfast, and after dinner). For the patient who is prescribed a self-care physical therapy program, it is recommended that the patient select the same time each day for the program (e.g., either morning or afternoon) with the same program continued into the weekend.

*Step 3: Compatible Regimen*

Selecting a regimen for the self-care behavior that is compatible with other daily activities is often the most difficult task facing the patient. Many of the desired self-care behaviors are incompatible with other daily activities, and special arrangements must be made to accommodate them. In these cases, the scheduled times for the self-care behaviors should require the least changes in the daily activities. For example many hypertensive patients who are trying to reduce the amount of dietary sodium consumed are confronted with the problem of integrating this new diet with a daily routine of business lunches. These patients might be encouraged to learn "best bets" for dishes that are low in sodium and choose them from the luncheon menu. Combined with an extremely low sodium breakfast and dinner, this strategy would yield an acceptable reduced daily intake of sodium. Accommodating the daily routine by the items available that contain the least amount of sodium may be the patient's best option.

*Step 4: Regimens with Minimal Side effects*

Given a choice, a regimen should include these activities that have the least aversive side effects for the patient. Although this may seem like common sense, it does not always happen. To illustrate, the patient who has been prescribed a regimen of physical activity may be encouraged to jog, swim, or bicycle, all reasonable aerobic activities. However, during certain seasons of the year, each of these outdoor activities may be extremely unpleasant or impractical. Care should be taken to select activities that are practical (e.g., brisk walking, jumping rope, running in time to music indoors, or ice skating) and enjoyable for the patient. Alternative activities also should be identified for use when problems are encountered.

## Step 5: Specification of Behavior

An important aspect of maintaining a self-care program is the precise specification of the behavior that the patient is expected to perform on a daily or weekly basis. Vague or ambiguous goals for a self-care program invite confusion and uncertainty as to whether or not progress is being made. For example, the clinician should choose as the target behavior for a weight loss program the patient's adherence to a specific level of the recommended diet (e.g., 18 of 21 meals per week, or better than 90%) rather than a certain number of pounds lost. The reason for this is that the patient directly controls what is eaten, while the patient's weight is a product of several factors, over some of which the patient has little control (e.g., metabolic rate, gain or loss of muscle mass). A self-care program should target those specific behaviors which the patient is able to control.

## Step 6: Monitoring Progress

Specific, short-term objectives have the additional advantage of providing the patient with a method for monitoring his own progress. A simple chart or tally of the frequency with which the patient achieves the behaviors specified in the regimen enables him to evaluate the degree of success. Several examples of self-observation systems are described in each of the succeeding chapters focusing on specific behavioral/medical problems. The opportunity for the patient to observe and evaluate himself is a fundamental feature of the well designed self-care regimen that promotes long-term adherence.

The regimen should also contain a brief description of the criteria that constitute non-adherence to the regimen. The patient should be aware of the boundaries of acceptable performance and have guidelines for determining whether or not he has relapsed. For example, a program for reducing the incidence of sleep disturbances might select the criteria of 3 restless nights in sequence as evidence that an active behavioral intervention should be reinstituted. This criterion allows for the occasional restless night, while raising concern before the insomnia becomes re-established as a problem.

## Step 7: Using the Natural Environment

In selecting an intervention to aid a patient establish a self-care regimen, it is important to consider whether or not it is likely that the regimen will be supported by the patient's natural environment once the clinician has withdrawn the intervention strategy. The behavioral intervention used by the clinician should be considered a temporary aid to initiate a new routine and establish the regimen as part of the patient's lifestyle. Ultimately, the patient and his environment must support the desired self-care regimen without the use of these aids. It is not likely that a regimen of self-care behaviors will be maintained if the natural environment contains little support for them. If these natural supporting mechanisms are not present, then they either need to be developed during the behavioral change program, or the clinician should seriously consider postponing the change program until they are present.

For instance, the clinician might initially use a series of "contracts" with the patient to establish the new self-care regimen. These contracts could specify the behaviors expected of the patient and indicate a reward if the patient is successful, or a mild punishment if the patient is not. Many weight loss programs require their patients to deposit a certain amount of money. A portion of the deposit is returned to the patient if he follows a prescribed diet for a specific length of time (e.g., a refund of $5.00 each week). If the patient does not adhere to the conditions of the contract, a portion of the deposit is forfeited (usually donated to a charitable organization). However, when the patient succeeds in achieving his goals, the clinician begins to withdraw this artificial strategy and allow the positive consequences in the natural environment to maintain the diet behavior. For a dieter natural consequences might be the appearance of a more enjoyable figure, new, smaller clothes, an enhanced sense of well-being, and the support of family or friends. If the patient's environment seems to lack this natural support, the clinician might encourage the patient to ask a friend to help and by becoming a partner in one of the initial contracts. The clinician and the patient actually teach the friend how to be a support person to the patient. The friend is then ready to provide some support during the maintenance phase of the program.

### Step 8: Continued Contact with Same Clinician

One of the most important strategies for improving the likelihood of the patient's maintenance of a self-care program is to ensure that the patient is seen by the same clinician at each clinic visit. Effective health behavioral counseling is based on the establishment of trust and rapport with the patient. This relationship is often difficult to establish in a single, brief meeting and will usually require several sessions to become firmly established.

Beyond the nature of the relationship, however, the effective counseling of the patient requires the clinician to acquire a large fund of knowledge about the patient (i.e., lifestyle, job, family, interpersonal relationships). Unlike the medical treatment of a patient, which usually depends less upon what the patient says and more on laboratory data and examination findings, patient counseling requires the clinician to draw upon information that is not usually recorded in the patient's chart, nor is accessible in a single clinic session. As the clinician learns more, the behavioral diagnosis becomes more refined, and the intervention more tailored to the individual patient. As a result, it is important that the same clinician follow an individual patient at each clinic visit to monitor the patient's progress in the self-care programs and help the patient adjust the program as needed.

## Three Types of Non-maintenance Problems

Patient non-maintenance often results from a combination of reasons; rarely is it the result of a single factor or set of conditions. Neither is patient non-maintenance always unexpected. Usually a patient's failure to maintain his program of self-care can be traced to the influence of the same factors that created difficulties for him during the initial changes in lifestyle. Three types of problems have already been identified. If the patient had difficulty deciding whether to attempt to follow the recommended self-care program, non-maintenance may result from a reconsideration of the original decision to take action. If the patient had difficulty establishing the self-care behavior as a habit, non-maintenance may be attributable to a change in the environment to which the patient was not able to adapt successfully. Finally, if the patient has been engaging in repeated self-debate, the non-maintenance may be attributable to a shift in the balance of positive and negative factors influencing the debate such that the negative factors now outweigh the positive ones.

The initial presence of each of these three types of problems increases the probability of non-maintenance. The clinician should be aware of the different kinds of maintenance difficulties associated with each of these three types of problems, and incorporate appropriate strategies into the counseling to help prevent non-maintenance attributable to these problems.

Non-maintenance may pose a problem even when the patient has not had any difficulty achieving the initial behavioral change. Some patients are able to cope with the minor difficulties that may arise during the initial achievement phase of the program. It is only later, during maintenance, that they have difficulty. In these cases the initial dynamic balance between the patient and the environment has changed, and because he lacks the skills necessary to cope with this change, the patient is unable to maintain the self-care program. In a sense, these patients experience the same problems that other patients do, except they experience them at a later time. Unfortunately, there is no method for distinguishing these patients from those who continue to be successful during the maintenance phase, and who never require counseling intervention by the clinician.

Because non-maintenance can result from multiple causes, the clinician must carefully distinguish among the different causes in order to develop an appropriate preventive or treatment program. To clearly diagnose the type of non-maintenance problem the patient is experiencing requires in-depth knowledge of the patient's daily activities and their interaction with the desired self-care regimen.

## Non-maintenance Associated with a Change in the Initial Decision to Acquire a Self-Care Behavior

Many patients have difficulty coming to the decision to follow a particular self-care routine. These patients may carefully consider the new recommended activities, and remain unconvinced of their long-term merits. For these patients the negative factors associated with the prescribed self-care behaviors seem to outweigh the value the patient places on the daily quality of life and the potential long-term benefits. This is a decision based on the patient's own personal values and philosophy. For example, the 60-year-old patient who has smoked for all of his life may remain unpersuaded of the desirability of stopping smoking for general health reasons. Rather, smoking is viewed as a small daily pleasure. However, after considerable thought the patient may be persuaded by his physician, family, or friends to quit smoking. Unfortunately, his decision may have resulted more from transitory social pressure that made the benefits of stopping smoking appear to outweigh the disadvantages. Later, after the patient has stopped smoking, he may again question its long-term benefits. As a result, the patient may return to smoking.

It is the reduction in the appeal of the stable, long-term positive consequences of a behavioral change that appears to shift a patient's decision toward a rejection of the self-care routine. In contrast to the other potential causes of non-maintenance, this type of non-maintenance results from a deliberate decision by the patient. He is fully aware of the decision and is able to offer a rationale for making it.

Such a change in the patient's decision to follow the self-care routine is most likely to occur when the patient has initially expressed reservations about altering his lifestyle. If the patient has been persuaded by others to make this fundamental change, there is an increased likelihood that he will repeatedly reassess the decision in terms of the stable positive and negative factors. The clinician should be alert to this possibility and should build in strategies to prevent a change in the patient's decision and to detect a change as soon as possible if it does occur.

### The Clinician's Approach

The clinician should clearly differentiate problems of non-maintenance associated with a change in the patient's initial decision to acquire a self-care behavior from other problems of non-maintenance. These problems require a very

Table 2. Counseling steps for maintenance problems associated with a change in the initial decision to acquire a self-care behavior

---

*Step 1: Diagnose change in initial decision.*
    Patient's problem should be clearly identified as a deliberate, conscious decision by the patient to stop following the self-care routine, resulting from the patient's evaluation of its long-term benefits and costs.

*Step 2: Identify factors.*
    Clinician should ask for the patient's perceptions of the specific long-term, stable, positive and negative factors affecting the decision to acquire a self-care behavior, as well as the short-term, fluid, positive and negative factors associated with following the program.

*Step 3: Present new or clarifying information.*
    Patient should be fully informed of the specific details of the treatment, its effects on the disease, and the likely result if treatment is not followed.

*Step 4: Correct faulty logic.*
    If patient is using faulty logic, the clinician should use appropriate persuasion to convince the patient of error.

*Step 5: Respect the patient's informed decision.*
    If patient has reached an informed decision about the self-care routine, the clinician should not attempt to change this decision even though it may conflict with the clinician's own values.

*Step 6: Maintain continued contact.*
    Clinician should continue to contact the patient at periodic intervals to monitor progress and provide support as needed.

---

different approach than either those problems of initiating a new behavioral change program or other non-maintenance problems. Further, once diagnosed, there are several techniques unlike those used with other types of problems that may help to resolve this type of non-maintenance problem (Table 2).

*Step 1: Diagnosis.* If asked, most patients openly admit that they have decided not to follow the self-care routine. This is a deliberate, conscious decision by the patient. A patient may not volunteer this information, however, and may instead simply continue following those recommendations with which he agrees and ignoring the others. As a result, he may not be following the self-care routine, but the clinician may not be aware that he is not doing so.

The diagnosis of non-maintenance due to a change in the initial decision to follow the self-care program is usually based on two observations. First, the patient has completely stopped following a particular self-care program. Usually there is a complete cessation rather than intermittent or inconsistent adherence to the program. Second, when asked, the patient's rationale for not following the program indicates the absence of strong, positive, stable factors for continuing. The patient rates other activities which are incompatible with the self-care behavior as having more personal value than the recommended routine.

*Step 2: Identify Factors.* If the clinician suspects that the patient's non-adherence is due to a change in the patient's decision to follow the self-care program, his initial approach should be to develop an understanding of the patient's rationale for this decision. The clinician needs to answer the following questions: "What rationale does the patient offer for the decision not to continue the self-care routine?", "What has changed in the patient's life that may have produced this new problem?", and "Why has this problem occurred now?" If the problem arises from a change in the patient's initial decision to follow the self-care routine, the patient often will offer a broad rationale reflecting his values and priorities. Statements such as, "I'm just not ready", or "I'm not willing to make the changes needed", or "I'd rather continue doing the things I'm currently doing", suggest that the patient is making a fundamental decision not to follow the self-care routine.

In order to diagnose the patient's problem as one relating to a change in the initial decision to follow the regimen, the clinician needs to solicit the patient's thoughts and "self-talk." What is the patient saying to himself or others as to why he is no longer following the self-care routine? This will likely evoke statements relating to the patient's values and preferred lifestyle in relation to the activities associated with the new routine. If the patient offers other reasons for not following the routine, the clinician should consider alternative diagnoses for the problem. For example, if the patient states, "I simply couldn't fit the routine into my day," the clinician might suspect that frequent self-debate is occurring. Or if the patient states "I forgot," the clinician might suspect problems in habit formation. These problems will be discussed later in this chapter.

*Step 3: Present New or Clarifying Information.* Once the clinician has determined that the patient's problem might be diagnosed as a change in the initial decision to follow the self-care routine, the next step is to consider whether the patient possesses accurate information regarding the disease and the treatment required in order to make an "informed decision." The clinician should ask the patient to explain in his own words his understanding of his medical condition and what effect the medical treatment is intended to have. The patient should possess both sufficient and accurate information. If not, the clinician needs to provide such information. With sufficient accurate information the patient may reconsider his decision and re-embrace the decision to follow the self-care routine.

*Step 4: Correct Faulty Logic.* In other cases, the patient's decision not to follow the recommended routine is not based on inaccurate or incomplete information but on faulty logic. That is, the patient possesses a clear understanding of the disease and its treatment, but comes into difficulty understanding the concept of probability which is inherent in the practice of medicine. Much of our medical knowledge is derived from observations of groups of patients and the identification of risk factors associated with the development, treatment, and prognosis of a given disease.

Although most medical clinicians have a reasonable understanding of probability and its relation to a risk factor, this concept creates confusion for many patients. Probability is a construct borrowed from biostatistics which describes a particular pattern of correlations between two sets of variables. In the case of a risk factor, the association is often between a physiological or medical variable and a disease condition. For example, it has been observed that the group of people who smoke cigarettes have a higher incidence of high blood pressure than the group of people who do not smoke. As a result, the biostatisticians describe cigarette smoking as being correlated with these medical conditions. In other words, cigarette smoking places the patient "at risk" of developing high blood pressure. The confusion for most patients is that this relationship is one of correlation and not of causation. That is, it cannot be said that cigarette smoking causes high blood pressure. In fact, many people who do not smoke have high blood pressure. Other people smoke but do not have high blood pressure. Further, this is an association that is observed in a group of patients and does not necessarily hold true for any particular individual. It is only true "on the average" that patients who smoke develop high blood pressure more often than patients who do not smoke.

Unfortunately, because many patients do not understand the concept of a risk factor, they rely on their personal observations to guide their decisions about their lifestyle and recommended changes in behavior. If, for example, another member of the family smoked cigarettes and lived to be 90 years old, or if they smoked and did not develop high blood pressure, the patient may accept this observation as evidence that cigarette smoking does not create serious health problems. These patients may benefit from the clinician's help in correcting this misinterpretation of these concepts. A correction of their faulty reasoning may lead to the patient's reconsideration of the decision not to follow the recommended self-care program.

*Step 5: Respect the Patient's Informed Decision.*   There is a small group of patients who possess complete, accurate information about their disease and its treatment, and further understand the concepts of probability and risk factors, yet reject the recommended self-care routine. These patients have arrived at a decision which is in concert with their own values and personal beliefs, but which does not correspond with the clinician's.

In such cases, if the clinician has determined that the patient has arrived at an informed decision, and declines to follow the self-care routine, it is the clinician's responsibility to respect and defer to the patient's decision. For example, an elderly patient who has smoked all of his life and who is dying of lung cancer may decide that the cessation of smoking and the adoption of a rigid dietary routine does not correspond with the way he wishes to live during his remaining months or years, even if it means shortening his life expectancy to a substantial degree. The patient retains the right to determine how he will lead his life, regardless of the clinician's own value system. The clinician's main concern in these cases is to be satisfied that the patient has truly reached an informed decision, and has not simply given up due to lack of skills or substantial difficulty in achieving the changes necessary. If there is any doubt, it may be wise for the clinician to request a consultation from a psychologist. Regardless of the outcome of the consultation, the clinician remains responsible for providing the best medical care available for the duration of the patient's illness.

*Step 6: Maintain Continued Contact.*   Whether the patient re-evaluates his decision and re-initiates the self-care routine or reaches an informed decision to reject the self-care program, the clinician should maintain relatively frequent contact with him during the succeeding weeks and months. The time immediately following the patient's re-valued decision whether or not to maintain the self-care routine is crucial to the patient's ultimate success. During this difficult time, the patient may benefit from the clinician's advice and encouragement. A little contact with the clinician during this period can have a substantial effect on the patient's long-term maintenance.

It is also wise to re-contact the patient who has decided not to re-initiate the self-care program. This can be done in a manner that communicates that the clinician's respect for the patient's decision, but also provides assurance that the clinician is available if the patient changes his mind or wishes to begin at least part of the recommended program. The clinician's re-contact dramatically states the clinician's concern for the patient's welfare.

### Non-maintenance Associated
### with Initial Habit Formation Problems

If the patient has had difficulty establishing a self-care behavior as a habit, there is an increased likelihood that he may experience difficulties in maintaining the routine as a habit over time. These difficulties often arise because the patient lacks the self-management skills to re-establish the habit once it is broken. The patient is successful in maintaining the routine only as long as the environment remains relatively stable. Once the environment changes and creates new or unexpected barriers for the patient, the patient may fail. Moreover, another competing behavior with greater immediate gratification may take its place. As a result, once the habit is broken, it does not become re-established.

Seemingly minor changes in the environment can have a dramatic effect on a self-care regimen that has become a habit because of 2 specific qualities of habits: (1) a habit occurs in response to specific cues in the environment with little thought, and (2) other behaviors with greater immediate gratification will take the place of the habit when it is not performed.

That habits occur in response to specific cues or signals in the environment with little thought means that the patient is performing the behavior as a routine, almost "automatically" when certain conditions occur in the environment. The patient has minimal conscious involvement in the activity. The habit exists in his daily routine because it has become comfortable and requires little effort or support. This is in contrast to other behaviors that the patient performs in a deliberate manner either because of their intrinsic positive qualities, or because of their desirable positive consequences (e.g., completing a report at work, playing cards, working in the garden). For example, the patient may start the self-care habit of eating low cholesterol meals while he is at home and at lunch in the local cafeteria. In familiar surroundings the habit of eating low-cholesterol foods occurs regularly in the same situation day after day with little deliberation. However, if the patient leaves these familiar surroundings (e.g., goes on a business trip) and eats with colleagues in a new setting (e.g., a restaurant never visited previously), the patient's usual daily pattern is disrupted. Those natural environmental cues that had been prompting the patient's choice of a low cholesterol meal (e.g., low fat milk in the refrigerator, "no-choice" meals prepared by a spouse, a tasty salad bar in the cafeteria at work) are absent. Further, social pressure from co-workers might encourage the selection of foods that are high in cholesterol. This might include explicit suggestions that he should "enjoy himself" or that the restaurant serves special gourmet foods, or, the more subtle pressure that everyone else is ordering foods that are high in cholesterol. As a result, the patient breaks his usual routine, and eats high cholesterol meals during the trip. A break in the habitual pattern might occur for other reasons, too. For instance, the patient may not be able to follow the normal routine due to unexpected changes in his daily work schedule, illness, or injury.

Once the habit is broken, it is not easy to re-establish. The reason for this difficulty is that in every situation, another behavior will take the place of the desired self-care behavior, and may have greater immediate positive consequences. This is exactly what happens when the patient stops smoking. The habit of smoking had been replaced by other, less damaging routines (e.g., gaining pleasure from handling a small substitute object, sucking on candy, using a muscle relaxation exercise). However, the powerful reinforcing qualities of cigarette smoking are immediately experienced when the patient smokes only a couple of cigarettes. As a result, the habit pattern of cigarette smoking returns. A similar situation exists with physical activity programs, sleep disturbances, weight loss programs, and drug regimens.

Table 3. Counseling steps for non-maintenance problems associated with initial habit formation problems

*Step 1: Diagnose initial habit formation as problem.*
　　Patient's problem should be clearly related to repeated failure to maintain the self-care routine as a habit.

*Step 2: Instruct patient in problem-solving skills.*
　　Patient should acquire an understanding of a simple six-step method for systematically analyzing and resolving a problem of habit maintenance.

*Step 3: Present rationale for effective strategy.*
　　Patient should be instructed in the reasons for the effectiveness of certain strategies in re-establishing a routine.

*Step 4: "Inoculate" the patient against future problems.*
　　Patient should receive some practice in solving potential future problems similar to the current problem so that they can be resolved without the clinician's assistance.

### The Clinician's Approach

Although many patients are able to adapt to a changing environment and re-establish the self-care routines as a habit, some are not as fortunate. These patients may profit from the clinician's guidance. Those patients who have had initial problems establishing a behavior as a habit are clearly at risk for failure if the environment changes. The clinician should consider offering specific counseling to these patients (Table 3).

*Step 1: Diagnosis.*　Non-maintenance resulting from a break in the habit pattern is usually the most common problem that patients encounter in long-term self-care routines. This kind of problem is preceded by an initial, stable pattern of adherence followed by a sudden cessation of the program. As discussed in later sections of this chapter, this pattern is similar to the one observed when the patient re-evaluates his initial decision to follow the program or when the patient experiences fatigue from studying.

Two factors distinguish a break in the habit pattern from other non-maintenance problems. First, a substantial change in the patient's daily routine has usually occurred. The patient has taken a vacation, been ill, just gotten married, separated from his spouse, or moved. Usually the patient can identify a major disruption in his usual activities that coincides with the cessation in the self-care program. This change may be temporary or permanent but in either case the patient has not been able to resume the self-care program.

The second factor that suggests that the problem is due to a break in the habit is that the patient expresses a clear desire to continue with the self-care routine. The patient would like to follow the program, but does not have the skills to develop a successful routine. As a result the patient is usually willing to cooperate with the clinician's suggestions and try a variety of strategies in order to find one that will be effective.

*Step 2: Instruct Patient in Problem-Solving Skills.*   Probably the most effective counseling technique for these patients is to involve them in the re-design of the self-care routine. The clinician should require the patient to be an active participant in the selection of the specific details for the new self-care regimen for two reasons. First, the patient will have to consider the possible advantages and disadvantages of various regimens and thereby learn to generate and assess the usefulness of alternatives. The patient will thus also gain practice in the process or problem solving which he can use when problems are encountered in the future. Second, the patient will develop a sense of ownership for the solution. That is, when successful, the patient will realize that he can exert control over his behavior and his environment. This attitude of ownership leading to a sense of mastery is very important for the patient to learn. Resuming a habit pattern after the environment has changed may severely test the patient's tolerance of frustration and require much perseverance before a successful program is developed.

In terms of specific counseling to accomplish these goals, the clinician should: (1) Clearly identify the problem for the patient, (2) Solicit the patient's suggestions for resolving the problem, (3) Discuss with the patient the potential benefits of each suggestion. Essentially, the counselor is teaching the patient the crucial steps in problem solving. Rather than simply prescribing a routine for the patient to follow, the clinician encourages him to take a major role in its design.

*Step 3: Present Rationale for the Effective Strategy.*   Much of counseling for behavior change is educational. The clinician instructs the patient how to acquire the desired self-care behavior, and educates the patient as to why the specific techniques used were successful. The rationale for this approach is to provide the patient with an understanding of the basic behavioral change process so that he can use the process in the future. Moreover, the patient needs to know why a particular technique was effective in order to be able to modify the technique in the future when confronted with unexpected problems. This education helps the patient resolve his own problems, and may effectively prevent a break in the habit pattern without requiring the clinician's involvement.

If the patient understands the rationale for a technique, then he can vary its application as conditions change. For example, a hypertensive patient who is experiencing difficulty taking a diuretic prior to breakfast might learn to place a cue (e.g., a reminder such as the pill bottle) on the breakfast table after dinner the previous evening. When the patient sees the pill bottle the next morning, he is reminded to take the medication. Once the cue is successful, the clinician should explicitly educate the patient as to the principles involved in selecting and using a cue. Specifically, the patient should learn that: (1) the cue must be noticeable, (2) the cue must be encountered immediately prior to the time when the desired behavior should occur, and (3) the cue should not be encountered at other times of the day. Using these guidelines, the patient should then be able to design a system of cues that would have the flexibility to adapt to a changing environment.

*Step 4: Inoculate the Patient Against Future Problems.*   Once the patient has successfully acquired a habit, and learned the principles behind the behavior change strategies involved, the clinician may further reduce the risk of non-maintenance by "inoculating" the patient against potential problems. This inoculation training involves challenging the patient with new problems that might be encountered. The clinician describes a specific problem, for instance, that requires the patient to use the newly acquired self-management skills to design a likely strategy to resolve the problem and maintain the self-care regimen. This "testing" of the patient prepares him to deal with unexpected problems without feeling dependent upon the clinician's help. With the potential problems identified, and possible solutions in mind, the patient can proceed with the self-care program with confidence and the skills to overcome difficulties.

## Non-maintenance Associated with Continuing Self-Debate

At least 25% of all patients report that their self-care behaviors never become habits. Instead, they state that they continually debate with themselves about whether or not they should follow the prescribed self-care routine. These patients do not lack the ability to follow the regimen. Rather, these patients have silent, daily arguments with themselves over whether or not they should follow the routine.

These self-debates usually center on changes in the environment or the patients' feelings at the time they should be following the self-care regimen. In Chapter 2, these transitory changes were described as fluid factors. They are fluid in the sense that their strength and even their presence can vary on a daily basis. Some examples of fluid factors are moods (e.g., fear, happiness, anger, depression), the actions of others (e.g., unexpected problems or demands), illness, or injury.

Everyone encounters unexpected events, some more frequently than others. It is not the occurrence of these events, per se, that poses a problem; rather it is their effect on the patient's decision whether or not to follow the desired routine. If the clinician suspects that the patient is self-debating during the early days of a new self-care program, special care should be taken to eliminate this self-debating because it is a likely source of future maintenance problems. This is true even if the patient is deciding in favor of the desired self-care routine.

Self-debating is a potential source of problems during maintenance because of the dynamic nature of the environment. The people and activities in our environment are in a state of continuing change. As a result new positive and negative consequences to the self-care behavior routine naturally evolve. Usually these new consequences are relatively weak in strength and have little effect, either on routines that are habitual, or deliberate behaviors that are associated with powerful incentives. However, other changes can have strong effects. For example, an overweight diabetic patient who has enjoyed some success in a weight loss program may find that his closest friend, who is also overweight, is choosing not to eat with him at lunch. This could be the result of the friend being increasingly uncomfortable with his own lack of success in weight loss, and the patient's obvious success.

These new consequences pose no problem to established habits. Once the self-care behavior has been established as a habit, the routine continues with little thought and is minimally affected by these events. However, these new consequences may affect the patient's decision to maintain the routine if he is engaged in continuing self-debate.

Self-debating indicates that the patient sees the positive and negative factors as equally compelling. The benefits and disadvantages of following the routine are about the same as not following the routine. The overall situation is neither overwhelmingly positive nor negative. As a result, the patient's decision can become influenced by relatively minor positive and negative fluid factors. The outcome of the patient's self-debate becomes dictated by the events of the moment.

### The Clinician's Approach

The clinician should use a four-step approach to counsel patients with this type of non-maintenance problem. These steps are: (1) Ascertain that the patient is self-debating, (2) Specify the positive and negative, stable and fluid factors present in the self-debate, (3) Intervene to eliminate the negative factors, and (4) Teach the patient problem-solving skills to cope with future problems (Table 4).

*Step 1: Diagnosis of Continuing Self-Debate.* The first step in counseling these patients is to determine that the patient is continuing to self-debate on a frequent basis. If asked, most patients who self-debate will freely admit that this is occurring. They will be familiar with the self-debate problem from discussions with the clinician when the self-care program was initiated. However, unless

Table 4. Counseling steps for maintenance problems associated with continuing
self-debate

---

*Step 1: Diagnose continuing self-debate.*
  Clinician should clearly establish that the patient's maintenance problem is a result of
    frequent self-debate as to whether or not the recommended self-care routine should be
    followed.

*Step 2: Identify factors.*
  Clinician should examine the patient's perceptions of the specific long-term, stable, posi-
    tive and negative factors affecting the decision to acquire a self-care behavior, as well
    as the short-term, fluid, positive and negative factors associated with following the pro-
    gram.

*Step 3: Eliminate negative stable factors.*
  Eliminating any negative stable factors is the most effective, long-lasting solution to a
    self-debate problem.

*Step 4: Instruct in problem-solving skills.*
  Patient should learn the basic six-step problem-solving process in order to resolve future
    self-debates in favor of following the desired regimen.

---

the clinician raises the issue, these patients may not volunteer to discuss their
self-debating.

*Step 2: Identification of Factors.*   Once the clinician has established that the
patient is continuing to self-debate, the next step is to identify the factors that
are contributing to the debate. This is perhaps the most difficult task for the
clinician, because most patients are not able to recall or conceptualize the
thoughts that occurred to them in a situation in the past. It is not common for
patients to be reflective and conscious of their particular thoughts.

As a result, the clinician may have to ask the patient to describe in detail the
routine that he followed on the previous day or the last time he was scheduled
for the self-care program. What did the patient do? How was the patient feeling
at the time? Does the patient recall any particular thoughts that occurred? The
patient's answers to these questions may provoke his recall of the details of the
self-debate that he was having at the time.

If the patient is vague or cannot remember clearly his specific thoughts, the
clinician should ask the patient to identify the next three scheduled times for
the routine. The clinician should request that the patient make a special point
of being aware of his thoughts about following the regimen over the next few
days. Is he self-debating? If so, how long does it last? How is it resolved? What
are the arguments, pro and con, that occur to him about whether or not to
follow the routine? Often it is extremely helpful to use a simple daily recording
form on which the patient notes his thoughts at the time.

The next step is to create a tally chart containing the positive and negative
factors that are influencing the patient's self-debate. This is a simple 2-column

| Factors with immediate effects | | | |
| Positive factors | Strength (1–10) | Negative factors | Strength (1–10) |
| --- | --- | --- | --- |
| 1. | | 1. | |
| 2. | | 2. | |
| 3. | | 3. | |
| 4. | | 4. | |
| 5. | | 5. | |
| Factors with delayed effects | | | |
| Positive factors | Strength (1–10) | Negative factors | Strength (1–10) |
| 1. | | 1. | |
| 2. | | 2. | |
| 3. | | 3. | |
| 4. | | 4. | |
| 5. | | 5. | |

Figure 1. Tally chart for analyzing a patient's self-debate.

list (Figure 1). Once the factors are sorted into the negative and positive categories, the patient indicates, on a scale of 1 to 10, each factor's relative strength, 1 being the weakest and 10 the strongest. Finally, the patient indicates the stability of each factor. If the factor tends to be a stable factor that changes little over time, it is given an S. If the factor tends to be a fluid factor that varies in strength or is sometimes present and other times absent, it is given an F. When complete, this tally chart will contain each of the factors effecting the patient's self-debate, indicate the relative balance achieved between the positive and negative factors, and suggest negative factors that might be targeted for removal.

*Step 3: Eliminate Negative Stable Factors.* The tally chart will identify those stable factors that are functioning as barriers for the patient. In most cases, the reduction or elimination of one or more of these negative factors will result in a marked improvement in the patient's maintenance. The overall balance of the advantages and disadvantages of following the self-care regimen will move toward maintenance. Further, the greater the strength of the negative factor that is eliminated, the more resistant the self-care routine will be to future non-maintenance due to self-debate.

Rather than eliminate negative factors, it may seem simpler to create more incentives for the patient to follow the self-care routine. This is often what is attempted. The rationale is that with greater advantages than disadvantages to following the routine, the patient will decide to follow the self-care program. As a result, motivating discussions are held with the patient by the physician, the nurse, members of the patient's family, or friends who attempt to persuade him to place greater value for personal, health, or social reasons on following the program. Unfortunately, these well-meaning attempts rarely lead to lasting success. Regardless of how desirable the advantages are, the patient still encounters the aspects of the program. As a result, although these motivational efforts may be successful initially, the patient eventually loses the incentive to stick to the program.

This situation is often seen with patients who have a chronic disease (e.g., hypertension, heart disease, cancer, diabetes) and who have been prescribed a medication with substantial side effects. After an initial period of perhaps excellent adherence, the frequency of following the medication regimen declines markedly. These patients report that they are aware of their disease, its prognosis, and the necessity of taking the prescribed medication; they also state that they are no longer willing to take the medication as prescribed. The clinician must identify each negative factor, and attempt to design a strategy that will reduce or eliminate the effect of the factor on the patient's self-care behavior.

The experience of hyperlipidemic patients who have been prescribed cholestyramine illustrates this problem and the clinician's appropriate counseling resp: nse. Cholestyramine is a lipid lowering drug that acts by extracting cholesterol from the bile as it moves through the gastrointestinal tract. Patients who are already troubled by gastrointestinal tract disorders such as indigestion, gas, or constipation may find that this medication aggravates their problems. Over time, the patient's self-debate whether or not to take the medication (which may involve many factors in addition to the side effects experienced) becomes increasingly resolved by not following the medication routine. The clinician's appropriate target for counseling is the chronic discomfort that the patient experiences even when the medication is not taken. Appropriate interventions may include a change in diet to reduce the consumption of irritating foods or to increase bulk; a change in beverage consumption to reduce the intake of liquids containing alcohol or caffeine and increase the intake of water; or a change in exercise pattern to improve bowel motility. Once these chronic discomforts are controlled and the side effects produced by the medication are minimized, the patient will be able to maintain the drug regimen.

*Step 4: Instruct the Patient in Problem-Solving Skills.*  Even though a major negative factor has been controlled or eliminated, the patient will continue to encounter changes in his environment which may influence his self-debate. Therefore, the patient should also be taught how to design a behavioral change program. This includes the following 6 steps: (1) identifying the problem, (2) generating alternative solutions, (3) weighing the likelihood of success for each solution, (4) trying one solution, (5) assessing its effects, and (6) revising the solution. These steps were discussed in detail in Chapter 3.

The clinician should point out that this is the process that was used to tackle the patient's initial problem of self-debating. Each step should be illustrated using the patient's own experience, if possible. The patient should be encouraged to describe each of the steps and how he might apply them to a new, hypothetical problem (e.g., a change in schedule, travel, holidays). In this way the patient leaves the counseling session with specific tools to use to resolve future barriers to maintenance. The patient may be able to prevent minor changes in the environment from becoming serious threats to the self-care routine.

### Resolving Non-maintenance Problems Discovered Late

Thus far we have discussed general preventive measures which can be used with any patient to promote maintenance. In addition, three specific non-maintenance problems have been discussed that can be anticipated as a continuation of problems first encountered when the patient began the self-care routine. In both of these situations, the clinician has become aware of the problem of non-maintenance early in the program.

With other patients, the clinician does not become aware that the patient is not following the recommended self-care routine, or is following the routine but not in a proper manner, until several months into the program. This often occurs because of infrequent clinic visits, the absence of sufficient time during a clinic visit to question the patient about the self-care routine, or because of the patient's reluctance to admit to the clinician that he is experiencing difficulty.

When discovered late, however, the problem becomes more difficult to resolve than if it had been attacked early. This is because now there is a history of lack of success for the patient. The fact that the patient was not following the self-care routine does not simply mean that the routine was absent from his daily schedule. It may also mean that the patient has attempted to follow the self-care routine in some manner, may have used some strategies with only partial or no success, and may now have developed specific negative attitudes toward the self-care routine and his ability to be succcessful with this type of program. The problem of non-maintenance has acquired an additional set of problems which the clinician must address in counseling the patient to re-start or improve adherence to the routine.

Non-maintenance problems discovered late are usually of 4 types: (1) the patient has not made the initial decision to follow the routine, (2) the patient is having difficulty establishing the routine as a habit, (3) the patient is self-debating, (4) the patient experiences "treatment fatigue." The first three of these problems have been discussed in detail in previous sections of this chapter. The only difference in the current situation is that initially the patient was experiencing these problems but the clinician was not aware of them. However, the clinician's treatment of these problems is identical to the steps outlined for their treatment when identified early. The following section discusses treatment fatigue.

## Treatment Fatigue

Treatment fatigue can be defined as the occurrence of initial satisfactory performance of a self-care routine followed by a significant decrease in adherence in the absence of obvious deterrents. When fatigued, patients report that they have lost their desire to follow the self-care routine. They "don't care about the routine," they "aren't interested," they "are tired of the program," or they "find the routine boring or tedious." It has been reported that for some aversive medication regimens, up to 15% of all patients experience regimen fatigue at some time during the first 3 years of their program.

Usually these patients cannot be identified early in a program. They appear to be doing well, and may have excellent maintenance to the routine over months or years. However, one day, usually without warning, they simply decide to stop following their routine.

Three causes are suspected for regimen fatigue. First, the self-care routine has lost its intrinsic appeal. The enjoyable qualities of the self-care routine have disappeared, and it is now seen simply as another task to be performed. Whereas initially the new routine may have been different and challenging, now it has lost its novelty. The initial feelings of self-control and accomplishment may have waned once the new routine was mastered. In short, the patient no longer enjoys the routine itself. For example, initially the patient might eagerly attend an aerobics exercise program early in the morning and find it new, different, and very much out of the ordinary. Gradually, however, if the patient does not derive sufficient pleasure from the exercises or their effects, the program can become an unpleasantly monotonous routine and the patient eventually can become fatigued.

The second cause of regimen fatigue is the gradual disappearance of some of the short-term, secondary benefits of the self-care program. The best wishes and support of family, friends, and co-workers for the patient's success in following the self-care routine no longer occur as often, if at all. In other words, the patient no longer experiences some of the added positive consequences of following the self-care routine. As a result the negative aspects of the program become more noticeable and aversive, and the patient decides not to follow the program any longer.

The third cause of regimen fatigue is the eventual decrease in the attention that the patient receives simply by virtue of being identified as having a particular disease. For some patients, the fact that they have a chronic disease (e.g., they are a "by-pass patient," "heart patient," "diabetic") sets them apart as unique among their family, friends, and co-workers. Initially, this uniqueness draws attention and notice. Often others express admiration for their ability to endure the disease or its treatement (e.g., the surgery, the demands of rehabilitation, the continuing pain or discomfort). In some cases the disease is even seen as an accepted condition associated with success in a difficult business situation (e.g., high blood pressure resulting from a high status, high pressured job). In a peculiar way, the patient is given higher status among co-workers for it. In either case, the patient is treated different by others.

Although this new "patient role" can be rewarding, for many patients with chronic conditions, its status wanes over time. Other people grow less interested in the patient's medical condition, and may begin to avoid discussing it. As this interest decreases, the patient also grows tired of the disease, and wishes he did not have it. As the self-care routines become increasingly annoying, the patient may decide simply not to follow them any more. This occurs partly because the routine lacks interest, and partly because it serves as a reminder to the patient that he has the disease.

## The Clinician's Approach

Treatment fatigue requires careful diagnosis to distinguish it from other causes of maintenance problems, particularly self-debate problems and changes in the patient's initial decision. Once diagnosed, however, the general approach to treatment fatigue is to increase the immediate positive aspects associated with the self-care routine, and to eliminate the immediate negative aspects. A five-step counseling process is recommended (Table 5).

Table 5. Counseling steps for non-maintenance problems associated with treatment fatigue

*Step 1: Diagnose treatment fatigue.*
   Patient's non-maintenance problem should be clearly established to be the result of treatment fatigue rather than of self-debate or habit failure.

*Step 2: Present new or clarifying information.*
   Patient should understand the potential long-term benefits of the self-care program.

*Step 3: Increase attractiveness of the self-care routine.*
   Patient's self-care routine should be adjusted to include strongly positive aspects, if possible.

*Step 4: Eliminate aversive aspects of the routine.*
   Patient's self-care routine should be adjusted to omit or minimize aspects that are unpleasant or uncomfortable for the patient.

*Step 5: Use self-help groups.*
   A self-help group can provide alternative, effective methods of overcoming typical problems in specific self-care routines and become a continuing source of support and encouragement for the patient.

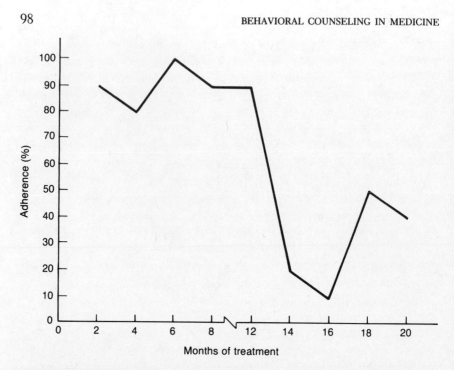

*Note:* Treatment fatigue is defined as a pattern of adherence to a self-care routine which is initially satisfactory, but is followed by a rapid significant decrease in adherence in the presence of patient's complaints of lack of interest in the program, and in the absence of obvious deterrents.

Figure 2. A pattern of adherence to a self-care routine suggesting that the patient experienced treatment fatigue with partial recovery.

*Step 1: Diagnosis.* To accurately diagnose treatment fatigue the clinician should first review the patient's pattern of adherence to the self-care. Treatment fatigue typically shows a pattern of initial, relatively stable, satisfactory performance followed by a rapid drop in adherence (Figure 2). This initial period of satisfactory performance may vary in length from weeks to years.

The patient's satisfactory performance is deceptive because if asked about the routine during this period, the patient will often report decreased interest in following the program and an increase in the number of difficulties that regularly have to be surmounted to be able to follow the routine. In other words, although it appears that the patient is doing well with the program, he is, in fact, succeeding only as the result of tolerating an increasingly aversive situation. Eventually the routine becomes too aversive and the patient stops, fatigued from the struggle. Most often, however, the patient will not voluntarily express these concerns, and, as a result, his decision to stop the program and expression of fatigue may come as a surprise to the clinician.

Because of this cognitive component of treatment fatigue, the diagnosis also depends upon the patient's statements of apathy regarding the routine, and the routine's increasing aversiveness. The patient should be asked to describe the self-care program in detail and the clinician should listen for the patient's feelings about the program. Does the patient seem to care about following the routine? Can the patient identify any pleasant or enjoyable aspects of following the routine? What does the patient believe is the likelihood that he will be able to follow the routine in the future? The patient's answers to these questions will distinguish the patient with treatment fatigue from the patient who is troubled with daily self-debates due to a changing environment, and from the patient who has re-evaluated his initial decision to follow the self-care program.

*Step 2: Present New or Clarifying Information.* As with any other non-maintenance problem, the clinician's first step is to ensure that the patient possesses complete and accurate information regarding the disease, its prognosis, the prescribed medical treatment, and the relationship between the disease and recommended self-care activities. In the case of treatment fatigue, however, it is particularly important that the patient understand the potential long-term benefits that may occur as a result of the self-care routine. These benefits are a major source of stable incentives for the patient to continue with a routine that may have grown uninteresting and lacking in immediate positive aspects. These long-term benefits provide the motivation for the patient to continue with the program, and to continue to work with the clinician to develop a more attractive self-care program.

*Step 3: Increase the Attractiveness of the Self-Care Routine.* If the patient's maintenance problem is clearly diagnosed as treatment fatigue, the primary goal of intervention should be to increase the inherent positive aspects of the self-care routine. The goal should be to identify a modification of the current routine or a new routine that has some intrinsically pleasing qualities for the patient. To do so requires a careful, detailed review of the patient's current routine to determine if any aspects of it are reinforcing. If so, these should be retained. In addition, the patient should be asked to help identify those types of activities or routines that are most attractive. For example, if the patient is fatigued from following a particular medication routine, a routine might be sought that has the patient taking the medication at a different time or drunk with a different liquid. If the patient is fatigued from following a particular low cholesterol diet, new recipes might be obtained from one of the gourmet low cholesterol, low salt cookbooks. Alternatively, a dietitian might be consulted to identify "trade-offs" which would allow the patient to eat highly desired foods in limited amounts by altering other aspects of the diet. If the patient is fatigued from attending an aerobics exercise program, alternative activities such as bicycling, swimming, skating, or walking might be explored. The important point of a new or modified program is that the patient should be able to find some aspect of it that is enjoyable, and it should remain so over time.

*Step 4: Eliminate Aversive Aspects of the Routine.*   In reviewing the routine, the clinician should also be alert to the patient's description of any negative or unpleasant aspects. If possible, these aspects should be reduced or eliminated. For example, the patient might indicate that the formal procedure of deep muscle relaxation is too noticeable to use during an anxiety provoking business meeting, and thus is only used before or after but not during the meeting. The clinician might offer to help the patient practice evoking the same feelings of relaxation when seated in a chair with his eyes open and without noticeable muscle contractions. In this way the patient can use the anxiety-reduction routine when needed and not be embarassed or uncomfortable using it.

*Step 5: Use Self-Help Groups.*   Self-help groups can be a particularly effective strategy for combating treatment fatigue. Membership in a group of patients who have the same or similar diseases may offer the patient alternative methods of coping with daily problems following a self-care routine. Group members share their own solutions to the problems they encounter and may provoke new ideas from other patients.

A self-help group also offers the support and understanding of others who have experienced the same problems maintaining difficult self-care routines. This support can help provide the patient with the necessary comfort, security, and courage to continue in a difficult situation. The caring and concern of a self-help group can also be extremely helpful to the patient in overcoming treatment fatigue.

The creation of a self-help group need not involve anything more difficult than inviting patients with similar diseases or treatments to an informal meeting once or twice a month. If structured as an educational discussion session, most patients are not uncomfortable attending, particularly if the clinician or someone from the clinic is leading the group discussion. However, patients who are having serious problems coping with their diagnosis, treatment, or their consequences on their personal life should be encouraged to consider joining a more formal group in therapy or seeking individual consultation from a psychologist.

# 6. Non-adherence to Medication Regimens

A patient's non-adherence to a prescribed medication regimen poses a serious problem in clinical practice. Non-adherence in individuals with acute problems can compromise their medical treatment and increase the possibility of further complications. Non-adherence in individuals with chronic health problems leaves them vulnerable to the progression of the disease and its effects.

Non-adherence presents the physician with a difficult decision. If the non-adherence is known, and the patient's symptoms are not improving, the physician must evaluate the effects of the inconsistent use of the medication and decide whether the patient's prescription should be changed. If the non-adherence is not known, and the patient's symptoms are not improving, the physician may decide to modify the patient's prescription to increase the dosage, change the frequency of administration, or switch to a more powerful medication. As a result, the patient may become over-medicated.

Many people have difficulty following their medication regimen, so it is not surprising that non-adherence is a common occurrence. It is estimated that between 20 and 80% of patients do not take their medication as prescribed. Although adherence levels vary across patients and regimens, approximately one-third of the patients consistently take their medication, one-third consistently do not take their medication, and one-third irregularly take their medication. If adherence level is plotted for a group of patients on the same medication, the resulting curve would appear to have a U or J shape.

Considerable research has focused on the phenomenon of patients' non-adherence. These studies have examined the relationship between non-adherence and characteristics of patients, characteristics of clinicians and clinics, and characteristics of regimens. These studies indicate that standard demographic variables such as the patient's age, sex, socio-economic status, educational level, religion, marital status, and race do not consistently predict adherence level. However, one patient-related characteristic that does appear to be consistently related to improved adherence is the presence of a supportive family member.

Patients with someone who supports them through treatment tend to do better than patients lacking such support.

The patient's relationship with the clinician and the clinic also appears to influence adherence. Improved adherence tends to occur when the clinician and the clinic staff are perceived as understanding, concerned, and empathic. Adherence also is improved if the patient sees the same clinician each visit. Not surprisingly, poor adherence is associated with increased waiting time in the clinic.

Characteristics of the medication regimen itself also can strongly influence the subsequent adherence level. Poor adherence is associated with reigmens that require multiple medications, frequent administration, or are prescribed along with several other lifestyle changes. Poor adherence also occurs if the regimen does not fit easily into the patient's routine, or if the patient has an irregular daily routine. Side effects of the medication, per se, do not seem to have a major effect on adherence if the patient is not alarmed by the symptoms, and if the clinician directly attends to them.

This research clearly implies that non-adherence is a direct result of the patient's response to the clinician, the clinic, and/or the medication regimen. As with other lifestyle changes, adherence to a prescribed medication regimen is determined by specific factors in the patient's environment. Thus, the clinician's response to a patient's non-adherence should be to develop an understanding of these factors and to intervene appropriately.

## The Behavioral Pattern Accompanying
## Adherence to a Medication Regimen

A medication regimen requires the patient to introduce a new routine into his daily activities that must be performed in a certain manner at a specific time. Clearly those medications that provide symptomatic relief are inherently reinforcing and will encourage the patient to continue to adhere to the regimen. Such medications, for example, include antacids which reduce the patient's indigestion, and antihistimines which relieve allergic reactions.

Unfortunately, many medications either provide no immediate symptomatic relief (e.g., theophylline which is taken to prevent asthma attacks) or have unpleasant side effects (e.g., a thiazide diuretic which increases urinary frequency and volume). The difficulty that many patients experience in attempting to start a regimen is that the immediate negative consequences of taking the medication outweigh the immediate positive consequences of doing so (Table 1). Even patients who understand and accept the necessity of taking the prescribed medication may discontinue it because the immediate negative consequences predominate.

Other factors can inhibit the patient from taking the medication as pre-

Table 1. Typical consequences of following a medication regimen for treatment of a chronic disease

|  | Consequences | |
|---|---|---|
|  | *Positive* | *Negative* |
| *Immediate* | Reduction of symptoms (if any) | Disruption of daily routine |
|  | Support from family, friends, or co-workers | Discomfort associated with the administration of the medication |
|  | Comfort from the knowledge that medical condition is being treated | Side effects of the medication |
|  |  | Criticism by family, friends, or co-workers |
|  |  | Cost to purchase or refill prescription |
| *Delayed* | Cure of the disease | Inconvenience of purchasing and storing medication |
|  | Control of disease progression | Problems related to the maintenance of equipment (if any) |
|  | Reduction in the risk of associated medical problems |  |
|  | Support from physician and clinic staff |  |

scribed. The patient may have to make special arrangements for storage and transportation of the medication (e.g., insulin must be kept away from extreme temperatures). The medication may require a special method of administration (e.g., a cream which must be allowed to be absorbed after application), or special timing in relation to food or sleep (e.g., antacids must be taken at least 1 hour after eating for maximum effect). The patient also may have to remember to take the medication at several different times throughout the day. All these factors can be disruptive and lead to non-adherence.

The balance of positive and negative factors is reversed when the patient does not take the prescribed dose of medication (Table 2). He avoids the chores of preparing and administering the medication, and any unpleasant side effects it might have. In addition, he avoids any negative social aspects of taking the medication. On balance, these immediate negative factors outweigh the positive factors for taking the medication. As a result the patient continues with his customary activities, and fails to follow the prescribed medication regimen.

## The Patient's Decision to Accept the Drug Treatment

The patient who suffers an acute medical problem with symptoms that are relieved by a prescribed medication does not need to be convinced of the wisdom

Table 2. Typical consequences of not following a medication regimen for treatment of a chronic disease

| | Consequences | |
|---|---|---|
| | Positive | Negative |
| Immediate | Avoid disruption of daily routine | Guilt that medical condition is not being treated |
| | Avoid discomfort of administering the medication | Continuation or reappearance of symptoms (if any) |
| | Avoid side effects of the medication | Criticism by family, friends, or co-workers |
| | Avoid criticism by family, friends, or co-workers | |
| | Save money by not purchasing or refilling prescription | |
| Delayed | None | Increased risk for continuation of the medical condition |
| | | Increased risk for progression of the medical condition |
| | | Increased risk for development of associated medical problems |
| | | Criticism by physician or clinic staff |

of following the drug regimen. The effects of the drug are readily experienced. When non-adherence to treatment for an acute illness does occur, it happens after the patient's symptoms have decreased or disappeared. This is observed, for example, in the treatment of acute infections with a 10-day regimen of antibiotics. The patient begins to feel better within a few days, his fever drops, and he returns to his usual activities. At this point the patient's adherence declines.

The situation is considerably different for the patient with a chronic disease or condition (e.g., hypertension, diabetes). Usually this patient has no problem initially deciding to follow the medication regimen as prescribed. Later, however, he may make a conscious decision to discontinue it. Although reasons vary, it is not uncommon for a patient to miss doses or to stop taking his medication completely for periods of time. This decision not to follow the prescribed medication regimen should be detected and treated as early as possible.

The clinician can help the patient make a conscious decision to follow the medication regimen by offering a clear explanation of the relationship between the prescribed drug and the chronic disease or condition. The clinician should avoid medical terminology as much as possible, explaining the medical problem and/or risks of disease using common terms (e.g., "heart disease" rather than "atherosclerosis," "high cholesterol" rather than "elevated lipids"). In all cases, the physician should establish that the medication regimen is essential to treat the patient's disease or condition and is not simply a recommendation.

The clinician also can be helpful by asking the patient to describe his understanding of the disease, the risk factors, the regimen, and the problems that the patient is likely to encounter while on the regimen. Occasionally the patient is misinformed or does not understand what the long-term course of treatment will be like. For example, a patient who starts a diuretic regimen and experiences increased urinary frequency may not understand that this is a temporary side effect of the drug that will disappear within a few weeks. In other cases, the patient may not understand the rationale behind the management of chronic disease, believing instead that the medication is curing the disease or condition rather than alleviating its symptoms.

Finally, it is most important that the clinician avoid attempting to scare the patient into following the medication regimen. Although the patient may indeed be at risk for serious medical complications, it is important that the clinician recognize that fear is a motivator only when it is at a moderate level. A high level of fear will have the unintended effect of inhibiting the patient's adherence, and may actually cause the patient to ignore his disease. As a result the patient may not only fail to follow the drug regimen, he also may decide to discontinue seeing the clinician. Therefore it is best that the clinician explain the patient's prognosis in a straightforward manner, indicating the continued effects of the disease in relation to the likelihood of their occurrence in this particular patient. Discussions of "worst case" possibilities should be avoided.

## The Initial Patient Contact

Not all patients experience problems following a long-term medication regimen. Those who do have problems encounter them at different points in the process of prescription, accommodation, and long-term maintenance. The clinician would like to know which patients will have the following problems, and when they will occur: (1) The patient has insufficient knowledge about the disease; (2) The patient rejects the medical diagnosis; (3) The patient deliberately decides not to follow the regimen; (4) The patient fails to establish the regimen as a habit; (5) The patient continues to self-debate whether or not to follow the regimen. If known in advance, the clinician then could use his clinical time to counsel only those patients who are "at risk of non-adherence" to their medication regimen, and allow the other patients to succeed on their own.

Unfortunately, we currently do not have the capability of making these predictions. Instead, it is recommended that the clinician provide guidance and support to all patients, but respond swiftly with intensive counseling as needed for those patients who begin to experience problems. The following section describes two specific actions that the clinician can take that require minimal time, and that will help the patient avoid subsequent problems: (1) educate the patient about the disease and the drug regimen, and (2) tailor the regimen to the patient's lifestyle.

## Patient Education

The clinician should ensure that the patient has obtained information about the disease, its long-term sequelae, and the effects of the drug, prior to leaving the clinic. This information may be given directly to the patient, in writing, through a slide/tape presentation, or through computerized patient education materials. In all cases, however, the patient should have the opportunity to ask questions of a member of the clinic staff about his specific case.

## Tailoring the Drug Regimen

In general, the patient's drug regimen should be adjusted to fit the patient's daily routine, within the parameters imposed by the pharmacokinetics of the drug prescribed. Usually there is some flexibility in either timing or dosage to achieve the maximum effect of the drug. If, for example, the patient has been prescribed a medication that should be taken once each day and the patient describes an irregular daily routine, the clinician might recommend that the medication be taken upon arising, rather than at the end of the day. Most people can exert more control over their activities immediatley after arising, than prior to retiring for the evening. Similarly, patients who must take a medication with one meal of the day can usually accomplish this more easily at breakfast than at lunch or dinner, which may involve friends, co-workers, or family. A brief discussion with the patient regarding his daily routine at the time the prescription is written may avoid obvious problems.

## Helping the Patient Start the Medication Regimen

After the patient has learned about the disease, the medication, and the medication regimen, he may recognize immediately that it will be difficult to follow through consistently with the regimen. In other cases, it is the clinician who may suspect that the patient will have difficulty. In either situation, the clinician can help the patient avoid likely problems by using the series of specific steps indicated in Table 3. The following section reviews each of these steps, and indicates what actions the clinician should take at each step.

Table 3. Steps to help a patient start a medication regimen

*Step* 1: *Review the patient's decision.*
  Clarify whether or not the patient has accepted the medical diagnosis and the need for the prescribed medication.

*Step* 2: *Review the potential difficulties.*
  Identify likely side effects of the medication.
  Identify likely disruption of usual daily routine caused by the medication regimen.
  Identify imminent disruption of the patient's daily routine due to travel, holiday, etc.

*Step* 3: *Select short-term and long-term goals.*
  Ensure that the patient understands the initial and final anticipated medication regimen.

*Step* 4: *Patient keeps a self-record.*
  Explain why and how the patient should use the Daily Medication Record.

*Step* 5: *Identify common, single-factor problems.*
  Identify whether the patient's difficulty is a problem of (1) forgetting, (2) travel, or (3) side effects.

*Step* 6: *Select a strategy to counter each common, single-factor problem.*
  Help the patient select a strategy to resolve the problem.

*Step* 7: *Rearrange the medication-related environment.*
  Review how the patient will arrange for the medication to be readily available.

*Step* 8: *Dispense a tailored medication regimen.*
  If possible, adjust the medication schedule to accommodate the patient's customary daily activities.

*Step* 9: *Select a starting date.*
  Ask the patient to select a specific time and day to obtain the prescribed medication and take the first dose.

*Step* 10: *Implement the medication regimen.*
  Instruct the patient to follow the medication regimen as planned. Provide the patient with written instructions describing the medication regimen.

*Step* 11: *Planned follow-up.*
  Instruct the patient to contact the clinician if any problems develop. Agree on date of the next clinic visit.

## Step 1: Review the Patient's Decision to Follow the Drug Regimen

The first concern should be whether or not the patient has accepted the need to follow the prescribed drug regimen. Two determinations should be made. First, has the patient accepted the fact that he has a particular disease, condition, or risk factor that may lead to a medical problem? The patient should fully understand his medical status. It may even be necessary to suggest that the patient consider obtaining a second opinion to verify the diagnosis. The patient should acknowledge that he has a particular medical problem and understand that it must be treated.

Second, the clinician should determine whether or not the patient has accepted the necessity of treating the medical condition with the prescribed medication. The patient should understand why the medication regimen is being recommended instead of other approaches (e.g., surgery, nutritional interventions). He should also accept that the prescribed medication regimen is the best course of action and agree to follow it as prescribed.

## Step 2: Review the Potential Difficulties

After the patient has made the decision to accept treatment, the clinician should discuss the potential difficulties he may encounter. This discussion should describe the side effects that most people experience. Side effects that are rarely encountered should not be mentioned initially. Instead, the patient should be encouraged to contact the clinician if any unusual symptoms are noticed after starting the regimen.

In addition, it should be indicated that following a medication regimen is not a trivial task. Everyone experiences some disruption of their daily routine as part of the process of starting a new daily activity. Soon however most people accommodate to the new regimen and the disruption diminishes. The patient should be encouraged to be tolerant during the initial week of the regimen and to allow the regimen to become part of his routine.

The clinician also should explore whether or not the patient anticipates being involved in any unusual activities during the first few days of starting the new medication regimen. If the patient is going to be traveling or on a holiday, it may be advisable to instruct the patient to begin the regimen upon his return to a normal daily schedule, if the patient's medical condition will not be compromised. This will make the initial discomfort of the new regimen less of a problem than if the patient must fit it into an unusual or uncontrollable daily schedule.

## Step 3: Select Short-Term and Long-Term Goals

In most drug regimens for chronic diseases, once the physician finds a therapeutic dose, the regimen will not change from week-to-week. The patient will continue on the same regimen indefinitely until the patient's condition changes. As a result, the short-term goal and the long-term goals of these medication regimens are identical.

In other cases, however, it is advisable to gradually increase the patient's dosage of medication until a therapeutic effect is obtained, or to allow the patient to accommodate to specific side effects of the medication as the dosage increases. For example, the antihyperlipidemic medication cholestyramine can be increased gradually over several weeks to allow the patient who is experiencing bloating to accommodate to this side effect. It should be clear, however, that once set, the patient's medication and dose should remain the same until the next visit. The patient should neither increase nor decrease the dose.

## Step 4: Patient Keeps a Self-Record

In order to determine the nature and frequency of a patient's problems with a medication regimen, it is very helpful to have him complete a Daily Medication Record for one week and return it to the clinic (see Figure 1). The patient records on this form each dose of medication he takes, and notes any problems he encounters. The clinician can rapidly review the form and readily determine whether or not the patient has been following the prescribed regimen. If there have been problems, the form may indicate when they occurred.

## Step 5: Identify Common, Single-Factor Problems

If the patient returns to the clinic and reports that he had difficulty following the medication regimen, the clinician should determine whether or not the patient's problem is a common, single-factor problem that can be solved by a simple intervention. Three common, single-factor problems are (1) not taking the medication because of side effects, (2) forgetting to take the medication at the proper time, (3) difficulty taking the medication when traveling.

These problems are considered single-factor problems because they result from one major factor. The clinician should suspect that one of these problems is present when the patient limits the discussion to these specific areas and mentions no other factors even after direct probing by the clinician. If, however, additional social or personal factors emerge, the clinician should proceed cautiously. The patient's problems may be complex and health behavioral counseling may be warranted.

## Step 6: Select a Strategy to Counter Each Common, Single-Factor Problem

If the patient experiences any of these common problems, the clinician should discuss it with the patient, and encourage him to select one of the simple strategies listed in Table 4. These strategies are discussed in detail in the next section. It is important, however, that the patient understand how to use the strategy, and agree to try it during the coming week. The clinician should be convinced that the patient understands the plan and can apply it in a variety of situations.

Table 4. Strategies for resolving common, single-factor problems

---

*Problem No. 1: Medication, or its administration, is unpleasant.*
 (1) Plan a stepped increase in the medication dosage to allow the patient to accommodate to its unpleasant effects.
 (2) Eliminate side effect–like symptoms that are unrelated to the medication.

*Problem No. 2: Patient forgets to take the medication.*
 (1) Put a "cue" in a prominent place where it will be noticed immediately before it is time to take the medication.
 (2) Use the Daily Medication Record to note when medication is taken.

*Problem No. 3: Patient has difficulty following the regimen when traveling.*
 (1) Make it easier to store and transport the medication by using a special, portable container.
 (2) Identify a cue that will be a reminder to take the medication along when traveling.

---

## Step 7: Rearrange the Medication-Related Environment

The patient should be encouraged to take appropriate steps to make it as easy as possible to follow the medication regimen. The key to this is to make the medication easily accessible. It should be in a location where the patient can obtain a day's dosage without difficulty. Any equipment or supplies that might be needed should be stored together with the medication so that the patient does not have to retrieve them from a different place. For example, if the medication is to be taken orally with a liquid, a supply of various juices, milk, or water, should be readily available. To further increase the ease of taking the medication, some patients prefer to separate each daily dose of medication into groups containing the number of pills to be taken at one dose. In this way they do not have to measure or count each dose every day. Each dose can be stored in an airtight plastic container. Some pill containers have 7 compartments, one for each day of the week. In this way, the correct dose is always ready for the patient to take. This container also is a convenient method to transport the medication when the patient is traveling.

## Step 8: Dispense a Tailored Medication Regimen

The clinician should tailor the medication regimen to the patient's usual daily routine whenever possible. The tailoring will greatly increase the likelihood that the patient will follow the regimen.

## Step 9: Select a Starting Date

The patient should be encouraged to identify when he will begin the medication regimen. Although this usually will be as soon as possible, occasionally the patient may not intend to purchase the medication for several days. The clinician should clarify when the patient plans to purchase the medication and when he will take the first dose.

### Step 10: Implement the Medication Regimen

The patient should be instructed to follow the medication regimen for a specific, brief length of time (e.g., 3 days) without change. This period will enable the patient to accommodate to the initial disruption of following a new routine. It also will identify recurrent side effects of the medication.

### Step 12: Planned Follow-up Contact

The patient should be instructed that after this brief initial period he should contact the clinician by telephone to review his progress. The clinician should tell the patient that it may be necessary to adjust the medication regimen but that the patient should not attempt this himself. At this follow-up contact the clinician must decide whether or not the patient is progressing satisfactorily, and whether more intensive counseling is needed.

## Specific Counseling Strategies for Common, Single-Factor Problems

Three common single-factor problems tend to interfere with the patient's adherence to a medication regimen. The problems are: (1) The medication has unpleasant side effects, (2) the patient forgets to take a dose of medication, and (3) the patient has difficulty in following the regimen when traveling. These problems usually can be attributed to a single primary factor, and respond to a simple intervention program. These problems do not require intensive health behavioral counseling. Rather, use of one of the simple strategies listed in Table 4 should be considered initially. Only if the patient continues to have difficulty should the clinician begin health behavior counseling.

### Problem No. 1: The Medication, or its Administration, Is Unpleasant

Often patients attribute their non-adherence to unpleasant side effects of the medication. Two strategies are used in this situation: (1) Design a stepped-program, or (2) eliminate the occurrence of the side effect-like symptoms that are not associated with the medication.

*Design a Stepped-Program.* A stepped-program contains a series of intermediate steps that the patient can tolerate that lead to the final regimen. The full regimen is introduced gradually rather than on the first day of the program.

This strategy is used when the clinician believes that the patient needs time to accommodate to the initial effects of the medication or the disruption of the routine. A stepped-program is used only when the medication dosage or frequency can be safely increased without placing the patient at risk medically during the initial weeks of the medication regimen. For example, the clinician might start the diabetic patient on a once-per-day insulin injection. Eventually, as the patient becomes accustomed to the medication, the clinician might then prescribe a regimen in which the patient takes two injections per day to achieve the level of blood glucose control desired.

*Eliminate Side Effect-Like Symptoms.* Some patients will have physical symptoms that are similar to the side effects of the medication but which are present even when the medication is not taken. These may be aggravated by the medication. The problem is that the patient attributes these symptoms to the medication, and decides not to continue with the medication regimen. For example, the patient may have headaches, dizziness, lethargy, indigestion, or sleep problems that are unrelated to the medication.

The clinician must differentiate those side effects which occur only when the medication is taken from those physical symptoms that occur at other times. Two critical questions should be asked: (1) Did the patient have these symptoms prior to starting the medication? (2) Does the patient notice these symptoms on days he does not take the medication? If the answer to either of these questions is yes, the clinician should attempt to control these symptoms without taking the patient off of the medication. For example, if the patient is complaining about constipation as a side effect of the medication, the patient's diet should be reviewed, and, if appropriate, dietary changes suggested. This might include the recommendation of increased consumption of high-fiber foods and liquids. In severe cases in which the medication may be contributing to the constipation, the clinician should consider taking the patient off of the medication until the constipation is controlled. If the patient is complaining of sleep disruption or nervousness, the clinician may decide to treat these problems (see Chapter 11) prior to returning the patient to the medication regimen.

### Problem No. 2: The Patient Forgets to Take the Medication

Many patients state that they forget to take a dose of medication. They report that at the time they were to take the medication they were involved in other activities and forgot it. Clearly for these patients, the medication regimen has not been established as a habit.

*Use a Cue.* The recommended strategy for resolving this problem is to identify a cue to remind the patient to take the medication at the proper time (see

Cues, Chapter 4). To be effective, the cue should be noticed by the patient just prior to the time to take the medication, and should not be encountered at other times of the day. Many patients use the medication bottle itself as a reminder. If they must take their medication at meal times, they simply leave the bottle on the table where meals are eaten. If the medication is to be taken at bedtime, it may be left some place where the patient is sure to look prior to retiring (e.g., on the nightstand or bureau). Some patients will simply write their medication schedule into their appointment book for the day. Other patients use a personal alarm on a watch or calculator, set to ring at the time they are to take their medication. It should be noted that cues generally are effective to initiate a new routine, but may lose their effectiveness as they become familiar. The patient may have to change cues frequently in order for the cue to remain noticeable.

*Ask the Patient to Keep a Self-Record.* The second strategy is to instruct the patient to enter on the Daily Medication Record whether or not he took his medication. Patients report that they remember to take their medication, as directed, when they are asked to keep a record. This form also reminds the patient that the clinician is interested in the patient's progress. However, record-keeping is similar to the use of cues in that when the novelty of the technique decreases, it loses its effectiveness. It also loses its effectiveness if the clinician does not seem to use the information collected by the patient.

If the patient reports that he is frequently forgetting to take the medication, the clinician should consider whether a more serious problem is present. The patient may be self-debating whether or not to take the medication. This problem can be characterized as a "Forget it" problem rather than "I forgot it." In this case, the clinician should explore the patient's initial decision to follow the regimen and examine the patient's ongoing self-debate. The problem of self-debate warrants the more intensive health behavioral counseling approach, described in a later section of this chapter.

*Problem No. 3: Patient Has Difficulty Following the Regimen When Traveling*

Another common problem occurs when the patient travels for business or on a vacation. The patient may report that he had an irregular daily schedule, and was not able to anticipate where he would be at the times he was to take his medication. As a result, his medication was not with him when he needed to take it. For example, the patient may have been prescribed a regimen to take the medication with dinner. However, at dinner he was on an airplane, and his medication was in his luggage.

*Use a Special Container for Travel.* Patients find that pre-planning for travel or holiday can circumvent this type of problem. A small airtight container can be used as a daily or weekly "pill box" to carry the day's dosage of medication. This can be placed unobtrusively in a coat pocket or purse. After the pills are placed in the container, a piece of cotton or tissue can be pushed into the container to prevent them from rattling.

*Use a Cue in the Patient's Luggage.* Between trips, the container should remain empty in the patient's luggage, shaving kit, or overnight case. In this way, the patient will not have to hunt for the container prior to his next trip. He also will be less likely to forget to take this medication along when he sees the container.

### Behavioral Counseling to Resolve Patient-Specific Problems

Patient-specific problems prevent many patients from following their prescribed medication regimen. These problems arise from multiple factors that are unique to the patient. As a result, the clinician must use intensive, health behavioral counseling to understand and resolve these difficulties.

The following section reviews each of the 11 steps in the health behavioral counseling process as it would be applied with patients who have difficulty following a prescribed medication regimen (Table 5).

### Step 1: Identify the Problem

The clinician's initial step should be to clarify the nature of the problem that the patient is encountering. Usually these problems can be classified as one of the following: (1) the patient does not understand the serious nature of the disease and the potential benefits of the medication, (2) the patient has decided not to follow the regimen, (3) the patient is having difficulty with one or more of the basic steps for starting the medication regimen, or (4) the patient has a problem that results from a combination of factors that are unique to him.

If the patient lacks information about the disease or its treatment, or if the patient does not appear to have made a definite decision to follow the regimen, the clinician should encourage the patient to re-read the patient education materials provided. The clinician might also provide additional information and answer questions that the patient might have. Health behavioral counseling should not be used at this point.

If the patient has problems with one or more of the initial steps for starting the program, the clinician should use the "Steps to Help a Patient Start a Medication Regimen" (Table 3). Behavioral counseling is not indicated until these steps have been completed.

Table 5. Eleven-step behavioral counseling for patients with problems adhering to a prescribed medication regimen

---

*Step 1: Identify the problem.*
  To what degree does each of the following problems seem to be present?
  (1) Lack of information about the disease and the benefits of the medication.
  (2) Absence of commitment to the initial decision to follow the medication regimen.
  (3) Difficulty implementing the steps to get started.
  (4) Difficulty establishing the regimen as a habit.
  (5) Continuing self-debate.

*Step 2: Clarify the goals of counseling.*
  (1) Review the expected duration of the medication regimen.
  (2) Review the nature of the counseling to be provided.

*Step 3: Collect information.*
  (1) Obtain detailed information from the Daily Medication Record.
  (2) Obtain additional information from the patient about the environmental factors that are either initiating or supporting his following and not following the medication regimen.

*Step 4: Develop a behavioral diagnosis.*
  Identify the primary relationship among the environmental factors surrounding the medication regimen that is either supporting the regimen or acting as a barrier to it.

*Step 5: Generate an intervention program.*
  (1) Keep the program simple.
  (2) Develop a program that includes a strategy both to support the medication regimen and to discourage the patient from not following the regimen.
  (3) Solicit the patient's ideas.
  (4) Give the patient a written copy of the program.

*Step 6: Intervene.*
  (1) Encourage the patient to use the program for at least 7 days in order to overcome the initial discomfort that accompanies a change in daily routine.
  (2) Instruct the patient to continue to use the Daily Medication Record.

*Step 7: Review the patient's progress.*
  Instruct the patient to contact the clinician in 7 days to review any problems encountered.

*Step 8: Generate a revised intervention program.*
  Modify the intervention program as needed and give the patient a written copy of it.

*Step 9: Reintervene.*
  Instruct the patient to use the revised intervention program for 7 days in order to accommodate to the new routine.

*Step 10: Develop a maintenance program.*
  Design a program with the patient to withdraw the artificial strategies that helped the patient initially.

*Step 11: Review the behavior change process.*
  (1) Review with the patient the strategies that seemed to be the most effective.
  (2) Identify the steps the patient should use to restart the medication regimen in the future, if necessary.
  (3) Give the patient a written list of the steps to be used to restart the program.

---

Behavioral counseling should be initiated when the patient has described problems that seem to be related to unique factors in the patient's family, social, or work situation. These factors are interfering with the patient's ability to establish the medication routine as a habit, or contribute to a continuing self-debate by the patient whether or not to follow the regimen.

### Step 2: Clarify the Goals of Counseling

It is important that the clinician and the patient share similar goals for the prescribed medication regimen. The patient should know whether the clinician is planning to change the current regimen over time. With some medications it is expected that the patient will accommodate to the present regimen and the dosage or type of medication will be modified over time. In addition, the patient should know whether the prescribed regimen is short-term, or is to be followed indefinitely. The patient must understand the overall goals of the treatment in order to understand the current regimen, and its relationship to the intermediate goals to be attained.

The goals of the counseling also should be reviewed with the patient. The clinician should explain that although together they will try to resolve the patient's difficulties, the goals of this counseling is for the patient eventually to take sole responsibility for following the medication regimen.

### Step 3: Collect Information

Two types of information are necessary to assess the patient's problem in following the prescribed medication regimen. First, the clinician needs information that accurately defines the behavioral profile for the medication taking. The frequency, duration, and quantity of medication taken should be recorded. This information can be recorded on the Daily Medication Record (see Figure 1). A completed form will indicate how much medication the patient is taking over what length of time each day.

Second, the clinician needs to develop a behavioral analysis (see Step 4 below) of the patient's current behavior (i.e., what the patient does instead of taking the medication) and the desired behavior (i.e., taking the medication as prescribed). The behavioral analysis should be a systematic, comprehensive listing of all antecedents that typically precede the behavior. It also should include the positive and negative, immediate and delayed consequences of the behavior (Table 6). The patient's Daily Medication Record is a particularly useful guide for the clinician to identify these factors. Information obtained from the form can be explored in detail with the patient.

Table 6. Examples of behavioral analysis

| Antecedents | Pos/Neg | Consequences |
|---|---|---|
| Current behavior: Patient does not take evening dose of medication | | |
| 6 p.m. | − | Mild guilt* |
| At desk in office | + | Feels justified because he was working late* |
| Feels tired | − | Recognizes that he is at increased risk for car-diovasular disease† |
| Angry he must work late | − | Angry that he had to work late* |
| Feels stressed | + | Did not interrupt his work to take medication so that he could finish work sooner* |
| Desired behavior: Patient takes evening dose of medication | | |
| 6 p.m. | + | Feels mildly pleased that his blood pressure is controlled* |
| At home | + | Feels pleased that his risk of developing car-diovascular disease is reduced† |
| Feels relaxed | − | Feels mildly unhappy that he has hyperten-sion* |

* Immediate consequence.
† Delayed consequence.

## Step 4: Develop a Behavioral Diagnosis

An effective intervention program is dependent upon an accurate behavioral diagnosis (see Chapter 4 for a detailed discussion of behavioral diagnosis). The diagnosis identifies the nature of the problem and determines the type of intervention to be developed. It is the clinician's assessment of the primary reason why the desired, new behavior of following the medication regimen is not occurring and why the current, customary behavior is occurring. Although there may be many factors involved in the patient's problem, the behavioral diagnosis clearly describes the primary "controlling factors" that are influencing the presence or absence of these behaviors. An example of a behavioral diagnosis for a patient-specific problem with medication adherence would be the following:

The patient's problem is that he is not taking his dose of antacid medication at lunch each day to control his peptic ulcer. A review of the patient's Daily Medication Record indicates that he eats lunch with co-workers each day in the company's cafeteria. He states that although he thinks about taking the medication and carries it with him in his coat pocket, he does not want to take the medication in front of his co-workers. He does not want them to know he must take the medication and think that he is "sick." He does take the medication after he returns to his desk, but often by then he has experienced some indigestion.

The clinician should review the behavioral diagnosis with the patient. The patient should have the opportunity to agree or disagree with the statement and to improve the clinician's understanding of the problem.

### Step 5: Generate an Intervention Program

The intervention program should contain two strategies. The first should be a strategy to promote and support the patient to take the medication as prescribed. This strategy should focus on eliminating the negative aspects of taking the medication and increasing the positive consequences for taking the medication. The second strategy should concentrate on those times when the patient does not follow the medication regimen. It should contain methods for both inserting negative consequences and deleting any positive consequences that may occur when the patient does not follow the medication regimen. It should be as simple as possible, requiring the fewest changes in the patient's lifestyle as possible.

The clinician should work with the patient to develop the intervention program. Although slower than simply giving the patient instructions on what to do, this collaborative problem solving will achieve better adherence over the long-term because the patient will understand the intervention program and have some ownership of it. After having thought through the problem and potential solutions with the clinician, the patient also will have a better understanding of his medication adherence problem. It is strongly recommended that a written list of the steps in the intervention program be given to the patient. This list avoids misunderstandings, and reduces the possibility of the patient simply forgetting part of the program.

### Step 6: Intervene

The patient should be instructed to follow the intervention program for a brief but specific period (e.g., 3 days). This interval should provide sufficient time for the medication to have an effect and for the patient to accommodate to the initial disruption in his schedule due to the new medication routine. Further, the patient will be able to differentiate the immediately experienced side effects of the medication from those that will remain over time. At the end of this period, the patient should re-contact the clinician. Of course the patient should be encouraged to contact the clinician sooner if he is having particular difficulty with the medication or the intervention program.

During the initial intervention period, the patient should be instructed to continue to record each dose of medication in the Daily Medication Record. This information will be used to assess the patient's progress and to identify continuing or new adherence problems. The form should be discontinued if the patient raises strong objections. In its place, the clinician should request that the patient contact the clinician by telephone approximately every 3 days in order to monitor his progress.

## Step 7: Review the Patient's Progress

The patient should be told when to re-contact the clinician for a follow-up visit. At this visit, the clinician should review the patient's Daily Medication Record and discuss any problems the patient experienced. The patient and the clinician should decide whether or not the behavioral diagnosis was accurate and how it should be modified, if at all. If the behavioral diagnosis is modified, the intervention program will need to be altered to increase its effectiveness.

## Step 8: Generate a Revised Intervention Program

The revised intervention program should be based on the improved behavioral diagnosis. The information collected by the patient during the initial phase of the program should help to identify those factors that are having the most influence on the patient's non-adherence. Working with the patient, a revised intervention program should evolve from the revised behavioral diagnosis. As before, the clinician should list the specific actions the patient should follow in the new intervention program for the coming week.

## Step 9: Re-intervene

The patient should follow the new intervention program for another brief but specific period (e.g., 3 days) prior to making any changes in it. During this period the patient should continue to collect information using the Daily Medication Record. As before, this information will be used to assess the revised behavioral diagnosis and to decide whether further adjustments are necessary in the intervention program.

## Step 10: Develop a Maintenance Program

Once the patient has achieved a stable, acceptable adherence pattern, the clinician should develop a maintenance program with him. By this time the medication regimen should be a routine. Most importantly, the patient's belief in the benefits of the regimen should be sufficient to sustain the program over time. Thus the program should be designed to systematically withdraw the artificial strategies used initially to promote the patient's adherence to the medication regimen.

*Step 11: Review the Behavior Change Program*

Because many patients encounter disruptions that interrupt the medication routine (e.g., illness, holidays, running out of medication) the patient should learn the steps that were used to help him get started on a regular medication schedule. Thus the patient needs a clear set of guidelines to use when he must restart the routine on his own.

The patient also should learn the steps that were used to resolve his particular problem. This step is important for two reasons. First, the patient should be prepared with a plan in case he re-encounters the same situation that caused the most recent problems. Second, the patient should recognize that he can use a logical, problem-solving process to resolve medication adherence problems that he may not have encountered in the past. It is to both the patient's and the clinician's benefit if the patient can resolve these problems. If the patient is successful, not only will he remain on the prescribed regimen, but also the clinician will not need to spend valuable time counseling this patient again.

## Counseling Strategies

There are several strategies that seem to be particularly helpful given a specific behavioral diagnosis for the patient's non-adherence to a medication regimen. These strategies attack the immediate positive or negative consequences that follow either the patient's taking of the medication or the activities that occur in its place.

It should be emphasized that these strategies should be used only after the clinician has completed a thorough evaluation of the patient's non-adherence problem and formulated a behavioral diagnosis. Misuse can render these strategies ineffective and may compromise the clinician's credibility with the patient.

*Strategies to Improve the Immediate Positive Consequences for Following the Medication Regimen (see Table 1)*

When the patient perceives that either few or insignificant immediate positive consequences occur when he does follow the medication regimen, he is less likely to continue to do so. The clinician may decide to inject a more powerful positive consequence into the situation.

*Guide the Patient to a Deliberate Decision.*   When a patient focuses only on the few immediate positive consequences of following the medication regimen, he may decide not to take a dose. The purpose of this strategy is to review with the patient all of the positive and negative, immediate and delayed consequences for following the medication regimen. The patient can literally list in writing each of these consequences. This exercise demonstrates the need for following the medication for the purpose of achieving long-term positive goals.

Once the patient has accepted the need to take the medication, the clinician should encourage him to make a deliberate decision to take it. This decision should be considered a permanent one. The patient should not review it at the time the medication is to be taken and should ignore any thoughts of reconsidering this decision at that time. Rather, he should focus his thoughts on relieving any discomfort he may have in taking the medication. If he wishes to review his decision he should know that he can do so with the clinician at the next clinic visit.

*Involve a Family Member to Support the Patient.* A family member, friend, or co-worker can provide helpful support to the patient in his efforts to follow the medication regimen. The patient should identify this person and ask him directly for support. This person's role is to encourage the patient to follow the regimen when the patient believes he will not be able to do so. It is important that the patient and support person agree upon a plan for the support person's intervention before a situation of non-adherence occurs. This will avoid resentment or hostility from the patient if the support person attempts to be directive in a manner that irritates the patient. For example, the patient might ask his spouse to observe for four consecutive nights whether or not he has taken his evening dose of medication prior to retiring. If the patient takes the medication, the spouse will make a comment such as, "I'm glad you were able to take your medication this evening" and then give him a kiss. If the patient does not take his medication, the spouse will agree to make no comment because the patient considers verbal reminders demeaning.

*Clinic Staff Provides Support.* An effective way of encouraging the patient to follow the medication regimen is for the clinic staff to take a genuine interest in his progress. They should be quick to take notice of substantial progress and offer support for his efforts. This support is most effective if the staff recognizes achievements that the patient considers substantial. Support that is offered for trivial progress tends to be rejected by the patient. In some cases it even may be considered insulting.

*Strategies to Counter Negative Consequences When the Medication Regimen Is Followed (Table 1)*

When the patient perceives that substantial immediate negative consequences occur when he does follow the medication regimen, he is less likely to continue to do so. A major source of negative consequences is criticism from family members, friends, or co-workers. The clinician should consider eliminating or reducing their occurrence.

*Educate the Person about the Patient's Medical Disease and Its Treatment.* The patient may be receiving criticism or ridicule from a family member, friend, or co-worker because the individual does not understand the nature of the patient's disease. The person may not be aware of the seriousness of the problem or the necessity of the prescribed treatment. Once this information is provided by the patient, the criticism may stop.

*Provide the Patient with Assertiveness Skills to Confront the Person.* In some cases, the family member, friend, or co-worker is criticizing or teasing the patient but does not realize the negative effect it is having on him. Often in these cases, the patient does not know how to effectively confront the person and ask that he stop his comments. In this situation, the clinician should help the patient to identify just what he might say to this person. In addition the patient should identify the worst and best results of such a confrontation. Once the patient feels comfortable confronting the worst possible situation, he gains the courage to talk with this person.

### Strategies to Remove or Minimize Positive Consequences When the Medication Regimen Is Not Followed (Table 2)

In some cases, the patient may not have actually experienced negative consequences for following the medication regimen but fears that he will and worries that he will not know how to handle the criticism. The patient avoids this situation by not following the regimen. A major source of feared negative consequences is criticism from family members, friends, or co-workers. The clinician should not attempt to persuade the patient that criticism will not occur. Rather, the clinician should provide the patient with skills for responding to possible criticism.

*Provide Skills in Managing Criticism.* If the clinician determines that the patient fears criticism, he should consider helping the patient reduce his fear by rehearsing his response with him. This can be accomplished by instructing the patient to verbalize the negative comments that he might hear and practice what he might say in response. This rehearsal also provides an inherent pairing of the feared criticism with a relaxed, comfortable state as the patient sits talking with the clinician. The clinician can be helpful by ensuring that the patient remains comfortable throughout the practice session and guiding him to imagine a wide range of possible criticisms. These possibilities would include what the patient would view as the "worst case." Having managed the situation with the clinician role playing the part of the critical friend or family member while the patient remains relatively relaxed, the patient should be able to use the rehearsed dialogue in the actual situation with his friends or family. However, prior to suggesting that the patient use the dialogue, the patient should be able to clearly state that his fear has been reduced by the rehearsal.

*Strategies to Counter Minimal Negative Consequences When the Regimen Is Not Followed (Table 2)*

Non-adherence to some medications results in few or no immediate negative consequences for the patient. As a result, the patient has less incentive to follow the regimen. In this situation, the patient may benefit from the creation of a mildly negative consequence that will occur if he does not follow the regimen. As with any artificial negative consequence, the event should serve more to encourage the patient's adherence than to punish his lack of adherence.

*Keeping a Self-Record.*   The patient may also benefit from noting in the Daily Medication Record each time he does not take the medication. It is suggested that he describe the situation at the time of non-adherence and the reason for not taking the drug. He can then review the form with the clinician at the next visit. This strategy can help the patient adhere to the medication regimen because most people report that it is much easier to take the medication than to write out why they did not take it. Further, knowing that the clinician will review the form and that he will have to describe the situations of non-adherence, a patient will tend to follow the regimen. The clinican should be careful to recognize, however, that when reviewing the form, it is not necessary to criticize the patient for failing to follow the regimen. A review of the form accompanied by probing to understand the situations of non-adherence is usually sufficient. This strategy has the added feature that it supplies the clinician with excellent information about the patient that will be helpful in subsequent counseling.

*Public Display of Progress.*   Another strategy is to develop with the patient a graph or chart of his progress in following the medication regimen. This graph would simply indicate the level of adherence each day and would be placed in a semi-public location where family members, friends, or co-workers might notice. The knowledge that non-adherence to the medication regimen may be known to others can act as a powerful negative consequence. Because of this, the clinician should exercise caution in the placement of the graph. If it is too threatening, not only may the patient discontinue keeping the graph, but he may not return to discuss the problem with the clinician. It is important, therefore, that prior to leaving the clinic the patient carefully consider the location of the graph, who might look at it, and how the patient would feel about those people learning of his non-adherence when it occurs.

## Case Illustration

The clinical application of the procedures discussed in this chapter is illustrated in the following simulated case. The case demonstrates how the clinician would help a patient start a medication regimen. It also describes how the clinician would use each of the 11 steps of health behavioral counseling to help resolve a patient-specific problem following the regimen. The case includes typical issues and problems encountered in the medical clinic with a patient's non-adherence to prescribed medication regimens.

### The Patient

The patient is a 45-year-old black man who works as a welder at an ironworks company. As part of a routine blood pressure screening program in his company he was found to have an elevated blood pressure of 142/90 mm Hg. He feels he is in excellent health and has no physical complaints. The patient is 5 feet, 11 inches tall and weighs 178 pounds. He does not smoke cigarettes. There is no family history of high blood pressure.

### Initial Visit

The patient came to the clinic for an evaluation of his elevated blood pressure by his personal physician. It was confirmed that he has essential hypertension. The patient's physical condition was explained to him and he was given written materials providing more information about high blood pressure, its relation to cardiovascular disease, and the rationale for treatment. The physician prescribed a thiazide diuretic, twice daily with meals, and was encouraged to reduce his dietary sodium intake. He was instructed to return for a follow-up visit in one month.

### Second Visit

The patient returned for his follow-up visit as scheduled. His blood pressure was still elevated at 134/86 mm Hg. The physician reviewed his physical status, his adherence to the medication regimen, and the side effects he had experienced. The patient explained that he had few side effects. However, he could not seem to remember to take all of his medication as planned. He reported that 3 or 4 evenings each week he simply forgot. Using a pill count, it also was estimated that the patient's overall adherence was approximately 60%. The physician decided that the patient would benefit from a more thorough review of his medication routine. Because the physician was scheduled to see other medical patients, he arranged for the patient to be seen immediately by the clinician, a member of the clinic staff trained in health behavioral counseling.

The physician briefly reviewed the case with the clinician. The clinician decided that initially he would use the "Steps to Help a Patient Start a Drug Regimen" (see Table 3).

*Step 1: Review the Patient's Decision to Follow the Drug Regimen.* The clinician determined that the patient had a basic understanding of high blood pressure. He was aware that his elevated blood pressure could not be cured, but needed to be controlled through medication and diet. He also knew that high blood pressure could lead to heart disease. The patient stated that he wanted to follow the drug regimen, but some days he simply forgot. The clinician decided that the patient was sincere in his desire to follow the prescribed drug regimen and offered to help the patient. The patient accepted this offer.

*Step 2: Review the Potential Difficulties of the Drug Regimen.* The clinician began by explaining that following a drug regimen is not an easy matter because the patient may have to change some of his habits to accommodate it. Although the initial process of change can be uncomfortable, the new regimen should soon become a routine.

The clinician also reviewed the type and extent of side effects of the medication that the patient was experiencing. The clinician repeated the physician's reassurance that these were not uncommon. Once the body accommodated to the drug, these initial side effects usually disappeared within 2 to 3 weeks.

The patient seemed to accept these initial side effects, and stated that he was willing to be patient during this initial period.

*Step 3: Select Short-Term and Long-Term Goals.* The clinician then discussed the drug regimen with the patient. He recommended that the patient's goal should be to take all doses of his medication in the evening as prescribed. The patient agreed that the change from taking the medication 55% of the time in the evening (i.e., 4 of 7 times) to taking the medication 100% of the time in the evening was not too large a step. Therefore, no intermediate goals would be used.

*Step 4: Patient Keeps a Self-Record.* The clinician reviewed the patient's drug routine using only the patient's description of those evenings when he missed taking a dose of medication. The clinician decided that because the patient could recall accurately whether or not he took each dose of medication each evening over the past week, there was no need to delay the intervention for additional information. However, the patient would use the Daily Medication Record during the next week to record each time he took his medication and, if not, why he was not able to take the medication.

*Step 5: Identify Common, Single-Factor Problems.*   The clinician and the patient reviewed each occurrence of the patient missing an evening dose of medication during the prior week. The patient missed a total of 6 doses. Two patterns emerged. On four of the evenings, the patient missed his dose because of forgetting. That is, the patient would return home from work at his usual time, would eat dinner, and watch television. He would not think about his medication until the next morning. The second pattern occurred when he worked overtime at the factory. At the normal quitting time, he would eat a sandwich for dinner and continue working for up to 3 hours. He would think about his medication, but it was at home.

*Step 6: Select a Strategy to Counter Each Common Single-Factor Problem.* The clinician and the patient discussed the problem of the patient's forgetting the medication and decided that a simple plan using a visible cue would help him to remember his evening dose at home. He would take the medication bottle from the bathroom where it has been, and place it at his usual place at the dinner table. This would not be conspicuous to others because there are other objects on the table, but it definitely would be noticeable to him.

The problem of working overtime required more discussion. However, the patient suggested that he could take a limited number of pills to work with him in another bottle and keep it in his locker. At his dinner break, he usually went to his locker, so he would be able to get the bottle easily. The clinician supported this idea.

*Step 7: Re-arrange the Medication-Related Environment.*   No further re-arrangement of the patient's environment was considered.

*Step 8: Dispense a Tailored Medication Regimen.*   The patient's drug regimen was not altered. He remained on a twice-daily schedule to take the medication with meals.

*Step 9: Select a Starting Date.*   The patient was instructed to begin the new medication routine immediately. The patient was to place the medication bottle on the table at home that evening. In addition, the clinician gave the patient a small, airtight bottle to take 5 pills with him to keep in his locker at work.

*Step 10: Implement the Medication Regimen.*   The patient agreed to follow the drug regimen as planned for 7 days. He would not change the intervention program during this period.

*Step 11: Plan Follow-up.*  The patient agreed to telephone the clinician in 7 days to discuss his progress. The patient also agreed to telephone the clinician if he had any difficulty with the program.

## Telephone Contact

The patient called, as planned, in one week. He reported that he had been able to take all of his medication when he was at home in the evenings. He was still not taking his medication at work, however. Although he had taken the pills to work, he just never has "gotten around to taking them." The clinician offered support for the patient's progress. He instructed the patient to continue with the program as they had agreed and that they would discuss the problem further at his upcoming visit with his clinician in one week.

## Third Visit

The patient returned for his follow-up visit as scheduled. The patient stated that he had not been able to take any of his medication at work. The clinician decided that health behavioral counseling was an appropriate approach for this problem.

*Step 1: Identify the Problem.*  Although the patient stated that his problem was "forgetting," further discussion revealed that he did not, in fact, forget to take the medication. He reported that when he worked overtime he was very tired and unhappy that he had to remain at work. The clinician clarified that the problem was not one of forgetting but rather a situation in which the patient remembered to take the medication but decided not to do so.

*Step 2: Clarify the Goals of Counseling.*  The patient stated that he would like to know of any suggestions that the clinician might have for resolving this problem. The clinician clarified the goals of treatment by indicating that he would work with the patient to resolve the problem but that the patient would have primary responsibility for making the changes suggested. The goal of the treatment would be for the patient to systematically explore with the clinician ways to resolve this problem until he was able to take all of his medication at work, when necessary. The patient agreed to this goal.

*Step 3: Collect Information.*  Through additional discussion and a review of his Daily Medication Record (see Figure 1), the patient indicated that when he worked overtime he felt angry and "put upon." When he thought of the medication, he felt that it was just something else that he had to do that he did not want to do. Therefore he did not take his medication. He felt "good" when he

Figure 1. A completed Daily Medication Record.

## Daily Medication Record Form

### Instructions

It is important that your physician has an accurate record of the medication that you take. This information will be helpful in your medical treatment. Use the attached Daily Medication Record Form to record each dose of medication you take. Use it also to record any problems you have.

Mark through the circle to indicate each dose of medication you take. Be sure to mark the record form immediately after taking the medication. Do not wait until the end of the day.

If you did not take a dose of medication, leave the circle blank for that day. Briefly note why you missed this dose in the area labeled "Comments". If you have any problems taking a dose of medication, make a note in this area. For example:

| Date | Day | Time | Dose #1 | Time | Dose #2 | Time | Dose #3 | Time | Dose #4 |
|------|-----|------|---------|------|---------|------|---------|------|---------|
| 6/3 | mon. | 8:00 | ⊘ | 12:15 | ⊘ | | ✳ | — | ◯ |

### Comments

✳ Forgot to take dose at dinner. Went out to eat.

Keep this Record Form with your medication. Return the Form to the clinic at each clinic visit.

---

## Daily Medication Record Form

Name _KLG_

Date of clinic visit _July 11, 1984_   Day: _Thursday_

Prescription:

Medication: _Diuretic_   Amount: _1 tablet 2x/day_

Time dose is taken: Dose #1 _7:00 am_/pm   Dose #2 _6:30 am_/pm
                    Dose #3 ___ am/pm       Dose #4 ___ am/pm

| Date | Day | Time | Dose #1 | Time | Dose #2 | Time | Dose #3 | Time | Dose #4 |
|------|-----|------|---------|------|---------|------|---------|------|---------|
| 7/11 | Th. | 7:12 | ⊘ | 6:45 | ⊘ | — | ◯ | — | ◯ |
| 7/12 | Fri | 9:15 | ⊘ | | ✳ | — | ◯ | — | ◯ |
| 7/13 | Sat. | 8:00 | ⊘ | 6:10 | ⊘ | — | ◯ | — | ◯ |
| 7/14 | Sun. | 7:30 | ⊘ | | ✳ | — | ◯ | — | ◯ |
| 7/15 | Mon. | 7:00 | ⊘ | | ✳ | — | ◯ | — | ◯ |
| 7/16 | Tues. | 7:15 | ⊘ | | — | — | ◯ | — | ◯ |
| 7/17 | Wed. | 7:05 | ⊘ | 6:15 | ⊘ | — | ◯ | — | ◯ |

### Comments:

✳ Worked late. Didn't take medication. ang.rg.

128

did not take the medication but later felt guilty about it. The clinician decided that there was sufficient information to formulate a behavioral diagnosis.

*Step 4: Develop a Behavioral Diagnosis.*   The information collected was organized into a table indicating the antecedents and consequences that appeared to surround both the instances when the patient took the medication and those occasions when he did not (see Table 6). This behavioral analysis included all factors available to the clinician.

The clinician used the behavioral analysis to identify those active factors that would comprise the behavioral diagnosis of this patient's problem. The clinician's behavioral diagnosis was that the patient was self-debating whether or not to take his medication in the evening when he worked overtime. The self-debate involved a number of positive and negative factors that occurred both immediately and over time. It was clear, however, that, on balance, the immediate consequences for not taking the medication were more positive than those consequences for taking the medication.

The clinician discussed this behavioral diagnosis with the patient. The patient agreed that the diagnosis was accurate. Together they reviewed all of the positive and negative, immediate and delayed consequences of his actions. The patient stated that he now understood the self-debate he was having.

*Step 5: Generate an Intervention Program.*   The clinician explained that the best treatment was for the patient to review this self-debate and try to imagine any situation in which it was better not to take the medication than to take the medication. The patient could not think of one. The clinician then encouraged the patient to make a deliberate decision to take his medication. The patient acknowledged that taking the medication, as prescribed, was the appropriate plan, regardless of any other factors. The clinician suggested that this decision, once final, should not be reconsidered even when the patient was tired, unhappy, or angry. To do so would invite a revised decision that might be illogical because it was based on the emotion of the moment. The patient agreed and said that he would ignore his personal self-debate because he knew what the correct decision was.

*Step 6: Intervene.*   The patient agreed to use the plan to ignore his self-debate when he was working overtime. He would "not let his foreman take control of his decisions about his medication." He would begin the plan the next day.

The patient was instructed to call the clinician on the day after the next day he had to work overtime. Together they would review what had happened.

The clinician wrote out each step of the intervention program as a behavioral prescription (Figure 2) and gave it to the patient.

---

**MICHAEL L. RUSSELL, Ph.D.**
Department of Internal Medicine
Baylor College of Medicine
Tel. 799-6032

---

**Program for Change**

For: _KLG_                              Date: _July 11, 1984_

1. keep 5 tablets of medication in a bottle in your locker at work.

2. Recall that after considering everything, you have made a decision to take your medication at work if you work late.

3. Ignore thoughts to self-debate whether or not to take your medication at work because you are upset.

4. Call me the day after the next time you have to work overtime.

---

Figure 2. Example of a behavioral prescription.

*Telephone Call*

The patient called the clinician two days later.

*Step 7: Review the Patient's Progress.*  The patient was very pleased that he took his medication. He stated proudly that he did not let his foreman "get to him." He expressed confidence that he would continue to take his medication as planned when he worked late.

*Step 8: Generate a Revised Intervention Program.*  No revision was made in the intervention program.

*Step 9: Re-intervene.*  The patient continued on the same program, as initially designed. He would see the clinician again on his next clinic visit in 4 weeks.

*Fourth Visit*

The patient returned for his follow-up visit as scheduled. His blood pressure was 120/80 mm Hg. He had taken his medication every day, as planned, except for one day when he ran out of medication at work. However, he replaced this medication the next day, and decided to take the bottle he used at work home with him when it was empty. It would serve as a reminder to fill it again.

*Step 10: Develop a Maintenance Program.*   Because the patient's intervention program did not involve artificial aids, it was continued as originally designed. The clinician believed that the program would not require modification in the near future.

*Step 11: Review the Behavior Change Program.*   The clinician reviewed with the patient the process used to resolve his medication adherence problems. These strategies were: (1) placing the medication in an easily accessible location where it would be seen, (2) taking some medication with him to work to take when he worked overtime, (3) listing the positive and negative, immediate and delayed consequences of following the prescribed medication regimen as compared with not following it, and (4) making a deliberate decision about the problem situation and ignoring any self-debate to change the decision. The patient re-stated that recognizing his self-debate and identifying the factors involved was very helpful. He volunteered that he would probably use this problem-solving strategy in other situations.

# 7. Adherence to Therapeutic Diets

Adequate nutrition is basic to life. The body requires minimum levels of a variety of nutrients to meet its metabolic needs and to generate energy. When a patient is healthy, adequate nutrition can be obtained from the range of foods that comprise the typical American diet.

When the patient is ill, adequate nutrition becomes a substantial concern for the clinician. If the patient is hospitalized due to acute illness, injury, or has had surgery, he may be provided with a temporary diet in the hospital that is nutritionally appropriate for the patient's compromised medical and physical status. The patient does not become involved in planning the modified diet in these acute situations and generally returns to his normal diet on discharge.

If, however, the patient has a chronic disease or condition, a normal diet may not meet the increased nutritional demands created by the disease (e.g., the patient with cirrhosis may require extra dietary protein) or may be too rich in certain nutrients and complicate the management of the disease (e.g., the patient with nephritis may benefit from a diet that is low in protein). In addition, the patient with chronic disease may be prescribed nutritional therapy to help arrest the continued development of the disease or to prevent the occurrence of a new disease. For example, hypertensive patients are frequently prescribed a diet that is low in sodium. Nutritional therapy requires the patient to make major modifications in his usual dietary patterns.

## The Problem: Non-adherence

It has been well documented that different prescribed diets place varying demands on the patient. The combined effect of these demands determines the ease of following the diet. For example, a comparison of a low-sodium diet, a low-cholesterol diet, and a low-calorie diet illustrates the relative influence of 7 factors on the adoption by patient of each diet (Table 1). As a result of the differing influences of these factors, patient adherence varies across diets. Although no studies have directly compared average patient non-adherence on

Table 1. Relative influence of selected behavioral factors on the adoption of three diets

| Behavioral factor | Cholesterol reduction | Sodium reduction | Weight loss |
|---|---|---|---|
| New knowledge needed | Moderate | Minimal | High |
| Changes in food preparation | Moderate | Few | Moderate |
| Foods to be avoided | Few | Many | Many |
| Effects on family | Moderate | Minimal | Moderate |
| Predominant reaction of others | Neutral | Neutral | Negative |
| Potential costs | Lower | Higher | Higher |
| Possible history of failure on the diet in the past | Low | Low | High |

different prescribed diets in similar clinicial settings, most studies report an average patient non-adherence level of 40 to 60%, regardless of the type of diet prescribed.

Patient non-adherence also varies when different patients are prescribed the same diet. For example, it has been reported that in a closely supervised dietary clinicial study, the distribution of adherence at one year of follow-up of patients who were prescribed a low cholesterol diet was "poor" for 16%, "fair" for 32%, "good" for 40%, and "excellent" for 12%.[1] This probably fairly represents the range of patient adherence to a single prescribed dietary program. It also corresponds with published reports that only 8% of physicians surveyed stated that they were "very successful" in helping their patients achieve dietary changes.[2]

## The Therapeutic Diet as a Lifestyle Change

The prescription of a therapeutic diet challenges most people with a difficult lifestyle change. There are two basic problems. One is that the individual must acquire basic information about the prescribed diet in order to understand its rationale and guidelines. The second problem is that the individual must integrate the therapeutic diet into his daily routine.

To appreciate the difficulty a patient confronts in understanding a therapeutic diet, consider the basic rationale for these diets. Essentially, a therapeutic diet requires the patient to change his typical pattern of eating certain foods in order to modify the amount of a particular nutrient consumed. The six categories of nutrients are (1) fats, (2) carbohydrates, (3) proteins, (4) minerals, (5) vitamins, and (6) water. A nutrient is an essential substance for the growth, maintenance, or repair of the body.

A supplemental therapeutic diet is prescribed to increase the consumption of certain foods in order to increase the intake of particular nutrients. A restrictive therapeutic diet is prescribed to reduce or eliminate entirely the consumption of certain foods in order to limit particular nutrients. To accomplish either of these dietary changes, the patient must acquire a basic knowledge of nutrition and the nutrients in all the foods he should eat in order to remain within the dietary guidelines. Usually the patient is given a detailed listing of those foods he must be sure to eat in sufficient quantities to receive the nutrients necessary, and/or a listing of those foods he must be sure to avoid because they contain nutrients which aggravate his medical condition or place him at increased risk for future medical problems.

The second problem is that the patient must change his current eating habits. This includes purchasing different foods, preparing foods differently, and selecting appropriate foods when a variety is offered (e.g., at a restaurant, party, or social events). The difficulties encountered by the patient in trying to integrate the new therapeutic diet into his lifestyle are most often the reason that the patient fails to follow the diet and eventually abandons it. This chapter describes these difficulties and how the clinician can help the patient overcome them.

A therapeutic diet places behavioral demands on the patient that are different from those of a weight loss diet. A restrictive therapeutic diet requires the patient to avoid eating specific foods, and if possible to substitute acceptable alternatives. Whereas weight loss programs will often tolerate almost any food in controlled quantities, therapeutic diets more often prohibit certain foods. For example, a restrictive therapeutic diet would focus on eliminating specific foods that exacerbate a specific condition (e.g., low sodium for hypertension, low cholesterol for hypercholesterolemia, or high fiber for colon cancer). Excess amounts of these nutrients place the patient at increased risk for the disease. The supplemental therapeutic diet also is unlike a weight loss diet in that it encourages the patient to increase his consumption of certain foods (e.g., high protein for tuberculosis, high iron for iron deficiency anemia, or high fiber for constipation), for example.

## The Behavioral Pattern Accompanying a Change in Diet

Most people maintain a relatively stable diet over time. We tend to choose the foods we eat from a certain set of only about 800 foods. These individual food preferences are developed at an early age and are dependent upon available foods, customs, religious beliefs, and to a lesser degree economic considerations.

Once established in childhood these eating patterns tend to be extremely resistant to change. People will continue to follow their eating patterns even when it becomes very difficult and/or costly to do so. This can be readily observed in

Table 2. Typical consequences of consuming a diet containing restricted foods

|  | Positive | Negative |
|---|---|---|
| Immediate | Pleasant taste | Potential for physiological reaction |
|  | Pleasant associations | Disapproval from others who are aware of the patient's dietary restrictions |
|  | Avoid thoughts of "wasting food" |  |
|  | Avoid thoughts of being "deprived" |  |
|  | Avoid informing others why certain foods must be avoided |  |
|  | Avoid potentially embarrassing social situations |  |
|  | Avoid remaining hungry |  |
|  | Maintain "quality of life" |  |
| Delayed | None | Excess of nutrient that increases the risk of disease |
|  |  | Excess of nutrient that increases the risk of medical complications |

the thriving imported foods business that depends, in part, on people from other countries who maintain their established food habits.

Over time, we come to associate pleasurable experiences with these foods. For example, we tend to eat traditional foods at special dinners with family or friends (e.g., special cuts of meat, ethnic foods, imported foods, foods that require considerable preparation). Similarly, stable food patterns may develop for the general type of meals eaten during the week. For the patient who has been prescribed a restrictive diet, the customary diet provides strong immediate positive consequences and few, if any, immediate negative consequences (Table 2). It is only over the long term that the consequences become predominantly negative. This situation encourages the patient to continue with his usual diet and will not be changed without a substantial shift in the factors that support the diet.

A similar situation exists for the patient who has been prescribed certain foods to increase his consumption of particular nutrients (Table 3). The patient's current diet is stable and supported by the same types of factors described above. The immediate consequences for not increasing the intake of particular foods are several, with few immediate negative consequences. It is only the long-term consequences of not receiving the nutrient that are negative. As a result, the patient may not include sufficient amounts of the prescribed foods over the

Table 3. Typical consequences of consuming a diet without prescribed supplements

|           | Positive | Negative |
|-----------|----------|----------|
| *Immediate* | Avoid time/effort needed to obtain required foods | Potential for physiological reaction |
|           | Consumption of other foods that taste better | |
|           | Avoid thoughts of being "deprived" | |
|           | Avoid telling others why certain foods must be eaten | |
|           | Avoid potentially embarrassing social situations | |
|           | Maintain "quality of life" | |
| *Delayed* | None | Deficiency in a nutrient resulting in the patient being at risk for a new disease |
|           | | Deficiency in a nutrient resulting in the patient being at risk for medical complications of current disease |

necessary period of time. Further, this pattern will not change without the introduction of new, powerful factors to create a substantial shift in its consequences.

Unfortunately, the introduction of the new prescribed diet provides few positive incentives for following the diet, and does not decrease the positive associations of the patient's current customary diet (Table 4). In fact, the new diet is often perceived negatively by the patient. This negative perception results from the predominantly negative consequences that immediately occur when the patient attempts to follow the diet. The immediate positive consequences are not sufficient to counter-balance the negative consequences.

Clearly a major factor determining whether or not the dietary recommendations will be followed is the degree to which the diet itself results in noticeable positive changes for the patient. Some diets will have a relatively rapid effect on the patient's symptoms. For example, a hypoallergic diet will rapidly reduce or eliminate the patient's allergic symptoms. A diabetic diet that controls high-calorie foods prevents diabetic ketoacidosis. The direct cause-effect relationship between the diet and his symptoms is clear to the patient. Other diets have delayed effects, or result in only a reduction in the patient's risk of future disease. For example, a diet that is low in sodium may contribute to lowered blood pressure for the patient with hypertension. A diet that is low in cholesterol may contribute to a reduced risk of cardiovascular disease for the

Table 4. Typical consequences of following a prescribed therapeutic diet

|  | Positive | Negative |
|---|---|---|
| *Immediate* | Avoidance of potential physio-logical reaction | Time/effort required to select foods |
|  |  | Embarrassment discussing why the diet must be followed |
|  |  | Disruption of usual food preparation routine |
|  |  | Disruption of usual food purchasing routine |
|  |  | Decreased flavor |
| *Delayed* | Reduction in risk of disease |  |
|  | Reduction in risk of medical complications of current disease |  |
|  | Improved physical health |  |
|  | Improved self-esteem |  |
|  | Pride in accomplishment |  |

patient with hyperlipidemia. These diets usually are more difficult for the patient to follow because their effects on the patient's medical condition are indirect or occur over time. In other cases they affect a disease process that is asymptomatic.

## The Patient's Decision to Accept the Dietary Prescription

The patient who has a medical condition that is directly affected by diet does not need to be convinced of the need to make a dietary change. The effects of the diet are immediate and usually sufficient to persuade the patient that a modification in diet is necessary. However, the patient for whom a dietary change will have a delayed effect (i.e., by reducing a risk factor) is usually the one who requires help; the effect of the diet on the patient's medical status may not be clear to the patient. This is particularly important when the patient must adopt a new diet that requires him to avoid desired foods or include foods that are not appetizing. As a result, these patients may not be convinced of the need for the prescribed diet.

Before proceeding with counseling it is important to determine whether or not the patient has made a conscious decision to adopt the prescribed diet. The patient should be able to clearly state that he has made this decision and indicate the reasons for having done so. These reasons must be sufficiently strong to overcome the initial discomfort in making a major change in lifestyle and to adopt the new dietary routine. For most dietary regimens these reasons relate to the long-term benefits of adhering to the diet. In some cases, however, immediate benefits of following the prescribed regimen can be identified. Examples of such benefits would be (1) reduce cost of using fresh foods in season as compared with frozen or canned foods that contain the additives or nutrients to be avoided (e.g., sodium, preservatives), (2) improved flavor using fresh foods as compared with commercially prepared foods, and (3) increased variety in foods as new recipes that conform to the dietary regimen are learned.

The clinician can prompt the patient to make a deliberate decision to adopt the new diet by emphasizing the medical reasons for doing so. The clinician also can encourage the patient to consider the potential problems that the patient might encounter in following the diet, and determine whether or not these problems are realistic. This discussion might reveal problems that the patient is anticipating and may indicate whether or not the patient believes that he can succeed in following the diet. If, at this point, the patient does not feel that he can follow the diet, it might be wise to explore these reasons further before the patient actually begins the diet.

In all cases, the clinician should make a direct, unequivocal statement to the patient about the diet. The clinician should make it clear that the diet is not simply a "recommendation" for the patient to follow. Rather, the clinician should be sure that the patient understands that adherence to the prescribed diet is a crucial part of the patient's medical care and that his medical condition will be improved by following it: The patient should recognize the direct relationship between the prescribed diet and his medical status. For example, the patient with hypertension should know that sodium has a direct effect on blood pressure in many people and that, therefore, a reduction in the amount of sodium he consumes may result in a significant reduction in his blood pressure.

As with all living patterns that place the patient at increased risk of disease, the clinician should not attempt to frighten the patient into changing his routine. Frightening consequences can actually be inhibiting because the patient refuses to think about them and ignores the diet. Instead, the clinician should present a realistic view of the potential consequences and, if possible, of the likelihood of their occurrence. Some patients may then assess the medical desirability of following the diet against the disruption created by the regimen and conclude that they do not wish to follow the diet at this time. The clinician should be prepared to accept this decision if the patient has given the situation careful consideration.

## Selecting a Therapeutic Diet for the Patient

A diet should be prescribed only by the physician who has complete knowledge of the patient's health status. Once the type of diet has been determined, however, the clinician may choose among several sources of information for the patient about the diet. These will be described in detail.

## Referral to a Dietitian

In most cases, the patient should be referred to a registered dietitian to receive patient education on the prescribed diet. The dietitian will review the patient's current dietary habits, instruct the patient in the fundamental concepts of the diet, and provide educational materials and helpful suggestions for following the diet. The dietitian also will review the patient's diet to ensure that it contains sufficient daily intake of required nutrients, vitamins, and minerals. Many dietitians have received training in counseling methods for helping the patient resolve difficulties in following a prescribed diet and can be strong allies in helping the patient adopt the necessary lifestyle changes.

## Diets from Professional Organizations

Many of the common diets have been standardized and are available from various national professional organizations including the American Heart Association, the American Kidney Foundation, and the American Diabetes Association. These materials usually are available at a nominal cost.

It is important for the clinician and the patient to distinguish these dietary programs from the popular dietary programs that are widely advertised. The popular programs usually have been developed from an individual's personal convictions and/or experience and have not been carefully reviewed by dietitians. In contrast, the dietary programs offered by the professional organizations usually are based on the current nutritional literature and have been reviewed by experienced dietitians.

## The Clinician's Role in the Patient's Therapeutic Diet

Although some patients experience little or no difficulty following a therapeutic diet, other patients describe insurmountable problems. Those that do have problems encounter them at different points in the dietary program. The dilemma for the clinician is to decide how much counseling should be offered to a patient beyond the minimum required to communicate the basics of the dietary regimen. The most efficient use of clinic time would be to spend time counseling only those patients who are either "at risk" for non-adherence to the regimen or who have begun to experience problems. As discussed in Chapter 2, "Counseling for Health Behavior Change," these problems usually occur in one of the following five areas: (1) insufficient knowledge of the regimen, (2) rejection of the medical diagnosis by the patient, (3) deliberate decision by the patient not to follow the regimen, (4) failure to establish the diet as a habit, and (5) continuing self-debate whether or not to follow the prescribed diet. Unfortunately, it is difficult to predict which patient will have problems following a therapeutic diet and, if so, what type of problem will occur. Therefore as a general policy, the clinician should follow a course of providing the minimal counseling necessary, while remaining prepared to respond rapidly to problems as they occur.

### Tailoring the Diet

As a general guideline, the clinician should attempt to tailor the prescribed diet to the patient's preferences and current habits. It should require as few changes as necessary to achieve the therapeutic goal. To accomplish this the patient should be encouraged to provide the clinician with a representative sample of his current dietary habits. If the prescribed diet requires the patient to avoid certain foods or nutrients that are part of the customary diet, acceptable substitute foods should be identified. For example, if the patient has been prescribed a low cholesterol diet, the clinician initially should identify the patient's food sources of saturated fat and cholesterol and then help the patient identify alternative foods (e.g., substitute lean for fatty meats, chicken or fish for luncheon meats). Because restrictive diets usually require the avoidance of most, but not all, foods containing a certain nutrient, the patient often can continue to enjoy certain foods in limited quantities, rather than rigidly avoiding all foods containing the nutrient. This individual tailoring of the diet to the patient requires the time and effort of both clinician and patient. However, the use of a Daily Food Record indicating the amount of each food the patient consumed at each meal over a 3-day period provides the necessary information for accomplishing this (see Figure 1). Extra time taken initially can lead to enhanced patient satisfaction and the avoidance of future problems.

### Dietary Instruction

Once the patient's current diet has been reviewed, the patient should receive instruction in the dietary program to be followed and appropriate supplemental materials. If a nutritionist is not available, the clinician should consider providing the materials and instruction himself. However, the clinician should be thoroughly familiar with the diet being prescribed prior to attempting to instruct the patient. Proper implementation of all of the prescribed dietary programs requires considerable knowledge. The patient never should be handed the dietary program materials and simply instructed to follow the program.

It is extremely important that appropriate instruction also be given to the individual who is responsible for meal preparation in the home if other than the patient. Personal contact or discussion by telephone with this person is important for two reasons. First, this person must understand the rationale and importance of the diet for the patient's health. It should be clear that the diet is being prescribed for the patient for medical reasons, and should not be considered simply a recommendation. Second, this person must acquire new knowledge and make changes in food purchasing and preparation. Although this information can be communicated by written materials it is important that the clinician be available to clarify the rationale for the diet and answer questions. If several patients are beginning the same diet, this can be accomplished efficiently by scheduling a group session and inviting patients and their family members.

## Helping the Patient Start a Therapeutic Diet

Once the patient has had an opportunity to review the dietary program or become convinced that the program has merit, he may anticipate problems in getting started with the program. After discussing the diet with the patient, the clinician also may suspect that the patient will have difficulty. If so, "Steps to Help a Patient Start a Therapeutic Diet" (Table 5) should be used. The following section discusses each of these steps, and indicates how the clinician should work with the patient at each one.

### Step 1: Review the Patient's Decision to Follow the Diet

The clinician's initial concern should be whether or not the patient has made a definite decision to follow the prescribed dietary program. This decision usually is more difficult for the patient than the decision to change other habits because most patients have not previously attempted to make this type or degree of dietary change. As a result, the patient may readily agree to follow the dietary program without truly understanding its importance or difficulty. When problems do arise, the patient may reconsider whether or not to follow the diet.

It is important therefore that the patient have a clear understanding of the rationale for following the diet, and sufficient knowledge of what he is to do. If the patient is uncertain, or the dietary program is ambiguous, he may decide not to follow it. Thus the clinician should review with the patient the reasons for following the diet and its effect on the patient's medical status. Further, the clinician should be certain that the patient knows that the clinician is prescribing the diet and not simply recommending it. Finally, the clinician should be assured that the patient has sufficient knowledge of the diet to be able to follow it with a high level of adherence until the patient returns for a follow-up visit.

Table 5. Steps to help a patient start a therapeutic dietary program

---

*Step 1: Review the patient's decision.*
Identify the patient's rationale for wanting to follow the prescribed diet.

*Step 2: Review the potential difficulties.*
Discuss the discomfort the patient may experience in following the diet.

*Step 3: Select short-term and long-term goals.*
Identify appropriate actions the patient can take.

*Step 4: Patient keeps a self-record.*
Explain why the patient should use the Daily Food Records for 3 days.

*Step 5: Analyze the content of the patient's current diet.*
Use the Daily Food Records to determine what foods the patient should attempt to increase, decrease, or omit from his diet.

*Step 6: Analyze the patient's eating patterns.*
Use the Daily Food Records to determine if the patient has a particular problem eating pattern.

*Step 7: Select a strategy to counter each problem eating pattern.*
Help the patient select a strategy to counter the problem eating patterns.

*Step 8: Rearrange the food-related environment.*
Minimize the physical barriers to following the diet and maximize those for non-diet foods.

*Step 9: Dispense the therapeutic diet.*
Provide the patient with a detailed, written description of the prescribed diet.

*Step 10: Select a starting date.*
Help the patient identify a day to begin the new dietary program.

*Step 11: Implement the therapeutic diet.*
Secure the patient's agreement to attempt the diet, without changes, for a 7-day period.

*Step 12: Plan follow-up.*
Recommend that the patient contact the clinician in 1 week.

---

## Step 2: Review the Potential Difficulties of Changing a Diet

Once the patient has agreed to adopt the diet, the clinician should review the potential difficulties that might be encountered during the initial days of following the diet. This review should emphasize two potential sources of difficulty that all patients confront. First, the clinician should discuss the initial discomfort and disruption that is created when any major changes are made in diet. These problems are caused by the need to adjust familiar patterns of eating. All foods and food-related activities (e.g., shopping, food preparation) should be reviewed to see whether or not they conform to the new dietary program. Once they are reviewed and a decision is made about each, the patient will be able to establish an alternative routine which can be maintained with less difficulty. Gradually those positive aspects of following the prescribed diet will be recognized, and the new diet can be supported over time.

The second type of problems are those that may arise due to an idiosyncratic daily schedule or activities that may act as temporary barriers to following the dietary program. For example, the patient might be aware of scheduled activities such as vacation, holidays, or business travel that could disrupt the initial dietary program. In such cases the patient should begin the diet when the normal daily routine resumes. For this reason, the clinician should ask the patient to identify those activities in the coming week(s) that he feels will create a major change in his routine daily activities.

## Step 3: Select Short-Term and Long-Term Goals

The clinician should identify a clear, objective, long-term goal for the patient's dietary program. It is important that the clinician and the patient agree upon the goal in order to avoid any misunderstanding about the purpose of the program. In addition, this goal should be measurable by the patient so that he knows how well he is doing at any time. In this way he can monitor his own progress and make adjustments in his diet to achieve the desired goals of the program.

Most therapeutic diets require major changes in patients' food consumption patterns. Therefore it is recommended that the clinician consider the number and magnitude of the changes that are being asked of the patient. As a general rule, the patient should be asked to make only three changes at any one time. If there are numerous changes, or if the changes are major, the clinician should design a stepwise program that will introduce the new diet gradually. For example, if the patient is prescribed a diet that is restricted to 2 grams of sodium per day and the patient is currently consuming 10 to 12 grams of sodium, the dietary program might be introduced in three steps. First, the patient would no longer add salt to food at the table and avoid obviously salted foods (e.g., potato chips). In addition, salt should no longer be added to food when it is cooked. The second step would be for the patient to avoid canned or frozen foods, and foods that have been pickled or cured. In the third phase, the patient would learn which of the common fresh or prepared foods are lower in sodium than other types or brands. In this way, the patient makes only a few changes at a time.

## Step 4: Patient Keeps a Self-Record

In order to tailor the prescribed diet to the patient's current food preferences and to identify the extent of the changes that will be required, the patient should keep a Daily Food Record (Figure 1). These records also will be used to determine the degree to which the patient's current diet differs from the prescribed diet and to identify any problem eating patterns the patient may have. The patient should be instructed to enter on the record all foods eaten during a 3-day period. This period should include at least one day on a weekend.

The patient's consistency in keeping the Daily Food Record also can be used as an indicator of the degree to which he will be able to follow the prescribed diet. If the patient is consistent and thorough, it is likely that he also will attend to the details of the new diet and have less difficulty following the prescribed regimen. If, however, the patient is inconsistent or considers the task unnecessary, or refuses to cooperate, the clinician should be alerted that the patient might have difficulty following the prescribed diet. If this occurs, the clinician should discuss the problem with the patient and require a completed set of Daily Food Records before the patient begins the diet.

### Step 5: Analyze the Content of the Patient's Current Diet

The Daily Food Record is the most accurate method of measuring the patient's current diet in terms of the nutrients that are critical to the prescribed diet. The clinician should review the patient's Records and calculate the intake of each targeted nutrient using the amounts of each food that is allowable (or contains a desired nutrient) on the prescribed diet. If necessary, detailed listings of nutrients, vitamins, and minerals are available in standard reference books for this purpose.[3]

The review of a patient's Daily Food Records can be time consuming, depending upon the targeted nutrients. However, the more accurate this calculation, the more guidance can be given to the patient. The clinician should recognize that these data are critical to the dietary program in order to determine the patient's short-term goals and to estimate the degree of changes necessary. The costs in terms of personnel time of calculating the nutrient analysis for a patient's diet must be considered as part of the required nutritional counseling.

Recently software programs for personal computers have become available that will perform a nutrient analysis quickly and accurately. The clinician should recognize, however, that these programs are only as good as the information about recipes and food components that was used for the calculations. The database should be sufficiently broad and detailed for clinical use. For instance, if the recipe for a particular food is not the one that is used by the patient, the clinician should be sure to enter the correct ingredients for analysis. If not, the food analyses will be inaccurate.

### Step 6: Analyze the Patient's Eating Patterns

In addition to providing information about what the patient eats, the Daily Food Records provide a useful summary of the patient's typical eating patterns. Because most people are unaware of their eating habits or how often they eat certain foods, they tend to underestimate the degree of difficulty they will have in following a prescribed diet because they do not recognize how their current eating patterns may interfere with the diet.

The Daily Food Records can be used to identify the patient's potential problem eating patterns and alert the clinician to areas that should be discussed with the patient. Common problem eating patterns are (1) occasional social pressure to eat certain foods, (2) eating at parties, and (3) unavailability of specific foods when eating away from home. The Food Record will identify these patterns; a specific plan may have to be developed to change them.

## Step 7: Select a Strategy to Counter Each Problem Eating Pattern

If the patient has a problem eating pattern, the clinician should discuss the pattern and help the patient to identify a strategy to eliminate the problem. A listing of potential strategies is contained in Table 6. These strategies are simple and require little explanation. The patient should select a strategy with which he is comfortable and develop a plan for using it prior to leaving the clinic session. The patient should be comfortable with the plan, and should know

Table 6. Strategies to resolve common problem eating patterns

---

*Problem No. 1: Social pressure to eat certain foods.*
  (1) If the diet requires supplements, meet the minimum requirements at other meals that day.
  (2) If the diet is restrictive, save a few portions from other meals that day to be used at this meal.
  (3) Select, when possible, his own food.
  (4) Leave excess or restricted foods on the plate.

*Problem No. 2: Eating at parties.*
  (1) If the diet is restrictive, save a few portions from other meals that day to use at the party.
  (2) Choose non-alcoholic beverages or limit alcohol consumption.
  (3) Stand away from the buffet and bar.
  (4) Select, when possible, his own food.
  (5) Leave excess or restricted foods on the plate.

*Problem No. 3: Unavailability of specific foods when eating away from home.*
  (1) If the patient is following a restrictive diet:
      (a) Make the best meal choice available.
      (b) Ask that meals be prepared in a manner that is acceptable.
      (c) Ask for substitute side dishes.
      (d) Ask that restricted foods be removed from the table.
      (e) Leave excess or restricted foods on the plate.
  (2) If the diet is to be supplemented:
      (a) Satisfy minimum daily requirements at home.
      (b) Make the best meal choice available.
      (c) Request substitute side dishes that contain the supplemental nutrient.

---

what to do in different situations. The clinician should review this plan with the patient and be satisfied that the patient has a thorough understanding of its purpose and the details of its use.

## Step 8: Rearrange the Food-Related Environment

Because the environment has such a powerful influence on diet, the patient should consider how the new diet will be affected by the food currently available in his surroundings. He should identify food not on the diet that will be tempting to eat.

Two specific, simple recommendations should be made. First, the patient should conduct a "pantry review" to identify food that is no longer permitted on the diet. This food should be discarded immediately. The patient should be discouraged from letting any food remain in order to "test my self-control." Later, when the patient has mastered the new diet, this food can be purchased as a test of self-control, if the patient thinks that is necessary.

The second suggestion is for the patient to purchase a variety of foods that are allowable on the prescribed diet. The immediate availability of these foods will help avoid further restrictions in the patient's meal choices. With more variety, the patient is encouraged to continue with the diet as prescribed.

## Step 9: Dispense the Therapeutic Diet

The patient should possess a detailed description of the prescribed diet program. The description should include the rationale, limitations, and allowable quantities of foods containing the targeted nutrients. These materials should be sufficiently detailed that the patient will be able to make a decision whether or not he is following the diet in almost all situations. The clinician should briefly review with the patient the contents of the written materials so that the patient knows where to find specific information.

The clinician must caution the patient that the diet should be followed as prescribed. The patient should be told that a diet that is either restricted or supplemented in certain nutrients should not be combined with other "diets" without consultation with the clinician. The patient can place himself at extreme risk if he follows other diets (e.g., calorie restriction for weight loss) or if he attempts to be more restrictive or add more supplements than recommended. The patient should understand that the prescribed diet is carefully balanced for nutrients and should not be changed. Moreover, any changes in the diet without the clinician's knowledge will result in a situation in which the clinician will not be able to make appropriate adjustments in the dietary program, if needed.

## Step 10: Select a Starting Date

The patient should select a specific day to start the prescribed diet. The first day of the program should be a routine one for the patient, without unusual stress or an uncontrollable schedule. If the start day is chosen to be a few days after the present clinic visit, the patient will have time to discard restricted foods and to purchase allowable foods.

## Step 11: Implement the Therapeutic Diet

The patient should be told that any changes in diet are always difficult due to the resulting changes in the daily routine; the new routine will be uncomfortable and disruptive. For these reasons alone, the patient should agree to adhere to the prescribed diet for seven days. This will provide the patient with seven opportunities to attempt to follow the prescribed diet at breakfast, lunch, and dinner. After one week, the patient should have accommodated to the new routine. If difficulties remain after seven days, the patient may be experiencing problems which require more intensive intervention. Therefore, the patient should re-contact the clinician after 1 week and together they will decide whether and how to modify the dietary program.

## Step 12: Plan Follow-up

The patient should be instructed to re-contact the clinician after 1 week, regardless of how well the dietary program is going. Preferably this re-contact will consist of a clinic visit; if this is inconvenient an extended telephone call may be sufficient. It is important that the clinician have the opportunity to review in detail the patient's progress and make modifications early in the program. The 1-week period also is important because the patient knows that if the dietary program is not going well, he has at most only 1 week before changes will be made. This knowledge should encourage the patient to continue with the dietary program and enable him to tolerate the initial disruption and discomfort.

## Common Problems

There are three common problems that patients confront while trying to follow a prescribed dietary regimen: (1) pressure from family, friends, or co-workers to eat certain foods which should be avoided, (2) eating at parties, (3) the unavailability of specific foods when eating away from home. These problems occur so often that they are frequently treated using one or more simple strategies rather than initiating the health behavioral counseling process (Table 6). If these strategies fail, consideration should be given to the possibility that aspects of the problem are unique to the patient and require in-depth evaluation and counseling.

### Social Pressure to Eat Certain Foods

Most patients report that it is more difficult to follow their prescribed dietary regimen when they are away from home. One common problem is social pressure to eat the same foods that others are eating at a group meal. This can be a problem both for patients who are trying to avoid certain foods as well as for those patients who are trying to increase the amount of dietary intake of a certain nutrient. They explain that it is very uncomfortable to refuse food that is offered. It also is difficult to obtain certain foods that are required by the diet. In either case, patients feel that others will be uncomfortable or the host will be offended if they do not eat what everyone else is eating or ask for a "special" meal. The explanation of the reasons for the special diet can lead to a discussion of the patient's medical condition, a situation which many people would rather avoid. As a result, the patient will simply accept the food that is offered, or not pursue those foods that are needed. If this problem occurs infrequently, it may have minimal impact on the patient's overall medical condition. However, if it occurs frequently, the patient must develop a program for managing it.

The problem of occasional social pressure to eat certain foods can be managed through a combined program of preparation and selection during the meal itself. This program is based on adjustments in other meals eaten during the day in anticipation of the increased intake of undesired foods, or the absence of desired foods. For example, a patient with diabetes would plan for a social dinner by taking the following preparatory steps: (1) ensure that breakfast, lunch, and afternoon snacks have resulted in an acceptable blood glucose level during the day, (2) consume a snack before attending the meal to avoid the problem of needing to eat because of low blood glucose level before dinner but having few items from which to choose, and (3) save one or more exchange units from breakfast or lunch for use at dinner. At the dinner, the patient would manage his food consumption by (1) selecting, when possible, those foods that are on his diet and selecting the "best" choices among foods that are not strictly on the diet but which are offered, (2) selecting reduced portions of foods that should be minimized, and (3) "tasting" but then leaving on his plate those foods that must be restricted.

If instead of being on a restrictive diet the patient is attempting to increase the amounts of certain nutrients, he also would follow a combined program of preparation and meal management at the social meal. For example, the patient with hypertension who has been prescribed a diet with increased potassium would prepare for a social dinner by ensuring that most of his daily requirement of potassium has been satisfied prior to the dinner. During the dinner he would select larger portions of those foods that contain potassium but not worry about reaching his minimum daily requirements through the food consumed at the dinner.

## Eating at Parties

Eating at parties can be a problem for those patients following a restricted diet. The problem occurs because of the availability of foods that are restricted combined with the patient's impaired judgment resulting from the consumption of alcoholic beverages. The patient may view the party as a "special occasion" during which the diet can be ignored. Complicating the problem is that frequently the patient cannot remember all that he has eaten. Of course the degree to which the patient can tolerate the consumption of restricted foods depends upon the patient's medical status, the amount of the restricted nutrient that is consumed during these "special occasions," and the frequency with which these events occur.

The patient should be encouraged to adopt a combined program of preparation and selection to manage his diet. For example, the patient with impaired gall bladder functioning who has been prescribed a low fat diet would prepare for a party by (1) ensuring that the meals eaten during the day of the party conform to the recommended restrictions and (2) eating a snack prior to the party to decrease his appetite and thereby decrease the attractiveness of the foods available at the party. During the party he would (1) choose non-alcoholic beverages or limit his alcohol consumption, (2) position himself away from the food and bar, (3) serve himself any food to be eaten, (4) select foods that are low in fat, and (5) leave foods on his plate that are high in fat.

## Unavailability of Specific Foods
## When Eating Away from Home

Another common problem is the unavailability of foods that comprise the diet when the patient is eating away from home. For the patient who is following a restricted diet, the problem is that the foods that are available are not recommended. For the patient who is attempting to supplement his diet, the foods that contain the targeted nutrient are not available. A combined program of preparation and selection during the meal also is recommended. The basis for this program is the view that the other meals during the day are adjusted in anticipation of increased intake of undesired foods, or the absence of required foods.

For example, if a patient with hyperlipidemia who has been prescribed a diet low in cholesterol and saturated fat knows that he will be attending a business luncheon, he would select a breakfast and dinner that is lower than usual in these components in order to accommodate, if necessary, the increased amounts contained in the lunch meal. The patient also would use several strategies during the meal. If the patient were following a restricted diet, he would minimize the amount of undesired food eaten including: (1) making the best meal choice available, even though it may be restricted on the diet (e.g., pan-fried fish rather than hamburger, (2) asking that a dish be prepared in a manner that is acceptable (e.g., broiling instead of frying, asking for salad dressing on the side), (3) asking for a substitute side dish that is acceptable on the patient's prescribed diet (e.g., baked patoato rather than french fries), (4) asking that restricted foods be removed from the table (e.g., butter), (5) leaving foods on the plate that are highest in the undesired nutrients, and (6) modifying the physical appearance of the food (e.g., by peeling off breading, scraping off gravy).

If the patient were following a diet supplemented in certain nutrients he would use a combination program that emphasizes preparation. For example, the pregnant patient who has an iron deficiency might be prescribed a diet that is enriched in foods high in iron and vitamin $B_{12}$. She would prepare for a social dinner by ensuring that her minimum daily requirements of iron and vitamin $B_{12}$ have been satisfied prior to the dinner. During the dinner she would select larger portions of those foods that contain iron and vitamin $B_{12}$, but not worry about reaching the prescribed daily requirements based on the foods consumed at the dinner.

### Behavioral Counseling to Resolve Patient-Specific Problems

Some patients who attempt to follow a prescribed diet encounter problems that are specific to their lifestyle, family, or personal habits. These patients require an individually tailored program that will either accommodate or resolve these problems.

The following sections describe how the clinician would use each step in the 11-step process of health behavioral counseling in a program to help patients resolve patient-specific problems in following a prescribed diet (Table 7).

### Step 1: Identify the Problem

Most often, patient-specific problems are encountered in one of the following areas: (1) the patient has difficulty in implementing one of the steps in the dietary program, (2) the patient continues to self-debate whether or not he should adhere to the presecribed diet, or (3) there are major negative factors in the patient's environment (e.g., lack of support from family, criticism of co-workers, other activities that have higher priority for the patient). The patient also may

Table 7. Eleven-step health behavioral counseling for patients with problems of dietary adherence

---

*Step 1: Identify the problem.*
  To what degree does each of the following seem to be present?
  (1) Absence of an initial decision to follow the diet.
  (2) Continuing self-debate whether to follow the diet.
  (3) Negative factors in the patient's environment that are punishing the patient for following the diet.

*Step 2: Clarify the goals of treatment.*
  (1) Identify both short-term and long-term dietary goals.
  (2) Identify specific actions the patient can take.

*Step 3: Collect information.*
  (1) Obtain detailed information from the 3-day Daily Food Records.
  (2) Obtain additional information from the patient about the environmental stimuli and consequences affecting the dietary program.

*Step 4: Develop a behavioral diagnosis.*
  Identify the consistent relationships among the primary and secondary factors surrounding the dietary program supporting it or acting as barriers to it.

*Step 5: Generate an intervention plan.*
  (1) Keep the plan simple.
  (2) Develop a plan that includes strategies both to support the diet and to discourage a return to prior eating patterns.

*Step 6: Intervene.*
  (1) Encourage the patient to use the intervention plan for at least 7 days in order to overcome the initial discomfort of changing a routine and to identify problems.
  (2) Instruct the patient to continue to keep the Daily Food Records.
  (3) List the steps of the intervention program in writing and give them to the patient.

*Step 7: Review the patient's progress.*
  Instruct the patient to contact the clinician in 7 days to review any problems encountered.

*Step 8: Generate a revised intervention program.*
  Modify the program as needed and give the patient a written copy of it.

*Step 9: Reintervene.*
  Instruct the patient to use the revised intervention program for at least 7 days in order to accommodate to the new routine.

*Step 10: Develop a maintenance program.*
  Design a program with the patient to withdraw the artificial strategies that helped the patient initially.

*Step 11: Review the behavior change process.*
  (1) Review with the patient the strategies that seemed to be the most effective.
  (2) Identify the steps the patient should use to restart the dietary program in the future, if necessary.
  (3) Give the patient a written list of these steps.

---

be experiencing several of these problems at the same time. A patient who has an extremely busy daily schedule also may have difficulty recording his daily food intake, and may even have difficulty coming to see the clinician to discuss these problems.

The clinician initially should clarify which of the three general types of problems the patient is experiencing: (1) the patient lacks information, (2) the patient has problems with one or more of the basic steps for starting the diet, or (3) the patient has a problem that is unique to him. If the patient needs additional information, he should be encouraged to reread the written materials describing the prescribed diet. If the patient has problems with one of the program's steps, the clinician might provide guidance (see "Steps to Help the Patient Start a Therapeutic Dietary Program" above). Only if the problem is patient-specific should the clinician initiate the health behavior counseling process.

### Step 2: Clarify the Goals of Treatment

The clinician should examine the patient's understanding of the short-term and long-term goals of treatment. Some patients may believe that they must follow an unrealistically stringent diet. Others may believe that the diet is more liberal than it actually is. Both the patient and the clinician must have a clear understanding of the diet's components in order for the patient to know whether or not he is within the guidelines.

The clinician also should review what is hoped to be accomplished through their counseling sessions. The patient must understand that he must make a deliberate decision to follow the diet. Further, the patient has the responsibility of taking appropriate actions to do so. The clinician's role is to work with the patient and help resolve problems that may occur.

### Step 3: Collect Information

The clinician needs two types of information to understand the patient's problem in following the prescribed diet. The first is a thorough description of the type and amounts of foods that the patient is currently eating. This information should be obtained from Daily Food Records (see Figure 1) collected over at least 3 days. These records will indicate the patient's typical diet and food consumption patterns. How close is the patient's current diet to the prescribed diet? Which foods will need to be restricted? Which foods can be increased?

The second type of information that the clinician needs is a detailed description of the positive and negative factors that the patient encounters prior to and immediately following meals when targeted foods (or nutrients) are eaten. Are there specific antecedent factors that are provoking the patient to eat foods that do not conform to the prescribed diet? Are there other factors that function as positive consequences to encourage the patient to continue with the customary diet, and not adhere to the prescribed diet? These data are collected from the patient's Daily Food Record, and from the clinic interview with the patient.

This accurate detailed information about the patient's diet also educates the patient about his current diet and eating patterns. Most patients are unaware of their dietary habits, and are surprised to learn the details of their nutritional intake. The process of collecting detailed records over a 3 day period also draws the patient's attention to his eating at every meal. Through this continuing surveillance the patient learns how his diet is influenced by his environment. This understanding prepares him for the intervention program to be developed subsequently.

## Step 4: Develop a Behavioral Diagnosis

An accurate behavioral diagnosis is crucial to a successful intervention program. The clinician must identify those factors that are promoting and supporting the current diet, as well as those factors that would discourage or punish the desired therapeutic diet. Included in an appropriate behavioral diagnosis would be a functional analysis of those factors that are contributing to the problems experienced by the patient. A typical behavioral diagnosis for a patient-specific problem in the category of self-debate would be:

> The patient's problem is that he exceeds the maximum amount of sodium allowed each day. The largest quantity of sodium is consumed prior to the dinner meal. A review of his dietary records indicates that over a 3 day period he consumed large amounts of salted snack foods eaten as appetizers. The patient states that he customarily has one or two cocktails prior to dinner, and his habit is to eat these foods. He reports that sometimes he can resist eating these foods, but usually he feels that after working hard all day he deserves a small reward.

## Step 5: Generate an Intervention Plan

The intervention plan should be designed so that a strategy is included that will make it easier for the patient to follow the prescribed diet and more difficult for the patient to follow his customary diet. The plan should be simple and, if possible, should include the patient's suggestions for resolving the problem. To illustrate, the following intervention plan might be developed for the patient described above:

> The patient recognized how his self-debate was interfering with following the diet. Therefore his first strategy was to clarify the issues of the self-debate and to acknowledge that it was his cocktail that he perceived as the daily reward, not the food.

> The second strategy was to acknowledge that he had more difficulty resisting highly salted foods after the first drink. It was then that he was more easily influenced by his thoughts of deserving the highly salted foods regardless of their effect on his medical status. Therefore, to eliminate this temptation he would replace the highly salted foods with acceptable low-salt foods. The absence of the highly salted food and the presence of acceptable alternatives should stop the debate.

This intervention plan was designed after the patient became aware of his self-debate. It includes a strategy to relabel the undesirable highly salted foods as an option rather than a deserved reward. It also includes a strategy to prevent the patient from eating highly salted snack foods once he has had a drink.

## Step 6: Intervene

The clinician should obtain the patient's agreement to attempt the new program for at least 7 days before considering a change. The 7-day period should provide the patient with several trials with the new program, and allows for the initial discomfort that accompanies any lifestyle change to dissipate.

During this time the patient should continue to complete the Daily Food Records. The information collected during this period will be used to make adjustments in the program when the patient discusses his progress with the clinician in a week. The records also may provide additional clues as to factors that are influencing the patient's dietary patterns.

As with any behavioral intervention program, the clinician should write out the specific steps the patient should take (see Figure 2). This explicit listing of what the patient should do will eliminate the possibility of the patient simply forgetting one or more of the actions he should take.

## Step 7: Review the Patient's Progress

After 1 week the patient should re-contact the clinician to discuss his progress. The patient should bring the Daily Food Records with him, and any other data that was to be collected. During this session, the clinician should review any problems that the patient had with the intervention program. An unambiguous decision should be made whether the patient should continue with the same program for another week or modifications should be made in the strategies used.

The 1-week follow-up session is critical to the ultimate success of the intervention program. It is important that any difficulties the patient encounters be rapidly resolved. Further, the clinician has the opportunity to revise the initial behavioral diagnosis based on additional information and perhaps improve the strategy selected. It also assures the patient that although he may be experiencing problems initially, he need only tolerate the program for 1 week before consideration is given to changing it. As a result, the patient is less likely to change the program on his own during the first few days of the intervention.

## Step 8: Generate a Revised Intervention

After reviewing the patient's progress and reconsidering the accuracy of the behavioral diagnosis, the clinician may decide to modify the intervention program. These revisions should be based on observations made by the patient, or the information collected on the daily record. The clinician should again write out the new program for the patient.

### Step 9: Re-intervene

The patient should agree to try the new program for 1 week without modifications. During this period the patient should continue to collect pertinent information on the Daily Food Records. After 1 week, the clinician and the patient can use these data to discuss further changes in the program.

### Steps 10 and 11: Develop a Maintenance Program and Review the Behavioral Change Process

After the dietary program has successfully been followed for one month, the clinician should discuss a maintenance program with the patient. The maintenance program should be designed as a permanent program that the patient can use indefinitely to follow the diet. As a result, any artificial strategies which depend upon the clinician must be withdrawn. At this point the positive medical and physical consequences of following the therapeutic diet should provide the patient with the incentive necessary to adhere to the diet. The patient should know that these consequences include maximizing longevity, reducing the likelihood of complications which would compromise the quality of life, and pride in self-management.

Another goal of the maintenance program is to ensure that the patient recognizes each of the steps that was used to help him begin and maintain the prescribed diet. By reviewing these steps the patient should be aware of those factors that tend to influence his eating patterns. Further, if the patient must re-start the diet following illness or a holiday, he has a good understanding of what he must do. Although the patient should be encouraged to resolve problems on his own, the clinician should also be sure the patient understands that he is available to help if the patient so desires.

### Specific Counseling Strategies

Many strategies have been used to help a patient adhere to a prescribed dietary regimen. There are several, however, that are particularly helpful. These strategies are designed to increase the attractiveness of following the diet, or to decrease the attractiveness of not following the diet. For dietary adherence this can be accomplished by increasing the positive consequences for the patient if he follows the prescribed diet, by decreasing the negative consequences for following the diet, or by providing unpleasant consequences if the patient continues to follow his customary diet.

Before attempting to use any of these strategies, the patient's problem should be thoroughly reviewed and an explicit behavioral diagnosis developed. Inappropriate application of these strategies not only can prove to be ineffective in resolving the patient's problem, but also can compromise the patient's continued cooperation in the program.

### Strategies to Increase Positive Consequences

One of the most frequently observed patterns when a patient is having difficulty following a prescribed diet is that he receives few or no positive consequences when he does follow the diet. To counter this problem, the intervention program might include a specific strategy to increase the number, frequency or type of positive consequences that he encounters when he follows the diet.

*Use a Contract.* A contract is simply an agreement by the patient that he will enjoy a modest pleasurable event if he follows the prescribed dietary regimen for a given number of days. For example, a patient might agree that if he follows a low-sodium diet as prescribed for 5 days, then he will allow himself to buy a magazine he enjoys but does not often purchase. The purpose of the contract is to provide relatively immediate consequences for the patient's new dietary regimen. The contract may be simply one the patient makes with himself, or it may involve a friend or family member. A more complete description of the use of contracts is contained in Chapter 4.

### Strategies to Increase Negative Consequences
### When the Diet Is Not Followed

The immediate consequences that occur naturally when the patient continues to eat his normal diet are generally very positive. The food tastes good to the patient; it is associated with pleasant activities in the past; it is readily available. Therefore it is sometimes necessary to identify a strategy that will increase the negative consequences to the patient when he follows his customary diet rather than the prescribed diet.

*Use a Contract.* A contract always specifies the positive consequences for following the diet. In addition, if the patient describes the customary diet as very attractive, the contract also might include a description of an unpleasant event if the patient does not follow the diet as agreed (e.g., donating a small amount of money to his "least favorite" organization). The unpleasant consequence should be modest, and serve more as a reminder to the patient than as a real punishment.

*Public Self-Monitoring.* Another effective strategy for providing a negative consequence for not following the diet is to have the patient select a public location to post his progress in following the dietary program. This might be at home or at work. This is appealing to some patients because the thought of their progress being monitored by others when they are not doing well is very unpleasant. The posting of a public record functions as a public commitment by the patient to make certain changes. This strategy provides immediate aversive consequences that are more powerful than the positive consequences of following the usual diet.

## Strategies to Remove or Minimize Negative Consequences When the Diet Is Followed

Patients frequently encounter negative consequences when they follow the prescribed diet. These negative consequences may arise from the diet itself, or they may result from the reactions of others. The prescribed diet may create too much disruption or be extremely distasteful for the patient. The patient may think that family members will complain about new foods being introduced into the family meals. In these cases the intervention plan should include a strategy to remove or minimize these negative consequences.

*Use a Stepped Program.* If the prescribed dietary program represents a significant change in the patient's eating patterns, the patient may be discouraged by the number and extent of the changes required. To overcome this problem, the clinician should carefully choose intermediate goals for the patient so that the diet is gradually introduced. Once the patient has become accustomed to the intial changes, other aspects of the diet can be added. To illustrate, a diet that is low in saturated fat would require changes in food preparation, food purchasing, food selection, and extensive knowledge of common recipes. The clinician might recommend that the diet be introduced in steps with the initial changes focusing on food selection (e.g., choosing broiled or baked meats, choosing margarine, avoiding high fat cheeses), and the next step concentrating on food preparation (e.g., using vegetable oil for cooking, using only egg whites).

*Provide the Patient with Assertiveness Skills.* Some patients express concern that their family members, friends, or co-workers will react negatively to their new diet. They fear that they will be criticized or ridiculed when following the diet. As a result, they do not want to discuss or follow the diet when they are with these people.

The clinician should discuss this problem with the patient directly. The patient may not know how to discuss the diet, or how to describe why he must follow the diet in a way that is reasonable and acceptable to his friends. In this case the patient might benefit from a rehearsal with the clinician of how he can discuss the diet. The patient can role play what he would say and the clinician can portray what his friend might say.

In other cases, the patient might need help in being sufficiently assertive to tell his friends of his new diet. The patient might benefit from a discussion of his own rights as an individual. He is justified in being concerned about his own health and the effect of his diet on his health status. The patient may need to recognize that friends, co-workers, and family will be supportive once they realize the nature and depth of the patient's commitment to the prescribed diet. Assertion skills training are described in more detail in Chapter 4, "Behavioral Counseling."

## Case Illustration

The following case illustration discusses how each of the initial steps for helping a patient get started on a dietary program can be used in the clinic. It also indicates how a clinician would apply the 11-step health behavioral counseling process to help a patient resolve a specific problem encountered when trying to follow the dietary program. The description of the patient was created to illustrate the major issues and common solutions used in the clinic.

### The Patient

The patient is a 39-year-old white male who works as the manager of a retail automobile parts supplier. He is in good health and asymptomatic. However, repeated laboratory analyses revealed an elevated total cholesterol level of 238 mg/dl with normal triglyceride levels of 115 mg/dl. The patient is 6 feet 2 inches tall and weighs 190 pounds. He is not overweight, and does not smoke cigarettes. The patient's family has a history of cardiovascular disease. The patient was considered to be at increased risk for cardiovascular disease and was prescribed a diet low in saturated fat, low cholesterol, and a phase I diet as recommended by the American Heart Association.

### Initial Visit

The clinician presented the patient with the results of his routine physical examination, and the assessment that he was at increased risk for developing cardiovascular disease because of his elevated cholesterol levels combined with a family history of heart disease. He therefore was prescribed a diet low in saturated fat and cholesterol. The patient understood the need for the diet and was given appropriate written materials describing the diet. The patient stated that he "knew nothing" about diets but would get his wife to help him. The patient was rescheduled for a return visit in 2 weeks.

## Second Visit

The patient reported that he was not doing too well on the diet. He stated that the diet was so complicated that he couldn't see how anyone could follow it. The clinician decided that initially he would use the "Steps to Help a Patient Start a Therapeutic Dietary Program" (see Table 7.5).

*Step 1: Review the Patient's Decision to Follow the Diet.* The clinician determined that the patient had been concerned about developing cardiovascular disease since his father had died of a heart attack at age 65. He was aware of his increased risk and expressed the desire to change his diet to reduce his cholesterol level. The clinician considered the patient to be sincere in his desire to change his diet, and offered to help him get started. The patient agreed willingly.

*Step 2: Review the Potential Difficulties of Changing a Diet.* The clinician cautioned the patient that changing his diet would not be a simple process, but it need not be difficult either. The clinician indicated that any major change in lifestyle was accompanied by an initial period of discomfort and disruption as new habits are being learned, and old habits discarded. Moreover, the patient's new diet also affected his wife and family with whom he ate breakfast and dinner. They would have to be involved in the program. The diet would require some effort by the patient, but once established, it would be no more difficult to follow than his current diet.

*Step 3: Select Short-Term and Long-Term Goals.* The clinician recommended that the patient follow a gradual program of changing his diet. Modest goals would be chosen initially, rather than making many large changes at one time. The clinician indicated that the long-term was a daily intake of total fat, 31% of total calories; saturated fat, 9% of total calories; polyunsaturated fat, 10% of total calories; and cholesterol, 200 milligrams. Intermediate goals would be developed based on the information that the patient collected about his diet over the next few days.

*Step 4: Patient Keeps a Self-Record.* Prior to making any changes in his diet, the patient agreed to record on Daily Food Records the amounts and types of foods that he ate for the next 3 days. The clinician explained that the patient should use these records to understand his current eating habits, and to identify

Daily Food Record

Today's Date Monday July 10, 1985

| TIME LOCATION OTHER | FOOD | AMOUNT |
|---|---|---|
| Breakfast 7:15 am kitchen, home | Fried egg | 1 |
| | Bacon strips | 2 |
| | Toast, buttered | 2 |
| | Strawberry jam | 1 tbs. |
| | Coffee, black | 2 cups |
| Office 10:00 am | Coffee, black | 1 cup. |
| Lunch 12:00 noon cafeteria, work | Fish fillet, fried | 4 oz. |
| | Potato, mashed | 1/2 cup |
| | green peas | 1/4 cup |
| | corn bread | 4" x 2" |
| | Ice tea | 8 oz. |
| | apple pie | 1 piece |
| Dinner 7:20 pm dining room, home | Chicken breast, fried with skin | 2 |
| | Rice with mushrooms | 1/2 cup |
| | Dinner rolls | 2 |
| | Coffee, black | 1 |
| | Watermellon | 1/8 |

Figure 1. Example of a Daily Food Record.

foods that are particularly high in saturated fat or cholesterol. The patient was scheduled for a follow-up visit in 1 week.

*Third Visit*

*Step 5: Analyze the Content of the Patient's Current Diet.* The clinicain reviewed the Daily Food Records and examined the amount of saturated fat and cholesterol the patient was currently eating (Figure 1). In addition an assessment was made of which foods the patient was eating that would have to be restricted, and substitutions made if possible. Using the standards made available, the clinician determined that there were major changes necessary at each meal. His breakfast consisted of eggs and a meat. His lunch usually contained one or more high fat, fried items. Finally, although his dinner meal appeared to be reasonable, it could be further improved if his wife could make a few changes in food preparation (e.g., substitute margarine for butter, remove skin from chicken).

*Step 6: Analyze the Patient's Eating Patterns.*    In reviewing the Daily Food Records, the clinician assessed whether or not the patient was encountering any of the common problems common to following a prescribed dietary program. During this review it became obvious that the patient lacked the essential nutritional information necessary to follow the diet.

The patient also discussed a second problem. He stated that although he thought he might be able to change his breakfasts, he did not see how he could change his lunches because he always ate lunch with his co-workers at a fast food restaurant, and there was nothing on the menu that fit the diet.

*Step 7: Select a Strategy to Counter Each Problem Eating Pattern.*    The clinician encouraged the patient and his wife to learn more about the prescribed diet by attending two instructional sessions with the clinic's dietitian. The dietitian would provide them with a review of the diet, additional educational materials, and answer any questions they had about food preparation or selection. The clinician would continue to work with the patient on his other problems.

The patient's lunch meal presented a more difficult, although common, problem. The clinician suspected that the patient's problem was more complicated than knowing how to select foods at lunch; the patient was feeling social pressure to eat with his co-workers, and select the same foods. However, the clinician decided to postpone discussion of this problem until a later session, after the dietitian had reviewed how to select foods when eating at a restaurant.

*Step 8: Re-arrange the Food-Related Environment.*    The clinician encouraged the patient to take two specific steps before starting the new diet program. First, the patient would conduct a "pantry review" using a list of foods to be available to understand about the diet, and discard foods that are high in saturated fat and cholesterol. In thinking about this strategy the patient identified the following items he knew were in his kitchen that he would throw out or give away: hard cheese, bacon, half and half used as a coffee creamer, lard for cooking, and some canned meat products (e.g., chili, corned beef).

The second step was that the patient would go to the grocery store and purchase specific foods that would substitute for the items that were restricted. He decided to purchase the following: vegetable oil for cooking, margarine, low-fat cheese, 2% milk, and cereal for breakfast.

*Step 9: Dispense the Therapeutic Diet.* The patient would receive detailed information about the diet from the dietitian. This would include tables indicating the amount of saturated fat and cholesterol in common foods, and recipes for common dishes that used low fat ingredients.

*Step 10: Select a Starting Date.* The patient was encouraged to select a starting date for the diet following the second session with the dietitian. This would occur in 2 days. The patient selected a Monday as the starting date, 5 days from the current visit day.

*Step 11: Implement the Therapeutic Diet.* The patient was instructed to follow the new diet for a period of at least 7 days and then return for a follow-up visit at the clinic. This period would provide seven opportunities to follow the new diet at each meal and the patient would have experienced many of the problems that will recur for him. The clinician also reminded the patient that any major lifestyle change would be disruptive and uncomfortable, so the patient must be tolerant for this week and not change the diet. The patient also agreed to keep a Daily Food Record for the 3 days prior to his follow-up visit to the clinic. At the return visit, the clinician and the patient would review the diet and any problems encountered. The patient agreed to this plan.

*Step 12: Plan Follow-up.* A return visit was scheduled in 8 days for the patient. The clinician stressed that the patient must return for this visit regardless of how well the diet seems to be going.

### Fourth Visit

The patient returned as scheduled, having followed the program developed at the previous clinic visit. The patient and his wife saw the dietitian for dietary instruction, discarded certain high-fat and cholesterol-rich foods, and purchased appropriate foods. His wife was learning to prepare foods that were low in saturated fat. He had changed his breakfast meal to consist of cereal with low-fat milk. The patient stated that his only problem was the lunch meal. The Daily Food Records revealed that his lunch meal had not changed. The clinician decided that it was appropriate to help the patient by using health behavior counseling (see Table 7).

*Step 1: Identify the Problem.* The patient initially stated that his problem was that there were no appropriate foods at the restaurant for lunch. Further exploration, however, revealed that the patient's main concern was that he did not want his co-workers to know that he was on a diet. He felt that they would not understand his explanation for his diet and they would either think that he had a "heart problem" or that he was a "health nut."

*Step 2: Clarify Goals of Treatment.* The patient stated that he wanted to reduce his chances of having a heart attack, but he did not want his co-workers to misunderstand why he was following the diet. He agreed to work with the clinician to find a way of managing this problem.

*Step 3: Collect Information.* The clinician decided that no additional information needed to be collected by the patient about this problem.

*Step 4: Develop a Behavioral Diagnosis.* The clinician's behavioral diagnosis of this patient was that the patient was experiencing moderate anxiety resulting from his thoughts about what his co-workers might say or do when they learned that he was on a diet. He felt that they would treat him differently and/or perhaps make jokes about his inability to eat "real food." Through discussions with the patient the clinician believed that these fears may be justified because the patient was lacking in the necessary social skills to explain adequately why he was on the diet.

*Step 5: Generate an Intervention Plan.* The clinician discussed with the patient how his co-workers' attitudes and actions might be influenced by how the patient describes the rationale for his diet and what he actually does. The patient agreed and together they developed a description of what the patient would do (e.g., select low-fat items from the menu, skip dessert and have fruit at the shop) and say (e.g., the patient's diet was to "lower cholesterol" which was "smart," not because he had a heart problem). The patient then practiced with the clinician what he might say to his co-workers.

*Step 6: Intervene.* The patient agreed to use the plan the next day when he would have lunch with only two of his co-workers. Gradually he would introduce the topic with others over the week. He would telephone the clinician at the end of the week. The clinician wrote this plan as a behavioral prescription (Figure 2) for the patient.

*Telephone Call*

The patient called the clinician at the end of the week as planned.

*Step 7: Review the Patient's Progress.* The patient described that he had briefly discussed the new diet with each of his co-workers, a few at a time, as they had

**MICHAEL L. RUSSELL, Ph.D.**
Department of Internal Medicine
Baylor College of Medicine
Tel. 799-6032

**Program for Change**

For: _D. S_                    Date: _July 11, 1985_

1. Continue on new low cholesterol diet for meals eaten at home.

2. Use rehearsed dialogue describing the new, low cholesterol diet as "smart" with one or two co-workers at lunch.

3. Select the best available foods at lunch.

4. Telephone me on Tuesday, July 18.

_M.L.Russell_

Figure 2. Example of a behavioral prescription.

planned. He was surprised that no one made a joke or tried to embarrass him. He was relieved and enthusiastic about his ability to follow the diet at lunch.

*Steps 8 and 9: Generate a Revised Intervention Plan (if needed), and Re-intervene.* The program did not need modification. The patient agreed to return for a clinic visit in 2 months.

*Fifth Visit*

The patient returned as scheduled for a blood analysis and routine clinic follow-up. His total cholesterol level was 218 mg/dl and triglyceride level was 95 mg/dl.

*Steps 10 and 11: Develop a Maintenance Program and Review the Behavior Change Program.* The patient reported that the lunch meal was still going well although he did express concern that he would like to make further changes in his lunch meals. He stated that he was tired of the few choices at the restaurant and had decided to bring a lunch to work. However, he was concerned that his co-workers would resent his not joining them at lunch each day. He asked the clinician for suggestions.

The clinician agreed that the plan for managing the lunch meal at the restaurant with his co-workers was successful; no further plan was necessary. However, the clinician did think the patient's desire to implement further changes in the lunch meal would require the patient to use a similar approach as before. Therefore the clinician reviewed with the patient each of the steps they had used together to design the initial plan, and then encouraged the patient to develop his own plan. With some discussion, the patient was able to do so successfully.

## References

1. Caggiula AW, Christakis G, Farrand M, Hulley SB, Johnson R, Lasser NL, Stamler J, Widdowson G: The multiple risk factor intervention trial: IV intervention on blood lipids. *Prev Med* 1981; 12:443–475.
2. Wechsler H, Levine S, Idelson RK, Rohman M, Taylor JO: The physician's role in health promotion—a survey of primary care practitioners. *N Eng J Med* 1983; 308:97–100.
3. Pennington JAT, Church HN: *Food Values of Portions Commonly Used*. Philadelphia, JP Lippincott, 1980.

# 8.  Weight Control

Obesity, Overweight, Health and Disease

In 1983, the U.S. Department of Health and Human Services reported that approximately 11 million men (19%) and 18 million women (28%) in the United States are obese.[1] That is, these individuals are in the upper 15% of all individuals in terms of total body fat as measured by skinfold thickness in several locations of the body using as a standard the values obtained from individuals in the age group of 20 to 29.

Obesity is usually distinguished from being overweight. Overweight is defined as excess body weight relative to height. Thus overweight reflects a combination of fat, bone, and muscle tissue mass, and is measured simply as the total weight for a given height. Approximately 13 million men (23%) and 19 million women (30%) in the United States are considered overweight because they are in the upper 15% of all individuals in terms of total body weight using as the standard the values obtained from individuals in the age group of 20 to 29.[1]

Although there is a substantial overlap between those who are obese and those who are overweight, some individuals are overweight for their height but are not necessarily obese (e.g., football players, weight lifters). Other individuals may not be overweight but still are obese by body fat measurement (i.e., little muscle mass and a relatively high percentage of adipose tissue) (Figure 1).

From a medical and public health viewpoint, obesity or overweight is of concern when it increases the patients' risk of morbidity or mortality. The Metropolitan Life Insurance Company has examined the height-weight values for those individuals with the lowest mortality rate. These height-weight values were published initially in 1959 and have been used widely as "desirable" weights for patients. This table was revised in 1983, and the idea of "desirability" was discarded because the old standards did not necessarily reflect the ideal weights for lowered morbidity. These revised values, presented in Table 1, represent simply the weight for a given height that has resulted in the greatest longevity.[2]

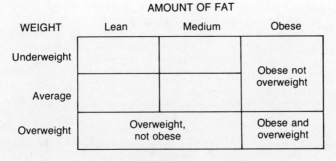

Figure 1. Comparison of obesity and overweight.

The effect of either obesity or overweight on morbidity varies depending on the patient's medical condition and other risks. However, it has generally been recognized that obesity is a risk factor for many health problems. Obesity places patients at increased risk for hypertension, adult-onset diabetes, hyperuricemia, and menstrual abnormalities. Further, obesity appears to be associated with endometrial carcinoma, degenerative joint disease, gallbladder disease, and atherosclerosis. Obesity also places patients at greater risk for anesthetic and major surgery.[3]

### Success in Losing Weight

Most obese patients are unable to achieve and maintain substantial weight loss. Less than 25% of patients who enter a weight loss program are able to lose 20 pounds or more. Typically, 80% of those patients who begin a weight loss program drop out before reaching their stated goal. Although these statistics are discouraging, effective methods have been identified.

The programs which have had the most success have been the behaviorally oriented programs which focus on changing eating habits rather than simply following a "diet." Most of these programs result in an average weight loss of 11 pounds in 10 to 12 weeks which is maintained for 1 year by over 40% of the patients. The weight loss program described in this chapter is a composite of behavioral methods which have been used effectively with medical patients over the last several years.

### Weight Loss as a Lifestyle Change

#### The Calorie Balance Equation

Excess weight is the result of a cumulative process of the patient having consumed more calories than the body has expended. This relationship can be viewed

Table 1. 1983 Metropolitan Life Insurance Company height
and weight tables for men and women *

| Height (in shoes) ‡ | Weight in pounds (in indoor clothing) † | | |
|---|---|---|---|
| | Frame | | |
| | Small | Medium | Large |
| **MEN** | | | |
| 5'2" | 128–134 | 131–141 | 138–150 |
| 5'3" | 130–136 | 133–143 | 140–153 |
| 5'4" | 132–138 | 135–145 | 142–156 |
| 5'5" | 134–140 | 137–148 | 144–160 |
| 5'6" | 136–142 | 139–151 | 146–164 |
| 5'7" | 138–145 | 142–154 | 149–168 |
| 5'8" | 140–148 | 145–157 | 152–172 |
| 5'9" | 142–151 | 148–160 | 155–176 |
| 5'10" | 144–154 | 151–163 | 158–180 |
| 5'11" | 146–157 | 154–166 | 161–184 |
| 6'0" | 149–160 | 157–170 | 164–188 |
| 6'1" | 152–164 | 160–174 | 168–192 |
| 6'2" | 155–168 | 164–178 | 172–197 |
| 6'3" | 158–172 | 167–182 | 176–202 |
| 6'4" | 162–176 | 171–187 | 181–207 |
| **WOMEN** | | | |
| 4'10" | 102–111 | 109–121 | 118–131 |
| 4'11" | 103–113 | 111–123 | 120–134 |
| 5'0" | 104–115 | 113–126 | 122–137 |
| 5'1" | 106–118 | 115–129 | 125–140 |
| 5'2" | 108–121 | 118–132 | 128–143 |
| 5'3" | 111–124 | 121–135 | 131–147 |
| 5'4" | 114–127 | 124–138 | 134–151 |
| 5'5" | 117–130 | 127–141 | 137–155 |
| 5'6" | 120–133 | 130–144 | 140–159 |
| 5'7" | 123–136 | 133–147 | 143–163 |
| 5'8" | 126–139 | 136–150 | 146–167 |
| 5'9" | 129–142 | 139–153 | 149–170 |
| 5'10" | 132–145 | 142–156 | 152–173 |
| 5'11" | 135–148 | 145–159 | 155–176 |
| 6'0" | 138–151 | 148–162 | 158–179 |

* From ref. 2., with permission, Metropolitan Life Insurance Company, 1983.
† In indoor clothing weighing 5 pounds for men and 3 pounds for women.
‡ In shoes with 1-inch heels.

as a calorie balance equation in which the calories obtained from food minus
the calories used in activity and metabolic processes equals the calories stored
as fat.

Calories ingested − Calories used = Calories stored
(from food)        (in activity)        (as fat)

If the patient's daily consumption of calories equals the total number of calories expended in daily activities and metabolic processes, then the number of excess calories is zero. No calories are stored as fat. As a result, the patient maintains the weight at which this balance is reached.

If the number of calories obtained from the foods eaten is more than the number of calories expended in daily activities and metabolic processes, then the patient gains weight. The calorie balance equation indicates that there are two ways for the balance to shift toward calorie storage as excess weight. First, the patient will gain weight if he begins to consume more calories than he expends, compared to the balance when his weight was stable. This situation occurs for many people during the holiday season when they consume more food than usual and gain weight.

Second, the patient will gain weight if he expends fewer calories then he consumes, compared to the balance when his weight was stable. This situation occurs when someone who usually has a very active daily schedule through which he expends considerable energy suddenly changes to a less active schedule and continues to consume the same amount of calories. For example, athletes experience weight gain after the sports season is over, or when they become injured. Upon retirement from an active profession, many people also experience weight gain when their activity level drops and their calorie consumption is maintained.

If, however, the number of calories used in daily activities and metabolic processes is greater than the number of calories consumed, then the body converts previously stored fat into energy. As a result, the patient loses weight. The rate for conversion of fat into energy is approximately the same for everyone: the expenditure of 3,500 calories into energy equals a weight loss of 1 pound.

It is important to recognize that weight loss can be accomplished by two processes. First, the patient will lose weight if he begins to consume fewer calories than he expends, compared to the balance when his weight was stable. This is the traditional calorie-based approach to weight loss. The patient is instructed to consume fewer calories, and weight loss will result. For example, if the patient consumes 500 fewer calories per day compared to the number of calories he consumed at a stable weight, he will have consumed 3,500 fewer calories after a 7-day period and should experience a weight loss of 1 pound.

Second, the patient also will lose weight if he expends more calories then he consumes, compared to the balance when his weight was stable. This situation will occur if the patient increases the amount of physical activity he performs each day. For example, a patient who uses an additional 500 calories each day will expend a total of 3,500 calories at the end of 7 days and should experience a weight loss of 1 pound.

The approach recommended in the following Weight Loss Diet Program is a combination of reducing the number of calories consumed, and increasing

Table 2. Typical positive and negative consequences of consuming excess calories

| | Consequences | |
| --- | --- | --- |
| | Positive | Negative |
| Immediate | Pleasurable taste | Guilt |
| | Reduction of tension | |
| | Social approval | |
| | Pleasurable associations | |
| | Avoiding feelings of "wasting food" | |
| | Avoiding feelings of hunger | |
| Delayed | None | Weight gain |
| | | Increased risk of certain diseases (e.g., hypertension, diabetes) |
| | | Unattractive appearance |
| | | Social disapproval |
| | | Physical discomfort |

the number of calories expended through physical activity. The weight loss diet emphasizes a balanced diet with modest calorie restriction. The accompanying physical activity program emphasizes a modest physical fitness program designed to expend calories and to promote improved feelings of well-being.

## The Weight Loss Pattern

When a patient's weight is stable, the number of calories consumed equals the number of calories expended. As a result, the patient is consuming sufficient calories every day to maintain the current weight.

Once the patient has become overweight, several factors contribute to the patient's continued consumption of sufficient calories to maintain a stable elevated weight. As with other behavior that is intrinsically pleasurable (e.g., alcohol consumption, cigarette smoking), the intake of an excessive number of calories either by too much food or high-calorie food, or both, is supported by its immediate positive consequences and the absence of immediate negative consequences (Table 2). The consumption of too much food or high-calorie food tends to be satisfying, is associated with pleasurable events in the past, and is often encountered in social situations. The immediate negative consequences are often only feelings of mild guilt, if the patient is aware of the number of

Table 3. Typical positive and negative consequences of following a
weight loss diet

| | Consequences | |
|---|---|---|
| | Positive | Negative |
| Immediate | Pride in accomplishment | Hunger sensations |
| | Improved self-image | Social disapproval for refusing foods |
| | | Avoidance of desirable foods |
| | | Disruption of usual daily routines |
| | | Embarrassment |
| | | Disruption of usual food-preparation routines |
| | | Disruption of usual food-purchasing routines |
| | | Withdrawal of effective method for managing stress |
| Delayed | Reduction of risk for cardiovascular disease | None |
| | Improved management of current disease | |
| | Improved stamina | |
| | Improved self-esteem | |
| | Improved appearance | |

calories being consumed. The risks of overconsumption of calories and resultant weight gain are only experienced over time and include negative consequences for health, appearance, and psychological status. Further, there are no long-term positive consequences. As a result, the short-term positive factors tend to favor the current eating patterns and the maintenance of the current weight.

When the overweight patient begins a weight loss diet, additional factors appear which favor a return to the original eating pattern. Whereas the long-term consequences of following the diet are overwhelmingly positive, the immediate consequences are often extremely negative (Table 3). As a result, the dieter experiences the weight loss program as extremely negative. Once the weight is lost, the patient feels he has succeeded and goes "off the diet." Unfortunately, in most weight loss programs, this means that the patient no longer follows a diet plan and returns to his previous eating patterns. Gradually the weight is regained, and the patient is faced with the same problem, except with perhaps less motivation to attempt another weight loss diet.

Alternatively the patient can follow a calorie-restricted diet combined with a modest physical fitness program and concentrate on changing lifestyle patterns in order to lose weight. Thus the patient learns how to change his eating patterns and to follow a diet which provides a pre-selected number of calories. When the desired weight is achieved, the calories can be adjusted upward to maintain the weight. For this patient, the diet and the physical activity program have become part of his daily routine. Moreover, the negative consequences for following the diet have decreased, and the long-term immediate benefits have had an opportunity to be experienced (e.g., a more attractive appearance, improved self-image, better-fitting clothes). As a result, the diet can be continued indefinitely.

### The Patient's Decision to Lose Weight

The overweight patient does not usually need to be convinced that he should lose weight. The overweight patient does, however, need to make a clear decision that he desires to lose weight at this time. In addition, the overweight patient needs to have a clear understanding of why he is ready now to make the necessary changes in his lifestyle and accept the discomfort of a new daily routine that includes the voluntarily avoidance of foods that are pleasurable. Examples of the non-medical benefits of weight loss that a patient might identify include better-fitting clothes, improved appearance, physical activities being easier, feeling more alert, feeling more relaxed, and improved self-esteem.

The clinician can encourage the patient to make this active decision by providing medical information that will support it. The clinician can also help the patient examine any barriers the patient perceives to initiating a weight loss program and determine whether these obstacles are real or imagined. A useful technique is to suggest that the patient record in writing the reasons he has decided to start a weight loss program and any reasons why he should not start the program. What factors are now present that were not present in the past, for example, six months ago? Examples of the types of factors that a patient might report include having exceeded a self-determined "upper weight limit," the termination of stress-producing activities, wanting to improve appearance by a certain date (e.g. wedding, vacation, reunion), inability to fit into certain clothes. This listing can be used as a basis for further discussions with the clinician. The clinician should consider whether or not the patient's reasons for beginning now will be sufficient to carry the patient through the uncomfortable initial stages of the weight loss program.

Regardless of the patient's reasons for deciding to lose weight and the precipitating factors for lowering weight now, the clinician should make a simple, direct statement that the patient should lose a specific amount of weight. The clinician should not equivocate. To ensure that the patient understands the clinician's prescription, the prescription should, if possible, be linked to a present medical condition of the patient, or to the risk at which the excess weight places the patient. For example, the patient with chronic low back pain should be told that the excess weight is probably a contributing factor to the back pain and that substantial weight loss may help his medical condition.

As with all medical conditions that place the patient at risk, the clinician should be careful not to use the possible consequences of the condition to the patient's health to threaten the patient into making a lifestyle change. Fear of future consequences may in fact immobilize the patient from taking action. Rather, the clinician must communicate realistic concerns to the patient, and allow the patient to make the decision to lose weight. If the patient decides not to begin a weight loss program at this time, he should know that the clinician will still continue to provide him medical care. Through the clinician's attitude of care and concern, the patient will understand that when he does make the decision to lose weight, the clinician is ready to help.

## The Patient's Weight Loss Diet Program

The Patient's Weight Loss Diet Program (see p. 200) is based on controlling the number of calories consumed each day. The diet provides the patient with a balanced diet, and encourages the inclusion of a variety of foods. Because the diet does not rely on special foods or require a restricted range of foods, it can be easily adjusted to increase the total number of calories consumed each day once the patient has achieved the desired weight. This diet is based on the recommendations of the American Heart Association.[4]

Although the Patient's Weight Loss Diet Program is based on caloric restriction, instead of strict "calorie counting," the patient keeps a record of the number of servings of food he consumes from each of the seven food groups. Each serving in a food group is defined in terms of an easily remembered quantity (e.g., 1 cup, 1 slice, 1 teaspoon). The sizes of one serving from each food group are presented in Table 4. The reason that the Patient's Weight Loss Diet Program uses servings is to reduce the amount of information about foods that the patient must acquire to follow the diet. It has been estimated that most people's daily diets comprise foods chosen from among approximately 800 foods. Although these foods differ in the number of calories per unit, foods within each food group generally contain approximately the same number of calories per unit. The Patient's Weight Loss Diet has been designed to use standard serving sizes in each food group and ignores small caloric differences among specific foods within a group. If the patient eats a variety of foods within each category, over time these small differences are averaged. As a result the patient loses weight

Table 4. Sizes of single servings of foods from each of the seven
food groups

| Food group | Amount |
| --- | --- |
| Milk group (170 calories) | 1 serving = 1 cup of whole milk |
| Vegetable group | 1 serving = ½ cup of vegetables<br>Group A = leafy vegetables<br>(negligible calories)<br>Group B = root vegetables<br>(35 calories)<br>Group C = beans, corn, potatoes<br>(70 calories) |
| Fruit group (40 calories) | 1 serving = one of the following:<br>1 cup of berries<br>1 small piece of fruit<br>(e.g. small apple or orange) |
| Bread group (70 calories) | 1 serving = one of the following:<br>1 piece of bread<br>1 roll<br>½ cup of noodles or rice<br>¾ cup of dry cereal |
| Meat group (75 calories) | 1 serving = 1 ounce of lean meat, fish, or poultry |
| Fat group (45 calories) | 1 serving = one of the following:<br>1 teaspoon (1 pat) of margarine or butter<br>1 teaspoon of vegetable oil<br>1 tablespooon of French dressing<br>6 small nuts |
| Free choice (75 calories) | 1 serving = one of the following:<br>1 glass wine<br>1 piece of fudge<br>4 hard candies<br>4 teaspoons of sugar |

and does not need to know more than the basic guidelines presented in
Table 4. However, if the patient routinely eats foods that are not easily classi-
fiable using these guidelines, a more detailed listing is presented in Appendix
B which can be photocopied and given to the patient.

The Patient's Weight Loss Diet Program has three different levels corresponding to the patient's initial weight (see p. 206).

If the patient weighs 100 to 139 pounds, Level I (1,235 calories) is recommended. If the patient weighs 140 to 199 pounds, Level II (1,800 calories) is
recommended. If the patient weighs over 200 pounds, Level III (3,000 calories)
is recommended. These three diets reduce the average daily caloric intake by
500 to 1,000 calories from the maintenance number of calories for individuals

within the specified weight ranges. A reduction of 500 to 1,000 calories per day will result in a reduction of 3,500 to 7,000 calories per week which will yield a weight loss of 1 to 2 pounds per week. This rate of weight loss is recommended because it does not place undue stress on the body, and it does not require drastic changes in the patient's eating habits. It does encourage a balanced diet and gradual changes which can become a permanent part of the patient's lifestyle.

The Patient's Weight Loss Diet Program also includes modest physical activity. The patient is encouraged to participate in vigorous, rhythmic physical activity three to four times each week for 30 to 40 minutes. During this period the patient should exercise at a level that will increase his heart rate to the target heart rate level for his age (see "Target Heart Rate Range", in Chapter 9), and maintain it at that level for the exercise period.

For the patient who desires to lose weight, the physical activity session provides several advantages in addition to improved cardiovascular fitness. First, this level of exercise will expend 150 to 200 calories per session. If the patient exercises four times per week, the additional 600 to 800 calories expended will result in the loss of approximately 1/4 pound each week. Second, most patients find that physical activity has a definite suppressing effect on appetite. The patient is less hungry following exercise. Third, many patients report feeling better about themselves, and are able to handle stress better when they have been following a regular exercise program. This psychological effect will help the patient resist using food to reduce tension or elevate his mood.

## The Clinician's Role

As with other programs requiring a change in lifestyle, patients have varying degrees of difficulty following a weight loss program. Some individuals have few problems losing the recommended amount of weight, once the clinician has made a clear statement of the need to do so. Other patients require continuing help and support from the clinician to be successful. Unfortunately it is usually difficult to predict who will succeed and who will not.

The problem for the clinician is to decide how much aid and counseling time should be spent with a particular patient to help him start and/or maintain a weight loss program. The dilemma is to avoid spending time with those patients who would have succeeded on their own, and at the same time, to avoid ignoring patients who need the extra guidance. Because there are no absolute guidelines, it is recommended that, in the absence of obvious barriers to the patient's success (e.g., the patient has a history of dietary failure; the patient has poor reading skills; the patient does not comprehend the diet program; the patient's family is not supportive), the clinician should follow a course of minimal involvement, with increasing involvement as needed.

Initially, the clinician should simply give the patient the Patient's Weight-Loss Diet Program (see p. 200) to read and follow on his own. The program is self-contained, including sufficient information for the patient to start a weight loss diet program on his own. The patient should be encouraged to tailor the program to his personal preferences and lifestyle, and to identify any problem eating patterns.

If this is insufficient, or if the clinician believes that the patient needs help in getting started, then the clinician should proceed through the following 12 steps to help the patient establish the weight loss program. Finally, if the patient experiences specific problems, the clinician should consider using health behavioral counseling to help the patient resolve them.

## Helping the Patient Start a Weight Loss Program

Although some patients will be able to implement the Patient's Weight Loss Program on their own, a larger number will have difficulty with one or more of the steps in the program. The following section provides guidelines for the clinician to help the patient design the initial program. It identifies common problems patients have with each of the steps and how the clinician might help the patient to resolve these. These steps are summarized in Table 5.

### Step 1: Review the Patient's Decision to Lose Weight

The patient's decision to lose weight should be carefully examined by the clinician. The reasons why the patient desires to lose weight are critical to the initial success of the program. The clinician should ask the patient what he hopes to achieve by losing weight. How does the patient imagine that his daily activities and lifestyle will be different after he has lost the desired weight? Why has the patient decided to lose weight now? What has provoked this decision? The clinician should decide whether or not these reasons are realistic, given the patient's current lifestyle. Has the patient considered the effort required to reach his goals? Does the patient view the goal as worth the effort?

This initial frank discussion with the patient not only will help clarify the patient's reasons for losing weight, it also will elicit a public statement of the patient's reasons for wanting to lose weight. This statement will be remembered by the patient and may prove to be helpful when he is struggling to follow the diet program.

If the patient has not clarified in his own mind why he wants to lose the weight, it is possible that the discomfort he will experience in the initial stages of the program will overcome his desire to lose weight, and the program will fail. The clinician should not encourage the patient to begin the program if it appears that the patient has not made a reasoned decision to lose weight. Rather,

Table 5. Steps to help a patient start the weight loss diet program

| | |
|---|---|
| *Step 1:* | *Review the patient's decision.* |
| | Identify the patient's rationale for wanting to lose weight now. |
| *Step 2:* | *Review the potential difficulties.* |
| | Discuss the discomfort the patient may experience in losing weight. |
| *Step 3:* | *Select short-term and long-term goals.* |
| | Identify appropriate actions that the patient can take. |
| *Step 4:* | *Patient keeps a self-record.* |
| | Explain how the patient should use the Daily Food Records for 3 days. |
| *Step 5:* | *Analyze the patient's eating patterns.* |
| | Use the Daily Food Records to determine if the patient has a particular problem eating pattern. |
| *Step 6:* | *Select a strategy to counter the problem eating pattern.* |
| | Help the patient to select a strategy to counter the problem eating pattern. |
| *Step 7:* | *Rearrange the food-related environment.* |
| | Minimize the physical barriers to following the diet and maximize those to "non-diet" eating. |
| *Step 8:* | *Select the proper weight loss diet.* |
| | Adjust the diet as needed if the patient's baseline weight is borderline between two of the diet categories. |
| *Step 9:* | *Select a physical activity program.* |
| | Identify a program for regular, vigorous aerobic activity. |
| *Step 10:* | *Select a starting date.* |
| | Help the patient choose the day to begin the program. |
| *Step 11:* | *Implement the weight loss program.* |
| | Secure the patient's agreement to attempt the diet without changes for 7 days. |
| *Step 12:* | *Planned follow-up.* |
| | Recommend that the patient contact the clinician in 1 week. |

the clinician might suggest that the patient consider the difficulties that such a program will create, and return to the clinic to begin the program when he feels ready to handle these difficulties.

### Step 2: Review the Potential Difficulties of Losing Weight

The clinician should discuss with the patient the normal pattern of pleasurable and uncomfortable factors that will be encountered in the Patient's Weight Loss Diet Program (see Table 3). The patient should know that the new diet will become a permanent diet, and that he will not be returning to his prior dietary habits. Initially these changes may be very difficult to accept because not only is the patient restricting his caloric intake, he may also be shifting to a balanced diet, and using various unfamiliar techniques to help him remain on the diet. As a result, the early phases of the diet will be uncomfortable. Eventually, however, the level of pleasure the patient experiences now with the foods he eats will return, although this pleasure will result from possibly different foods or recipes.

The patient should know that the behavioral approach to weight loss is to provide specific aids to help him during the early stage of the dietary program and to counteract problem eating patterns that lead to weight gain. The strategies are temporary, however, and it is anticipated that eventually the dietary routine will become part of his lifestyle, and will require no more effort to follow than the patient expends on his current diet.

### Step 3: Select Short-Term and Long-Term Goals

The patient's first decision is to select an appropriate goal for the weight loss program. This goal should specify how much weight the patient desires to lose, and the amount of time allowed for doing so. The goal should not demand that the patient lose more than 1.5 pounds per week. For example, a patient might choose to lose 20 pounds to achieve his ideal weight, and decide to attempt this over a 15 to 20 week period. A table of ideal weights for men and women, by height, is included in the patient materials.

Some patients desire to lose weight at a faster rate. Many popular weight loss programs promise large weight losses in very short amounts of time, and the patient may not understand why this program cannot do so. Diets with severe calorie restriction can cause nutritional and metabolic imbalances which may risk damage to the cardiovascular system, the kidneys, and the liver. Other weight loss programs rely on water loss to achieve dramatic weight loss results, which are, of course, transitory. The recommended program offers a safe rate for permanent weight loss without jeopardizing the patient's health during the program.

### Step 4: Patient Keeps a Self-Record

The patient is strongly encouraged to keep a daily record of the amounts of each of the foods eaten during a 5-day period. This period should include at least 1 day on the weekend. This food record is essential to determine what the patient's current eating habits are, and to identify any problem eating patterns that he may have. A blank Daily Food Record is presented in the Appendix.

The patient's response to keeping a Daily Food Record is a good indicator of whether or not the patient will be successful in the weight loss program to come. Although the task of recording each food and amount eaten is somewhat annoying, it is considerably easier than the task of following the diet itself. If the patient is either not willing to complete the food record, or only records foods on some days, the clinician should re-consider whether or not the patient should be encouraged to begin the diet at this time. The clinician should directly confront the patient with this issue. If the patient desires to continue with the program, the clinician should instruct him to repeat the assignment to complete the Daily Food Record. Neither the clinician nor the patient will be able to determine the patient's typical eating habit patterns without this information.

## Step 5: Analyze the Patient's Eating Patterns

Most people are not aware of their own eating habits and are surprised by the results of the Daily Food Records. They discover that foods they thought were rarely eaten are eaten more frequently than they thought. They also discover that the total calories eaten on the average day often exceeds what they would have estimated. Finally, they identify foods that they eat "out of habit" or "without noticing," and that could easily be omitted from their diet. Keeping an accurate Daily Food Record is a useful technique to prompt the patient to follow the prescribed diet.

The information collected on the Daily Food Records also will reveal if the patient has a problem eating pattern. Many patients have one or more of the following patterns: binge eating, rapid eating, and eating too much at parties or at restaurants. These patterns are discussed in the following section, "Common Problems with the Weight Loss Diet Program."

## Step 6: Select a Strategy to Counter the Problem Eating Pattern

Once the patient's problem eating pattern(s) have been identified, the clinician should review with the patient the list of strategies that may be helpful in counteracting each pattern (see Table 6). The patient should select a strategy with which he is comfortable and develop a plan for using it. It is important that the patient leave the session with the details of how he will use the strategy. If he leaves without having explored these details, it is unlikely that he will do this on his own at home, and the program may fail. The clinician also can be helpful by gently but directly asking pointed questions how the patient plans to overcome possible problems in using the strategy. If necessary, the clinician should suggest a way of using the strategy that has been successful for other patients.

## Step 7: Re-arrange the Food-related Environment

Regardless of whether or not the patient has a problem eating pattern, he should be encouraged to review his food-related environment and re-arrange it to support the new diet. The intent of this step is to eliminate or minimize physical barriers to following the diet, and maximize the likelihood of success.

Two specific simple recommendations should be made. First, the patient should prepare or purchase a variety of foods that are allowed in large quantities. These foods are low in calories, and the patient can eat them as snacks without worrying about the relatively small number of total calories they contain (e.g., cucumber spears, unsalted popcorn). A complete listing of suggestions is included in the patient's materials.

The second suggestion is to remove high-calorie foods from the home and office. If it is not possible to do this at home, in order to accommodate family members' eating habits, then it is suggested that these foods be removed from their original wrapping and placed in non-transparent containers so that the patient will not repeatedly see them.

### Step 8: Select the Proper Weight Loss Diet

The patient is instructed to choose one of the 3 diets according to his current weight. Each of them provides a balanced diet with caloric restrictions to achieve a weight loss of approximately 1 to 2 pounds each week.

The patient should be discouraged from further restrictions of the diet beyond these guidelines. An overly restricted diet not only requires close medical monitoring, it also places extraordinary demands upon the patient which increase the likelihood that the patient will not follow it.

### Step 9: Select a Physical Activity Program

The Patient's Weight Loss Diet Program is not only a reduced calorie diet. It also includes regular, vigorous physical activity. The physical activity is included for several reasons. First, the physical activity does expend some calories. Although the number of calories expended are not usually sufficient to have a substantial impact on weight, it does help some. Approximately 100 to 110 calories are expended for each mile covered by walking or jogging. Second, physical activity tends to suppress the appetite. Patients do not feel as hungry during the day if they have exercised in the morning. Third, physical activity tends to increase the body's metabolic rate and maintain the elevated rate for several hours. This increase counteracts the body's natural tendency during a decrease in caloric intake to decrease the metabolic rate to conserve calories. Finally, and perhaps most importantly, physical activity tends to have several positive effects on the patient's mood which can have a strong influence on the weight loss program. Once the physical activity routine is established, patients report feeling more alert, more relaxed, and less hungry during the day. Thus not only are some of the barriers to following the diet reduced or eliminated (e.g., eating in response to feelings of stress or depression), but due to improved mood, the patient is better able to cope with those problems that are encountered in following the diet. It is for these reasons that the physical activity program should be strongly supported by the clinician. The patient should not be led to believe that physical activity is an optional part of the program.

The most common error made in selecting a physical activity is to begin with a program that is too difficult for the patient. The key guideline in selecting a program with an appropriate level and duration of physical activity is that the program should be modest, with gradual increases over time. The patient should not have to strain or experience fatigue at any point in the program. A conservative approach is strongly recommended in order that the patient can accommodate physically to the program, and retain a positive attitude about participating in it.

The patient's materials provide a description of a basic walking program that is recommended for use in this diet. For those individuals who need to begin at a higher level, Chapter 9, "Physical Activity," provides guidelines for establishing an appropriate program. Included in that chapter are suggestions for working with the patient who is having difficulties starting the basic program.

### Step 10: Select a Starting Date

The patient should be encouraged to select a specific day to begin the Weight Loss Diet Program. The program should not be started during a time of stress for the patient, or when the patient knows that his schedule will be irregular or uncontrollable. It is best if the patient selects a routine day to minimize the difficulty in simply starting the program.

### Step 11: Implement the Weight Loss Program

The patient should be reminded that the new weight loss program will cause some disruption of his routine, and for that reason alone he will experience some initial discomfort. Therefore, the patient should attempt to follow the program for at least a 7-day period prior to making any major changes. In this time the patient will have experienced breakfast, lunch, and dinner during each day of the week and on the weekend and should begin to accommodate to the new routines. Seven days is usually the minimum required to begin to detect problems that may continue as barriers for the patient. It also is true that the second week often is more difficult for the patient than the first week because the initial enthusiasm for the new diet has begun to decrease. For these reasons, the patient should be instructed not to make changes in the diet prior to talking with the clinician.

*Step 12: Plan Follow-up*

The clinician should encourage the patient to call the clinician after 1 week. This re-contact does not need to be a long conversation. Often a brief discussion is sufficient. The purpose of the re-contact is for the patient and the clinician to review the program, and to make any adjustments that might be needed. If necessary, a clinic visit can be scheduled to resolve more difficult problems. The advantage of this telephone contact is that the patient knows that if he is having difficulty, at worst, he will only have to follow the diet until the re-contact with the clinician. This provides the opportunity for the initial discomfort to decrease, and the patient to accommodate to the new program. A second advantage is that the clinician is alerted early to any problems that the patient might be having, and has the opportunity to resolve them before the patient decides to quit the program.

## Common Problems with the Weight Loss Diet Program

There are several problems that patients commonly encounter when following a weight loss diet. These problems are (1) social pressure to return to prior eating habits, (2) binge eating, (3) rapid eating, (4) eating at restaurants when fatigued, (5) eating when socially overwhelmed, and (6) not being able to "get back on the diet" after an unusual day during which the diet was not followed. These problems are not patient-specific, rather they are single factor problems that prevent the patient from losing weight. Often they can be substantially reduced or eliminated using one or more simple strategies without initiating the in-depth health behavioral counseling process (see Table 6).

*Social Pressure to Exceed Dietary Limitations*

Many patients report that they would like to follow the diet but they feel pressure from their family or friends to return to their prior eating habits. These patients are extremely uncomfortable refusing food from others. They explain that their friends or family members would be offended if they did so.

The problem in most cases is that the patient does not wish to make a public issue of his diet and, in order to avoid any discussion or embarrassment, accepts the food offered. Four suggestions could be offered by the clinician. First, whenever possible, the patient should be encouraged to contact prior to the meal(s) the friend or family member with whom he expects social pressure to eat foods he would prefer to avoid, and explain that he has been prescribed a special diet. The diet requires that he must limit his portions, and occasionally avoid certain foods. The patient does not need to request special foods. Rather,

Table 6. Strategies for resolving common problems

---

*Problem No. 1: Social pressure to exceed dietary limitations.*
   (1) Explain diet to host before meal.
   (2) Save a few servings from other meals for the meal.
   (3) Leave excess food on plate.
   (4) Consider avoiding situations in which there would be social pressure to exceed diet's
      restrictions.

*Problem No. 2: Binge eating.*
   (1) Practice waiting 15 minutes, when hungry, before eating.
   (2) Practice interrupting a meal for 3 to 5 minutes before continuing.
   (3) Have large quantities of low-calorie, "free choice" items available.

*Problem No. 3: Rapid eating.*
   (1) Place the fork on the plate between each bite.
   (2) Concentrate on tasting each bite.
   (3) Allow sufficient time to eat.
   (4) Avoid scheduling other activities during mealtime.

*Problem No. 4: Eating at parties.*
   (1) Choose a nonalcoholic beverage; limit alcohol consumption.
   (2) Stand away from buffet and bar.
   (3) Select, when possible, own food.
   (4) Save servings from other meals that day.
   (5) Choose low-calorie desserts.

*Problem No. 5: Eating at restaurants.*
   (1) Select foods that are the best choices available.
   (2) When the meal arrives, estimate allowable serving sizes and set aside excess.
   (3) Request that undesired foods be removed from the table.

*Problem No. 6: Resuming the diet.*
   (1) Follow the diet as closely as possible every day.
   (2) Approach each day individually.
   (3) Refer to original diet prescription.

---

the patient need only explain that he will be limiting the foods he eats, and that he may leave some food.

The second step is that if the patient knows that he will be attending a special occasion (e.g., a dinner, a celebration), he should save some of the servings from the morning and noon to have available for the evening meal. It is preferable for the patient to shift servings than to exceed the total number of daily servings allowed.

The third step that the patient may use is simply to leave the excess food on his plate. Usually at a social meal the host is more interested in everyone tasting a food that was specially prepared, than having everyone finish all the food that was served.

Fourth, in extreme cases, the patient may feel that he is unable to resist the food that is offered by others, or that this social pressure will occur frequently.

The patient should consider avoiding meals with those individuals when this problem is likely to arise during the initial weeks of the program. This may require the patient to change his schedule in other ways too. For example, the patient may eat at different times or plan activities that will take him away from the meals with others (e.g., shopping, errands, exercise).

## Binge Eating

Binge eating is a common eating problem in which the patient eats large quantities of food in a relatively brief amount of time, usually by himself. The binge might begin with eating a slice of pie and end only when the entire pie has been eaten. The binge may last for hours or for days. The binge has a disastrous effect on the weight loss program and on the individual's sense of self-control. The binge pattern can be difficult to detect because it may occur intermittently, and the patient may be reluctant to list all the foods eaten. Therefore, it is good practice to review each meal with the patient.

The binge eating pattern can be overcome if the patient learns a strategy to interrupt the binge. These strategies must be practiced prior to the binge to be effective: (1) wait at least 15 minutes from the time the desire is noticed before eating, (2) practice interrupting a meal for 3 to 5 minutes before continuing eating, (3) prepare large quantities of snacks that are "free choice" items on the diet which can be eaten if the desire to binge eat is too strong to resist.

## Rapid Eating

Rapid eating is frequently encountered in men and women in high pressure jobs. They complete their meals in the shortest possible time. Unfortunately rapid eating leads to overeating. The problem is that it takes approximately 15 to 20 minutes for ingested food to affect the sensation of hunger. The patient may continue eating beyond the amount of food necessary or on the weight loss diet program. Rapid eating also can lead to indigestion and gas due to the air swallowed with the food. Rapid eating may be suspected if the patient's Daily Food Record indicates less than 15 minutes to complete a meal, complaints of indigestion or gas, and eating more at meals than desired due to "hunger."

The strategies for countering the pattern of rapid eating are all designed to slow the patient's eating. They are: (1) place the fork down on the plate between bites, (2) concentrate on tasting each bite of food, (3) schedule sufficient time to eat the meal, and (4) avoid scheduling other activities to do while eating.

*Eating at Parties*

Eating at parties becomes a problem when the patient overeats or overdrinks. Usually food selection is not a major problem because there are often choices that fit the weight loss diet. The problem is that many patients consider social functions as "exceptions" to their usual routine, and do not wish to follow the diet program during these occasions. As a result they eat and drink as they wish. Because the pattern of eating at parties is usually an infrequent one, often patients will not remember all they had to eat, and thus the Daily Food Record may not reflect all that was eaten or drunk at a social gathering.

The strategies used for eating at parties are designed to encourage the patient to choose food and drink wisely and to adjust the distribution of servings for the day in order to accommodate the additional food that may be consumed. The patient should consider (1) limiting alcohol consumption to two drinks or less, (2) standing away from the buffet and bar, (3) serving himself, (4) saving two or three bread and fat servings for the party, and (5) choosing low calorie desserts.

*Eating at Restaurants*

Many patients complain that although they are able to follow the diet program when they are eating at home, they cannot follow the diet when they are eating at a restaurant. They say that they do not know the serving sizes of the foods on the menu, or that they cannot find the right combination of foods, or that they find themselves eating more than they should have, or that they feel they must eat all food served. Usually overeating at a restaurant is readily detected on the Daily Food Record.

The clinician should approach this problem from the standpoint that although the patient does not control the food that is served, he does control what he eats. The patient always has the choice of whether or not to eat a particular food and the amount to be eaten. Therefore, the patient should approach eating in a restaurant using the following simple guidelines.

1. The patient should choose those foods that most closely fit into his diet. If no food seems to be acceptable, he should make the best guess as to which foods come closest to the dietary requirements. In no case should the patient simply abandon the diet because none of the choices fits the diet exactly or feel he must not eat.
2. When the food arrives at the table, the patient should estimate the appropriate serving size for each of the foods served, and set aside any excess amounts. The patient should be reminded that it is not only acceptable, but desirable to leave excess foods uneaten.
3. The patient also should be encouraged to request that the waiter remove from the table any foods that the patient does not wish to eat or have avail-

able as temptations. For example, the waiter may be asked to remove the bread, the crackers, or a side dish that is served with the meal but which the patient does not wish to eat, such as french fries.

### Difficulty "Getting Back On the Diet" After a Day Off the Diet

Some patients believe that once they go on a diet they must remain on the diet until they have lost the weight. If they "go off the diet", then they have failed. Moreover, they believe that it is too difficult to re-start their program to make another attempt. As a result, if the patient encounters a day during which he cannot follow the diet, he may not only not follow the diet for that day, he may decide there is no reason to continue. This, of course, is wrong.

The clinician should be sure that the patient understands that the diet in the Patient's Weight Loss Diet Program is a balanced diet with a restricted total caloric intake. The diet can be followed indefinitely and in fact will be the basis of the maintenance diet, although with increased caloric intake. Therefore, if the patient encounters a day when the diet cannot be followed, the patient should be encouraged to follow these simple guidelines:

1. Follow the diet as well as possible every day.
2. If the diet cannot be followed on a particular day, forget the day. The only setback is that it will take a bit longer to reach the desired weight loss than had originally been planned.
3. Approach each day separately. Do not let yesterday's problems following the diet program affect today's efforts to follow the diet program.
4. Refer to the steps from the original diet plan to get started again.

The important point the patient should remember is that it is not expected that he should be able to follow the diet under all conditions at all times. If the patient is fortunate enough not to encounter difficult days, fine. If, however, the patient does experience unforeseen conditions and cannot reasonably follow the diet, it is not a catastrophe. The patient has not failed. The diet has not failed. Rather, it is simply not reasonable for the patient to be expected to follow a diet under all conditions. Of course, the patient must make an honest appraisal of the situation, and not use this flexibility as an excuse to not follow the diet deliberately.

### Behavioral Counseling to Resolve Patient-Specific Problems

Many patients who attempt to lose weight do not succeed. Even patients who try to follow the steps in the Patient's Weight Loss Diet Program may find that they have specific personal, family, or lifestyle conditions that present insurmountable barriers to their program. For example, the patient may have a family who is resistant to any change in the foods they normally eat. Another patient may be sabotaged in his efforts to lose weight by a spouse who also is overweight.

The following sections describe how the clinician would use health behavioral counseling to help patients with specific problems. These patients may respond to the 11-step counseling process presented in Table 7.

## Step 1: Identify the Problem

Patient-specific problems in starting and maintaining a weight loss program usually occur in one of the following areas: (1) difficulty in implementing one of the steps in the program, (2) continuing self-debate whether or not to follow the diet at a particular meal, or (3) negative factors in the environment (e.g., lack of support or criticism, peer pressure to eat additional servings of certain foods, stress). The patient also may encounter several of these problems at the same time. For example, the patient who has difficulty categorizing a food or its portion may also have co-workers who are critical of any attempts by the patient to lose weight, and, as a result, self-debates whether he should try to follow the diet.

The first step is to clarify the nature of the patient's problem. The patient should be asked to describe each of the difficulties he has had with the diet, and the clinician should quickly determine which of the following general approaches should be followed: (1) the patient should be encouraged to re-read the patient materials and follow the recommended program on his own, (2) the clinician will need to guide the patient through the program to ensure that each step is properly designed and implemented, or (3) the clinician needs to use health behavior counseling to help the patient resolve patient-specific problem.

## Step 2: Clarify the Goals for Treatment

The clinician should determine whether the patient has selected appropriate short-term and long-term goals for the Weight Loss Diet Program. Some patients have unrealistic expectations in terms of the rate of weight loss. For example, a patient may wish to lose 20 pounds in 1 month. Others have the unrealistic expectation that once they have lost the unwanted weight, their weight problem has been solved. They expect to receive a temporary program to lose weight, and be able to return to their prior eating habits when they go "off the diet."

The Weight Loss Diet Program can be characterized by its reliance on gradual, safe, weight loss, with the emphasis on the patient adopting new eating patterns which will be sustained after the desired weight is achieved. The pa-

Table 7. Eleven-step health behavioral counseling for patients with problems losing weight

---

*Step 1: Identify the problem.*
To what degree does each of the following seem to be present?
(1) Absence of an initial decision to lose weight.
(2) Continuing self-debate as to whether to lose weight.
(3) Negative factors in the patient's environment that are punishing him for following the weight loss program.

*Step 2: Clarify goals of treatment.*
(1) Identify both short-term and long-term weight loss goals.
(2) Identify specific actions the patient can take.

*Step 3: Collect information.*
(1) Obtain detailed information from the 5-day Daily Food Records.
(2) Obtain additional information from the patient about the environmental stimuli and consequences affecting the weight loss program.

*Step 4: Develop a behavioral diagnosis.*
Identify the consistent relationships among the primary and secondary factors surrounding the weight loss program that are either supporting it or acting as barriers to it.

*Step 5: Generate an intervention plan.*
(1) Keep the plan simple.
(2) Develop a plan that includes strategies both to support the weight loss program and to discourage a return to prior eating patterns.

*Step 6: Intervene.*
(1) Encourage the patient to use the intervention plan for at least 7 days in order to overcome the initial discomfort of changing a routine and to identify problems.
(2) Instruct the patient to continue to keep Daily Food Records.
(3) List the steps of the intervention program in writing and give them to the patient.

*Step 7: Review the patient's progress.*
Instruct the patient to contact the clinician in 7 days to review any problems encountered.

*Step 8: Generate a revised intervention.*
Modify the program as needed and give the patient a written copy of it.

*Step 9: Reintervene.*
Instruct the patient to use the revised intervention program for at least 7 days in order to accommodate to the new routine.

*Step 10: Develop a maintenance program.*
Design a program with the patient to withdraw the artificial strategies that helped the patient initially.

*Step 11: Review the behavior change process.*
(1) Review with the patient the strategies that seemed to be the most effective.
(2) Identify the steps the patient should use to restart the weight loss program in the future, if necessary.
(3) Give the patient a written list of these steps.

---

tient's goals should relate to the behavioral changes that the patient can control, not to weight loss per se. An appropriate intermediate goal would be for the patient to follow the prescribed weight loss program for 7 consecutive days. The patient should know that the program requires the patient to choose to make a permanent change in his eating patterns. The counseling that the clinician offers will be helpful, but it is expected that the patient will "do the work" of following the diet and succeed as a result of his own efforts.

## Step 3: Collect Information

Two types of information are needed to understand the patient's eating patterns and possible problems in following the weight loss diet. First, accurate information is needed regarding the type and amounts of each food that is eaten during a given period of time. This information can be collected using the Daily Food Record (see Appendix) and should be used to construct a behavioral profile of the patient's food consumption. How much food is the patient eating? How often is the patient eating? How do the types of food eaten compare with the recommended distribution of servings?

The second type of information needed is a description of the positive and negative factors the patient experienced prior to and immediately following eating. This information is used to identify recurring factors that appear to provoke eating, and other factors that appear to reinforce its occurrence. These patterns will contribute to the development of a behavioral diagnosis of the patient's problem eating patterns.

The collection of accurate, detailed information about the patient's eating patterns also serves to educate the patient about his eating. Most patients are not aware of their eating habits or those factors that are encouraging them to eat. They are usually surprised to learn how much food they eat, how often they are eating, and the factors that are provoking their eating. The process of data collection draws attention to the patient's eating habits, and prepares him to attend to the amount and types of foods eaten that form the basis of the Patient's Weight Loss Diet Program. This self-observation also "demystifies" the program. The patients learns the direct relationship between the foods eaten and factors in the patient's environment.

## Step 4: Develop a Behavioral Diagnosis

The success of the lifestyle intervention program will depend upon the accurate identification of the factors that are stimulating the patient's problem eating, as well as the factors that support the patient's problem eating habit. An appropriate behavioral diagnosis will contain a description of these factors and their functional relationship to the problem eating pattern. A typical behavioral diagnosis for a patient-specific problem in the category of negative factors in the environment is:

The patient's problem is that he exceeds his allotted number of servings at three of five dinners during the week and at both dinners on the weekend. These meals are prepared by his wife and eaten with his two teenage sons. He reports that he does not wish to impose his weight loss diet on his family. He also does not want to waste food by not eating what he is served. He reports that his wife feels that his weight loss diet is "his problem" and that she will not change her cooking to meet his needs. He is able to follow the diet at breakfast and lunch, which he eats at work.

## Step 5: Generate an Intervention Plan

The intervention plan should be designed to eliminate or reduce the effects of the factors that are provoking and supporting the problem eating pattern. Further, the plan should include strategies to prompt appropriate eating patterns, and support them whenever they occur. The plan should be as simple as possible. For example, the patient described in the behavioral diagnosis above might develop the following plan for himself:

1. The patient will arrange to explain in detail to his wife why he must follow the prescribed diet and how the diet relates to his current medical status.
2. The patient will show his wife how much of each food group he would like at dinner and provide her with an easy method of measuring each food. If she is not willing to measure foods for him, he will estimate the amount of food he is allowing himself and return the rest to the kitchen before the meal.
3. The patient will not ask that the family change their usual eating habits.
4. The patient will ask his wife if she would like to walk with him in the evenings after dinner.

This intervention is designed to eliminate the wife's possible objections to the husband's diet by providing her with information as to its importance to the patient, by not requiring changes in the family meal routine, and by providing him with a plan for returning food if the servings are too large without offending the wife. In addition, it offers the possibility of the wife becoming more involved in the program in the future if she enjoys the evening walks and sees the benefits for the husband.

## Step 6: Intervene

The patient should be instructed to try the intervention for at least 7 days before considering a change in the routine. The 7-day period should provide sufficient opportunity to detect problems in the program, while allowing enough time for the initial discomfort of the new routine to diminish.

The clinician also should consider requesting that the patient continue to record his daily consumption of food, just as he did during the initial observation period. The information collected during the initial week of the intervention program will be the basis upon which modifications to the program can be made. It will provide more accurate and reliable information than if the patient simply attempts to recall what happens over this period. This additional information may also clarify or confirm problem eating patterns that were detected during the initial observations. An additional intervention plan designed to eliminate these newly emerging problems also may be required.

As with all behavioral interventions, the clinician should write the plan as a "Behavioral Prescription" for the patient. This explicit listing of what the patient will do will avoid misunderstandings between the clinician and the patient. It will also increase the chances that the patient will follow all of the changes agreed upon during the session. No suggestions will be forgotten.

## Step 7: Review the Patient's Progress

At the end of the 7-day period the patient should contact the clinician to review the program's progress. At this time the patient should describe any problems he has had. In addition the patient's Daily Food Record Forms should be reviewed in detail. If the patient is experiencing few problems, the clinician may suggest that he continue the program without changes. If the patient is experiencing problems, however, the clinician will need to re-assess the behavioral diagnosis and consider modifying the intervention plan.

This early review is an important step in the initial phase of the patient's program. Any problems that the patient experiences should be addressed as soon as possible. With a date in mind when his problems will be reviewed, a patient often can accept the initial discomfort and follow the program until that day. This gives the program a chance to have an effect, and provides specific information that will be used to modify the program.

## Step 8: Generate a Revised Intervention

If the clinician re-assesses the behavioral diagnosis and develops a new intervention plan with the patient, the same guidelines used with the initial intervention should be followed. The patient should continue to record the foods eaten on the Daily Food Record Form. The patient also should be given a written behavioral prescription with each step clearly described.

## Step 9: Re-intervene

The patient should agree to try the intervention for a fixed period of time, such as 7 days. At that time the patient will contact the clinician to review the program. The patient should agree not to make any changes in the program until he has talked with the clinician.

*Steps 10 and 11: Develop a Maintenance Program*
*and Review the Behavior Change Process*

Once the patient has followed the weight loss diet for a 1-month period, a maintenance program should be developed. The maintenance program has the goal of gradually withdrawing each of the artificial strategies used to start the weight loss diet, and enable the natural consequences of following the program to continue to support it. These consequences would include a pride in seeing a definite weight loss, and an improved mood resulting from the regular exercise program.

The second part of the maintenance program is to review with the patient the strategies that seemed to be the most helpful for him. The purpose of this review is to give complete control over the patient's program to the patient, while at the same time showing the patient how he was able to resolve initial problems. The patient should be encouraged to reuse these strategies if he finds that he encounters problems in the future. If the patient is not able to solve a subsequent problem, he should feel welcome to call the clinician for help.

## Specific Counseling Strategies

Several counseling strategies can help resolve a patient-specific problem eating pattern. These strategies either increase the positive consequences of following the desired diet, or provide for aversive consequences for not doing so. The decision to use one of these strategies should be made after a thorough behavioral diagnosis has been made. If misapplied, the strategy not only can be ineffective, but it can result in the patient losing motivation to continue with the program.

*Strategies to Increase Positive Consequences*

If the behavioral diagnosis indicates that the patient is receiving few or no positive consequences for following the desired diet, the clinician may decide to use one of the following strategies:

*Use a Contract.*   A contract states that the patient will receive a reward if he follows the diet for a specified length of time. The contract may allow for the patient to treat himself to a new shirt if he follows the diet for 7 consecutive days, for example. This tangible result provides an incentive in addition to losing weight to follow the diet. It is important that the short-term goals of the program be stated in terms of behavior that the patient can effect. For example, an acceptable goal would be the patient's adherence to the diet, while an unacceptable goal would be weight loss, because the patient does not directly control his weight. Rather, he controls what he eats.

This contract might be made between the patient and himself, or between the patient and a family member. The added advantage of making the contract with a family member is that it involves someone who can encourage the patient during the week to follow the diet. A blank contract is presented in the Appendix.

*Provide the Patient with Assertive Skills.*   Some patients fear that their co-workers or family members will be critical of their efforts to follow the diet program. This fear will prevent them from testing whether or not this belief is true. The patient will avoid discussing the diet or following the diet when he is with these individuals.

The clinician can be helpful by discussing the patient's reluctance to talk about the diet with these people. In most cases, the problem is that the patient does not know how to tell these people about the diet program. The clinician can rehearse with the patient how, when, where, and what the patient might say to them. This rehearsal need not take long, but the patient should have the opportunity to talk with the clinician just as he might discuss the diet program with someone else. For a more detailed discussion of this assertion training, see Chapter 4.

### Strategies to Increase Negative Consequences of Not Following the Diet Program

As has been discussed earlier, it is the short-term consequences of eating that seem to have the most powerful influence on the patient's eating patterns. The following strategies provide immediate negative consequences to the patient who does not follow the diet program.

*Use a Contract.*   The best contracts provide not only positive consequences for following the diet program, but also include modest aversive consequences for not following the program. These aversive consequences usually involve a monetary deposit with a friend or family member. The patient agrees that the deposit of, for example, $25 will be donated to a "least favorite charity" if the patient fails to perform to the contract's standards. For example, the patient might identify the Democratic Party as his least favorite charity and agree that every week he does not follow the diet program, $5 should be sent to them by the friend.

*Public Self-Monitoring.*   Some patients find that posting a weight chart in a public location and marking whether or not they followed the diet program is extremely motivating. The patient wants to avoid the peer pressure when he does not follow the program, and enjoys the support when he does follow the program. This public chart should not be for recording weight loss because of the lack of correspondence each week between following the diet and whether or not weight loss is experienced.

### Case Illustration

The following case illustration describes a patient who might be seen in an out-patient medical clinic. The case has been constructed to illustrate most of the major aspects of designing a weight loss program for a patient, and how typical problems might be resolved. This patient represents a composite of the characteristics and problems presented by patients commonly seeking a weight loss program.

### The Patient

This 47-year-old male patient has been diagnosed as having type II (adult-onset) diabetes mellitus. The patient is 5 feet 10 inches tall, of medium build, and weighs 183 pounds. He is 20 pounds over the upper limit of the weight range for his height using the Metropolitan Life Insurance Company Standards. He does not exercise regularly, although he does play golf occasionally. He does not smoke.

### First Visit

*Step 1: Review the Patient's Decision to Lose Weight.* The patient's initial inquiry about a weight loss program occurred following the clinician's discussion of his type II diabetes. He learned that he had a relative insulin deficiency and that his diabetes might be controlled by weight loss. He stated that if weight loss would help to control his diabetes he definitely wished to lose weight. He also said that he had wanted to lose weight for several years, but could not seem to bring it down more than 10 pounds. Every time he was able to lose weight he seemed to regain it within a few months. The clinician believed that the patient was sincere in his decision to lose weight.

*Step 2: Review the Difficulties of Losing Weight.* The patient was concerned that because he had not been able to lose weight in the past, he would not be successful this time. He stated that he usually grew tired of eating only salads and did not want to give up the "good foods" he enjoyed. He asked for a "diet pill" to help him. The clinician explained that the weight loss diet was not difficult to follow, but that it does require time to lose weight. The patient would not feel deprived of food, nor would there be many restrictions regarding the type of foods he could eat. The diet was a balanced, calorie-restricted diet. Further, the clinician emphasized that the patient had two goals: (1) to lose the weight, and (2) to change his eating habits permanently. A "diet pill" would not help him to permanently change his eating habits, and was not recommended.

*Step 3: Select Short-Term and Long-Term Goals.* The clinician stated that the recommended weight loss program would result in loss of 1.0 to 2.0 pound weight loss per week. As a result the patient should achieve his long-term goal of a 20-pound reduction in about 20 weeks, depending on his adherence and how his body adjusts to the diet. Once the patient began the diet phase of the program he agreed that he would follow the diet for 7 consecutive days prior to making any changes in the program.

*Step 4: Patient Keeps a Self-Record.* Prior to starting the diet, the patient agreed to the amount and type of food he ate during the next 5 days. He would return in 1 week for a follow-up visit.

*Second Visit*

*Step 5: Analyze the Patient's Eating Pattern.* The clinician reviewed with the patient the Daily Food Record the patient had collected over a 5-day period. It was clear from these records that the patient frequently ate high-calorie snacks mid-morning and occasionally mid-afternoon. In addition the patient typically consumed high-calorie lunches in the cafeteria at work. The patient was surprised how often he ate high-calorie snacks.

*Step 6: Select a Strategy to Counter the Problem Eating Pattern.* The patient decided to substitute low-calorie snacks for the high-calorie snacks at the office. He said that he could easily give up the pastry during the morning coffee break. If he found that he was hungry mid-morning, he would eat a banana. For an afternoon snack, he would purchase a low-calorie soft drink. If he was hungry in the mid-afternoon he would have an apple.

Through discussion with the clinician it was clear that the patient needed knowledge about serving sizes and the acceptable number of serving sizes to achieve weight loss. The clinician urged the patient to review in detail the discussion of these in the patient's materials. The clinician hoped that with more information the patient would be able to make more appropriate choices in the cafeteria at lunch.

*Step 7: Re-arrange the Food-Related Environment.* Because the patient's snacks were a source of a large number of calories, the clinician reviewed with the patient how he might also re-arrange his home environment to help with his weight loss program. The clinician discussed how to re-arrange the environment, and the patient agreed to use each of the strategies suggested in the Patient's Weight Loss Diet Program.

*Step 8: Select the Proper Weight Loss Diet.* The patient's initial weight was 183 pounds, 20 pounds over the upper range of the weight for his height using the Metropolitan Life Insurance Company Standards. The proper weight loss diet for this patient was Diet Plan II.

*Step 9: Select a Physical Fitness Program.* The clinician discussed the need for incorporating a modest physical fitness program into the Weight Loss Program. Because the patient was overweight and had little aerobic capacity, the clinician recommended that the patient follow a simple, brisk walking program, 20 minutes every other day. The brisk walking program would expend additional calories and could be easily incorporated into the patient's daily morning activities. Further, the patient said that he would not feel embarrassed by brisk walking. He confided that he had been discouraged from joining a formal exercise program because they usually started at a level that was too strenuous for him and required clothes that revealed his excess weight (e.g., gym shorts, T-shirt).

*Step 10: Select a Starting Date.* The patient determined that he would need 3 days to purchase the snack foods for his new program. He decided to begin the program on the fourth day after the present clinic session.

*Step 11: Implement the Weight Loss Program.* The patient agreed to continue on the Weight Loss Diet Program for 7 days. He stated that he realized that the program would cause some discomfort initially simply due to the changes required in his daily activities; however, he would not change the program during this initial period. To ensure that there would be no misunderstanding of what the patient was to do during the coming week, each activity was listed as a "behavioral prescription" (Figure 2).

*Step 12: Plan Follow-up.* The patient agreed to re-schedule a visit with the clinician on the eighth day following the start of his program. If, prior to this time, the patient felt he needed to change the program, or was having difficulty getting started, he agreed to contact the clinician by telephone.

### Third Visit

The patient returned to the clinic as scheduled. His weight loss program was proceeding well. He had no problems implementing each of the suggestions

**MICHAEL L. RUSSELL, Ph.D.**
Department of Internal Medicine
Baylor College of Medicine
Tel. 799-6032

**Program for Change**

For: *D. S.*                                    Date: *May 15, 1985*

1. *Prepare a variety of allowable snack foods.*

2. *Remove high calorie snack foods from home and office.*

3. *Follow The "Patient's Weight Loss Diet Program II. Begin on next monday (may 20).*

4. *Plan to walk briskly for 25 minutes every other day.*

Figure 2. Example of a written behavioral prescription for weight loss.

discussed in the last clinic visit. However, he reported that at times when he felt very stressed he would return to eating the high-calorie snack foods. The clinician decided that it would be best to approach this problem using the 11-step health behavior counseling process (see Table 7).

*Step 1: Identify the Problem.* The patient reported that beginning Thursday afternoons and continuing through Friday, he felt increasingly anxious. He associated this stress with the completion of the weekly report for his boss. He stated that as his anxiety increased, he found that he became hungry, and would eat the recommended snack, and then have a high-calorie food in addition (e.g., a chocolate milk shake).

*Step 2: Clarify Goals for Treatment.* The patient stated that he desired to lose weight but that he could not control his stress without eating. He agreed that if he could control the stress he would not need to eat at these times. The goal for treatment was to learn an alternative method to counter the stress in place of eating high-calorie snacks.

*Step 3: Collect Information.* After further discussion with the patient, the clinician decided that additional data collection was not necessary prior to implementing an intervention. However, the patient would begin to record those times when he felt particularly stressed (i.e., greater than 5 on a 10-point scale in which 1 = no anxiety, 10 = extreme anxiety).

*Step 4: Develop a Behavioral Diagnosis.*   The patient's eating of high-calorie snack foods appeared to be directly related to the stress the patient was experiencing. The food would reduce the feelings of stress and anxiety.

*Step 5: Generate an Intervention Plan.*   The clinician decided that the patient would benefit from learning deep muscle relaxation. If he could acquire this skill, he would be able to reduce the feelings of stress without eating. The patient was eager to learn this technique. The clinician gave the patient the self-instructions for achieving deep muscle relaxation, and instructed the patient to practice the technique once in the morning and once in the evening at his desk at the office.

*Step 6: Intervene.*   The patient was to follow the intervention program for 7 days. In 1 week, the patient was to re-contact the clinician by telephone to discuss the patient's progress.

## Telephone Call

The patient telephoned in 1 week, as planned.

*Step 7: Review the Patient's Progress.*   The patient reported that he was continuing to follow the Weight Loss Diet II as originally planned. In addition he felt that the deep muscle relaxation procedure was helping to control his anxiety. The patient also stated he was only practicing the technique once each day.

*Step 8: Generate a Revised Intervention.*   The program appeared to be effective as originally designed. The clinician did, however, strongly urge the patient to practice the deep muscle relaxation twice each day.

*Step 9: Re-intervene.*   The patient continued with the original program. He agreed to schedule a follow-up visit in 3 months to review his progress.

## Fourth Visit

The patient returned for a follow-up visit in 3 months. At that time he had lost 15 pounds and expressed confidence that he would reach his goal of 20 pounds.

*Steps 10 and 11: Develop a Maintenance Program and Review the Behavior Change Process.* The clinician congratulated the patient on his progress to date and agreed that the patient probably would achieve his goal. Therefore it was appropriate at this visit to review the dietary program that the patient would follow once he achieved his goal weight.

The clinician also reviewed with the patient the specific steps that the patient had followed in overcoming his problem eating patterns. These included (1) using the Daily Food Record to identify problem eating patterns, (2) having low-calorie snacks available at home and at the office, (3) choosing "best choices" from the lunches at the cafeteria, (4) using the deep muscle relaxation technique instead of eating when he felt stressed, and (5) following a regular program of brisk walking. The patient stated that he recognized these techniques as the most helpful to him, and would incorporate them into a future program he might need to maintain his ideal weight.

## References

1. National Center for Health Statistics: Obese and overweight adults in the United States. *National Health Survey*, series 11, no. 230, 1983.
2. Metropolitan Life Insurance Company: Metropolitan height and weight tables for men and women, 1983. *Stat Bull Metrop Life Found* 1983; 64:2.
3. Bray GA (ed): *Obesity in America*. Washington, DC, US Government Printing Office, 1979.
4. American Heart Association: *Your Mild Sodium-Restricted Diet: Weight Loss*. Dallas, American Heart Association, 1969.

# The Weight Loss Diet Program

**Excess Weight: What Is It?**

Excess weight is the result of your body's efforts to accommodate the extra calories you take in from the food you eat. Slowly over time you obtained more calories from the food you ate than your body used in your daily activities. Excess weight is really stored calories. The relation between the food you eat and the weight you gain can be seen in the Calorie Balance Equation:

$$\text{Calories eaten} - \text{Calories used} = \text{Calories stored}$$
$$\text{(from food)} \qquad \text{(in activity)} \qquad \text{(as fat)}$$

This equation is a biological law for everyone. It says that if you consume more calories than you use, the excess calories will be stored in your body as fat. If, however, you reduce the number of calories you consume below the number you expend each day in your daily activities, then your body will use up some of the calories that have been stored as fat.

Some people are surprised to learn that this relationship is as true today as it was yesterday and will be tomorrow. What is surprising to them is that excess weight is not something that "happened to them in the past," but, rather, is being maintained by their current eating habits. That's right. Their eating patterns today are supporting their excess weight.

The Weight Loss Diet Program is based on the fact that if you can learn to gain control of your eating habits, you can gain control of the Calorie Balance Equation to achieve and maintain the weight you desire. This is why the program is not a "diet" you use temporarily simply to lose weight. Rather, it is a program designed to put you in control of your eating habits. You gain new eating habits during the period of weight loss that you will continue with when you have achieved your goal weight.

Flexibility has been built into the Weight Loss Diet Program because it is designed to become a permanent part of your life. The program encourages

200

you to tailor your new eating habits to your lifestyle. It offers a wide variety of foods. In fact, there are few foods that must be avoided. Only those that are extremely high in calories have been excluded. Almost any food in appropriate amounts can be accommodated in the program diet. Similarly, there is no miracle food or combination of foods in the program. The diet is based on established nutritional principles that provide balanced meals with controlled caloric values so you can lose weight safely.

## Your Decision

The decision to begin a weight loss program is one that will offer you many benefits, including:

- feeling better about yourself
- clothes fitting better
- physical activities becoming easier
- feeling more alert
- feeling more relaxed
- potentially reducing your blood pressure

However, a weight loss program that is successful in helping you achieve and maintain a lower weight requires effort. You will need to make fundamental changes in your lifestyle. For most people, major changes in their daily routines are awkward, frustrating, and uncomfortable until they become habitual.

Your decision to lose weight and possibly experience the discomfort of a new daily routine is a good decision for you only if you are taking these steps because you care about yourself and your health. You are committing yourself to this program because you want to. Family members and friends can be very helpful to you, but it is your program to follow.

You may find that your commitment to the program will be tested severely during the weeks to come. You may find yourself in situations in which other people will attempt to persuade you to change your program or stop it altogether. You should prepare for this now.

*Step 1: Mention to Your Family and Friends with Whom You Eat That*
*You Will Be Starting the Weight Loss Diet Program and Will Be*
*Making Some Changes in Your Eating Patterns*

Alert your family and friends that you will be making some changes in your eating habits in the near future and prepare them for your refusal to continue with your old eating patterns. You might rehearse what you would say to refuse additional food or high-calorie snacks that do not fit in your program. You will

Summary checklist for the Weight Loss Diet Program

---

*Goal:* Your goal in the Weight Loss Diet Program is to achieve and maintain a weight loss of
_____ pounds from your current weight.

WEEK 1:

*Step* 1: Mention to your family and friends who you eat with that you will be starting the
weight loss program and you will be making some changes in your eating
patterns.

*Step* 2: Select a starting date for your weight loss program.

*Step* 3: Complete a Daily Food Record, starting with yesterday's meals, and continue for at
least 3 days.

*Step* 4: Prepare or purchase a variety of foods that are allowed in large quantities on your
weight loss diet.

*Step* 5: Remove high-calorie snack foods from your home and from your desk at the office.

WEEK 2:

*Step* 6: Select the appropriate level of the Weight Loss Diet Program.

*Step* 7: Distribute the number of servings you are allowed for each Food Group into the
morning, afternoon, and evening periods to suite your taste.

*Step* 8: Review your Daily Food Records to identify problem eating habits.

*Step* 9: Make a contract with yourself to achieve your goal of following the diet program.

*Step* 10: Record your progress in following the weight loss program each day.

---

find that in many public situations, you do not even need to explain that you
are on a weight loss program. Simply stating in a firm manner that you do not
want the food will be sufficient. An alternative strategy is to accept the food,
take a small bite, and then leave the rest on your plate.

## Gradual Changes

Losing weight gradually is not difficult, but it does require time. Just as your
excess weight was slowly acquired, your weight loss should be gradual but definite. You can change your eating habits without feeling deprived or going on
a diet of special foods. But you must do a little preparation.

The Weight Loss Diet Program helps you make these changes over a 2-week
period. Each week has a specific set of goals (see the summary checklist).

## Week 1: Preparing for the Program

Before you begin your new weight loss program you should make a few simple
preparations to make this change in your eating habits as easy as possible. Many
people fail in their efforts to change their eating habits because they were not
prepared before they began.

## Step 2: Select a Specific Starting Date for Your Program

Your new weight loss program may require you to make fundamental changes in your eating habits. You should plan carefully and be prepared for changing this part of your lifestyle.

You should pick a date within the next 7 days to begin your weight loss program. Choose a day that you know you will not be attending any social or business events involving food. Also allow a day or two to adequately prepare your environment for your new program. Once you have chosen a day, mark it on your calendar. The day you choose will mark the end of your old eating habits and the beginning of new ones, which you control.

## Step 3: Complete a 1-Week Food Record Starting with Yesterday's Meals and Continue for at Least 3 Days Until Your Starting Date

Most people do not pay much attention to their eating habits. This is because they are so well established in our daily routines that, except for individual choices, we do not think much about them. We eat breakfast, lunch, dinner, and sometimes snacks without much thought. More often than not, we are not aware of our eating patterns.

The time between today and your starting date is your opportunity to observe your typical eating habits and patterns. Do not try to change your eating habits this week; simply record them. Once you have clearly identified these patterns, you can begin to build a program to accommodate your preferences, eliminate undesirable habits, and achieve your weight goal.

In the example of a completed Daily Food Record for one day presented here, the person had eaten about 2,500 calories on that day. This is the number of calories required to maintain the weight of a 195-pound man or woman whose lifestyle usually includes little physical activity. Anyone weighing less than that who regularly consumes this number of calories will gain weight over time. Remember the Calorie Balance Equation! For example, if you weigh 165 pounds and this is a typical day for you, you will gain about 3 pounds over 1 month.

More important, however, is the pattern of eating that is evident from the Food Record. Are the calories appropriately distributed among the 7 food groups (i.e., Meats, Vegetables, Milk, Fruits, Breads, Fats, and Free Choice)? In this example it is clear that most of the calories are coming from meat dishes, deserts, and snacks. Few calories are coming from vegetables, fruits, and milk.

Is there a pattern of when the calories are consumed? In this example, most of the calories are consumed after the lunch meal. Almost 70% of the total calories are eaten in the afternoon and evening.

Your eating pattern will be unique to your lifestyle and tastes. In Week 2 of

DAILY FOOD RECORD

TODAY'S DATE: Monday, March 29, 1986

| Time Place Others | Hunger (1–10) | Food | Amount |
|---|---|---|---|
| 6:25 to 6:40 a.m. kitchen (alone) | 2 | wheat toast margarine jam orange juice coffee (black) | 2 slices 2 pats 1 tsp. 6 oz. 2 cups |
| 10:15 to 10:30 a.m. office (alone) | | coffee | 1 cup |
| 12:35 to 1:10 p.m. cafeteria (friend) | 5 | wheat bread mayonnaise tuna fish cheese (cheddar) diet drink | 2 slices 1 tbs. 3 ounces 1 ounce 12 ounces |
| 3:25 to 3:40 p.m. cafeteria (friend) | 3 | yogurt | 1 cup |
| 6:30 to 7:15 p.m. den (spouse) | 3 | gin & tonic unsalted nuts | 1½ oz. alcohol 1½ ounces |
| 7:20 to 7:45 p.m. kitchen (family) | 4 | 2 pork chops green beans baked potato roll margarine ice tea sugar ice cream | 6 ounces total ⅔ cup 1 medium 2 pats 10 ounces 1 tsp. 1 cup |

Example of a completed Daily Food Record.

the Weight Loss Diet Program, you will use your Daily Food Record to identify your current eating patterns.

*Step 4: Prepare or Purchase a Variety of Foods That Are Allowed in Large Quantities on Your Weight Loss Program*

Your current environment is supporting your current eating habits. The following changes will help to ease the adjustment to new eating habits by arranging your environment to support them rather than oppose them.

Place the following items in a convenient location, in a clear container (e.g., glass jar). In this way, when you want a snack, acceptable snack foods will be readily available. Some suggested snack foods are:

- unsalted popcorn (in plastic bags)
- unsalted potato chips (in plastic bags)
- melba toast
- carrot sticks
- small apples
- cucumber spears
- radishes

### Step 5: Remove High-calorie Snack Foods from Your Home and from Your Desk at the Office

If you currently eat high-calorie snacks, throw them out. The first few weeks of your program will be easier if you can avoid placing yourself in tempting situations. By not having these high-calorie foods around, you will not find yourself "debating" whether or not you should eat them.

If you feel that you must have high-calorie snacks available for other family members, remove them from their usual containers and place them in an unmarked, nontransparent container (e.g., plastic storage box). Place the container out of sight on a cupboard shelf that you do not use often. In this way you will not be seeing these foods repeatedly.

### Week 2: Starting the Program

### Step 6: Identify the Proper Weight Loss Diet for You

*Servings.* The Weight Loss Diet Program is based on your controlling the number of servings of different foods you eat each day. You are allowed a certain number of servings from each of the 7 Food Groups for each day's meals, depending on your current weight. A serving is an easy way to remember your diet without having to count calories. You simply record how many servings you eat at each meal.

The amount of food equal to one serving is easy to remember. The amount of food in one serving in each Food Group is accurate for most foods in the group. However, there are a few exceptions which you should know. See the List of Specific Foods by Serving Sizes on p. 210.

*The Weight Loss Diet.* Notice that the program limits the total number of servings you eat in each Food Group each *day*, not each meal. As a result, you control the number of servings you have at each meal so long as you follow two simple rules:

1. Do not exceed the total number of servings you are allowed each day from each Food Group. The number of servings you are allowed in each Food Group has been carefully determined according to your current weight.
2. Eat at least one serving of meat, one serving of bread, and one serving of fruit at each meal. The Weight Loss Diet Program is based on balanced meals to ensure proper nutrition. Eating three balanced meals also reduces between-meal hunger.

Your current weight determines which of the three levels of the diet is correct for you:

> If you weigh 100–139 pounds, use: Level I
> If you weigh 140–200 pounds, use: Level II
> If you weigh over 200 pounds, use: Level III

Each level specifies the number of servings you are allowed from each of the 7 Food Groups. In this way you can readily keep track of the number of servings you have had and shift servings from one meal to another as needed.

You should follow only the diet program recommended for your current weight. It has been designed to help you lose weight at a rate of about 1 pound a week. It will provide you with a balanced diet and sufficient calories to maintain your usual level of daily activity. It is important that your weight loss be gradual. The program provides enough time for your new eating habits to become permanent and for your new, lower weight to become firmly established.

### Step 7: Distribute the Number of Servings You Are Allowed from Each Food Group into the Morning, Afternoon, and Evening Periods, to Suit Your Taste

Notice that the number of servings from each Food Group marked Morning, Noon, or Night. These are recommendations based on most people's preferences. You may wish to modify the number of servings at each meal to suit your taste. However, the total number of servings from each Food Group must *not* exceed the number listed. For example, if you know that you always eat more servings of Bread and Meat in the evening and fewer servings in the afternoon than are listed on the chart, you can move the appropriate number of servings from the Afternoon total to the Evening total. Or, if on a particular day you do not happen to eat the full number of servings of Bread reserved for the Morning, you can save them to eat later in the day.

The servings have been divided among the Morning, Afternoon, and Evening. Some people enjoy a substantial snack in the midmorning, midafternoon, or late evening. Snacking is acceptable on the Weight Loss Diet Program, but you must set aside the proper number of servings for your snack. For

The Weight Loss Diet Program: 3 levels

LEVEL I (1,235 calories)
(weight: less than 140 pounds)

| Food group | Daily servings | Suggested distribution | | |
|---|---|---|---|---|
| | | Morning | Afternoon | Evening |
| Milk (skim) | 2 | 1 | 1 | 0 |
| Vegetable (at least one each from groups A, B, and C)* | 3 | 0 | 1 | 2 |
| Fruit | 4 | 1 | 1 | 2 |
| Bread | 5 | 1 | 2 | 2 |
| Meat | 5 | 1 | 1 | 3 |
| Fat | None | | | |
| Free Choice | 1 | 1 | 0 | 0 |

LEVEL II (1,800 calories)
(weight: 140–199 pounds)

| Food group | Daily servings | Suggested distribution | | |
|---|---|---|---|---|
| | | Morning | Afternoon | Evening |
| Milk | 2 | 1 | 1 | 0 |
| Vegetable (at least one each from groups A, B, and C)* | 3 | 0 | 1 | 2 |
| Fruit | 4 | 1 | 1 | 2 |
| Bread | 7 | 2 | 2 | 3 |
| Meat | 5 | 1 | 1 | 3 |
| Fat | 4 | 1 | 1 | 2 |
| Free Choice | 2 | 0 | 1 | 1 |

LEVEL III (3,000 calories)
(weight: over 200 pounds)

| Food group | Daily serving | Suggested distribution | | |
|---|---|---|---|---|
| | | Morning | Afternoon | Evening |
| Milk | 4 | 1 | 1 | 2 |
| Vegetable (at least one each from groups A, B, and C)* | 6 | 0 | 3 | 3 |
| Fruit | 8 | 2 | 2 | 4 |
| Bread | 10 | 2 | 4 | 4 |
| Meat | 10 | 2 | 2 | 6 |
| Fat | 4 | 1 | 1 | 2 |
| Free Choice | 2 | 0 | 1 | 1 |

* See List of Specific Foods by Serving Sizes, p. 210.

example, if you would like to have an apple and some cheese as an afternoon snack, simply set aside one fruit serving and one milk serving from your daily total.

By recording the number of servings you eat at each meal, you can keep track of the total number of servings you have had in each Food Group and shift servings from one meal to another as needed. But remember, you can only shift servings *within* a single day, not from one day to the next.

### Step 8: Review Your Daily Food Records
### to Identify Problem Eating Habits

Before you begin your Weight Loss Diet Program, use the following steps to review your Daily Food Records. Determine if you currently have a problem eating pattern.

1. Identify the Food Group for each item you recorded. Mark the Food Group in the "Food Group" column in the Daily Food Record.
2. Using the List of Specific Foods by Serving Size determine how many servings from each Food Group you ate at each meal. Mark the number of servings by each item in the column labeled "Servings" in the Daily Food Record.
3. Place all of the Daily Food Records side by side on a table and compare the number of servings you ate from each Food Group for Breakfast each day. For example, if you kept Daily Food Records for 5 days, compare the number of servings you had at each meal on each of the 5 days:

- Are the number of servings in each of the Food Groups different for each day?
- Did you tend to eat larger meals when you were with friends or family?
- Did you have 2 or more snacks during the day?
- Did you spend less than 15 minutes eating any of your meals?

If you answered YES to any of these questions you may have an eating pattern that will interfere with your weight loss program. You should discuss your eating habits with your clinician. There are specific techniques for resolving these difficulties.

### Step 9: Make a Contract with Yourself to Achieve Your Goal of
### Following the Weight Loss Diet Program

Right now you may be saying to yourself, "I don't see any problems with this new program. It should be easy for me since I really want to lose weight." Fine. Unfortunately, many well-intentioned people have needed more than just the

A PERSONAL CONTRACT

Activity: *Following the Weight Loss Diet Program II*

Level of Performance: *I will not exceed the allowable number of servings in each Food Group.*

Consequences

If I follow the routine for *7 days* as outlined above, then I will provide myself with the small reward of:

*Going to the museum on Saturday afternoon*

As further encouragement to follow the routine, if I do not do so, then I promise to: *Donate $5.00 to the Republican Party.*

In addition, *my friend Sue* has agreed to help me by doing the following: *Holding my check for $5.00 to mail if I am not successful*

*Johnson*
Signature

*April 5, 1985*
Date

Example of a completed Self-Contract.

desire to change their eating habits. They have found that their decision to lose weight wasn't enough to get them through the tough times when they were tempted to return to their old eating habits.

Many patients have discovered that a helpful tool to get them started during the first few weeks is a Self-Contract. A Self-Contract is simply a written agreement with yourself that you will follow your weight loss program as outlined herein. When you do follow the program for a certain number of consecutive days (e.g., 5 days in a row), you can indulge yourself a little: Following the program earns you something that you personally enjoy. It need not be costly or complicated, simply something you enjoy but rarely take the time for. You can select almost anything you enjoy. Except food. Examples might be:

- going to a movie
- reading a book
- visiting a friend

- going to the zoo
- calling a friend who lives out of town
- browsing in a favorite store
- taking a long, hot bath

The Self-Contract is designed to help you through those days when it seems very difficult to stay with the program. But, if you miss a day, don't give up. Immediately review your day. What happened to prevent you from reaching your goal? How can you rearrange your environment so that will not happen again?

Remember, the Self-Contract concerns only the total number of days *in a row* that you follow the diet program. So, you can begin again the next day— but with a difference. Now you have changed your environment to avoid or eliminate the problem.

*Step 10: Record Your Progress in Following*
*the Weight Loss Diet Program*

The Weight Loss Diet Program is designed to enable you to lose approximately 1 pound each week. It is important that you not lose weight faster than that so you can adapt to your new eating habits.

Your progress in the program, however, should not be measured only by weight loss. Although that is the ultimate goal of the program, you cannot control your weight. You *can* control what you eat. Your progress should be examined in terms of how well you are able to follow the diet program. Your goal is to fol-low the diet program every day.

It is helpful to record each day whether or not you followed the program. In this way, you can measure your progress and identify days of the week that are routinely difficult for you. You will be able to follow your successes also.

List of specific foods by serving size within the 7 food groups

---

*Note:* Each individual item listed is equal to one serving.

WHOLE MILK (170 calories)

| | |
|---|---|
| Whole milk | 1 cup |
| Whole buttermilk | 1 cup |
| Whole milk (evaporated) | 1 cup |
| Nonfat milk (from powder) | 1 cup (plus 2 fat servings) |
| Nonfat buttermilk | 1 cup (plus 2 fat servings) |
| Skim milk | 1 cup (plus 2 fat servings) |
| Yogurt (plain) | ¾ cup |
| Ice milk | ⅓ cup |

SKIM MILK (85 calories)

| | |
|---|---|
| Nonfat milk (from powder) | 1 cup |
| Nonfat buttermilk | 1 cup |
| Skim milk | 1 cup |

VEGETABLES
*Group A (negligible calories)*

½ cup of any of the following:

| | |
|---|---|
| Asparagus | Lettuce |
| Broccoli | Mushrooms |
| Brussels sprouts | Okra |
| Cabbage | Peppers, red or green |
| Cauliflower | Radishes |
| Chicory | Squash, summer (yellow, zucchini, etc.) |
| Cucumber | Tomato juice (low-sodium) |
| Eggplant | Tomatoes |
| Endive | Turnip greens |
| Escarole | Wax beans |
| Green beans | |

*Group B (35 calories)*

½ cup of any of the following:
Onions
Peas (fresh or low-sodium, canned)
Pumpkin
Rutabaga (yellow turnip)
Squash, winter (acorn, Hubbard, etc.)

*Group C (70 calories)*

| | |
|---|---|
| Beans, lima or navy (fresh or dried) | ½ cup cooked |
| Beans, baked (no pork) | ¼ cup |
| Corn | ⅓ cup or 1 small ear |
| Parsnips | ⅔ cup |
| Peas (split, green or yellow, cowpeas, etc.) | ½ cup cooked |
| Potato, white | 1 small |
| Potato, mashed | ½ cup |
| Sweet potato | ¼ cup or ½ small |

FRUITS (40 calories)

| | |
|---|---|
| Apple | 1 small |
| Apple sauce | ½ cup |
| Apricots (dried) | 4 halves |
| Apricots (fresh) | 2 medium |
| Banana | ½ small |
| Cherries | 10 large |
| Dates | 2 |
| Fig | 1 medium |
| Fruit cup or mixed fruit | ½ cup |
| Grapefruit | ½ small |
| Grapes | 12 |
| Mango | ½ small |
| Orange | 1 small |
| Papaya | ⅓ medium |
| Peach | 1 medium |

List of specific foods by serving size within the 7 food groups (*continued*)

*Note:* Each individual item listed is equal to one serving.

| | |
|---|---|
| Pear | 1 small |
| Pineapple | ½ cup diced or 2 spears |
| Plums | 2 medium |
| Prunes | 2 medium |
| Raisins | 2 tablespoons |
| Rhubarb (sweetened) | 2 tablespoons |
| Tangerine | 1 large |

*Juices*

| | |
|---|---|
| Apple juice or cider | ⅓ cup |
| Apricot nectar | ¼ cup |
| Cranberry juice (sweetened) | ⅓ cup |
| Grapefruit juice | ½ cup |
| Grape juice | ¼ cup |
| Orange juice | ½ cup |
| Pineapple juice | ⅓ cup |
| Prune juice | ¼ cup |
| Tangerine juice | ½ cup |

*Berries*

| | |
|---|---|
| Blackberries | 1 cup |
| Blueberries | ⅔ cup |
| Cranberries | 1 tablespoon |
| Raspberries | 1 cup |
| Strawberries | 1 cup |

*Melons*

| | |
|---|---|
| Cantaloupe | ¼ small |
| Honeydew melon | ⅛ medium |
| Watermelon | ½ cup |

*Note:* Fresh lemons and limes may be used as desired. Unsweetened cranberries and cranberry juice and unsweetened rhubarb may also be used as desired.

BREADS (70 calories)
*Breads & Rolls*

| | |
|---|---|
| Bread (any type) | 1 slice |
| Cornbread | 1 piece (3″ × 3″) |
| Biscuit | 1 medium |
| Muffin | 1 medium |
| Roll | 1 medium |

*Crackers*

| | |
|---|---|
| Melba toast | 4 pieces |
| Unsalted crackers | 5 (2″ × 2″ square) |
| Graham crackers | 2 |

*Cereals (dry)*

| | |
|---|---|
| Any dry cereal | ¾ cup |
| Shredded wheat | ⅔ biscuit |

*Cereals (cooked)*

| | |
|---|---|
| Any | ½ cup |

*Pasta*

Any (e.g., spaghetti, noodles)                    ½ cup

*Rice*

Any                                               ½ cup

*Ingredients in Baked Goods*

Barley                                            1½ tablespoons (uncooked)
Cornmeal                                          2 tablespoons
Cornstarch                                        2½ tablespoons
Flour                                             2½ tablespoons
Tapioca                                           2 tablespoons

*Miscellaneous*

Griddle cakes                                     2 (3″)
Matzo                                             1 (5″ × 5″)
Popcorn (unsalted)                                1½ cups
Waffles                                           1 (3″ × 3″)

MEATS (75 calories)
*Meat or Poultry*                                 1 ounce, cooked
Any *except* smoked salted or koshered meats such as:
bacon
bologna
chipped beef
corned beef
frankfurters
ham
luncheon meats
salt pork
sausage
smoked tongue

*Note:* 4 ounces of raw meat, boned, equals 3 ounces of cooked meat.
     5 ounces of raw meat with bone equals 3 ounces of cooked meat.

Typically, a 3-ounce serving equals:
1 pork chop
2 lamb chops (rib)
1 leg and 1 thigh of chicken
½ breast of chicken
2 meat patties (2″ thick, 2″ diameter)
2 thin slices of roast meat (3″ × 3″)

*Fish*

Whole or fillet                                   1 ounce, cooked
Any *except* salted or smoked fish, such as:
anchovies
caviar
salted and dried cod
herring
smoked oysters
sardines

*Cheese*

Any unprocessed, hard cheese                      1 ounce
Unsalted cottage cheese                           ¼ cup

List of specific foods by serving size within the 7 food groups (*continued*)

*Note:* Each individual item listed is equal to one serving.

*Miscellaneous*

| | |
|---|---|
| Egg | 1 |
| Peanut butter (low-sodium) | 2 tablespoons |

FAT (45 calories)

| | |
|---|---|
| Avocado | ⅛ of 4″ avocado |
| Butter | 1 teaspoon |
| Cream, heavy (sweet or sour) | 1 tablespoon |
| Cream, light (sweet or sour) | 2 tablespoons |
| Fat or oil for cooking | 1 teaspoon |
| French dressing | 1 tablespoon |
| Margarine | 1 teaspoon |
| Mayonnaise | 1 teaspoon |
| Nuts, unsalted | 6 small |

FREE CHOICE (75 calories)

| | |
|---|---|
| Bread (any item on list) | 1 serving |
| Candy | 1 piece fudge |
| | or, 4 pieces hard candy |
| | or, 2 large gumdrops |
| | or, 3 marshmallows |
| | or, 10 jelly beans |
| Fat (any item on list) | 2 servings |
| Fruit (any item on list) | 2 servings |
| Sugar | 4 teaspoons |
| Syrup, honey, jelly, jam, marmalade | 4 teaspoons |
| Vegetable (any item on list) | 1 serving |
| Wine, any | 1 glass (3 oz.) |

# 9. Physical Activity

Epidemiological studies have repeatedly identified an association between a sedentary lifestyle and an increase in incidence of cardiovascular disease. Individuals who engage in routine physical activity, either at work or during leisure time, experience less disease and have an increased likelihood of survival if disease does occur.

The investigators of the Framingham Study[1] reported that of a group of 207 men who were followed for 10 years, individuals who were more active physically had a lower rate of cardiovascular disease as compared with men who were sedentary. In a 22-year study of 3,686 longshoremen, researchers reported a strong association between low energy expenditure in physical exercise and the risk of fatal heart attack.[2] Those workers who engaged in duties requiring vigorous physical activity had a reduced risk of fatal heart attack. Similarly, in a study of bus conductors and drivers in London, the conductors, who walked up and down the aisles of the bus collecting fares, had 30% less heart disease than did the drivers.[3]

Studies of athletes have offered some support for the suggestion that the reduced incidence of cardiovascular disease associated with physical activity is not due simply to their superior athletic ability. Individuals who participated in athletics in college and abandoned their sport after leaving college were at increased risk of cardiovascular disease later in life from cigarette smoking, overweight, and alcohol use. In contrast, a study of Finnish ski champions reported that, on the average, they enjoyed a 4- to 5-year increase in lifespan, compared with the rest of the population.[4] This suggests that individuals who continue to exercise and maintain a lean body weight are at lower risk of cardiovascular disease, regardless of their natural athletic abilities.

Unfortunately neither these studies nor any other published study has proven that participating in regular vigorous physical activity reduces the chances of cardiovascular disease. All of these studies simply indicate that there is a strong correlation between the two. A possible explanation is that it is people who are healthier to start with who participate in physical fitness programs. It is their naturally healthier status that reduces their chance of heart attack, not their physical activities.

However, a high degree of physical fitness is not only associated with a reduced chance of cardiovascular disease; it also appears to have other benefits. Participation in regular physical activities contributes to weight loss by expending calories and often suppressing appetite. Weight loss is highly recommended in the management of high blood pressure and diabetes. Regular exercise seems to help in the treatment of sleep disorders and stress, and in cigarette smoking cessation programs. A regular physical fitness program also seems to promote feelings of well-being, and has even been reported to be a useful adjunct in therapy for depression.

Given the desirability of regular physical activity, it is unfortunate that 51% of Americans 20 years of age and over report that they do not engage in regular exercise.[5] Further, more than one-third of these nonexercising individuals mistakenly believe that they are more active than other people in their age group.

In sum, although there appears to be a strong association between regular, vigorous physical activity and reduced incidence of cardiovascular disease, causation has not been proven. Research studies have not been able to separate the effects of self-selection (by the exercise participants) from the effects of the physical exercise itself. However, physical activity also appears to have a beneficial effect on other important aspects of the patient's medical and psychological status. Clinicians must weigh the results of current research studies and assess their applicability for individual patients. Then, if they do recommend increased physical fitness programs for patients, they must face the challenge of helping them achieve and maintain the desired levels of physical activity.

## Exercising for Physical Fitness

The amount of physical activity prescribed for an individual patient will vary depending upon the patient's current cardiovascular fitness and medical status. Before a specific program of physical exercise for any patient over 35 years of age is recommended, the patient should undergo a physical examination and possibly a graded exercise tolerance test.

If there are no contraindications to exercise, the clinician should prescribe the level of physical activity recommended by both the American Heart Association and the National Heart, Lung, and Blood Institute, that is, regular exercise of moderate intensity (50 to 75% of capacity) performed 15 to 30 minutes every other day. It is perhaps surprising that this relatively small percentage of the patient's time would yield such great benefits, but the body has a tremendous capacity to adapt to the increased physiological demands placed on it.

In response to increased physical exercise, the body attempts to maintain physiological homeostasis. Initially, a temporary disruption in the homeostatic balance results in an immediate attempt to return the system to balance. The major determinant of the balance within the cardiovascular system is the amount of oxygen available at the cellular level. For example, if a patient attempts a demanding physical activity, such as rapidly walking up three flights of stairs, the cardiovascular system responds to the increased demands for energy from the leg muscles by increasing the amount of oxygen transported to them. Because an increase in oxygen transport is most easily accomplished by an increase in cardiac output, the stair climbing results in a transitory increase in heart rate and respiration. Such infrequent, transitory, increased energy demands are accommodated by a shift toward the system's maximum output. As the homostatic balance of oxygen returns, the cardiovascular system returns to its pre-work level of output.

However, if the increased demands on the cardiovascular system occur repeatedly, another, quite different accommodation process occurs. In addition to responding to the immediate demand of the increased work load, the cardiovascular system slowly begins to adapt and reset its homeostatic balance point. When a patient starts a steady physical fitness program, significant changes occur in his cardiovascular system that enable him to perform more easily physical activities that previously required more effort. Following these changes, a climb of three flights of stairs is less demanding on the patient. The patient has accommodated, physiologically, to an increased level of work.

A progressive physical fitness program can effectively influence the cardiovascular system's capacity for work by modifying two factors: (1) the ability of the cardiovascular system to transport oxygen to the muscles, and (2) the ability of muscle tissue to use the oxygen provided. These factors are the major limits to the body's capacity to sustain physical activity. Therefore, an improvement in either factor (or both) will significantly improve the cardiovascular system's ability to respond to extraordinary demands.

The ability of the cardiovascular system to transport oxygen to the muscles is improved by the heart's increased stroke volume (as compared with its stroke volume before the exercise program). The heart is strengthened and pumps more blood during each stroke. As a result, at any given heart rate, the heart is pumping more oxygen-carrying blood to the muscle tissues. Therefore, when extra demand is placed on the cardiovascular system to perform a strenuous task, the system has a greater capacity to respond.

A progressive physical fitness program also results in more oxygen being removed from the blood by muscle tissue. The differential oxygen content between arterial blood and venous blood can improve by 8% or more. Although the exact mechanism for this increased differential is not known, it is suspected that the improvement is related to an enhanced ability of the mitochondria in the muscle cells to use the oxygen that is delivered to them.

It is important to note that this physiological accommodation occurs as a result of frequent, mild-to-moderate physical exertion. The fitness program need not, and indeed should not, be daily strenuous exertion. Rather, functional conditioning of the cardiovascular system is better accomplished by three sessions of exercise per week, each 30 to 40 minutes long, during which the heart rate remains within a range of 65 to 75% of the maximum rate for the individual's age. Maintaining this modest level of physical activity initiates the cardiovascular systems accommodation, yet does not demand too much effort or discomfort for the patient. The patient can be assured that the effort expended during the first week of the program should be the maximum effort demanded at any time.

The accommodation by the cardiovascular system to increased work continues until an individual's physiological limit, determined by heredity, is reached. At that point, the individual's heart rate cannot increase in response to a greater work load, no matter how long the individual performs at that level. Beyond this plateau, the only improvement will be an increase in the amount of time that the individual can function at that work load. In practical terms, the degree of physical fitness discussed in this chapter (and recommended for most patients) will not bring them close to their physiological limits.

### Selecting a Physical Activity

Although physical fitness is a combination of strength, flexibility, aerobic capacity, and endurance, it is important to remember that it is increased aerobic capacity that has been associated with a reduction in risk of cardiovascular disease and with other medical benefits. Therefore, the goal of the physical activity program is to improve the functioning of the cardiovascular system. The patient should be encouraged to select aerobic activities for the physical fitness program.

Aerobic activities are characterized as rhythmic, vigorous, and capable of being sustained for 30 to 40 minutes (Table 1). The patient is not limited only to the aerobic activities listed in Table 1, however. Any activity that elevates and sustains the patient's heart rate within the target heart rate range can be selected.

The target heart rate range is the level at which the individual is using the optimum amount of oxygen. It is approximately 65 to 75% of the patient's maximum obtainable heart rate. The patient's target heart rate range can be estimated by taking 65 to 75% of the difference between 220 and the patient's age. For example, the target heart rate range for a 42-year-old patient is 65 to 75% of (220 − 42), or 116 to 133 beats per minute (which is equivalent to 29 to 33 beats per 15 seconds). Alternatively, the patient's target heart rate range can be identified using Table 2.

Table 1. Examples of aerobic and nonaerobic activities *

| Aerobic | Nonaerobic |
| --- | --- |
| Walking | Baseball |
| Jogging | Bowling |
| Bicycling | Golf |
| Hiking (up hill) | Volleyball |
| Swimming | Football |
| Stationary cycling | Tennis |
| Skating | Sailing |
| Cross-country skiing | House or garden work |
| Jumping rope | Lifting weights |
| Aerobic dance | Surfing |
| Basketball | Shopping |
| Soccer | Horseback riding |
| Kyaking, rowing, or canoeing | Water skiing |
| Ice hockey | Hunting or fishing |
| Calisthenics | Motorcycle trail riding |

* An aerobic activity requires repetitive, rhythmic motion and is capable
of raising and maintaining the heart rate at the target heart rate level for 30
minutes. An activity is considered nonaerobic if it fails either to raise the
patient's heart rate to the target heart rate value or to maintain it at that
level for 30 minutes.

Using the target heart rate range, a progressive physical fitness program can
be constructed from any one or a combination of aerobic activities. The program should be tailored to the patient's current fitness level and then gradually
increase the aerobic demand while monitoring the patient's heart rate. Examples of progressive physical fitness programs are given in Table 3.

Table 2. Table of target heart rate ranges

| Age (years) | Target heart rate range, per minute (65–75% of maximum) | Target heart rate range, per 15 seconds (60–75% of maximum) |
| --- | --- | --- |
| 20 | 130–150 beats | 32–37 beats |
| 25 | 127–146 beats | 32–37 beats |
| 30 | 124–143 beats | 31–36 beats |
| 35 | 120–139 beats | 30–35 beats |
| 40 | 117–135 beats | 29–34 beats |
| 45 | 114–131 beats | 28–33 beats |
| 50 | 111–128 beats | 28–32 beats |
| 55 | 107–124 beats | 27–31 beats |
| 60 | 104–120 beats | 26–30 beats |
| 65 | 101–116 beats | 25–29 beats |
| 70 | 98–113 beats | 24–28 beats |

Table 3. Two sample progressive physical fitness programs*

| | Warm-up | Target heart rate range exercising | Cool-down | Total time |
|---|---|---|---|---|
| **Walking program** | | | | |
| **Week 1** | | | | |
| Session A | Walk slowly 5 min | Then walk briskly 5 min | Then walk slowly 5 min | 15 min |
| Session B | Repeat above pattern | | | |
| Session C | Repeat above pattern | | | |

*Continue with at least three exercises during each week of the program:*

| | | | | |
|---|---|---|---|---|
| Week 2 | Walk slowly 5 min | Walk briskly 7 min | Walk slowly 5 min | 17 min |
| Week 3 | Walk slowly 5 min | Walk briskly 9 min | Walk slowly 5 min | 19 min |
| Week 4 | Walk slowly 5 min | Walk briskly 11 min | Walk slowly 5 min | 21 min |
| Week 5 | Walk slowly 5 min | Walk briskly 13 min | Walk slowly 5 min | 23 min |
| Week 6 | Walk slowly 5 min | Walk briskly 15 min | Walk slowly 5 min | 25 min |
| Week 7 | Walk slowly 5 min | Walk briskly 18 min | Walk slowly 5 min | 28 min |
| Week 8 | Walk slowly 5 min | Walk briskly 20 min | Walk slowly 5 min | 30 min |
| Week 9 | Walk slowly 5 min | Walk briskly 23 min | Walk slowly 5 min | 33 min |
| Week 10 | Walk slowly 5 min | Walk briskly 26 min | Walk slowly 5 min | 36 min |
| Week 11 | Walk slowly 5 min | Walk briskly 28 min | Walk slowly 5 min | 38 min |
| Week 12 | Walk slowly 5 min | Walk briskly 30 min | Walk slowly 5 min | 40 min |

Week 13 on:
Check your pulse periodically to see if you are exercising within your target heart rate range. As you get more in shape, try exercising within the upper range of your target heart rate range. Remember that your goal is to continue getting the benefits you are seeking and to enjoy your activity.

| | | | | |
|---|---|---|---|---|
| **Walking/Jogging program** | | | | |
| **Week 1** | | | | |
| Session A | Stretch and limber up for 5 min | Then walk 10 min (Try not to stop) | Then walk slowly 3 min and stretch 2 min | 20 min |
| Session B | Repeat above pattern | | | |
| Session C | Repeat above pattern | | | |

*Continue with at least three exercise sessions during each week of the program:*

| | | | | |
|---|---|---|---|---|
| Week 2 | Stretch and limber 5 min | Walk 5 min/jog 1 min/ walk 5 min/jog 1 min | Walk slowly 3 min/ stretch 2 min | 22 min |
| Week 3 | Stretch and limber 5 min | Walk 5 min/jog 3 min/ walk 5 min/jog 3 min | Walk slowly 3 min/ stretch 2 min | 26 min |
| Week 4 | Stretch and limber 5 min | Walk 4 min/jog 5 min/ walk 4 min/jog 5 min | Walk slowly 3 min/ stretch 2 min | 28 min |

| | Warm-up | Target heart rate range exercising | Cool-down | Total time |
|---|---|---|---|---|
| Week 5 | Stretch and limber 5 min | Walk 4 min/jog 5 min/ walk 4 min/jog 5 min | Walk slowly 3 min/ stretch 2 min | 28 min |
| Week 6 | Stretch and limber 5 min | Walk 4 min/jog 6 min/ walk 4 min/jog 6 min | Walk slowly 3 min/ stretch 2 min | 30 min |
| Week 7 | Stretch and limber 5 min | Walk 4 min/jog 7 min/ walk 4 min/jog 7 min | Walk slowly 3 min/ stretch 2 min | 32 min |
| Week 8 | Stretch and limber 5 min | Walk 4 min/jog 8 min/ walk 4 min/jog 8 min | Walk slowly 3 min/ stretch 2 min | 34 min |
| Week 9 | Stretch and limber 5 min | Walk 4 min/jog 9 min/ walk 4 min/jog 9 min | Walk slowly 3 min/ stretch 2 min | 36 min |
| Week 10 | Stretch and limber 5 min | Walk 4 min/jog 13 min | Walk slowly 3 min/ stretch 2 min | 27 min |
| Week 11 | Stretch and limber 5 min | Walk 4 min/jog 15 min | Walk slowly 3 min/ stretch 2 min | 29 min |
| Week 12 | Stretch and limber 5 min | Walk 4 min/jog 17 min | Walk slowly 3 min/ stretch 2 min | 31 min |
| Week 13 | Stretch and limber 5 min | Walk 2 min/jog slowly 2 min/jog 17 min | Walk slowly 3 min/ stetch 2 min | 31 min |
| Week 14 | Stretch and limber 5 min | Walk 1 min/jog slowly 3 min/jog 17 min | Walk slowly 3 min/ stretch 2 min | 31 min |
| Week 15 | Stretch and limber 5 min | Jog slowly 3 min/ jog 17 min | Walk slowly 3 min/ stretch 2 min | 30 min |

Week 16 on:
Check your pulse periodically to see if you are exercising within your target heart rate range. As you become more fit, try exercising within the upper range of your target heart rate range. Remember that your goal is to continue getting the benefits you are seeking and to enjoy your activity.

*From *Exercise and Your Heart*. Office of Prevention, Education and Control, National Heart, Lung, and Blood Institute. NIH publication No. 81-1677, May 1981.

## The Physical Fitness Program

When encouraged to start a physical fitness program, most patients will require only information and guidelines about how to do it. However, the clinician can be extremely helpful to the patient if, in recommending a physical activity program, the following five steps are taken.

### Step 1: Explain the Benefits of Physical Activity

First, the clinician should identify the anticipated benefits of increased physical fitness. The explanation should be brief and relate primarily to the patient's own medical and physical status. For example, a patient with hypertension might be told, "Many people with hypertension are able to reduce their high blood pressure through weight loss, reduction of sodium intake, and a modest physical fitness program. If your blood pressure drops, we might be able to reduce the amount of your medication. However, we cannot be sure, and we will not know until you have made these changes and maintained them over time. I would strongly recommend that you adopt a program that includes vigorous, rhythmic physical activity three times each week for 30 to 40 minutes. I would be glad to help you design such a program, if you wish . . ."

### Step 2: Select an Aerobic Activity

The patient should be provided with instruction about aerobic activities. Several publications are available to help the patient do so.

### Step 3: Identify Target Heart Rate

The patient should be educated about the importance of reaching and maintaining a pulse rate within the target heart rate range. The clinician should calculate this value for the patient (using the formula or Table 2).

### Step 4: Measure Pulse Rate

The patient should be taught how to find and measure his own pulse rate. Some patients find the carotid pulse most easily, others the radial pulse. The clinician should take the patient's pulse at the same time the patient does and verify that the patient is using the correct procedure. It is important that the clinician spend the few minutes necessary to do this with the patient because it emphasizes the importance of monitoring the pulse rate and ensures that the patient can find the pulse and accurately calculate the pulse rate.

### Step 5: Offer Suggestions as to How to Get Started

The clinician might offer suggestions that have proven helpful to other patients making a major change in lifestyle. A list of suggestions for starting and maintaining a physical fitness program are contained in Table 4.

### Step 6: Follow-up

The final step is maintaining a follow-up program over time. The program should include activities that are interesting to the patient and potentially helpful. The clinician should be aware, however, that often the follow-up program will fail and the patient will require more counseling.

Table 4. Getting started, keeping going: Guidelines for patients*

*To get started:*
1. Carefully select the three times for your physical fitness program.
2. Consider your physical fitness session an "appointment" with yourself.
3. Place your clothes and equipment together so you know where they are.
4. Alert your friends and family about the times you have scheduled for your fitness sessions.
5. Do not begin some other activity just before a fitness session unless you know you can finish it in time to begin exercising.
6. If you need a reminder, set an alarm.
7. If you find yourself considering skipping a session, make yourself a "fair deal" by waiting until after you have started the activity before you make your decision.
8. Remember that you will usually feel better after the fitness session, regardless of how you feel beforehand.

*To keep going:*
1. Have an alternative activity chosen for the times when you cannot follow your preferred routine.
2. Put variety into your fitness activities.
3. Explore ways of prolonging and enhancing the pleasant feelings of relaxation and freedom that come with exercising regularly.
4. Talk with other people who are participating in a regular fitness program to get ideas.
5. Consider exercising with a friend.
6. Consider joining a group or class.
7. Consider an organized swim, ride, or run with people at the YMCA or bicycle club.
8. If you have been ill or injured and have stopped your program, restart your regular routine of three 30–40 minute sessions each week as soon as possible, but start slowly.
9. Adjust your program as you progress, but don't strain.

*From Russell ML: *Getting Started, Keeping Going.* Houston, The LIFE/Heart Program.

## The Behavioral Pattern Accompanying a Physical Fitness Program

When patients fail to establish a routine physical fitness program, it is almost always because of the difficulty of changing their lifestyle as the program requires, not of the physical activity itself. From the perspective of changing behavior, a progressive physical activity program has a fundamentally different scheme from the other health programs discussed in this book (Table 5). Once established, the physical activity program, if properly designed, provided immediate positive consequences for the patient, as well as long-term benefits. That is, it has immediate effects such as increased alertness, an enhanced sense of well-being, and physical pleasure from the movement itself. Many people who exercise regularly report that they simply feel better after their exercise session and that the physical activity routine is pleasurable in itself. This contrasts markedly with the unpleasant and frustrating consequences often associated with initiating changes in other health behaviors, such as taking medication (Chapter 6), changing diet (Chapter 7), losing weight (Chapter 8), or stopping smoking (Chapter 10). For physical activity, the natural consequences tend to encourage the patients to continue with their program.

Table 5. Immediate and delayed consequences affecting a physical fitness program versus other behavior change programs

|  | Strength of immediate consequences | | Strength of delayed consequences | |
|---|---|---|---|---|
|  | Positive | Aversive | Positive | Aversive |
| Physical fitness program | High | Moderate | High | Low |
| Other lifestyle programs (e.g., smoking cessation, weight loss, medication adherence) | Low | Moderate/High | High | Low |

The problem facing the patient who would like to begin a physical fitness program is that prior to starting the program, its consequences are perceived to be more aversive than positive. Patients' perceptions of a physical fitness program often include negative associations such as embarrassment, soreness, boredom, fatigue, and lack of time. They rarely consider the consequences.

The goal of the initial counseling should be to change the balance of the perceived positive and negative associations of physical activity. The patient should be informed of the consequences typically experienced by patients who start physical fitness programs. Often the patient does not know what is expected in an exercise regimen. Once the patient understands the modest level and nature of the physical activities that are recommended (e.g., 3 sessions per week of 30 to 40 minutes duration); that the program will be tailored to the patient's rate of accommodation; and that there are many benefits of exercise (e.g., loss of fatty tissue, enhanced self-esteem, reduced anxiety, increased stamina), the patient may decide to initiate a program without further counseling from the clinician. Other patients, however, may require help in overcoming unique personal circumstances that prevent them from starting a physical fitness program.

Many of the patient's negative associations with a physical fitness program can be eliminated with some forethought and planning. Interesting activities should be identified, convenient and inexpensive exercise facilities in the community (e.g., parks, schools, playgrounds) should be located, and an appropriate schedule for the fitness program should be designed. Ideally, the physician will attempt to tip the balance of negative and positive factors influencing the patient's decision to initiate a physical fitness program by simultaneously eliminating negative factors and enhancing positive ones.

### Helping a Patient Design a Physical Fitness Program

In contrast to those patients who need only information and encouragement to be successful, some patients need the clinician's help to learn how to design a

Table 6. Behavioral components of a basic physical fitness program

---

*Step 1: Review the patient's decision.*
   Make sure the patient is committed to his decision to initiate and maintain the program.

*Step 2: Select short-term and long-term goals.*
   Help the patient select specific, realistic long-term goal(s) and short-term objectives.

*Step 3: Select a compatible activity.*
   Help the patient choose a physical activity that is inherently satisfying.

*Step 4: Identify alternative activities.*
   Ensure that the patient has identified an alternative activity to do when it is not possible
      to participate in the preferred activity.

*Step 5: Design a compatible routine.*
   Help the patient design a routine that is compatible with the patient's daily schedule.

*Step 6: Monitor the program.*
   Make sure the patient has a method for monitoring progress.

*Step 7: Rearrange the environment.*
   The patient should ensure that his social and physical environment supports the new
      physical fitness program.

*Step 8: Plan follow-up.*
   Make sure the patient understands how and when the patient and clinician will discuss
      the patient's progress in the program.

---

physical fitness routine that will work for them. With these patients, the clinician should determine whether or not each of the basic steps of a successful program have been included in the plan (Table 6). The clinician can help the patient develop those that are missing and improve those that are not sound.

## Step 1: Evaluate the Patient's Decision to Start a Physical Fitness Program

A permanent behavior change cannot be attained without the patient's acceptance of the rationale for the program. The patient must decide that the goals of the new activities are desirable and that he is willing to try to achieve them.

It is important that the clinician determine the patient's reasons for beginning the new physical fitness program. The key question to be asked is: Do the reason(s) for beginning the program appear to be strong enough to help the patient overcome the initial discomfort and disruption created in the daily schedule? This initial decision and willingness to try to begin a new fitness program must sustain the patient through any initial doubts or desire to quit. The clinician should ask the patient to discuss how he decided to begin the program and to describe the program's specific goals. This will help the patient clarify what is to be accomplished and provide a clear summary of goals that can be recalled by the patient if doubts about the decision begin to occur. The clinician can be most helpful by clearly summarizing and paraphrasing the reasons the patient desires to make this change. It will also result in an explicit "public" statement of the patient's commitment to the new program.

The discussion need not be lengthy. The clinician should ask a few specific questions, such as "What prompted you to start this physical fitness program?," "What differences do you think increased physical fitness will have on the performance of your day-to-day activities?"

## Step 2: Select Short-Term Goals and Long-Term Objectives

The next step is to ask the patient to list both the specific long-term goals and the short-term objectives of the program. Ill-defined or unrealistic objectives will become apparent, and should be reviewed, including the following:

1. To lose a substantial amount of weight within a short time. A weight loss of 1 pound per week by exercise alone would require the equivalent of running approximately 35 miles or bicycling approximately 90 miles.
2. To dramatically improve strength. An aerobic fitness program will substantially improve stamina but will not markedly improve strength.
3. To progress rapidly and go farther, faster. The key to success in a physical activity program is slow, gradual progress. An increase of 10% per week is the recommended maximum.
4. To solve personal/social problems, such as to gain the respect of others, impress friends, win competitive events. For most individuals beginning a physical fitness program, these goals may be attainable over time; however, it is unrealistic to base the decision to begin the program on these reasons. If they occur, fine. They add to the enjoyment of the program. However, they should not be the reason for starting the program.

Some realistic objectives for beginning a physical fitness program include:

1. To improve one's ability to perform routine physical activities.
2. To gradually achieve a measure of fitness that enables one to participate in other activities. For example, individuals who enjoy skiing in the winter or individuals who enjoy hiking in the summer often will maintain a physical activity program off-season so that they may enjoy their sport even more.
3. To enhance alertness and sense of relaxation. Most patients report that they simply feel better when they have engaged in some form of physical activity.
4. To reduce tension and/or anxiety.
5. To engage in an activity that removes one from the ordinary daily routine and allows one to put aside the problems of the day.

Because the overall goal of the physical fitness program is to initiate and maintain a set of activities that provides a "training effect" for the individual, it is important to define the performance criteria for each patient. The activities should be balanced to provide the necessary training effect but should not tax or cause the patient discomfort. The program should be designed to stress the body moderately and then allow the body's natural accommodation process to occur. The initial step should be one that the patient can easily complete on the first day. This should be the guideline for every day. The level of activity should be based on the body's ability to accommodate to the stress of increased physical activity. It should not be based on what the patient believes he should be able to perform. It is important to explain to the patient the reason for selecting a level of activity that may feel "easy" for him. Selecting the proper level of activity will not only provide the most benefits physiologically, it will also tend to give the patient a psychological incentive to continue with the program.

Rather than follow a predetermined schedule of stages which are measured by the number of weeks that the patient has been in the program, it is far better to base the decision as to the rate of progress on the patient's own accommodation to the current level of the program. The stepped program presented in Table 3 only suggests a schedule measured in weeks. The patient should progress only as fast as his body allows. The schedule is only a general guide, not a set of weekly objectives to be attained. If the evaluation of the patient's progress is based on physiology, the program will not require too much effort on the patient's. From a phychological perspective, if the patient knows that the program will never require more effort than is currently expected, he is more likely to continue.

### Step 3: Select a Compatible Activity

The third major step is to capitalize on activities that are enjoyable or satisfying for the patient. The patient should be encouraged to review the list of activities that provide cardiovascular conditioning (Table 1) and select two or three that are appealing. The selection of an activity that is enjoyable for the patient may be the most critical step in developing a lasting physical fitness program. Many patients will begin a program but give little thought to the activity they choose, other than that they have seen others doing it or that they believe it is "good" for them. This approach should be discouraged. The patient has a choice, and the more enjoyable the activity is, the more likely it will be that the patient will continue the program, even if problems and setbacks occur.

### Step 4: Identify Alternative Activities

The patient should select one or two alternative activities to substitute for the regular activities on days when it is simply not possible to engage in the original preferred program. For example, a patient who attends an aerobics class three times each week may find that overtime work forces him to miss a class. Rather than simply skipping the class and not exercising, the patient could substitute stationary bicycling, jumping rope, walking, or jogging later in the evening or the next morning. The patient should always keep ready the necessary clothing and equipment so he can shift to the alternative program with minimal difficulty.

*Step 5: Design a Compatible Routine*

It is important that the physical fitness program be scheduled for periods when other demands on the patient's time are minimal. For a patient who works a typical 9-to-5 day, this could mean that the program uses early morning hours before breakfast, or the lunch hour, or after-work hours. An early morning exercise routine has many advantages, including stimulating an alertness that will continue through the morning and occurring when there is less competition for the use of facilities (e.g., pool, gym, track). However, it has the disadvantages of being affected by the patient's activities of the previous night (e.g., alcohol consumption, lack of sleep, late hours), being the coldest time of day, and, in areas where it is dark, of being the least safe time of day. Exercising at lunchtime has other advantages and disadvantages: It provides a break from the work routine, tends to decrease hunger (which aids weight control), and provides the opportunity to exercise with friends or colleagues, if desired. Its disadvantages can include difficulty locating appropriate shower and changing facilities, having to travel from work to exercise and back within a limited lunch break, and potentially missing social interaction with other employees who do not exercise. Many people choose the evening for their exercise routines. An evening schedule has the advantage of tending to reduce the stress and tension that have built up during the day. It also tends to be warmer than the morning but not as hot as noon. In addition, some people are better able to simply "get out the door" in the evening. Unfortunately, there is a greater likelihood of unanticipated changes in the daily routine that will conflict with the evening exercise routine. In addition, it tends to be the most popular time for people to use exercise facilities.

These considerations illustrate that there is not single "best" time for everyone's physical activity program. The patient should select a time that seems best for his usual daily routine. This time should be adjusted, however, if conflicts are encountered or anticipated. For example, if overtime on the job is anticipated, a switch from an evening to a morning program would avoid a break in the physical activity routine. Changing the schedule at the seasons change is also common: Morning schedules tend to be more popular in the summer, and evening or noontime schedules more popular in the winter.

## Step 6: Monitor the Program

The selection of an appropriate initial level of physical activity requires a method of accurately monitoring the patient's current level of activity. Measuring the patient's pulse rate is the best way to do this because it indicates the amount of stress that current physical activity is placing on the cardiovascular system.

## Step 7: Rearrange the Environment

Achieving and maintaining a regular physical activity program requires that the patient overcome two different sets of problems. First, the patient must fit the physical fitness program into his daily schedule and overcome any disruptions it creates. The patient should not only set aside the time for physical activity but should also be prepared to protect this time as being personally important. A high priority should be assigned to the program. Spouses or other family members may need to be reminded that the physical activity program is not leisure time. Rather, it is an active, vital part of the patient's week. The family's recognition of the importance of the patient's commitment to exercise can prevent conflicts.

The second set of problems involves the initiation and conduct of the program itself. It is as easy as possible to engage. Eliminate the minor annoyances and hassles that create barriers to participation. For example, it is a good idea to set aside all the clothing and equipment needed for the program. This can easily be done by placing them in a special drawer, box, sports bag, or shopping bag. With the clothing and equipment readily available, frustrating delay in starting the activity each day can be avoided. Preparation for the activity itself is also very helpful. Encourage the patient to plan ahead of time where to run, bike, ski, or walk. If possible, the distance should be determined by driving the route in a car. If the patient will be using public facilities, he should identify the hours that the facilities are least crowded or determine what to expect during the hours selected.

Often patients cannot seem to get started. This frequently results from their mistaken belief that before beginning a physical activity, one should be "in the mood" and feel ready to exercise. Because people who are not regularly exercising seldom experience this feeling, there is little likelihood that the patient will begin or continue a program. Therefore, it is recommended that the patient select a particular day and time to begin the new physical activity program, and agree to start the program as scheduled regardless of how he feels physiologically or psychologically that day. Once the patient begins the program and experiences the physical and psychological changes that do occur, he may begin to eagerly anticipate each session.

*Step 8: Plan Follow-up Contact with the Clinician*

Because so many patients have difficulty beginning a physical fitness program, it is helpful to ask the patient to recontact the clinic in about 3 weeks to report progress. This need not be a formal visit to the clinic. A brief telephone call is usually sufficient for the clinician to be satisfied that the patient is progressing smoothly in establishing the fitness program. If the patient is having trouble, however, the clinician can offer helpful suggestions over the phone. This telephone contact is particularly important after only 3 weeks because the clinician may be able to redirect the patient's program if it is not succeeding. If this contact were not made until several months later, and the patient had had difficulty getting started, the patient might not only have given up on the program but also might be less willing to begin again. Therefore, the patient should leave the first clinic visit with the assurance that the clinician wants to be informed of his progress and with clear instructions when to report in.

### Common Problems

There are several problems which involve only a single, major factor that are common among patients beginning a physical fitness program: (1) initial discomfort adjusting to a new schedule, (2) embarrassment when exercising in public, (3) boredom, and (4) lack of time. These problems often can be remedied without initiating in-depth behavioral counseling. Usually, a simple suggestion to eliminate or reduce the effect of the single factor will be sufficient. However, the clinician should be confident that the patient's difficulties truly result from a single factor and are not the result of a more complex interaction of factors.

*Initial Discomfort Adjusting to a New Routine*

Although the physical discomfort experienced during the initial weeks of a new physical activity program can be minimized or avoided, the patient must recognize that there will be minor irritations and frustrations. He must be willing to endure some discomfort until the new program becomes routine. While the patient is accommodating physiologically to the new physical activities, he is also accommodating psychologically. He is engaging in a new set of activities that are unfamiliar and feel awkward, and he may have to change established habits. For instance, he may choose to awaken earlier than usual, postpone a drink immediately after work, or to schedule time at lunch for the program.

It is often helpful for the patient to make a commitment to pursue the physical activity routine for a specific length of time and suspend judgment about its effects. For example, a patient might agree to participate in the program for

Table 7. Strategies for resolving problems of embarrassment about the physical fitness program

*Strategy No. 1: Minimize public exposure and unwanted attention.*

(1) Choose a natural physical activity such as brisk walking rather than a sport such as jogging or an obvious exercise program (aerobic calesthenics). This could be walking in a shopping mall, or walking the dog around the neighborhood.
(2) Consider an exercise that can be done at home, such as stationary bicycling, aerobic dancercise to a record or tape, or possibly swimming.
(3) Avoid wearing flashy athletic clothes.
(4) Use public facilities at nonpeak hours.

*Strategy No. 2: Exercise with someone who will offer "moral support."*

(1) Join a group class at work, a local hospital, school, YMCA, or church.
(2) Ask a friend or family member to accompany you.

*Strategy No. 3: Be assertive and defend your right to make a lifestyle change.*

(1) Rehearse an assertive statement about the fitness program to use in reply to co-workers or family members who ask questions. For example, "It is unfortunate that you do not enjoy exercising. I find it very relaxing and plan my day so I can do it. I prefer exercising to other activities (e.g., drinking, eating, working) at that time."

*Avoid:*

• Wearing a full warm-up suit in hot weather just to "cover up"; this is extremely dangerous because of the risk of heat exhaustion.
• Exercising in isolated or dark public places.
• Attempting to exercise at someone else's pace. Set your own pace and stick to it.

3 weeks before deciding to make major changes in the program or to abandon it. This 3-week commitment will minimize the patient's constant reevaluation of the program on a day-to-day basis—which is particularly important during the early, difficult weeks—and will sustain the patient's participation in the program until some progress is made. The patient should have experienced some of the immediate benefits of the program, and some noticeable physiological accommodation should have been achieved without additional effort by him. The patient will experience slow, gradual improvement, and should be encouraged by this to continue exercising.

*Embarrassment*

Some patients are extremely uncomfortable exercising in public because of their excess weight, self-consciousness, or particular body features (e.g., birthmarks, surgical scars). This embarrassment may prevent them from openly discussing their concerns with the clinician. However, if the clinician suspects that the patient is reluctant to engage in public exercise, he can encourage the patient to (1) design a physical fitness program that avoids public exposure, (2) join a group of other patients who have similar characterisitics (e.g., overweight or with similar medical histories), and (3) accept the physical fitness program as something that the patient has a right to do for himself, regardless of what other people think. Specific suggestions for dealing with embarrassment are listed in Table 7.

### Boredom

Some patients stop exercising after a relatively brief time because they grow bored with the routine. They say that "swimming laps is dull," or "I don't enjoy running in circles," or "there is no nice place to bicycle." Such patients tend to emphasize the importance of the entertainment value of the fitness program.

The clinician can help the patient confront this problem by (1) working with the patient to increase the pleasurable aspects of whatever physical fitness activity is chosen, and (2) encouraging the patient to add variety to the fitness routine, with music or with new routines each day. Several specific suggestions are listed in Table 8. This listing also includes suggestions regarding what the patient should be encouraged to avoid doing.

### Lack of Time

Perhaps the most frequent problem patients have is their inability to find time to exercise. These patients have the desire to exercise and may enjoy their exercise routine once they get into it, but they cannot seem to work the fitness program into their regular schedule. The clinician can suggest that they (1) select a specific time that appears to be free of conflicts (i.e., avoid allowing the fitness program to be scheduled "as time is available"), and (2) identify an alternative activity (e.g., jumping rope, jogging in place) to be substituted if the primary program must be cancelled. A list of specific suggestions is presented in Table 9.

The clinician should approach the patient's complaint about lack of time with caution and be sure that it is not, in fact, an excuse for not exercising because of lack of interest. He should rule out the possibility that the patient simply does not place a high enough priority on the fitness program to find the time for it. If this is the case, the clinician should review the patient's decision to participate in the program.

### Behavioral Counseling to Resolve Patient-Specific Problems

In spite of a carefully designed physical fitness routine, some patients encounter difficulties that cannot be readily resolved by the suggestions described above. The clinician must assess, diagnose, and intervene in each case individually to successfully resolve such problems using the 11-step health behavior counseling process (Table 10, and described in detail in Chapters 2 and 4).

Table 8. Strategies for resolving problems of boredom with the physical fitness program

*Strategy No. 1: Increase pleasant aspects of the program.*

(1) Consider exercising with a friend or family member.
(2) Consider joining a group for occasional activities (e.g., bicycling, hike, walk, run).
(3) Detect and examine the pleasurable thoughts and feelings experienced while exercising and after the exercise session. Can these be enhanced or prolonged?
(4) Consider getting involved in a self-paced exercise-for-charity program in which a sponsor donates a given amount of money to a charity depending on the amount of exercise you complete in a certain time (e.g., $.10 per mile walked during 1 month donated to the American Heart Association).

*Strategy No. 2: Put variety into your program.*

(1) Switch to an alternative activity (e.g., bicycling instead of jogging, walking instead of swimming).
(2) Seek an alternative setting for the usual activity (e.g., a new bicycle route, a different swimming pool, a new jogging trail).
(3) Talk with other individuals who are doing the same type of exercise to see how they add variety to their fitness program.

*Avoid:*

• Continuing with an exercise that is boring.
• Discussing your feelings of boredom with friends or family members who do not exercise. They might agree that exercising is a negative experience and discourage you from continuing with your program.
• Examine the likelihood that you will discontinue the program in the near future.
• Ignore statements that all physical fitness programs are boring when you have only attempted one.

Table 9. Strategies for resolving problems of lacking time for the physical fitness program

*Strategy No. 1: Carefully select the schedule for the program.*

(1) Schedule the fitness program at times for which there is little likelihood of conflict.
(2) Identify a "back-up" time for exercising if the primary time is not available.
(3) Schedule these three primary times on the weekly calendar as "appointments" that should not be broken.
(4) Record what is done during each physical fitness session on a weekly calendar.

*Strategy No. 2: Identify an "all-purpose" alternative activity.*

(1) Select an alternative activity that can be done any time (e.g., jogging in place, jumping rope, brisk walking).
(2) Select a day to try the alternative activity in place of the primary activity to make sure it is suitable.

*Avoid:*

• "Doubling up" on exercise sessions to make up a missed session. This will lead to frustration and possibly injury. Instead, use the back-up time or activity. If necessary, skip the session.
• Exercising only on weekends. This will not promote the cardiovascular fitness level desired. Schedule three sessions during the week.
• Exercising if you are not feeling well or are extremely tired, or if the weather is inclement. Be flexible and use the back-up activity or time.

Table 10.  Eleven-step behavioral counseling for patients with problems adhering to a physical fitness program

*Step  1:  Identify the problem.*
To what degree does each of the following seem to be present?
(1) Absence of an initial decision to start exercising.
(2) Failure to establish the physical fitness program as a habit.
(3) Continuing self-debate.
(4) Fatigue with program.

*Step  2:  Clarify the goals of treatment.*
Identify appropriate long-term goals and short-term objectives.

*Step  3:  Collect information.*
(1) Determine if the patient wants to discuss personal details of his lifestyle.
(2) Obtain details of each activity session.
(3) Instruct the patient to collect additional information in a daily log.

*Step  4:  Develop a behavioral diagnosis.*
Identify the relationships among the primary and secondary factors surrounding the physical activity program supporting or inhibiting it.

*Step  5:  Generate an intervention plan.*
(1) Keep the plan simple.
(2) Identify a program that will eliminate or reduce aversive factors associated with the physical fitness program.

*Step  6:  Intervene.*
(1) Encourage the patient to agree to use the intervention plan for at least one scheduled physical activity session.
(2) Write out the plan and give it to the patient.

*Step  7:  Review the patient's progress.*
(1) Collect data regarding the patient's ability to use the intervention plan and to follow the schedule for the physical fitness program.
(2) If there does not appear to be any change, consider modifying the behavioral diagnosis.

*Step  8:  Generate a revised intervention plan.*
Write out the revised program for the patient.

*Step  9:  Reintervene.*
Encourage the patient to agree to use the intervention plan for at least one scheduled physical activity session.

*Step  10:  Develop a maintenance program.*
(1) Gradually withdraw attention and support for the patient's maintenance of the program.
(2) Encourage the patient to withdraw any artificial aids used to initiate the program.
(3) Require that the patient take increasing responsibility for modifying the program or designing a new program to overcome any problems.

*Step  11:  Review the behavior change process.*
(1) Review with the patient the strategies that seemed to be the most effective.
(2) Review how to restart the fitness program if it is stopped for any reason.
(3) Write out the steps used in restarting the fitness program.

## Step 1: Identify the Problem

Patients' problems adhering to a physical fitness program can be classified into four major types: (1) lack of commitment to the initial decision to follow the fitness routine, (2) failure to establish the fitness routine as a habit, (3) continuing self-debate, or (4) fatigue. Often, the patient's problem may involve aspects of all of these and the clinician would be wise to investigate the influence of each. For example, a patient having several problems may state that he tried to follow the fitness routine but after 1 week gave it up because he could not find a good place to exercise and, although he enjoyed exercising, it was too much trouble to do as often as he should. This patient's problem may be one or a combination of several of these problems, possibly compounded by one of the following: (1) his decision to exercise was based only on a desire to please his physician, (2) the routine was not clearly specified, (3) the routine was not tailored to his daily activities, and (4) the routine was not adjusted to his level of fitness.

## Step 2: Clarify the Goals of Treatment

The clinician should verify that the patient has both an appropriate long-term goal and appropriate weekly objectives. The patient should begin with activities that are well within his physical limits and progress at his own rate (but no greater than a 10% increase per week). For example, a patient selects a long-term goal of exercising three times per week for 30 to 40 minutes in her target heart rate range. The first week might consist of three sessions of stretching, brisk walking for 10 minutes in the target heart range, and then a cool-down period. Each successive week she could increase, by no greater than 10% of the previous week's level, the time spent exercising at the target heart rate range.

## Step 3: Collect Information

Most patients are able to report accurately the activity and the amount of time they spent in each session. However, unless the patient has been educated about heart rate, the patient may not be able to accurately judge the relative intensity of the activity. The patient's pulse rate is the only accurate means of judging how vigorous the activity is for that individual. The clinician should be sure that the patient understands the concept of the target heart rate range and can take an accurate pulse. Otherwise, the patient can easily stray above or below a desirable level of activity. Too much vigorous activity, and the patient will become fatigued or injured. Too little activity, and the patient will not benefit.

The clinician can suggest that the patient keep a daily log about the physical fitness program. This will help the clinician describe a behavioral profile and

| Date | Time | Activity | Duration | Distance | Pulse | Comments |
|------|------|----------|----------|----------|-------|----------|
| 1/4 | 5:25pm | Walk/Jog | 30 min. | 2 miles. | 120/128 | Feels good to be outside! |
| 1/6 | 5:35pm | Walk/Jog | 30 min. | 2 miles | 118/124 | Legs a little bit stiff from iron. |
| 1/8 | 5:35pm | Walk/Jog | 25 min. | 1 3/4 mils | 120/24 | Took it slow. Feel good. |
| 1/11 | | Skipped | | | | |
| 1/13 | 5:25pm | Walk/Jog | 30 min. | 2.0 miles | 122/126 | ok but BORED |
| 1/15 | 5:35pm | Walk/Jog | 30 min | 2.0 miles | 124/128 | This is dull. |

Figure 1. Example of a patient's weekly log of physical activity.

develop a functional analysis of the fitness routine as it relates to the patient's other activities. The daily log is used to record the activity, its duration, the distance covered, the patient's pulse rate, and the patient's thoughts about the session (Figure 1).

The most difficult problem in collecting information from a patient who is not following a physical fitness routine is that the patient (and occasionally the clinician) may be uncomfortable discussing personal topics. These can include details of the patient's leisure activities, job routine, the reactions of family members to the patient's planned program, and the patient's feelings about his lack of success. The clinician must recognize that some patients ask for help but do not expect to discuss these areas. The clinician should explore the general nature of the problem, and then, if necessary, explain to the patient that to fully understand the problem, they will have to talk about some "personal" subjects. The clinician should inquire if the patient is willing to do so. In this way the patient is informed of the intent of the questioning and has the opportunity to continue the session or not.

### Step 4: Develop a Behavioral Diagnosis

It is usually not difficult to develop an accurate behavioral diagnosis of a patient's failure to follow the physical fitness program. With a brief discussion, the patient usually is able to accurately identify the critical events surrounding the physical activity program that support or inhibit it. Once these factors are identified and their relationships clarified, the behavioral analysis can readily be developed. For example, a patient's problem is that he is not following a physical activity schedule as planned. A review of his daily schedule shows that he will exercise only when the weather is pleasant, not if it is raining or cold outside.

## Step 5: Generate an Intervention Plan

The intervention plan should be as simple as possible. It should be directed toward either the antecedents or consequences of the fitness program, resolving or reducing the effects of the factors that prevent the patient from following it. The plan should enable the natural, positive benefits of participating in the program to support its continuation. For example, if it is clear that a patient has selected an activity that is convenient but not enjoyable (e.g., it reminds him of forced exercises in school or the military), the patient should be encouraged to vary the exercise routine or select an alternative activity.

## Step 6: Intervene

The intervention should be planned to be attempted for at least 1 week. The patient's agreement to attempt the new program for that long affords him sufficient opportunity to determine if the intervention will be effective in a variety of situations, not simply one day, or more than one week.

It is very important that the clinician take the time to write out the behavior change program for the patient. The patient should leave the session with a "behavioral prescription" that lists each task to be accomplished. An example of a behavior change program for a patient having difficulty with a physical fitness program is presented in Figure 2. It leaves little room for the patient to be mistaken or confused about what he is to do in the coming days and weeks.

## Step 7: Review the Patient's Progress

The clinician should review the results of the fitness program and the behavioral intervention with the patient. Two types of data should be considered: first, the frequency and intensity of the patient's participation in the physical fitness program. Was there a change in these? Second, the clinician should review the manner in which the patient used the behavior change intervention. How did the patient make the changes suggested?

If there was a change in the patient's participation in the physical fitness program, then the clinician should consider continuing with the same behavior change program and reviewing the data again later. However, if the patient used

**MICHAEL L. RUSSELL, Ph.D.**
Department of Internal Medicine
Baylor College of Medicine
Tel. 799-6032

**Program for Change**

For: _J. D._                          Date: _2/1/84_

1. Select an <u>aerobic</u> activity for your physical fitness program.

2. Follow a physical fitness routine of 3 sessions of 30-40 minutes each week.

3. Take your pulse rate half way through and again at the end of each session. DO NOT EXCEED YOUR TARGET HEART RATE RANGE OF 114 to 131 beats/min.

4. Record your session in your log book.

5. Call me in 10 days.                 _M. Russell_

Figure 2. Example of a behavioral prescription for a physical fitness program.

the behavior change strategies as described by the clinician and there was no substantial change, then the clinician should reconsider the initial behavioral diagnosis. Additional information may be needed to more clearly understand the functional relationships present. A change in the behavioral diagnosis may necessitate revising the intervention.

## Step 8: Generate a Revised Intervention Plan

If a revised intervention is developed, the clinician should be sure to write out the new program, step by step, in a behavioral prescription. The new written program is needed because the patient may not understand how the new program differs from the old. Often, it is the clinician's implied or unstated assumptions about what the patient will do that lead to the patient's failure to follow the behavior change program.

## Step 9: Reintervene

As with the initial intervention, the patient should be asked to attempt the new behavior change program for at least 1 week before considering changing it. This is the minimum amount of time needed to know whether the new intervention will be successful or not. The patient might be encouraged to tele-phone the clinician to discuss the results of this trial and any possible modifi-cations needed at the end of this period.

## Step 10: Develop a Maintenance Program

The final goal of a behavior change program is for the patient to be able to maintain the lifestyle change over time. When the patient has successfully fol-lowed the physical fitness program for at least 6 weeks, the clinician should begin to develop a program to help the patient continue indefinitely. For a physical fitness program, this is usually a relatively simple matter because of the inherent reinforcing qualities of physical activity. By 6 weeks, the patient should have experienced some of the pleasurable physiological changes associ-ated with regular exercise (decreased tension, increased alertness, general sense of well-being) and will have developed a routine that fits into his schedule.

There are three strategies that will help the patient maintain the program on his own. The first is for the clinician to reduce gradually the attention and sup-port that the patient may have needed to begin the program. The clinician should begin to treat the physical fitness program as any other aspect of the patient's lifestyle rather than as a "special" one.

Second, the clinician should encourage the patient to remove the artificial strategies that were introduced to get the patient started. For example, if a pa-tient had been making contracts with herself or others, she should try to forgo these. If a patient had been setting up a reinforcement system of, for example, purchasing new sports equipment (e.g., shoes, tennis balls, running shorts) as she progressed, she should now purchase these items only when needed or de-sired.

Finally, the clinician should acknowledge any problems the patient contin-ues to have but increasingly require him to generate the solutions to them. In a relatively short time, the patient should have full responsibility for all adjust-ments in the program so that his dependence on the clinician will be reduced. The clinician can still monitor the effects of the patient's adjustments and offer suggestions if he becomes stuck. For example, by this time, the patient should have established a workable schedule for exercising at home during his routine work week. The clinician should encourage the patient to develop a workable plan for exercising when his schedule is disrupted. The experience that the pa-tient gets from resolving these problems will greatly contribute to the patient's ability to develop solutions to future problems and maintain the fitness program as a permanent aspect of his lifestyle.

## Step 11: Review the Behavior Change Process

A major challenge in helping patients maintain a fitness program is preparing them to resume the program if it is interrupted (e.g., due to illness). Two suggestions are offered. First, the clinician should review with the patient the specific behavior change interventions that seemed to be the most effective and confirm that the patient knows what to do and how to implement these strategies.

Second, the clinician should ask the patient what he would do to restart the program, specifically, the activities, the duration, and the distance. The details of what physical activity to start with and at what level should be identified. For example, a patient who had reached a level of swimming for 30 minutes three times a week, may need to begin by swimming only 10 minutes a session the first week. The patient who was jogging for 35 minutes per session may have to restart by briskly walking for the same amount of time during the first week if he has stopped the program for several weeks.

Finally, the clinicial should write out the details of both what the patient should do to resume the physical fitness program and the behavior change strategies that helped get him started. This written statement should also include the strategies the patient currently is using to maintain the program. In this way, the patient will have all of the information necessary to restart the physical fitness program without having to depend on the clinician.

## Specific Counseling Strategies

The clinician has many specific intervention strategies which can be helpful in resolving a particular behavioral change problem (see Table 11). Counseling strategies should be used only after a behavioral analysis of the patient's problem has been formulated. Otherwise, not only might the strategy fail, but the patient might lose his motivation to continue with the program. It cannot be emphasized too strongly that the behavior change recommendation be based on the guidelines discussed in this chapter. A behavioral prescription should be given the same careful consideration that is used to select a drug prescription.

### Prompt the Desired Behavior

The strategies in this group are designed to prompt the patient to exercise at the prescribed time. The cue should have three characteristics: (1) it should be unique, (2) it should be positioned so that it is noticed by the patient just before a particular action is to be taken, and (3) it should not be prominent at other times. Examples of cues for a physical fitness program are an "appointment" for the physical fitness program written into the patient's appointment book, a personal alarm set to ring at the time scheduled for the physical fitness program, and a special marker (e.g., a colorful sticker) placed on the patient's calendar at the time or days set for the physical fitness program.

Table 11. Counseling strategies for patient-specific problems with a physical fitness program

| Problem | Suggested counseling strategy |
|---|---|
| Patient forgets regimen | Use a cue |
| Patient reports few or no positive consequences associated with the physical fitness program | Increase positive qualities of activity<br>Use a self-contract<br>Schedule group activities<br>Increase sensitivity to pleasurable feelings |
| Patient reports negative consequences associated with the physical fitness program | Avoid fatigue<br>Reschedule time for routine |

*Increase Positive Consequences*

If the behavioral diagnosis indicates that the patient is aware of few or no positive consequences of the physical fitness program, the clinician can use one of three strategies:

*Increase Innate Positive Qualities of the Activity.* The physical activity should be enjoyable for the patient, or another activity should be found. Adding variety to a particular routine can also be helpful (e.g., a new route, a new facility, a rearrangement of the activity).

*Use a Contract.* The patient may find a formal or informal self-contract helpful for specifying a reward to be received once the physical activity program has been established. An example of a contract is shown in Figure 3.

*Suggest Group Activities.* The patient may receive needed attention and reinforcement by joining a group activity program. The support from others in the group can be a very strong aid in keeping the patient involved in the activity. Many patients arrange to exercise with a friend one day of the week. The companionship can help the patient continue the program during the most difficult times.

*Increase Sensitivity to Pleasurable Feelings.* In focusing on the physical performance of an activity, many patients fail to notice the pleasure that can accompany or follow the activity. The patient should be encouraged to concentrate on the pleasurable feelings of moving, breathing, and working their muscles, and of the environment (e.g., the wind, the fog). Once the patient has identified and experienced these feelings, he should be encouraged to experiment with ways to enhance them. What activities tend to produce these feelings? What

```
┌─────────────────────────────────────────────────────────────────┐
│                      A PERSONAL CONTRACT                          │
│                                                                   │
│   Activity:   Jogging on streets near home.                       │
│                                                                   │
│                                                                   │
│   Level of Performance:  3 times per week for 30 to 40 minutes    │
│   each. My pulse rate will remain within my Target                │
│   Heart Rate Range of 114 to 131 beats per minute.                │
│                                                                   │
│   Consequences                                                    │
│   If I follow the routine for  2 weeks        as outlined above, then │
│   I will provide myself with the small reward of:                 │
│                                                                   │
│     Going to see a movie of my choice.                            │
│                                                                   │
│                                                                   │
│   As further encouragement to follow the routine, if I do not do so, │
│   then I promise to:  Donate the price of the movie ticket ($5.00) │
│    to the American Heart Association.                             │
│                                                                   │
│                                                                   │
│                            _____                    │
│                               Signature                           │
│                            _____                    │
│                                1/18/84                            │
│                               Date                                │
└─────────────────────────────────────────────────────────────────┘
```

Figure 3. Example of a self-contract for a physical fitness routine.

increases their intensity? Many people find that ultimately they continue to participate in a physical fitness program because they come to enjoy and expect these pleasurable sensations.

### Decrease Negative Consequences

The most common problem patients encounter in physical fitness programs is that they experience aversive events during or after the physical activity. Three strategies are recommended:

*Avoid Fatigue.* The patient should be instructed to avoid becoming fatigued during any part of the physical fitness program. The routine should be designed so that the patient's heart rate stays within the target heart rate range. If the patient is not fatigued at the start of the activity (e.g., from lack of sleep or alcohol consumption) and is aware of becoming tired during the activity, he should be instructed to stop the exercise session. This prevents the activity from becoming associated with unpleasant thoughts and feelings. Because the patient stops the session before becoming fatigued, he will be eager to return to the activity.

*Avoid Pain.* The patient confronts a real danger in exercising if he feels pain. If pain is felt, and it is greater than experienced before, the patient should stop the activity. This is particularly common when beginning a group work-out at a gym of an exercise class. Sometimes the new member becomes very sore early and then quits. Instead, a new class should be joined that will begin where the patient is comfortable.

*Re-schedule Activity.* If the physical fitness program has been poorly scheduled and conflicts with other activities, the patient may become frustrated and unhappy. He should select a time for the program when there is little likelihood of conflict.

## Case Illustration

The following case description presents a typical patient whose case illustrates most of the major aspects of designing a physical fitness program and of resolving problems.

### The Patient

A 37-year-old man is being treated for hypertension. The condition was diagnosed 1 year ago by his physician. His blood pressure is currently under good control by medication (his most recent blood pressure reading was 125/82). The patient is approximately 25 pounds over his ideal weight, and has not exercised regularly since he played baseball in college.

### First Visit

As part of the overall management of the patient's high blood pressure, his physician encouraged him to begin a modest physical fitness program of 30 minutes of vigorous exercise three times each week. The patient was given the booklet *Exercise and Your Health*, describing how to begin a physical fitness program. In addition, the physician gave the patient the list of suggestions, "Getting Started, Keeping Going," in Table 4. He was then referred to staff in his own clinic for follow-up.

### Second Visit

The patient returned to the clinic for a follow-up visit 1 month later. He stated that he could not seem to follow a regular routine of physical exercise. He said that between the demands of his job and his family, and the time he needed to relax, there was no time left for exercising. He asked the clinician for suggestions. The clinician reviewed each of the eight basic behavioral components in the well-designed physical fitness program (see Table 6).

*Step 1: Review the Patient's Decision.*    The patient stated that he agreed with his physician's recommendation and wanted to "get back in shape." He understood that exercise could help reduce his blood pressure and also hoped that he would be better able to cope with some of the tension he felt at work.

*Step 2: Select Long-Term Goals and Short-Term Objectives.*    The patient's long-term goal was "to get back in shape like I was in school." The patient's short-term objective was "to get out and exercise more." The patient did not have any more specific plans.

In terms of a clinical assessment, these were unacceptable. The patient's long-term goal should be realistic, and the short-term objectives should contain a specific statement of what the patient expects to achieve in the first week and in each of the next few weeks. Therefore, the clinician reviewed with the patient what an acceptable long-term goal was and how the short-term objectives help to achieve it. After a brief discussion, the patient selected a new long-term goal: "to exercise three times per week for 40 minutes." His new short-term objective was "to start, this week, exercising three times per week for 20 minutes."

*Step 3: Select a Compatible Activity.*    The patient had selected running, but, it was clear to the clinician that the patient did not enjoy his running program. He described it as "boring" and "mindless." Therefore, the clinician discussed other activities with him to find one he might find more enjoyable. The patient decided to try swimming during the next few months. He stated that he always enjoyed swimming but rarely seemed to go to a pool anymore.

*Step 4: Identify Alternative Activities.*    The patient stated that he had not, as yet, identified an alternative activity to use if he was unable to run or swim. The patient chose to purchase an inexpensive stationary bicycle that would be placed in the den so he could easily use it when desired.

*Step 5: Design a Compatible Routine.*    The patient indicated that he had not identified a specific time for his exercise program but tried to exercise on the afternoons he arrived home on time from work. This haphazardness made it highly unlikely that he exercised at all. The clinician suggested that he identify three specific times during the week to exercise. The patient selected Monday, Wednesday, and Friday, from 5:45 to 6:00 p.m.

*Level 6: Monitoring the Program.* After each exercise session, the patient was advised to make a brief note in his daily calendar about the session, including what he did, how far he went, and how long it took. The patient was encouraged to continue to keep this record.

*Step 7: Rearrange the Environment.* The patient stated that he had told his wife of his physical fitness program. He also had placed his running clothes on a special set of wall hooks near the door in the utility room of his house. While these efforts seemed adequate, the patient did not indicate what his wife's reaction was to the program. Also, new arrangements would have to be made for the equipment and clothing needed for the new swimming program.

The patient said that he would obtain a locker at the YMCA pool near his office and leave his swimming clothes there.

*Step 8: Plan Follow-up.* The patient agreed to call the clinic in 1 week to report his progress with the new physical fitness program. Specifically, he was to tell the clinic nurse when he had exercised, how long he had exercised, and if he anticipated any problems in the next week. If he had encountered a problem or anticipated having a problem in the next week, the clinician would call him back.

## Third Visit

The patient returned for a follow-up visit 2 months later and reported that he was doing better with the physical fitness program. He showed the clinician his daily log, which revealed that the patient was exercising two or three times each week. The patient stated, however, that he was not sure he would be able to continue with the same schedule because his wife was not happy that the family dinner had to be delayed until he arrived home from the pool.

The clinician determined that this was a patient-specific problem that warranted health behavior counseling. The clinician used the 11-step Behavioral Counseling process as follows:

*Step 1: Identify the Problem.* The patient indicated that his wife had become increasingly critical of his physical fitness program in the last two to three weeks. He reported that she had told him, "It's not fair to the rest of us to wait for dinner while you swim," and "You are too old to become a 'jock' again," and "You are just going to hurt yourself." The patient said that he had tried to ignore her and follow his routine. He did not feel that he could continue to do so, however.

The clinician concluded that the patient's basic problem was that he was be-

ginning to self-debate whether or not to continue with the program. It was becoming increasingly likely that he would decide against it.

*Step 2: Clarify the Goals of Treatment.*   The treatment goal was to design a
revised fitness program that would reduce the patient's wife's objections to it.

*Step 3: Collect Information.*   After discussing this problem with the patient,
the clinician decided that no additional information was needed to design an
intervention program.

*Step 4: Develop a Behavioral Diagnosis.*   The clinician concluded that the
patient's problem was that his wife's criticism was becoming too negative and
was increasing the likelihood that the patient would decide to quit his exercise
program.

*Step 5: Generate an Intervention Plan.*   The clinician decided that a three-
part intervention might be most successful. The intervention would be designed to decrease the wife's negative comments, encourage her to participate
in the program if she desired, and eliminate the situation creating the conflict.
First, the patient's wife would be informed about the relationship between physical
fitness and high blood pressure. The patient said that he had not done this, but
that this information might best come from the clinician. The clinician agreed
to call the patient's wife. Second, the clinician suggested finding an alternative
time for the program. The patient felt that the evening was best for him, but
he could see how it was disrupting the family routine and agreed to try an early
morning schedule for 3 weeks to see how it worked. Third, the clinician suggested that the patient and his wife find an aerobic activity they could do together on the weekend (e.g., bicycling or brisk walking).

*Step 6: Intervene.*   The patient agreed to this plan and to report by telephone
in 1 week how it had worked. The clinician called the patient's wife that afternoon.

## Telephone Call

One week later, the patient reported that the program seemed to be working.
He and his wife had been bicycling the previous two Saturday mornings, and
he felt that he was accommodating to the early-morning swimming.

*Steps 7, 8, and 9: Review the Patient's Progress, Generate a Revised Intervention
Plan, and Reintervene.*   The clinician did not change the behavioral diagnosis, modify the intervention plan, or reintervene with a new plan.

*Fourth Visit*

The patient returned to the clinic 2 months later for a blood pressure check. He reported that the program was going well. He had maintained a program of three physical fitness sessions a week, and his wife not only was no longer criticizing his program, but also enjoyed the bicycling on the weekends.

*Step 10: Develop a Maintenance Program.*   No artificial strategies had been used in this case, so none had to be withdrawn.

*Step 11: Review the Behavior Change Process.*   The clinician reviewed with the patient the problem of his self-debate. The patient understood how both positive and negative factors tended to influence him and realized that, if he self-debated in the future, he would have to identify the negative factors affecting his program and reduce or eliminate them.

When asked if he anticipated any future problems, the patient expressed concern about being able to continue with the program if he had to travel out of town for several days. In anticipation of this, the patient designed a routine for himself in which he would either use a hotel swimming pool or jog in place in his room for 25 minutes.

## References

1. The Framingham Study
2. Paffenbarger RS Jr, Laughlin ME, Gima AS, et al: Work activity of longshoremen as related to death from coronary heart disease and stroke. *N Eng J Med* 1970; 282:1109–1114.
3. Morris JN, Kagan A, Pattison DC, et al: Incidence and prediction of ischaemic heart-disease in London busmen. *Lancet* 1966; 2:553–559.
4. Karvonen MJ, Klemola H, Virkajarvi J, et al: Longevity of endurance skiers. *Med Sci Sports Exerc* 1974; 6:49–51.
5. Exercise and participation in sports among persons 20 years of age and over: United States, 1975. *Advancedata* 19, 1978.

# 10. Smoking Cessation

The per capita consumption of cigarettes by adults in the United States rose steadily throughout the first half of the twentieth century until, in 1964, the Surgeon General linked cigarette smoking with specific health risks.[1] Since then, the percentage of adults who smoke cigarettes has continued to fall. In 1965, approximately 52% of white American men smoked, compared with 42% in 1976 and 38% in 1980. The change in rates for black men is similar, but at a level approximately 10% higher. For both white and black women, the rate was 34% in 1965, compared with 32% in 1976 and 29% in 1980.[2]

Although it is encouraging that the prevalence of cigarette smoking is declining, the fact that more than one-third of all Americans smoke continues to be a major public health concern. In 1979, the Surgeon General reviewed the scientific literature on cigarette smoking and concluded that cigarette smoking is the most significant preventable risk factor for premature death and disability in the United States.[3]

The specific physiological and medical effects of cigarette smoking have been reviewed in detail elsewhere[3,4] and will not be repeated here. However, the conclusions of these reviews should be clear. Cigarette smoking is strongly associated with cardiovascular disease. Smokers have an increased risk of fatal and nonfatal myocardial infarction, occlusive atherosclerotic peripheral vascular disease, and sudden cardiac death. Cigarette smoking also is clearly linked to cancer. Smokers have an increased incidence of cancer of those tissues that come in direct contact with the cigarette smoke, including lung, mouth, larynx, and esophagus, and of organs that receive the by-products of cigarette smoke, such as bladder, pancreas, and kidney. Further, cigarette smoking has been associated with decreased lung function, a greater incidence of chronic obstructive pulmonary disease, and acute respiratory disease. The clinician should be aware of the literature on smoking and be able to communicate these findings to patients.

## The Patient's Decision to Stop Smoking

Most patients who smoke are aware that cigarette smoking places them at risk for medical problems. This message is not new. However, many people who smoke develop a rationale for ignoring this clear message. They want to believe that they can continue to smoke because they are somehow different from those smokers who develop medical problems. They are young, or strong, or never seem to be ill, or their parents lived long lives. For these or similar reasons, they believe that they are an exception and can continue to smoke.

These patients make a conscious decision to smoke. They will continue to smoke until they are convinced that it is unwise to do so. Once they decide to stop smoking, they stop. In fact, most patients who stop smoking do so on their own, without professional help. Such patients do not need a formal smoking cessation program.

Other people say that they want to stop smoking but they do not make the commitment to stop. It is important, therefore, to determine why the patient wishes to stop smoking. Ask the patient to write down the reasons he desires to quit. This will encourage the patient to formalize his reasons and can be used as a basis for discussion.

Regardless of the patient's rationale for quitting, the clinician should make a direct, explicit recommendation that the patient stop smoking. The patient should not doubt that his physical health is at risk as long as he continues to smoke. The clinician should state the facts about the immediate as well as the long-term hazards of continuing to smoke for each individual patient. For example, a young patient might be informed that the carbon monoxide in cigarette smoke has an immediate effect on heart and brain tissue. A pregnant patient might be told that carbon monoxide from the cigarette smoke reaches her fetus and could affect its development.

Although the potential medical effects of cigarette smoking are severe, the clinician should be careful to avoid trying to scare the patient into quitting. The clinician should present the consequences of smoking as possibilities and not absolutes. This is important for two reasons. First, it has been recognized that although fear can be a powerful motivator, too much fear can have an inhibiting effect. The patient will ignore the information because it is too threatening and will continue to smoke. The second reason for presenting this information as potential consequences rather than absolute certainties is that there are many people who, for reasons that are not fully understood, do not develop disease even after years of cigarette smoking. Patients may know of relatives or friends for whom this is true. If so, the patient may tend to discredit the clinician's data about smoking and be less willing in the future to accept other recommendations from the clinician.

On the positive side, the clinician should be sure to note that, to the best of our knowledge, the physiological effects of smoking can be reversed. Usually, within 12 months of quitting, the patient's blood chemistries will return to normal, lung capacity will increase, tar deposits in the lungs will disappear, and the risk of medical disease will be equivalent to that of patients who have never smoked.

Perhaps most importantly, the clinician should clearly indicate that he expects the patient to make up his mind. Care should be taken so that the patient does not feel he will be condemned by the clinician if the recommendations are not followed. The clinician should separate his opinion of the patient's cigarette smoking, of which the clinician may strongly disapprove, from that of the patient as a person. Throughout these sessions the clinician should recognize that the patient has the right to continue to smoke and if he chooses to do so, that does not mean that the patient is lacking in any psychological or moral way. Neither does it mean that the clinician–patient relationship should change. The clinician can continue to provide medical care for the patient, and treat him with respect and dignity, and at the same time recommend that the patient stop smoking.

### Smoking Cessation as a Lifestyle Change

When a patient fails the attempt to stop smoking, it is usually due to a combination of factors, which, on balance, favor continuing to smoke rather than stopping. As with other habitual activities of intrinsic pleasure (e.g., overeating, alcoholism, drug abuse), cigarette smoking is a behavior that has many immediate positive consequences and few immediate negative consequences (Table 1). It is only the long-term consequences that are highly negative.

When the smoker attempts to quit, however, the immediate consequences are predominantly negative, and it is only the long-term consequences that are overwhelmingly positive (Table 2). As a result, the smoker who quits may initially experience smoking cessation as extremely negative and resume smoking during this early period. If the patient is able to refrain from smoking during this time, many of the immediate negative factors will decrease (Figure 1).

The emphasis of the Smoking Cessation Program described here is on providing aids that will help the patient through this initial difficult period.

### The Smoking Cessation Program

Once the clinician has stated the need for the patient to stop smoking, he should decide how much help the patient needs to quit. Because counseling for smoking cessation is time consuming for both the clinician and the patient, and because many people are able to quit on their own, the best approach is provide

Table 1. Typical consequences of cigarette smoking

| | Consequences | |
| | Positive | Negative |
| --- | --- | --- |
| Immediate | Physiological sensations | "Smoker's breath" |
| | Pleasure of a familiar habit | Discomfort of others |
| | Anxiety reduction | Social disapproval |
| | Reduction or elimination of physiological withdrawal symptoms | |
| | Reduction or elimination of psychological withdrawal symptoms | |
| | Images of positive personal characteristics (e.g., status, glamour, beauty) | |
| | Feelings of belonging to a group | |
| Delayed | None | Chronic cough |
| | | Stained fingers and/or teeth |
| | | Cost of cigarettes |
| | | Increased risk of cancer, cardiovascular or lung disease |
| | | Poor stamina |

Table 2. Typical consequences of quitting cigarette smoking

| | Consequences | |
| | Positive | Negative |
| --- | --- | --- |
| Immediate | Pride in accomplishment | Physiological withdrawal symptoms |
| | Social approval | Psychological withdrawal symptoms |
| | | Social disapproval |
| | | Absence of a familiar routine |
| Delayed | Reduction of risk of cancer, cardiovascular or lung disease | Social disapproval |
| | Saving of money otherwise spent on cigarettes | |

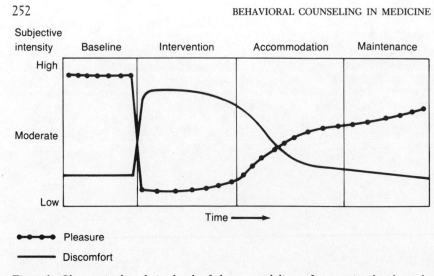

Figure 1. Changes in the relative levels of pleasure and discomfort associated with smoking cessation.

the patient with the materials for the Smoking Cessation Program and allow him to follow it independently. If the patient is not successful or asks for guidance, then the clinician should consider helping the patient start the program.

The Smoking Cessation Program (Table 3) is a simple program consisting of five components that incorporate the methods that have been proven to be the most effective for most people who stop smoking. The program places particular emphasis on the patient's own efforts to quit. It requires neither special training nor equipment, and involves little or no medical risk. The basic steps in this program have been recommended by the National Heart, Lung, and Blood Institute[5] and the American Cancer Society.[6]

*Step 1: Patient Keeps a Self-Record*

If the patient accepts the clinician's recommendation to stop smoking, he should be instructed how to use the Daily Smoking Record to note both the number of cigarettes smoked and the number of urges to smoke (Figure 2). The purpose of monitoring the number of cigarettes smoked each day is to determine the exact level of smoking and the particular situations in which the patient smokes. This information will be used to select an intervention and to assess the degree of the patient's success.

By monitoring his urges to smoke, the patient becomes aware of any self-debate about whether or not to smoke and also has a record of the number of times he decides *not* to smoke. The patient's awareness of self-debate draws his attention to the fact that he has a choice. Once the patient becomes aware of

Table 3. The Smoking Cessation Program

---

*Step 1: Note the following information, for at least 2 days, in the Daily Smoking Record.*
  (1) Each urge you have to smoke.
  (2) Each cigarette you smoke.
  (3) The time you smoke.
  (4) Where you smoke.
  (5) One of the 6 reasons for smoking (i.e., pleasure in handling the cigarette, physiological need, accentuation of pleasure, tension reduction, habit, or stimulation).
  (6) Rating of the importance of the cigarette (0 = none, 10 = extreme).

*Step 2: Use the Smoking Pattern Analysis Chart to determine the characteristics of your cigarette smoking.*
  (1) Tally the number of times you recorded each of the 6 reasons for smoking. The most frequently marked pattern is probably your most common smoking pattern.
  (2) List the cigarettes that you rated "high" (score of 8, 9, or 10) in importance. These cigarettes will be the ones that you will find it most difficult to do without. If you decide to "taper off" your smoking, these cigarettes should be the last ones eliminated.
  (3) List the cigarettes that you rated "low" (score of 0, 1, or 2) in importance. These cigarettes are the ones that you will find it the easiest to do without. If you decide to "taper off," these should be the first ones eliminated.
  (4) List the situations in which you had the urge to smoke but resisted. Try to determine how you were able to resist the urge. You may be able to use this strategy with other urges to smoke.

*Step 3: Select a smoking cessation aid.*
  Select from the list of smoking cessation aids those suggestions that relate to your most frequent reasons for smoking. Select aids that you will be comfortable trying.

*Step 4: Select a quitting date.*
  Choose a day to stop smoking; it should be one on which you have no special activities planned.

*Step 5: Plan follow-up.*
  Schedule a follow-up visit with the clinician.

---

this, he should begin to realize that, contrary to the common belief among smokers, an individual can influence his smoking pattern. Further, the patient's urges to smoke will become the target of specific intervention strategies later in the program.

The Daily Smoking Record also requires the patient to note how much importance he attaches to each cigarette. The degree of importance ranges from 1 (extremely low) to 10 (extremely high) and is defined simply as the strength of the desire the patient feels to have the cigarette. Recording this information makes the patient aware that many times he is smoking "without thinking" and could very well forgo a cigarette. This information will be used later in designing an intervention strategy.

The column labeled "Reason" on the Daily Smoking Record is for the patient's evaluation of why a particular cigarette was smoked. The patient chooses from among the six reasons described below.

DAILY SMOKING LOG

Day: _____

| U/C* | Time | Location | Importance rating (0–10) | Reason** |
|------|------|----------|--------------------------|----------|
| ___ | ___ | _____ | _____ | _____ |
| ___ | ___ | _____ | _____ | _____ |
| ___ | ___ | _____ | _____ | _____ |
| ___ | ___ | _____ | _____ | _____ |
| ___ | ___ | _____ | _____ | _____ |
| ___ | ___ | _____ | _____ | _____ |
| ___ | ___ | _____ | _____ | _____ |
| ___ | ___ | _____ | _____ | _____ |
| ___ | ___ | _____ | _____ | _____ |
| ___ | ___ | _____ | _____ | _____ |
| ___ | ___ | _____ | _____ | _____ |
| ___ | ___ | _____ | _____ | _____ |
| ___ | ___ | _____ | _____ | _____ |
| ___ | ___ | _____ | _____ | _____ |
| ___ | ___ | _____ | _____ | _____ |
| ___ | ___ | _____ | _____ | _____ |
| ___ | ___ | _____ | _____ | _____ |
| ___ | ___ | _____ | _____ | _____ |

*U = Urge
C = Cigarette

**Reasons:
1 = To handle something
2 = Physical craving
3 = To accentuate pleasure

4 = To reduce tension
5 = As a habit
6 = As stimulation
7 = Other (describe)

Figure 2. Daily Smoking Record.

*Pleasure in Handling the Cigarette.*    Some cigarettes are smoked because the patient derives pleasure from the simple ritual of taking out a pack of cigarettes, lighting one, and handling it while it is burning. The patient is aware of smoking and enjoys the activities that surround it. Cigarettes are often smoked for this reason during leisure time, or when the patient is only slightly involved in some other activity.

*Physiological Need.*    Patients smoke many cigarettes because of a physiological need. The mildly disturbing sensations of withdrawal from nicotine provoke continued smoking. Cigarettes are usually smoked for this reason after a certain amount of time has passed since the last cigarette, regardless of other activities.

*Stimulation.*   Patients often smoke to increase their alertness or to wake up. Frequently, cigarettes are smoked for this reason in the early morning, or during a morning or afternoon break from work.

*Accentuation of Pleasure.*   Often, patients smoke when they are at leisure to enhance the feelings of relaxation. These situations might include smoking in the evening while watching television, after a meal, or while reading.

*Tension Reduction.*   Patients frequently will smoke to ease the anxiety or fear they experience in certain situations. Smoking has a calming effect that helps them handle the stressful situation.

*Habit.*   The reason patients most commonly cite for smoking is that it simply is a habit. They smoke cigarettes because it is part of their routine, and they are only vaguely aware that they are lighting and smoking them while they are absorbed in other activities.

The patient should record, over at least a 2-day period, every cigarette smoked. The days on which the record is kept should be typical ones, including a weekday and a weekend day. They do not have to be consecutive but should be fairly close together (e.g., Thursday and Saturday, Sunday and Tuesday. The patient should carry the Daily Smoking Record with him and make notes at the time he smokes or has an urge, not later in the day. The more accurate the information in the Daily Smoking Record, the more likely it is that a true pattern of the patient's smoking will emerge, and the easier it will be for the patient to quit.

## Step 2: Analyze the Smoking Pattern

The 2-day Daily Smoking Record provides information that is crucial to the analysis of the patient's personal smoking pattern. The nature of the pattern determines the type of intervention used.

The patient should follow the steps in the Smoking Pattern Analysis Chart (Figure 3). First, the patient should tally the number of times he smoked a cigarette for each of the six basic reasons. This will indicate the one or two primary reasons the patient is currently smoking. Second, the patient should list all of the situations which were rated either 8, 9, or 10 in terms of importance. These situations will require special consideration in the intervention strategy. The patient should also list situations which were rated 1, 2 or 3 (Figure 3) in importance. These may be eliminated easily, without use of a special intervention.

Finally, the patient should list those situations in which he felt the urge to smoke but decided not to, and should identify why he resisted the urge. If he

*Step 1: Tally the number of times each of the 6 reasons for smoking was marked on the Daily Smoking Record.*

Tally

1. Handling     _____
2. Physiological need     _____
3. Accentuate pleasure     _____
4. Tension reduction     _____
5. Habit     _____
6. Stimulation     _____
   Other     _____

*Step 2: List all situations for which the cigarette was rated "high" (8, 9, or 10) in importance.*

1. _____
2. _____
3. _____
4. _____
5. _____

*Step 3: List all situations for which the cigarette was rated "low" (0, 1, or 2) in importance.*

1. _____
2. _____
3. _____
4. _____
5. _____

*Step 4: List any situations in which you recorded an urge to smoke but resisted it. Note any special strategy used.*

        Situation                           Strategy

1. _____    1. _____
2. _____    2. _____
3. _____    3. _____
4. _____    4. _____
5. _____    5. _____

Figure 3. Smoking Pattern Analysis Chart.

deliberately used a particular technique, this should be noted and considered for inclusion in the intervention plan.

### Step 3: Select a Smoking Cessation Aid

Once the patient's typical smoking pattern has been identified, one or more aids can be selected that will help support his quitting. The patient should be aware that no technique has been developed that will prevent him from experiencing at least some discomfort when he stops smoking. The techniques listed are simply aids to reduce the discomfort and make cessation easier. The following sections discuss why the aids described for each of the major smoking patterns are effective. A list of the specific aids, by smoking pattern, is contained in Table 4. It should be emphasized that the patient should review this list and

Table 4. Smoking cessation aids, listed by primary reason for smoking

*Smoking Pattern No. 1: Pleasure in handling the cigarette.*
Select an object or activity to handle that is similar to a cigarette:
   (1) A pen or pencil.
   (2) A drinking straw.
   (3) A plastic stir-stick.
   (4) A string of beads.
   (5) A large paper clip.
   (6) A pen knife or nail clipper.


*Smoking Pattern No. 2: Physiological craving.*
Because the physiological withdrawal from cigarettes lasts only a few days, these aids are designed to help you resist the urge to smoke:
   (1) Throw out all cigarettes and matchbooks you have left.
   (2) Place ashtrays on a shelf that requires effort to reach.
   (3) Purchase small candies, throat lozenges, or gum with strong flavors (e.g., peppermint, spearmint, licorice, ginger, anise). Use a breath freshener, mouthwash, or spray. Chew sunflower seeds.
   (4) When you have the urge to smoke, breathe deeply with the lips pursed and momentarily hold your breath, as you would if you were smoking.
   (5) Drink ice water.
   (6) Avoid alcoholic beverages (because of their strong association with cigarette smoking and because they can impair your judgment).


*Smoking Pattern No. 3: Stimulation.*
These aids, rather than a cigarette, refresh and stimulate you:
   (1) Wash face, neck, and hands in cool water.
   (2) Use an eyewash to refresh tired eyes.
   (3) Stand up and stretch arms above head.
   (4) Walk up one or more flights of stairs.
   (5) Do 10 push-ups.
   (6) Drink cold fruit juice.
   (7) Drink ice water.


*Smoking Pattern No. 4: Accentuation of pleasure.*
These aids encourage you to focus on the pleasurable sensations of an activity (e.g., eating, reading, having sex, drinking, physical activity) in place of the cigarette:
   (1) Take a "mental photograph" of the situation that you will remember later.
   (2) Take note of the subtle flavors of the foods you eat.
   (3) Take one sip of a drink or one bite of food and enjoy its texture and flavor for as long as possible.
   (4) Focus on your pleasurable feelings and try to prolong them as long as possible.


*Smoking Pattern No. 5: Tension reduction.*
These aids help reduce feelings of stress:
   (1) Reduce the amount of caffeine you consume by limiting the number of cups of coffee, cola, and tea you drink.
   (2) Engage in a physical activity suited to your level of physical fitness.
   (3) Substitute a favorite food or drink (in moderation) for a cigarette.
   (4) Avoid situations you know are stressful during the initial 2 to 3 weeks of the smoking cessation program.
   (5) Plan to get a good night's sleep each night during the first few days, beginning with the night before the quitting date.

Table 4. Smoking cessation aids, listed by primary reason for smoking (*continued*)

---

*Smoking Pattern No. 6: Habit.*

These aids help make you aware of each cigarette so you will have to decide whether or not to smoke it:

   (1) If you decide to "taper off," place your cigarettes in a different container.
   (2) If you decide to "taper off," place cigarettes in a different location (e.g., pocket, purse).
   (3) If you decide to "taper off," do not carry matches so you will have to ask others for a light.
   (4) Throw out your cigarettes; you will have to ask for a cigarette from a friend if you want one.
   (5) Change cigarette brands so you will notice each cigarette you smoke.

---

select an aid that seems best suited to his particular tastes. Each of the aids listed for a particular smoking pattern functions similarly.

*Aids for Pattern No. 1: Pleasure in Handling the Cigarette.*   These are substitute objects that provide tactile stimulation. Any object can be used, providing it is portable, unobtrusive, and similar in general shape, weight, and texture to a cigarette.

*Aids for Pattern No. 2: Physiological Craving.*   These are designed to help the patient resist the temptation to smoke once he has quit by making it more difficult to resume smoking.

*Aids for Pattern No. 3: Stimulation.*   Patients who derive pleasure from the stimulating qualities of cigarette smoking can substitute activities that provide similar sensations. These aids emphasize a substitute physical activity for smoking, other than eating. Eating tends to be a stimulus to smoke (and can also lead to weight gain).

*Aids for Pattern No. 4: Accentuation of Pleasure.*   These are designed to help the patient become more aware of the pleasurable aspects of certain situations and focus on enhancing them. In this way the patient can learn to enjoy these times without a cigarette.

*Aids for Pattern No. 5: Tension Reduction.*   The aids listed for tension reduction provide alternatives to smoking for reducing the level. These techniques must be practiced so that the patient can use them with only minimal disruption of his ongoing activities.

*Aids for Pattern No. 6: Habit.*   Because the patient smokes habitual cigarettes with little thought or pleasure, they will not be missed. These aids are designed to disrupt the habit and draw the patient's attention to the cigarette smoking so that he has the opportunity to make the decision to smoke or not. Cigarettes smoked out of habit are usually resisted fairly easily.

## Step 4: Select a Quitting Date

The patient should select a quitting date after which he pledges that he will no longer smoke. The day chosen should be one that will be fairly routine. Avoid days on which there are special activities, social events, travel, or holidays planned for that date.

## Step 5: Plan Follow-up

Before the patient leaves the clinic, a date should be set to follow up on the patient's experience with the smoking cessation program. This follow-up should be about 3 days after the quitting date. Because the patient will spend at least 2 days keeping a self-record (see Step 1), the follow-up day should be 7 days from the date of the current clinic visit. The follow-up can be part of a routine visit to the clinic for medical purposes or it can be accomplished by telephone.

The purpose of the follow-up is to provide a specific opportunity to review the success of the smoking cessation program and to resolve any problems the patient has encountered. The clinician can also offer encouragement to the patient during what is the most difficult time of the program. By picking a specific date for follow-up, the patient makes an agreement with the clinician to begin the program before the follow-up contact date. In this way, the patient has further encouragement to initiate the program.

### Helping a Patient Start a Smoking Cessation Program

Even though the steps in the Smoking Cessation Program are clear, many patients will not be able to design a smoking cessation program on their own. The following guidelines should help the clinician design a smoking cessation program with the patient (Table 5).

## Step 1: Review the Patient's Decision to Stop Smoking

First, clarify why the patient has decided to stop smoking at this time. What does the patient identify as the reason(s) he has chosen to quit? Does the patient sound as if he is committed to his decision to quit smoking, or is it more likely that his decision is based on superficial or transitory reasons (e.g., social pressure from friends, the urging of the physician)? Before designing a smoking cessation program the clinician should be convinced that the patient's decision is definite. During the early phase of the Smoking Cessation Program, the patient may self-debate whether or not to continue with a program that is uncomfortable. If the initial decision is not a firm one, then the patient is likely to resume smoking rather than abstain. If the patient has not made a firm decision to stop

Table 5.  Steps to help a patient start the Smoking Cessation Program

*Step 1: Review the patient's decision.*
   Identify the patient's rationale for quitting.

*Step 2: Review potential difficulties.*
   Discuss the difficulties the patient might experience in quitting.

*Step 3: Select short-term and long-term goals.*
   Explain how the patient should use the Daily Smoking Record.

*Step 4: Analyze the patient's smoking pattern.*
   Use the Smoking Pattern Analysis Chart to identify the patient's typical smoking patterns.

*Step 5: Select a smoking cessation aid.*
   Help the patient choose a smoking cessation aid.

*Step 6: Select a quitting date.*
   Help the patient choose a quitting date.

*Step 7: Monitor the patient's progress.*
   Encourage the patient to continue to keep the Daily Smoking Record to identify successes and failures.

*Step 8: Plan follow-up.*
   Schedule follow-up contact (by telephone or in the clinic) for approximately 10 days after the quitting date.

---

smoking, the clinician should discuss the patient's perceptions of the positive and negative factors associated with smoking and with quitting. The patient should be cautioned not to start the Smoking Cessation Program until he has firmly decided to quit.

## Step 2: Discuss the Potential Difficulties of Quitting Smoking

The patient should understand the pattern of alternating pleasure and discomfort he can expect to encounter during the Smoking Cessation Program (Figure 1). While he is smoking, the level of pleasure will be high. When he quits, the pleasure drops markedly and the level of discomfort rises dramatically. It is this period, immediately following smoking cessation, that is the most difficult. However, as the patient accommodates physiologically, psychologically, and behaviorally to a daily routine without cigarettes, the pleasure level steadily rises while the discomfort level declines.

The behavioral approach to smoking cessation provides specific aids to help the patient counter the discomfort experienced during the days immediately following quitting. The aids correspond to the smoking patterns the patient followed and are meant to be used temporarily. None eliminates the discomfort completely; neither do the aids provide the high level of intrinsic pleasure smoking used to give the patient. However, they do help the patient tolerate the discomfort and successfully achieve complete withdrawal from cigarettes.

## Step 3: Select Short-Term and Long-Term Goals

The clinician should urge the patient to conscientiously keep the Daily Smoking Record for 2 days. The patient should understand the importance of this step and not skip over it to begin the Smoking Cessation Program immediately.

The patient's response to this "homework" assignment is sometimes predictive of whether or not the patient will be able to follow the Smoking Cessation Program. Although recording each cigarette smoked requires some effort by the patient and does tend to be annoying at times, the disruption this simple task creates is very much less than that which the full Smoking Cessation Program will create. If the patient is not willing to use the Daily Smoking Record or does not complete it as instructed, the clinician should consider whether or not the patient will be able to follow the full program and whether this is the best time for the patient to be quitting smoking. An explicit commitment to follow the program, as designed, must be obtained from the patient.

Step 3 concludes the initial interview with the patient. The patient should be scheduled for a follow-up appointment in 1 week to continue with Steps 4 to 7.

## Step 4: Analyze the Patient's Smoking Pattern

In the follow-up interview, the clinician should review with the patient the completed Daily Smoking Record and Smoking Pattern Analysis Chart to identify the patient's usual smoking pattern. The clinician also should identify any other patterns that occurred more than three times each day.

The accuracy of this pattern analysis has a major effect on whether the specific smoking cessation aids will be effective. Misdiagnosis of the patient's smoking pattern will likely lead to failure of the program. Unfortunately, most patients do not understand how a smoking pattern relates to the use of a specific smoking cessation aid. He may consider one aid to be as effective as any other and may choose one for the wrong reasons (e.g., the aid is popular, it is inexpensive, it worked for a friend). The patient's use of an inappropriate (and therefore ineffective) aid may lead him to believe that since that aid is as good as any other and it didn't work, then the patient's failure to stop smoking must be the result of his inability to change. Thus the patient will be unlikely to try to quit smoking again soon.

## Step 5: Select a Smoking Cessation Aid

Once the patient's smoking patterns have been identified, the patient should review the list of smoking cessation aids (Table 4) and select one for each smoking pattern. The clinician should help the patient identify a specific plan for using each aid and should be satisfied that the patient is leaving the interview with a detailed plan, not simply a general idea of what to do. The aid or technique also must fit into the patient's daily routine. If the aid is unrealistic (e.g., a patient selects a physical activity break as a substitute for a cigarette break, yet the clinician is aware that the patient's daily work schedule will not easily accommodate this), then the patient should be urged to select another one.

In some cases, the clinician may need to help the patient to tailor the aid to his lifestyle. For example, a patient may select the aid, "Avoid situations in which others smoke." If a patient decides not to join co-workers who smoke at the office during coffee breaks and lunch, the clinician should encourage the patient to make a list of alternative activities for these times (e.g., shopping trips, brisk walking, visiting a museum).

## Step 6: Select a Quitting Date

The patient should select a quitting date that is at least 2 days but not more than 1 week from the date of the second interview. This allows for some anticipation and preparation time yet the patient can still start the program while he is eager to make a change. The quitting date should be a routine day for the patient. It is also helpful if no special activities are planned for the week after the quitting date.

The patient should use the time between the second interview and the quitting date to prepare for the smoking cessation program. Family, friends, or co-workers who might be supportive of the patient's efforts to stop smoking should be informed. Special foods (e.g., low-calorie snacks such as sugarless gum, hard candies, unsalted popcorn) and materials to be used as aids (e.g., stickers to use as cues, a small charm or special coin to handle instead of a cigarette) should be prepared or purchased.

## Step 7: Monitor the Patient's Progress

The patient should be instructed to complete the Daily Smoking Record each day, beginning with the quitting date. If the patient is unable to stop smoking, or is able to eliminate only certain types of cigarettes (e.g., cigarettes smoked as a habit), then the clinician will need to help the patient. The Daily Smoking Record will show the number of cigarettes smoked along with other information that will be helpful in behavioral counseling, which is discussed later in this chapter.

## Step 8: Plan Follow-up

The patient should be scheduled for a follow-up visit with the clinician in approximately 7 days from the date of the second clinic visit. It may be part of a regular clinic visit or be conducted by telephone.

The purpose of this contact is to let the clinician communicate concern and support to the patient and to recognize his accomplishments. The patient may have greater motivation to begin the program if he knows that there will be subsequent contact with the clinician to check on his progress. If the patient is experiencing difficulties getting started, then the clinician will have the opportunity to modify the program and resolve problems early on.

## Weight Gain: A Common Problem

Weight gain after quitting smoking is a common problem for many patients. An average weight gain of 5.0 to 7.5 lb. can be anticipated. Patients who gain more than this may become extremely distressed and consider resuming smoking simply to lose the weight. Although the physiological basis for this weight gain is not entirely clear, it is suspected that the stimulation from the nicotine in the cigarettes suppresses the appetite. Further, smoking cessation often leads to enhanced taste and smell, which may in turn increase the patient's enjoyment of food.

Because weight gain is such a common phenomenon and of concern to most patients, it is important that the patient receive some dietary guidance before quitting smoking. The patient should be alerted to the possibility of feeling hungry more often. Moreover, the patient should be prepared to follow a diet that allows him to eat more but without a substantial increase in calories. Low-calorie snacks, smoking cessation aids, and balanced meals are all important.

If the patient currently does not have a balanced diet, or has one that includes foods that are high in fats and calories, the clinician might consider referring the patient for dietary counseling before initiating the Smoking Cessation Program. The patient could then learn about a balanced diet and be prepared with proper foods and snacks during the smoking cessation program. In this way the weight gain could be avoided or at least minimized.

## Behavioral Counseling to Resolve Patient-Specific Problems

Some patients' failure to quit smoking can be traced to specific personal, family, or lifestyle conditions that are only minimally affected by the usual smoking cessation aids. For example, a patient whose co-workers all smoke or a patient who is under considerable and persistent stress at work and at home may need more help than is provided in the steps outlined so far.

The following 11 steps of behavioral counseling (Table 6) should be used to help patients who have not been successful with the basic Smoking Cessation Program.

Table 6. Eleven-step behavioral counseling for patients having problems with the Smoking Cessation Program

---

Step  1: *Identify the problem.*
To what degree does each of the following seem to be present?
(1) Absence of commitment to the initial decision.
(2) Continuing self-debate.
(3) Negative factors in the environment that are punishing the patient for trying to quit smoking.

Step  2: *Clarify the goals of treatment.*
(1) What are the patient's short-term goals?
(2) What are the patient's long-term goals?

Step  3: *Collect information.*
(1) Obtain detailed information from the 2-day Daily Smoking Record.
(2) Obtain additional information about the environmental stimuli and consequences affecting the patient's cigarette smoking.

Step  4: *Develop a behavioral diagnosis.*
Identify the consistent relationships among the primary and secondary factors surrounding the cigarette smoking supporting or inhibiting it.

Step  5: *Generate an intervention plan.*
(1) Keep the plan simple.
(2) Identify strategies that will inhibit cigarette smoking and make not smoking more attractive.

Step  6: *Intervene.*
(1) Encourage the patient to agree to use the intervention plan for at least 3 days in order to overcome the physical withdrawal symptoms and allow the new routine to become established.
(2) Encourage the patient to continue to collect information in the Daily Smoking Record about any cigarettes smoked.
(3) Write out the intervention plan and give it to the patient.

Step  7: *Review the patient's progress.*
(1) Request that the patient call the clinician on the second day of the program, so that any problems can be detected early on.
(2) Request that the patient contact the clinician 10 days after the start of the program to assess his or her progress and revise the behavioral diagnosis, if necessary.

Step  8: *Generate a revised intervention plan.*
Write out the revised program for the patient.

Step  9: *Reintervene.*
Encourage the patient to agree to use the revised intervention plan for at least 3 days in order to accommodate to the new routine.

Step 10: *Develop a maintenance program.*
Develop a plan to withdraw any artificial aids used to stop smoking.

Step 11: *Review the behavior change process.*
(1) Review with the patient the strategies that seemed to be most effective.
(2) Identify the steps the patient should use to restart the smoking cessation program, if necessary.
(3) Write out the details of how to restart the smoking cessation plan and give them to the patient.

## Step 1: Identify the Problem

Patients' problems with initiating and maintaining a smoking cessation program usually fall into one of three general categories: (1) difficulty implementing one of the steps of the program, (2) continuing self-debate whether or not to smoke, or (3) negative factors in the environment (e.g., lack of support, criticism, peer pressure to smoke). Often the patient's problem involves a combination of categories, for example, a patient who keeps a poor record of his smoking patterns and who reports that he is uncomfortable not smoking when he is with friends at a party.

The clinician must clarify with the patient the problem or problems that occurred when the patient attempted to stop smoking. Together they should explore each of these potential problems as the patient may not be able to conceptualize his problems easily in this manner. Once the patient's general problem(s) is identified, the next step is to obtain more specific details about it.

## Step 2: Clarify the Goals of Treatment

Although the goal of the Smoking Cessation Program may seem self-evident to the clinician, it may not be to the patient. Some patients who request a smoking cessation program do not really wish to stop smoking; rather, they want a "half-way goal" at which they can continue to smoke but in a more medically acceptable way. For example, they hope to reduce the number or type of cigarettes they smoke but intend to continue to smoke. This situation is frequently seen with other substances with addictive properties. The alcoholic desires to reduce the amount of alcohol consumed but not stop drinking; the heroin or cocaine user hopes to limit daily intake but not stop altogether.

If the patient has selected a half-way goal as the aim of treatment and the clinician is not aware of it, it is likely that the clinician will be frustrated and the program unsuccessful. Although reducing the number of cigarettes smoked per day and switching to a cigarette lower in tar and nicotine is medically advisable, the Smoking Cessation Program is designed for the patient to achieve and maintain abstinence. It is not designed to help the patient achieve half-way goals. Even if a patient achieves a half-way goal, it is highly likely that he will back into his previous smoking pattern. No program has yet proven to be effective in helping patients merely reduce smoking.

## Step 3: Collect Information

The clinician needs two types of information to understand the patient's smoking pattern and problems. The first is the Daily Smoking Record.

The clinician also needs information to formulate a behavioral diagnosis of the patient's problem. (The procedure for developing a behavioral diagnosis is described in detail in Chapter 4.) To develop a behavioral diagnosis for the patient who smokes, the clinician must examine both the cigarette smoking and the patient's attempts to quit within the context of the patient's other activities and environment. The clinician may obtain most of this information through discussions with the patient. However, when the patient is vague or not sure, additional information may be obtained using a modification of the Daily Smoking Record. For example, a patient may not be aware of the variety of activities during which she smokes during the day. The clinician might instruct her to describe the activity instead of simply noting the place where she smoked in the Daily Smoking Record.

The collection of accurate, detailed information is extremely important at this phase of counseling. This information will shape the clinician's behavioral diagnosis and the recommended treatment. Most important, the patient is also learning that cigarette smoking is not simply a habit which occurs and is sustained by itself. The patient becomes increasingly self-observant and begins to recognize that it is influenced by other activities and the environment. The patient will then be able to understand the "implement–evaluate–modify" approach used by the clinician to help the patient stop smoking and collaborate with the clinician in identifying potential intervention strategies.

### Step 4: Develop a Behavioral Diagnosis

An effective lifestyle change depends upon an accurate diagnosis. The behavioral diagnosis will determine what strategy is chosen to resolve the patient's difficulty with the Smoking Cessation Program. It is a succinct description of the functional relationship between the factors in the environment and the target behavior. The behavioral diagnosis identifies activities that provoke the behavior and the factors in the environment that support it. The following is an example of a behavioral diagnosis:

> A patient's smoking was prompted by sitting with friends who smoke at lunch. The smoking is supported by the patient's wish to avoid telling his friends that he is stopping smoking. The patient believes that his friends would interpret his stopping smoking as a rejection of them or of their lifestyle.

Usually, the behavioral diagnosis is a more exact statement of the patient's unique difficulty within one of the three main problem areas (i.e., a problem implementing one of the steps in the program, continuing self-debate, or negative factors in the environment). Several behavioral diagnoses may have to be developed for a single patient: for example, one for the patient's difficulty with withdrawal symptoms, one for the criticism he gets from others, and one for his continuing self-debate.

*Step 5: Generate an Intervention Plan*

The intervention plan should be a combination of strategies designed to reduce or eliminate factors that prompt and support the cigarette smoking and to attempt to introduce elements into the patient's daily routine that will promote and support non-smoking activities. Both smoking and non-smoking activities should be addressed.

Because the goal of the Smoking Cessation Program is complete abstinence, the intervention plan should contain a strategy to resolve each of the patient's difficulties. An intervention plan that focuses on only one problem at a time is not likely to be successful. The clinician and patient should identify a strategy for each problem before the overall program is begun (i.e., before the quitting date).

A potential problem with this comprehensive approach is that if the patient has multiple problems, the list of strategies may become very lengthy. Unfortunately, the more changes that the patient must make, the less likely it is that the program will succeed. Therefore, the entire program should be reviewed before implementing it to determine if the patient will be able to manage all of the changes recommended.

If more than three changes are being suggested, the program should initially address changes that are not directly related to the number of cigarettes smoked each day. For example, if a patient habitually smokes while drinking coffee, and he drinks five or more cups of coffee each day, a pre-smoking-cessation goal might be to restrict the number of cups of coffee consumed to one or two per day. If successful, this could contribute substantially to the smoking cessation program. A patient might be encouraged to begin a daily program of brisk walking for 20 minutes before lunch. This would contribute to an enhanced sense of physical well-being and perhaps function as a substitute for cigarettes usually smoked early in the afternoon to increase alertness.

*Step 6: Intervene*

The patient should be asked to follow the intervention program for a minimum of 3 days. These 3 days will be the most difficult for the patient because of nicotine withdrawal combined with the psychological changes that accompany any new behavior and the disruption in normal routine. Therefore, the patient's commitment to attempt the program for 3 days is crucial. No changes should be made in the program during this time.

Because cigarette smoking is a behavior that normally occurs often during a day, the intervention should be closely monitored by the patient during the first days. The patient may be asked to keep a Daily Smoking Record of his urges to smoke as well as recurrent thoughts about cigarette smoking. This helps the

**MICHAEL L. RUSSELL, Ph.D.**
Department of Internal Medicine
Baylor College of Medicine
Tel. 799-6032

**Program for Change**

For: *M.K.*                    Date: *4/2/84*

1. Limit beverages with caffeine to 2 cups of coffee at breakfast.
2. Change cigarette brands.
3. Record in the Daily Smoking Log each cigarette smoked, every day.
4. Complete the Smoking Pattern analysis Chart the day before your next clinic visit.
5. Schedule a clinic visit in 10 days.

                                    *M.J.Russell*

Figure 4. Example of a behavioral prescription for the smoking cessation program.

patient express his discomfort, and provides the clinician with an accurate record of the difficulties the patient has in implementing the cessation program.

As with other lifestyle changes, the specific actions that the patient is to take during the smoking cessation program should be clearly written as a "behavioral prescription" (Figure 4). This explicit list of what the patient should do leaves little room for misunderstanding after the patient has left the clinic.

*Step 7: Review the Patient's Progress*

The patient should be instructed to contact the clinician during the second day of the behavior change program. This contact may be brief and made by telephone. Its purpose is to monitor the patient's progress in following the new program and to encourage him during this difficult phase.

If the patient is having difficulty following the program, the clinician should determine if all problems have been identified and whether the behavioral diagnoses developed for the known problems are accurate. Then, if necessary, the clinician can use this opportunity to modify the program based on the pa-

tient's experience so far. This will avoid the situation in which the patient decides on his own to modify or stop the program.

### Step 8: Generate a Revised Intervention Plan

If a new or revised program is designed, it should be written in detail for the
patient, regardless of how simple the changes suggested might be. Usually several possible changes are discussed, and patients often do not remember all that
is said in the clinic interview. This avoids any confusion the patient might have
about what he should do in the next few days.

### Step 9: Reintervene

The patient should be asked to make a commitment to try the new program for
at least three days before considering any changes. This will allow for the initial
accommodation to occur, and also will postpone any self-debate. The patient
should agree to contact the clinician in 2–3 days to discuss his progress and
make any changes deemed necessary.

### Steps 10 and 11: Develop a Maintenance Program
### and Review the Behavior Change Process

Once the patient has achieved abstinence from cigarette smoking for at least 1
month, a maintenance program should be developed. It should have two parts.
The first part is a plan for withdrawing all artificial aids that had helped the
patient stop smoking. The patient should be able to cope with all situations and
not smoke, without using any of the special strategies used initially.

The second part is a specific program for the patient to follow if he feels that
the temptation to return to smoking is becoming too great. This program will
vary from patient to patient, but it should involve reinstituting the artificial
strategies that helped the patient stop smoking in the first place. The strategies
should be written down so that the patient can take the list home. Finally, the
patient should be encouraged to contact the clinician for help in either preventing a lapse or in reinstituting the cessation program.

### Specific Counseling Strategies

Some patients do not succeed with the smoking cessation program because of
unique, patient-specific factors. In these cases, the patient's smoking is controlled by powerful environmental factors that encourage him to continue to
smoke and render the basic Smoking Cessation Program ineffective. Many pa-

Table 7. Counseling strategies for patient-specific problems in the Smoking Cessation Program

| Problem | Strategies |
|---|---|
| Patient reports no support or a negative reaction from family or co-workers | Use a self-contract. |
| | Acquire assertiveness skills. |
| Patient reports that cigarette smoking is too tempting | Use a self-contract. |
| | Arrange the environment so that it is difficult to smoke |
| | Arrange the environment so that it is unpleasant to smoke |

tients report that they want to stop smoking, tried to stop, but did not succeed because they "need to smoke because of the stress [they] are under at work," or they "can't stop smoking as long as [their spouse] continues to smoke," or they think they don't have enough "willpower."

The clinician has several counseling strategies (Table 7) that can be helpful in resolving these problems. These strategies would be used at Step 6 in the behavioral counseling process. The clinician should be cautious in using them, however, and have already made a behavioral diagnosis. If a strategy is misapplied, it may be ineffective and result in the patient's losing his motivation to continue with the program.

### Increase Positive Consequences

If the behavioral diagnosis indicates that the patient is aware of no positive consequences or of only negative ones, the clinician might consider using one of the following strategies:

*Use a Contract.* A formal or informal self-contract is helpful for specifying explicit positive consequences that will occur if the patient follows the Smoking Cessation Program for a given period of time. The contract also can be used to promote the support of family members or co-workers. An example of a self-contract is presented in Figure 5.

*Provide the Patient with Assertiveness Skills.* Some patients have not actually experienced negative reactions from their family or co-workers but fear that they will. In most cases, this fear is based on the patient's unwillingness to assert his personal preference because of an unrealistic belief that the response from the family or co-workers will be unpleasant or hostile. The clinician can help the patient by rehearsing what he might do and say in these situations. The patient can be asked to role play briefly with the clinician exactly how he would tell

PERSONAL CONTRACT

Activity: *Stopping cigarette smoking*

Level of Performance: *Complete stopping of smoking cigarettes for one week (ie Monday to monday)*

Consequences:

If I follow the routine (described above) for *1 week*

then I will provide myself with the small reward of:

*Purchasing a new tie on Monday with the $9⁰⁰ I saved from not smoking.*

As further encouragement to follow my routine, if I do not do so,

then I promise to:

*Donate $9⁰⁰ on monday to the Republican Party*

*m Kearl*

signature

*4/16/84*

date

Figure 5. Example of a self-contract for smoking cessation.

people about his decision to stop smoking and how he would react to mildly negative questions asked by the clinician. This role playing need not take more than 3 to 5 minutes and can easily be accomplished in a clinic visit. It can reduce the patient's anxiety about discussing the topic and usually enables the patient to carry out the intervention program as planned. A more detailed discussion of assertiveness training is contained in Chapter 4.

*Increase Negative Consequences*

Although the long-term negative consequences of smoking are well known, it is more often the short-term consequences that actually result in smoking cessation. The following strategies help provide immediate negative consequences for smoking.

*Use a Contract.*   The self-contract for smoking cessation should specify a negative consequence that will occur if the patient does not adhere to the agreed-upon regimen. For example, a patient agrees to deposit $40 with a friend before stopping smoking. The positive consequence of not smoking is to receive a return of $10 each week. If the patient does smoke during that week, however, the $10 is sent by the friend to the patient's "least favorite" charity or nonprofit organization.

*Rearrange the Environment.*   The patient can rearrange his home or office so that cigarette smoking becomes extremely difficult or unpleasant. The more effort and trouble the patient must go through to be able to smoke, the easier it will be to forgo smoking those cigarettes that are rated low in importance. For example, a patient can remove all ashtrays from sight and place them on the upper shelf of a cabinet, place her cigarette lighter in a locked drawer, and throw out all matchbooks, as well as remove all cigarettes from her home and office.

### Case Illustration

The following case illustration describes a typical patient who might be seen in an outpatient medical clinic. It illustrates most major aspects of designing a smoking cessation program and how to resolve problems.

### The Patient

A 34-year-old woman has no physical complaints and scheduled the present clinic visit for a general physical examination. She was found to be in good physical health.

### First Visit

As part of the general medical history, the patient reported that she currently smoked approximately 1 pack of "low tar," filter cigarettes each day. She has a 20-year history of cigarette smoking. When asked about her smoking, she stated that she had been thinking about quitting and had tried to quit in the past but failed. She reported trying "the special plastic filters that reduce the amount of smoke you get," but said that after 4 days she "could not seem to get used to the last filter" and never actually quit. She said that she was getting worried about her smoking and its effects on her health, and would "really like to stop."

She asked if the clinician had any suggestions. The clinician followed the steps outlined in Table 5.

*Step 1: Review the Patient's Rationale for Stopping Smoking.* The clinician reviewed with the patient her desire to stop smoking. She stated that she disliked her "smoker's cough" and was worried that her smoking would affect the health of her 2-year-old daughter. She also was aware that smoking was "risky" because she was taking birth control pills. The clinician determined that she had good reasons for quitting and had reached this decision on her own. She supported her decision and clearly stated her recommendation that the patient stop smoking. She also indicated her willingness to help.

*Step 2: Discuss the Potential Difficulties of Quitting Smoking.* The patient felt that it would be too difficult for her to stop smoking on her own. She was aware that the physical withdrawal symptoms would be uncomfortable. In addition, she said that most of her friends and co-workers smoked and she felt that they would be "hurt" if she no longer joined them in cigarette breaks. This, in turn, would make her very uncomfortable.

It was clear that the patient was not likely to be able to follow the Smoking Cessation Program on her own. Therefore, the clinician offered to guide her through the program if the patient agreed to return to the clinic for two additional visits to monitor her progress. The patient agreed to this plan.

*Step 3: Patient Keeps a Self-Record.* The clinician then discussed the Smoking Cessation Program with the patient and answered her questions. She taught her how to use the Daily Smoking Record for the next 2 days and how to use the Smoking Pattern Analysis Chart. Both were to be completed before she returned for her next visit, scheduled in 1 week.

*Second Visit*

The patient returned for a follow-up visit one week later.

*Step 4: Analyze the Patient's Smoking Pattern.* The clinician reviewed with the patient the Daily Smoking Record and the Smoking Pattern Analysis Chart. It was clear that the patient's most frequent smoking pattern was for relaxation (10 of 20 times, or 50%; 10 of 21 times, or 47.6%). All of these incidents were rated 8, 9, or 10 in importance. The patient explained that she "had a very stressful office job with two bosses giving her assignments." The next most frequent pattern was smoking for stimulation, specifically taking a cigarette break with co-workers (4 of 20 times or 20%; 6 of 21 times or 28.6%). These were rated 6, 7, or 8 in importance. The patient only recorded one urge to smoke, which she overcame while watching television one evening at home.

*Step 5: Select a Smoking Cessation Aid.* The patient reviewed the list of smoking cessation aids for the smoking pattern of tension reduction and decided to reduce the current number of beverages with caffeine that she drank from 10 per day to two or three. This should have an immediate calming effect. For the smoking pattern of stimulation, she decided to walk downstairs, around the floor of the building, and then upstairs again. She would also purchase fruit juice for a snack.

*Step 6: Select a Quitting Date.* The patient stated that the coming week would be "extra stressful" at work. However, the following Monday would be the first of at least 3 routine days. She decided that Sunday would be her last smoking day; her quitting day would be Monday.

*Step 7: Monitor the Patient's Progress.* The clinician instructed the patient to monitor her smoking cessation program by using the Daily Smoking Record. She was to note all urges she had to smoke, as well as any cigarettes she smoked. The patient was scheduled for a return visit on the Friday of the week she would quit smoking.

### Third Visit

The patient returned to the clinic as scheduled. Her smoking cessation program was only partially successful. She had not been able to completely stop smoking during her breaks with co-workers. The clinician determined that the patient was struggling with a patient-specific problem that warranted health behavior counseling. The clinician used the 11-step health behavior counseling process (Table 6).

*Step 1: Identify the Problem.* The patient indicated that she did not want to ignore her co-workers during lunches and breaks. When she was with them, she did not feel that she could not smoke.

*Step 2: Clarify the Goals of Treatment.* The patient stated that she wanted to quit smoking completely but that she did not wish to offend her friends.

*Step 3: Collect Information.* After discussing the problem with the patient, the clinician determined that additional data collection was not necessary. The clinician was able to formulate a behavioral diagnosis from the information she already had.

*Step 4: Develop a Behavioral Diagnosis.* From a behavioral perspective, the clinician concluded that the patient's desire to continue to socialize with her co-workers was very strong. Further, she did not wish to offend her friends. The clinician believed that the patient might be willing to stop smoking with friends if she learned social skills for handling this situation tactfully.

*Step 5: Generate an Intervention Plan.* The clinician decided that the patient should continue with the program that was already being used successfully by the patient. In addition, the clinician would help the patient rehearse what she would say and do with her co-workers during their lunch and break times. This was accomplished in the clinic interview. The patient developed an explanation of her desire to quit smoking, and framed her reason in terms of her daughter's health and well-being and her hope that her friends would help her. She also developed a plan for what to say if cigarettes were offered to her. After three rehearsals, the patient felt very comfortable and was eager to try it out on her friends.

*Step 6: Intervene.* The patient would begin the new plan on the following Monday morning; she agreed to not change it for 5 days. She also agreed to call the clinician the following Friday afternoon to report how well the plan worked.

*Step 7: Review the Patient's Progress.* The patient called the following Friday and reported that her friends had not been as concerned about her stopping smoking as she had feared. She said that she was pleased that several of them individually had wished her luck in her program. She had not had a cigarette all week.

*Steps 8 and 9: Generate a Revised Intervention Plan and Reintervene.* There was no need to develop a new plan.

*Step 10: Develop a Maintenance Program.* The clinician and the patient decided to continue with the program as designed for one month. At the end of the month, they would reassess the patient's progress and decide if a formal maintenance program was needed.

*Fourth Visit*

One month after the patient's quitting date, she returned for a brief, final visit with the clinician. The clinician reviewed the patient's progress in the Smoking Cessation Program and learned that she had tried one cigarette approximately a week earlier and found that it was not at all satisfying. She reported that she tried to smoke only one but that it had made her somewhat nauseous. She did not anticipate any future problems in "staying off" cigarette smoking.

*Step 11: Review the Behavior Change Process.* The clinician reviewed with the patient each of the steps in the Smoking Cessation Program. The patient was given another copy of each of the materials used in the program. She understood that if she lapsed and began smoking again, she should use these materials to restart her smoking cessation program on her own. She also knew that if she had any trouble, the clinician would be available to help.

### References

1. United States Public Health Service: *Smoking and Health: Report of the Advisory Committee to the Surgeon General of the Public Health Service.* Washington, DC, US Government Printing Office, 1964.
2. United States Public Health Service: *Health, United States, 1981.* DHEW PHS 82-1232. Washington, DC, US Government Printing Office, 1981.
3. United States Public Health Service: *Smoking and Health, 1979. A Report of the Surgeon General.* DHEW PHS 79-50066. Washington, DC, US Government Printing Office, 1979.
4. American Cancer Society: *Dangers of Smoking, Benefits of Quitting.* New York, NY, American Cancer Society, 1980.
5. National Heart, Lung, and Blood Institute: *The Physician's Guide: How to Help Your Hypertensive Patients Stop Smoking.* NIH publication No. 83-1271. Washington, DC, US Government Printing Office, 1983.
6. American Cancer Society: *I Quit Kit* (no. 2028). New York, NY, American Cancer Society, 1977.

# 11. Management of Stress Reactions

Stress reactions are one of the most frequently encountered psychobehavioral problems in the outpatient medical clinic. Healthy individuals may complain of symptoms such as headache, indigestion, heart palpitations, skin rashes, bowel disturbances, sleep difficulties, nervousness, inability to concentrate, and behaviors of excess (e.g., weight loss or gain, chain smoking, abuse of alcohol). These symptoms can frustrate the physician when no medical diagnosis can be confirmed, whatever treatment is tried provides only temporary relief, and each time the patient is placed in a stressful situation, the symptoms recur.

The effect of stressful events on patients with an active disease is much more serious, however, than the discomfort they cause. Stressful events can disrupt the individual's efforts to adhere to a prescribed treatment regimen because other acitivites acquire greater priority than the regimen. This can confound the patient's treatment and possibly compromise his health. Because the patient's physiological reaction to stressful events can involve almost any body system, abnormal laboratory values can result that may mask or mislead the physician about the patient's true condition. Moreover, it is suspected that reactions to stressful events can aggravate many diseases and conditions and complicate their management. Finally, because of their powerful influence throughout the body, the patient's stress reactions may play a substantial role in precipitating many illnesses (Table 1).

### Stressors, Stress Perceptions, Stress Reactions, and Coping Skills

Helping the patient who complains of stress is difficult, in part, because of the confusion surrounding the meaning of "stress." The term *stress* has been used interchangeably to describe an event in the environment, an individual's perception that an event poses a threat to him, and the individual's reaction to his perception. To avoid this confusion, the term stress will not be used in this chapter. Instead, the terms *stressor, stress perception, stress reaction* and *coping response* will be employed (Figure 1). A *stressor* is an event in the environment

Table 1. Examples of medical diseases and conditions that can
be precipitated and/or aggravated by stress reactions

| Disease/condition | Precipitated | Aggravated |
|---|---|---|
| Cardiovascular | | |
| Coronary heart disease | X | X |
| Hypertension | ? | X |
| Hyperlipidemia | ? | X |
| Stroke | X | X |
| Childbirth | X | X |
| Gastrointestinal | | |
| Acid indigestion | X | X |
| Colonitis | ? | X |
| Ulcer | X | X |
| Genital-urinary | | |
| Sexual dysfunction | X | X |
| Infectious diseases | X | X |
| Major surgery | 0 | X |
| Neurological | | |
| Chronic pain | X | X |
| Burn pain | 0 | X |
| Epilepsy | X | X |
| Facial muscle pain | X | X |
| Migraine headache | X | X |
| Respiratory | | |
| Asthma | ? | X |
| Emphysema | ? | X |
| Rheumatoid arthritis | ? | ? |

X, probably; 0, probably not; ?, not known.

that triggers an individual's perception that the event is potentially threatening. This *stress perception* is the psychological state that reflects the individual's concern about the potential loss of something that is highly valued (e.g., money, status, a friend, health). A *stress reaction* is the individual's involuntary psychiological, psychological, and behavioral response to the stressor. An individual's *coping responses* are the behavioral, cognitive, or affective strategies used to reduce the discomfort of the stress reaction and to avoid it in the future.

Stressors can be grouped into four basic types. The first type of stressors are acute, time-limited events, which recur only infrequently for an individual. An example is a job interview. The second type of stressors are prolonged, time-limited situations, which continue over time but eventually resolve themselves and recur only infrequently. Examples are pregnancy or an acute illness. The third type of stressors are acute, recurrent events, which occur, resolve themselves, and frequently recur for the individual over time. Examples are having

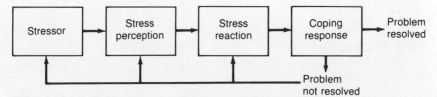

Figure 1. Relationship between stressors, stress perceptions, stress reactions, and coping responses.

to prepare a monthly report for a supervisor or visiting relatives on weekends. The fourth type of stressors are chronic events: situations that are continually present for the patient over time. Examples are a chronic medical disease or a handicap. In the medical outpatient clinic, the clinician will encounter all four types of stressors. Of most concern, however, are the chronic stressors that result in repeated acute or sustained stress reactions.

One of the difficulties in understanding the phenomenon of stress reactions has been the assumption that certain events (i.e., stressors) create stress perceptions and therefore the same stress reactions for everyone. More recently, it has been recognized that individuals differ markedly in their reactions to the same event. An event that functions as a stressor for one individual does not necessarily do so for another. Further, an individual may perceive an event as a stressor at one point in time but not at another. The event does not have to have negative connotations to be perceived as stressful. Some positive events can be perceived as threatening and create a stress reaction, such as a new job, a recent marriage, or the birth of a child. It should be remembered that an event is perceived as a stressor not because of its specific characteristics but because of the meaning given to the event by the person experiencing it.

It is extremely difficult to predict who will respond to a particular event with a stress perception and subsequently a stress reaction because many variables influence the perception of an event as stressful. These variables include an individual's personality, psychosocial history, medical history, current biological status, and personal coping resources. The variables interact with social factors such as the presence and support of others and the individual's environment. The patient's perception of the stressor also is affected by his assessment of its significance in terms of his well-being and his assessment of whether or not he can manage the situation.

From a medical perspective, it is the patient's stress reaction that is of most concern. Stress reactions can cause widespread physiological reactions which affect the cardiovascular system (e.g., elevate heart rate, respiration, or blood pressure), the neuroendocrine system (e.g., elevate epinephrine, norepinephrine, or adrenal corticoid levels), the gastrointestinal system (e.g., increase gastric motility or secretion), and the central and peripheral nervous systems. The stress reaction also can have psychological effects such as decreased adaptiveness, negative affect, narrowed ability to concentrate, and hypervigilance. Emotional effects frequently reported include feelings of apprehension, fear, tension, and confusion.

It is important to distinguish a stress reaction from an anxiety reaction. Clinically, they are very different and require distinct treatments. A patient experiences a stress reaction in response to a specific stressor in the environment, which he perceives as threatening and only partially within his power to control. In contrast, an anxiety reaction is a state in which the patient may have subjective physiological and psychological symptoms similar to a stress reaction but for which there is no clear stressor. An anxiety reaction is more diffuse than a stress reaction and cannot be attributed to a specific event. It arises from within the patient and may indicate a psychological disorder. Patients with anxiety should be referred for psychological evaluation.

## Management of Stress Reactions as a Lifestyle Change

Not all stress reactions render an individual unable to function. It is the strength of the stress reaction and whether it leads to an appropriate coping response that determine its effect. Both an extremely strong stress reaction and the absence of any stress reaction are destructive for an individual; both can lead to ineffective coping responses. Indeed, the absence of stress reactions might be considered the functional death of a living organism. Without stress perception leading to stress reactions, the individual is unable to respond to his environment, as in a vegetative coma and in certain psychiatric disorders such as catatonia. Some minimal stress perception and reactions are necessary. The individual must be able to perceive potential threats to his life, for example, and to be able to obtain essentials for survival (e.g., food, water, shelter) (Figure 2). Stress can help the individual perform at his best and successfully cope with problems. But extreme and protracted stress reactions threaten a patient's health

Figure 2. Continuum of stress reactions.

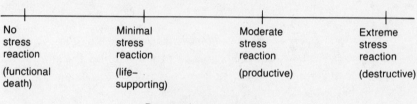

| No stress reaction | Minimal stress reaction | Moderate stress reaction | Extreme stress reaction |
|---|---|---|---|
| (functional death) | (life-supporting) | (productive) | (destructive) |

Degree of stress reaction

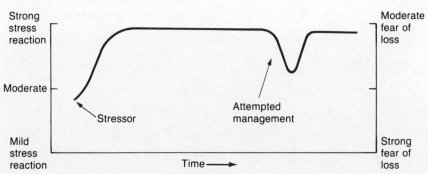

Figure 3. Relationship between fear of loss and intensity of stress reaction.

by immobolizing him, preventing an appropriate coping response, and thus resulting in serious medical consequences.

Because a stress reaction is extremely unpleasant, it may be puzzling why it is sustained. A stress reaction is believed to recur because it serves a useful function; the stress reaction is an aroused, alert state that prepares the individual for action in response to the perceived threat. The individual is ready either to "fight" to take control and cope with the situation, or to take "flight" from the situation.

Once someone becomes familiar with a stressful situation, his aroused state is sustained as long as he perceives that the stressors continue to exist, because he fears the loss of something of value—real property, status, self-esteem. Further, the aroused, stressful state is actually more comfortable than the alternative of being unprepared to confront the perceived problem. If the patient becomes less alert or attentive to the stressors, the fear of loss increases (Figure 3) and the patient is forced back into the alert, aroused state. Once the individual perceives a threat and realizes that he has little control over it, the stress reaction is sustained until either the individual withdraws from the situation or the problem is solved.

The difficulty in treating stress reactions, and the primary reason why "self-treatment" is usually not successful, is that the patient experiences such a high level of discomfort in the presence of the stressor that he is unwilling to risk the possibility that it may increase. A new technique that may fail is rejected in favor of the familiar, although inadequate, current method of coping with the situation.

## Health Behavior Counseling

Stress reactions differ from most of the other health behavior problems discussed in this book. A stress reaction is an involuntary response to a problem,

Table 2. Eleven-step behavioral counseling to resolve patient-specific problems in stress management

---

*Step 1: Identify the problem.*
    (1) Determine whether or not the patient recognizes that he is experiencing stress reactions.
    (2) Determine whether or not the patient understands the effect of stress on his medical condition.

*Step 2: Clarify the goals of treatment.*
    (1) Review the goal of treatment—the reduction or elimination of the patient's stress reactions.
    (2) Review the nature of the counseling to be provided.

*Step 3: Collect information.*
    (1) Obtain detailed information from the Daily Stress Record.
    (2) Obtain additional information from the patient about the environmental factors initiating or supporting the stress reactions.

*Step 4: Develop a behavioral diagnosis.*
    Identify the primary relationships among the environmental factors associated with the stress reactions supporting or helping control the reactions.

*Step 5: Generate an intervention plan.*
    (1) Provide training as needed in:
        (a) Problem-solving skills.
        (b) Assertiveness skills.
        (c) Muscle relaxation skills.
    (2) Design the intervention plan to be implemented by the patient.
    (3) Keep the plan simple.
    (4) Solicit the patient's suggestions.
    (5) Give the patient a written copy of the plan.

*Step 6: Intervene.*
    (1) Agree on the specific number of times that the patient should use the plan before considering changing it.
    (2) Instruct the patient to continue to use the Daily Stress Record.

*Step 7: Review the patient's progress.*
    Instruct the patient to contact the clinician in a certain number of days (e.g., 7 days) to review any problems encountered.

*Step 8: Generate a revised intervention plan.*
    Modify the intervention program as needed and give the patient a written copy of it.

*Step 9: Reintervene.*
    Instruct the patient to use the revised intervention plan a specific number of times before considering changing it.

*Step 10: Develop a maintenance program.*
    Design a program with the patient to withdraw those artificial strategies that helped him or her initially.

*Step 11: Review the behavior change process.*
    (1) Review with the patient the strategies that seemed to be most effective.
    (2) Identify the steps the patient should use to restart the stress management program in the future, if necessary.
    (3) Give the patient a written list of the steps to be used to restart the program.

---

whereas the other behaviors described are under the voluntary control of the patient. The patient does not choose to have a stress reaction in the same way he chooses whether or not to diet, to take medication, to exercise, or to refrain from smoking. A stress reaction is an aspect of the patient's current behavior that he views as undesirable but is unable to control. The goal of health behavior counseling for stress reactions is to bring them under voluntary control and reduce or eliminate them.

Most patients recognize that they experience stress reactions in response to situations at work, with their family, in personal matters, or with friends. They would like to reduce their feelings of discomfort if, by doing so, they also could successfully manage the situation. The problem is that most people are unsuccessful when they try to resolve the situations that produce the stressors. They also do not know how to manage their reactions effectively.

The following section describes how the clinician would use health behavior counseling (Table 2) to help a patient manage stress reactions. The clinician should become involved immediately in the patient's intervention program once the diagnosis of a stress reaction is made. No general program is recommended for the patient to try on his own initially. Because this process can be costly in terms of clinical time, both the clinician and the patient must be prepared to invest this time in the counseling. Therefore, it is strongly recommended that the clinician discuss with the patient the nature of the proposed treatment and the time and effort required before beginning.

### Step 1: Identify the Problem

The initial step in managing a stress reaction is to determine whether or not the patient recognizes that he is experiencing this reaction and that it is detrimental to his medical condition. Although most patients acknowledge that the stress reaction occurs and believe that such reactions are "not good" for them, they may not understand the direct effects on their physical health. It is important that the clinician establish his concern about these reactions by making a definitive statement regarding the need to reduce or eliminate them. He should also indicate his willingness to counsel the patient to help reduce or eliminate stressful situations.

Some patients may not expect to discuss their stress reactions, or their management, during the initial visit. It may be best to introduce the topic of managing stress reactions during the first visit but then suggest that the patient schedule another visit to discuss it in detail. This strategy helps the clinician keep on schedule that day and also increases the likelihood that only patients who have decided to make changes in their stressful activities will be counseled. Patients who are not prepared to discuss their problems the first day may think about it and accept counseling at the next visit.

*Step 2: Clarify the Goals of Treatment*

The clinician might consider the goal of treatment to be to eliminate or reduce stress reactions to a level at which they no longer affect the patient's medical condition. However, the patient may not share this goal. He may wish to control the stress reaction only if it is possible to do so without disrupting other aspects of his life. For example, a patient may experience extreme stress reactions in response to demands that he perform well at his job. Although the patient may wish to control his stress reactions, he is not be willing to do so if it will compromise his job performance. It is extremely important, therefore, that the patient and the clinician share the same goals. Because many of the stressful events in patients' lives involve their personal values, it is important that the treatment goals be compatible with these values and that the clinician and the patient are in agreement about this.

The clinician should explain to the patient the type of counseling that he will offer. The patient should understand that the counseling will be a collaborative undertaking in which the patient collects data, tries an intervention program developed together with the clinician, and then discusses the results with the clinician. The patient should also understand that he will have primary responsibility for implementing the intervention plan. Although the clinician will guide him in designing the plan, the patient will be expected to follow through.

*Step 3: Collect Information*

The clinician needs two types of information about the patient's stress reactions. The first is a profile of the stress reactions, including their frequency, duration, and intensity. Although the patient usually can provide a general description of these characteristics, the clinician should ask him to keep a Daily Stress Record of each instance of a stress reaction (Figure 4).

The clinician also needs a detailed description of the situations in which the patient experiences the stress reactions. Sometimes the patient may experience the same reaction in more than one situation. Each situation should be reviewed separately, in detail, to identify the different stressors.

The clinician should develop a behavioral analysis for each situation which lists all the antecedents and consequences of the stress reaction that the patient can identify. The clinician needs to probe not only for what was significant in the environment, but also what the patient's thoughts and feelings were at the time of each reaction. Because stress reactions frequently involve the patient's fears of what may happen (but usually does not), the clinician should be sure to ask about what the patient believes are the likely negative outcomes of the situation. If the patient is not able to identify these fears, he should be in-

DAILY STRESS LOG

TODAY'S DATE  _Tuesday  5·21·85_____

| Time | Location | People | Feelings | Thoughts | Results |
|------|----------|--------|----------|----------|---------|
| 10am | Store | Clerks Supervisor | Anxious! Perspiring | I need to change the display area for the sale. | Started to work on it. |
| 2³⁰pm | Store | Customers | Rushed | I need to train my clerks. | Waited on customers |
| 4³⁰pm | Store (Leaving) | Co-workers Clerks Customers | Anxious | Why do customers show up at the close of business?? | Waited on customers |
| 5³⁰pm | In car | Alone | Fatigued | I should have worked with the new computerized system today. | Promised to do it tomorrow. |

Figure 4. Example of a Daily Stress Record.

structed to record in the Daily Stress Record his thoughts about the possible negative outcomes after the same stress reaction occurs again.

### Step 4: Develop a Behavioral Diagnosis

Although patients perceive many different types of situations as stressors, the problems that are frequently encountered in the outpatient clinic can be divided into three major types: behavioral, affective, and cognitive stress management.

In behavioral stress management problems it is the patient's own behavior (or absence of certain behavior) that creates the stress reaction. He lacks the specific skills or knowledge needed to manage the situation effectively so he experiences a stress reaction. An example is a patient who experiences a stress reaction when asked to make a public presentation because she "does not know what to say." Another example is a father of a young child who lacks the parenting skills to manage the child's behavior. In both these cases, if the patient could learn the appropriate skills, the situation could be changed and the stress reaction eliminated. Whether or not the patient possesses the appropriate skills for managing the situation should be included in the behavioral diagnosis.

In affective stress management problems, the patient is in a situation that he cannot change and experiences a stress reaction that he cannot reduce. For example, a patient experiences a stress reaction when he visits his family. He is not able to alter substantially the attitudes or behavior of his family members and he lacks the ability to eliminate his stress reactions. Whether or not the patient can change or eliminate his stressful reactions should be included in the behavioral diagnosis.

Patients with cognitive stress management problems are afraid to assert their right to decide what they will do. They simply are unable to refuse the requests of others. Most of them can identify what actions they would like to take but they fear the negative responses of others if they do act on their own. For example, the clinician seeing a patient who is experiencing stress reactions due to demands at work should determine whether the patient is able to express his legitimate desires or whether his co-workers are imposing unreasonable demands on him. The patient experiences a stress reaction because he agrees to the unreasonable demands and is frustrated and angry at doing so. Whether or not the patient possesses appropriate assertiveness skills should be included in the behavioral diagnosis.

Once the general type of problem is identified, it is important to develop a behavioral diagnosis for the specific problems that the patient is experiencing. The behavioral diagnosis identifies the primary factors that are provoking and maintaining the patient's stress reactions and indicates those that prevent the patient from managing them. Although many factors may be involved, it identifies the primary "controlling factors" that appear to be central to the patient's problem. For example, the following behavioral diagnosis describes a patient-specific problem involving a stress reaction:

> A patient experiences a stress reaction at home due to his financial situation. A review of the patient's Daily Stress Record reveals that, in the evening when he returns from work, his wife frequently complains that his modest salary will not cover their expenses.

The behavioral diagnosis is:

> When discussing his financial situation with his wife, the patient fears that he cannot pay their bills and he experiences a stress reaction. The patient possesses appropriate behavioral and cognitive skills but does not have an effective method for managing his affective responses.

Once the clinician develops the behavioral diagnosis, he should review it with the patient. The patient should be encouraged to refine or modify the diagnosis until it is clear and accurately stated.

It is very important that the clinician exercise caution in developing a behavioral diagnosis for a patient with a stress reaction. Stress reactions can involve complex relationships between the patient and other individuals. They also can accompany other more serious psychological problems. The clinician should carefully assess the situation and decide if the patient's problem is caused only by stress and if the interventions described below are appropriate. In some cases, the clinician should consider referring the patient for psychological evaluation and possibly treatment. Guidelines for referral are discussed later.

## Step 5: Generate an Intervention Plan

The intervention plan should flow directly from the behavioral diagnosis, which identifies the area in which the patient seems to be having the most difficulty (i.e., behavioral, affective, or cognitive). If the problem is primarily behavioral, a problem-solving strategy should be considered; if the problem is primarily affective, muscle relaxation training should be considered, and if the problem is primarily cognitive, assertiveness training should be recommended. Specific intervention programs for problem solving, muscle relaxation, and assertive skills are described in the following section.

The behavioral diagnosis also describes the specific situation in which the patient encounters the stress reactions. The intervention plan should indicate how the patient can appropriately apply new skills in these situations. The clinician should work with the patient to design the particular steps that will start the patient with the least stressful situations and progress through increasingly more stressful situations.

Each step in the program should be written in a "behavioral prescription" for the patient (Figure 5). The prescription should describe how and when the patient is to practice and apply the new skills. This avoids the potential problem of the patient misunderstanding the intervention program or forgetting a step. The written list can also serve as a record of helpful techniques that can be used later in designing a maintenance program.

## Step 6: Intervene

The patient should be asked to use the intervention program as designed, working through the less stressful to the more stressful situations. It is often helpful to encourage him to attempt to use the stress management program at least three times before deciding that it is not successful because the newness of the program may cause the patient some discomfort. If, however, after three tries the program still is uncomfortable, the patient should contact the clinician to review the program.

During this initial period the patient should continue using the Daily Stress

**MICHAEL L. RUSSELL, Ph.D.**
Department of Internal Medicine
Baylor College of Medicine
Tel. 799-6032

**Program for Change**

For: _PCS_____     Date: _5-20-85_____

*1. Keep a Daily Stress Log each day for the next week.*

*2. Record each occurrence of a stress reaction (i.e. nervousness, acid indigestion, fatigue). Indicate the situation and your thoughts.*

*3. Schedule a return visit in one week.*

Figure 5. Example of a behavioral prescription for stress management.

Record to note his thoughts, feelings, and behavior in the situations that had previously caused a stress reaction. This information will be used to monitor the patient's progress and to help determine what, if any, modifications should be made in the behavioral diagnosis and/or the intervention plan.

### Step 7: Review the Patient's Progress

Regardless of how well the program is going, the patient should be instructed to get in touch with the clinician in about three weeks. This contact may take place either during a routine follow-up medical visit to the clinic or by telephone. Its purpose is to provide the clinician with information about how the patient is using the program, and whether or not he has had any trouble. If so, the clinician should inquire how the patient overcame the problems. This follow-up also will reveal whether or not the patient has continued with the program as agreed, or has stopped using it. The clinician may be able to help the patient resume the program or may need to schedule another counseling session to discuss the problem.

*Step 8: Generate a Revised Intervention Plan*

The clinician should base the revised intervention program on his new under-standing of the problem. This understanding should, in turn, be reflected in a modified behavioral diagnosis that identifies the primary factors that appear to be controlling the patient's stress reactions.

If a revised intervention plan is designed, the clinician must make sure that the patient has a list of the steps. This is particularly important if the clinician and the patient have discussed a number of possible alternatives before deciding on a particular change.

*Step 9: Reintervene*

The revised intervention should be initiated slowly, just as the original inter-vention was attempted. The patient should use the revised intervention at least three times in order to accommodate to the new routine. After following the revised intervention for 3 weeks, the patient should contact the clinician to re-view his progress. This cycle of revised interventions should be repeated until one is developed that substantially reduces or eliminates the patient's stress re-actions in the situations originally identified.

*Step 10: Develop a Maintenance Program*

After the patient has reduced or eliminated the stress reactions, the clinician should help him gradually withdraw any artificial strategies that were used. The patient should increasingly rely on natural cues to prompt his use of the stress management methods. If muscle relaxation was used, the patient should be able to create the feelings of relaxation without needing to use the full formal pro-gram. If the patient learned assertiveness skills, he should be able to develop an assertive statement without extensive rehearsal. In other words, the patient should be able to use the stress management skills easily and habitually.

*Step 11: Review the Behavior Change Process*

The final step is to formally review with the patient all the aspects of the stress management program to identify the basic steps that helped the patient and to discuss what the patient did at each step. The patient should be given a written summary of these steps so that he can refer to them if other stress-producing situations are encountered. The patient may be able to eliminate future stress reactions when they first appear, rather than allowing them to become inca-pacitating. Finally, the patient should be encouraged to contact the clinician as soon as possible if he experiences any problems and needs help.

## Basic Counseling Strategies

Three strategies are particularly effective in helping patients manage stress reactions: (1) problem-solving training, (2) muscle relaxation training, and (3) assertiveness training. The problem-solving training is designed to identify a solution that would eliminate the stressor. The muscle relaxation training program helps the patient manage the feelings accompanying the stress reaction. The assertiveness training enables the patient to change directly the situation that contains the stressors. These programs may be used alone or in combination, as indicated by the behavioral diagnosis. The clinician should use these interventions only after he has completed a thorough evaluation of the patient's stress management problem and formulated a behavioral diagnosis. If misused, these programs will be ineffective and may compromise the clinician's credibility with the patient.

### Problem-Solving Training

Some patients experience strong stress reactions because they lack the information or skills to cope effectively with certain situations. The patient perceives the situation as stressful because he feels he cannot change it. He does not know what to do. Problem-solving training is a systematic, 10-step method to change the situation producing the stress reaction (Table 3). The clinician should guide patients through the process but allow them to make their own choices at each step.

*Step 1: Identify the Problem.* The clinician and the patient must agree on what the problem is. The patient should be encouraged to describe in detail the situation that is bothering him. If indeed stress management counseling is the appropriate treatment, it should become clear to the clinician that the patient would not experience these stress reactions if he possessed the skills to handle the situation. The clinician should describe approaches the patient can use to cope with the stress reactions and ask if the patient agrees that these would help. For example, a diabetic patient may have a stress reaction when she travels because she fears having an insulin reaction in an unfamiliar place. The patient needs knowledge of alternative ways to manage her blood glucose levels when she travels.

*Step 2: Collect Information.* It is often necessary for the patient to collect additional information so that he will better understand the situation and be able to make informed choices. For example, the diabetic patient described above might be instructed to read a booklet on diabetes to learn how and why insulin reactions occur.

Table 3. Eleven-step problem-solving training
program

---

*Step* 1: Identify the problem.

*Step* 2: Collect information.

*Step* 3: Generate alternative solutions.

*Step* 4: Consider the consequences of each solution.

*Step* 5: Review the patient's personal values.

*Step* 6: Select a solution.

*Step* 7: Intervene.

*Step* 8: Review the patient's progress.

*Step* 9: Select a revised or alternative solution.

*Step* 10: Reintervene.

*Step* 11: Review the problem-solving steps.

---

*Step 3: Generate Alternative Solutions.*   The clinician should help the patient develop several alternative solutions. Initially, any potential solution that comes to mind should be listed, without attempting to evaluate its feasibility of effectiveness. This encourages the patient to suggest possibilities freely without being inhibited and unnecessarily rejecting good ideas. In the example of the patient with diabetes, she might consider various combinations of food, exercise, and insulin injections on the days she travels that would yield good blood glucose control and avert an insulin reaction.

*Step 4: Consider the Consequences of Each Solution.*   The patient should then consider the positive and negative consequences that would be associated with each solution, including the advantages or benefits and disadvantages or costs.

*Step 5: Review Personal Values.*   The clinician should encourage the patient to judge the degree to which each of the potential solutions involves his personal values. With patients who are not comfortable raising this issue themselves, the clinician should ask direct questions; otherwise, they may agree to a program that they do not intend to follow. For example, the patient with diabetes may consider eating regular and appropriate meals while traveling. However, this may not be possible without discussing her diabetes with the co-workers with whom she travels. Because she believes that diabetes is a personal problem, not for public discussion, she may not be able to implement this solution.

*Step 6: Select a Solution.*   The patient should select the solution that is comfortable. Even if the clinician has some doubts about its effectiveness, the patient should be encouraged to try the approach he thinks is best. He should also know that if it does not work, the next step will be to review the situation and choose another solution.

*Step 7: Intervene.*   The patient should agree to try the solution and contact the clinician to discuss the results by telephone or in a return clinic visit. It is important that this discussion occur as soon as possible after the patient tries the program.

*Step 8: Review the Patient's Progress.*   When the patient contacts the clinician, they should review exactly what has occurred. The patient should recall his actions, discussions, and feelings. The patient should be asked about both the positive and the negative consequences of using the solution. This is important because the patient may make a conclusion that is not warranted by what actually occurred. The clinician needs this information to help the patient review the plan or to encourage the patient to select another solution to the problem. The diabetic patient, for example, might have chosen to alter her morning dose of insulin to accommodate a snack instead of a full lunch; she also might have decided to pack high-sugar snacks to eat if she feels an insulin reaction coming on.

*Step 9: Select a Revised or Alternative Solution.*   Using the information he provided and the subsequent conclusions discussed with the clinician, the patient should either revise the initial solution or select an alternative one. Again, the patient should know that if the revised or alternative solution does not work, the plan will be reviewed and another solution tried.

*Step 10: Reintervene.*   As in step 7, the patient should agree to try the solution and contact the clinician by telephone or in a return clinic visit to discuss the results. It is important, however, that the discussion occur as soon as possible after the patient tries the program.

*Step 11: Review the Problem-Solving Steps.*   Once the situation that had been producing the stress reactions has been resolved, the clinician should review the problem-solving steps with the patient. If the patient encounters other situations that produce similar stress reactions, he should consider trying to solve the problem himself. If unsuccessful, he should be assured that the clinician is available to help.

## Muscle Relaxation Training

Muscle relaxation training is a six-step program designed to teach the patient how to achieve a deeply relaxed state and then how to use this technique to reduce the stress reaction associated with specific stressors (Table 4). The pro-

Table 4. Six-step muscle relaxation training program

---

*Step 1:* Prepare the patient.

*Step 2:* Create a hierarchy of stressful situations.

*Step 3:* Practice imagining each stressful situation.

*Step 4:* Acquire the ability to rapidly achieve muscle relaxation.

*Step 5:* Use muscle relaxation and imagine the hierarchy of stressful situations.

*Step 6:* Use muscle relaxation and actually experience the hierarchy of stressful situations.

---

gram is designed to disassociate the stress reaction from the provoking stressors. It is based on the observation that patients can reduce their stress reactions whether or not the stressors that provoke the reactions change. The program also should be used to reduce a patient's stress reaction to secondary stressors (i.e., events, people, objects) that may not be directly related to the original stressors but to which the patient's stress reaction has become generalized.

*Step 1: Prepare the Patient.*   The patient should be given a complete, clear description of the rationale for the muscle relaxation training program. It is extremely important that the patient understand each step of the program and what to expect. The clinician should be satisfied that the patient agrees with the program's goals. If the patient has doubts or expresses reluctance, the clinician should discuss these concerns before proceeding. The patient should also be aware that although he will be introduced to each step in the training program in the clinic, it is the patient's responsibility to practice the skills at home. Because the relaxation training program depends on the patient's complete involvement, the clinician should feel that he has a good rapport with the patient.

*Step 2: Create a Hierarchy of Stressful Situations.*   The patient should be asked to create a hierarchy of stressful situations. The patient should assign a value of 10 to the most stressful situation. Next, the patient should identify a minimally stressful situation for which the patient recalls feeling only the slightest stress reaction and which he was able to manage; this should be assigned a value of 1. The clinician and the patient should then identify stressful situations corresponding to levels 2 through 9. More than one situation can be assigned to each level. When the list is complete, the patient should review it and make sure the situations are in the proper order.

*Step 3: Practice Imagining Each Stressful Situation.*   Beginning with the situation producing the least stress reaction (i.e., level 1), the clinician should help the patient to imagine each situation in detail as if he were actually in it. The clinician should be sure the patient is not only describing the general situation but can actually "see" the situation including minor details (colors, objects, odors). The patient should be able to identify a fair amount of detail. The clinician should be confident that the patient can imagine himself in the situation, and is not simply talking about it objectively without placing himself in it. At each step the clinician should take notes regarding the specifics mentioned by the patient; these will be helpful in recalling the scene later.

Some patients have difficulty imagining a situation in detail. It is sometimes helpful to give the patient a "homework" assignment that requires him to deliberately place himself in each situation and note the details. He should develop a list of phrases and words that accurately describe the situation to be used at the next clinic visit. Some patients can visualize a situation if they have in hand an item that they associate with it (e.g., a quarterly report associated with stress reactions at work; a checkbook associated with stress reactions caused by financial problems). Others are helped by looking at a photograph of the person who is viewed as the cause of the stress reaction.

*Step 4: Acquire the Ability to Rapidly Achieve Muscle Relaxation.* The patient should be taught how to achieve muscle relaxation, that is, how to (1) detect muscle tension and (2) relax these muscle groups that are tense. To learn these skills, the patient should be guided through a sequence of tensing and then relaxing the major muscle groups in the body. The patient focuses on the differences between the feeling of muscle tension and the feeling of muscle relaxation. This training introduces the patient to the very comfortable feelings of complete muscle relaxation and shows him how to achieve this state. The patient also learns how the feelings of relaxation can be maintained by imagining a pleasant, soothing scene.

Once the patient has learned to detect muscle tension and to relax his muscles, the next step is to learn how to add the technique of focused breathing to enhance the relaxation. The purpose of focused breathing is to force the patient to attend to the rhythm of his breathing and to exert voluntary control over it. The patient imagines the air smoothly flowing in and out of his lungs in a slow, rhythmic manner and deliberately attempts to slow his breathing. The patient learns to count backward from 20 with each breath taken, so that when he reaches the number 0, he is completely relaxed and breathing slowly and smoothly. Focused breathing also directs attention away from the stressors that were producing the stress reaction. This helps break the sometimes repetitive thoughts about the stressors that continue to provoke the patient's stress reaction.

The next step is to increase the speed with which the patient can achieve the relaxed state and to help him do so without disrupting normal daily activities. This is accomplished by directing him to use systematic muscle scanning instead of progressing through the formal sequence of tensing and relaxing each major muscle group. Systematic muscle scanning focuses attention on each of the large muscle groups to detect even the slightest tension and then to reduce it. This process rapidly decreases the time required to achieve complete muscle relaxation because the patient only attends to muscles that are tense. Systematic muscle scanning is then coupled with focused breathing. When these two techniques can be used easily in sequence, the final step is to practice using them with eyes open while sitting in a chair, while talking with a friend, and while engaged in routine daily activities. With practice, many patients can use these techniques and achieve muscle relaxation within a few seconds. To facilitate the development of this skill, some clinicians provide the patient with an audiorecording of the muscle relaxation procedures to use in practice sessions at home. The audiorecording helps the patient proceed through the correct sequence of exercises.

*Step 5: Use Muscle Relaxation and Imagine the Hierarchy of Stressful Situations.* Beginning with the least stressful situation (i.e., level 1), the clinician guides the patient to achieve the relaxed state, while imagining the stressful situation. The patient is instructed to cope with each situation by using muscle relaxation and focused breathing to reduce any stress reaction that occurs. This pairing of the relaxed state with the imagined stressful situation continues until the patient is able to imagine comfortably each situation in the hierarchy.

The process should proceed only as rapidly as the patient can relax successfully while imagining a stressful situation. If the patient begins to feel that he cannot overcome the stress reaction while imagining a stressful situation, he should raise his hand slightly to notify the clinician. The patient should be instructed to stop imagining the scene and to return to the relaxed state. Occasionally, even after several attempts, the patient will not be able to achieve the relaxed state while imagining a particular stressful situation. It may be necessary to develop an intermediate step that contains some, but not all, of the elements of the situation. The patient should attempt to manage the intermediate situation and then move on to the one causing difficulty.

*Step 6: Use Muscle Relaxation and Actually Experience the Hierarchy of Stressful Situations.* This is the final step in the training program. The patient is instructed to use his ability to achieve muscle relaxation in each of the actual stressful situations on the hierarchy. Beginning with the situation producing the least stress reaction (i.e., level 1), the patient should deliberately place himself in the situation, and scan to detect any muscle tension and reduce it. Once the first situation is mastered, the patient should attempt the second situation. The patient's progression through the hierarchy should be carefully monitored and discussed with the clinician. Usually, only one or two situations should be attempted between discussions so that the patient does not progress too rapidly and encounter a stressful situation that he cannot manage. In some cases, it may also be necessary for the patient to practice the imagined stressful situation again in the clinic before encountering the actual situation.

Some clinicians prefer to combine steps 5 and 6, and alternate the patient's practicing imagining several scenes with the patient's using the relaxation techniques in the actual situations. This should be considered for patients who have difficulty developing realistic images of the specific scenes.

### Assertiveness Training

The six-step assertiveness training program is designed to provide the patient with effective social skills that will help him achieve specific personal objectives (Table 5). Some patients need these skills to change the situation that is producing the stressors. The use of assertiveness skills eliminates the stressors and the resultant stress reactions. Assertiveness training helps the patient identify the specific actions of others that have a negative effect on him, to insist that they be changed, and to describe how he would like them changed. The program also helps the patient assess the realistic positive and negative consequences of using assertiveness skills.

*Step 1: Prepare the Patient.* The patient should be told that his stress reaction results, in part, from his current inability to insist on changes in others' behavior that is having a negative effect on him. Most patients readily acknowledge that this is an accurate description of their situation. Many know what they would like to do or say in the situation but fear that severe negative consequences will result if they do what they feel. For example, a patient might feel that his employer makes unfair demands of him but he is fearful of saying anything in response and, as a result, experiences a stress reaction.

It is extremely important that the clinician have a good rapport with the patient. The patient should feel free to discuss his reactions to the dialogues that will be developed and his concerns about using them in an actual situation. If the patient has any doubts or expresses reluctance, the clinician should discuss them before proceeding.

*Step 2: Clearly Describe Each Stressful Situation.* The next step is to obtain a clear description of each situation in which the patient is unassertive and experiences some degree of a stress reaction. The patient should explain to the clinician why he believes that he cannot challenge the individual(s) who are creating the stressful situation. The clinician should explore the likely positive and negative consequences of the patient's being assertive in these situations. The patient should identify the "worst case," the "best case," and the "most likely case." This questioning is essential because in some situations it would not be in the patient's best interest to use assertiveness skills. More often, how-

Table 5.  Six-step assertiveness training program

*Step 1:* Prepare the patient.

*Step 2:* Clearly describe each stressful situation.

*Step 3:* Create a hierarchy of the stressful situations.

*Step 4:* Describe the process for developing an assertive statement.

*Step 5:* Develop an assertive statement for each stressful situation, using imagined situations.

*Step 6:* Use an assertive statement in each actual stressful situation.

ever, once he carefully considers a situation, the patient will recognize that the risk of a negative outcome is far outweighed by the potential positive consequences. It is important that the patient is comfortable with the decision to try to change each situation that is discussed.

*Step 3: Create a Hierarchy of Stressful Situations.*   The patient should be asked to create a hierarchy of the problem situations, beginning with the most stressful one, which the patient should assign a value of 10. Next, the patient should identify a situation in which he is assertive but feels slightly uncomfortable being so; this should be assigned the value of 1. The clinician and the patient should then identify other problem situations for levels 2 through 9. More than one situation can be assigned to each level. When this list is complete, the patient should review it and make sure the situations are in the proper order.

*Step 4: Describe the Process for Developing an Assertive Statement.*   Next, the clinician teaches the patient how to create an assertive statement to use in the stressful situations. The goal of this step is to prepare a rehearsed monologue which the patient believes is accurate and appropriate to use to change the situation. If the statement is carefully thought through, the likelihood that the "worst case" situation will occur is reduced, and the patient will not fear making comments that he will regret later.

The assertive statement describes (1) the problem behavior, (2) the patient's objection, (3) an alternative behavior, and (4) positive consequences for the alternative behavior. The clinician can help the patient develop what to say, but the patient should be encouraged to use his own words. The clinician should emphasize that it is more important to remember to include the four basic components when making an assertive statement than to memorize a statement.

The first component should be an accurate, objective description of the other person's actions or statements that cause the patient's stress reaction. It is extremely important that this description be as objective as possible; it should not imply judgment about the other person's feelings, motives, or values. It should be a simple description of what the person said or did: for example, "Yesterday you asked me to stay late at the office to finish a report that you needed for today's meeting."

The second component is a statement of the patient's objections to the problem behavior. Again, this should not imply any judgment of what the other person should feel, think, or believe. To continue the above example, the statement could be, "I feel irritated that you did not give me more notice that the report was needed for the meeting."

The third component is a description of a specific alternative behavior that would be acceptable to the patient and which would involve minimal loss to the other person. It is important that the alternative behavior be a single, relatively small change, since smaller changes can be accommodated more readily than larger ones. Over time, through a series of small steps, the larger changes can be achieved. To continue the example, this suggestion could be, "I need at least one full day to prepare the report for you."

Finally, the assertive statement should contain a description of the positive consequences that will result if the alternative behavior is adopted. The positive consequences should be actions over which the patient, but not the other person, has control. Although the positive consequences will not usually be the reason that the other individual decides to adopt the alternative behavior, they may give him another incentive. To finish the example, the statement could be, "If you give me a full day to prepare the report I will be able to do a first-rate job for you, and the report will be accurate and complete."

*Step 5: Develop an Assertive Statement for Each Stressful Situation Using Imagined Situations.* After the clinician explains the rationale for and components of the assertive statement, the patient should create an assertive statement for each stressful situation in the hierarchy. The patient should begin with the situation at the bottom of the hierarchy (i.e., level 1) and proceed through the most difficult situation (i.e., level 10). The patient should create his own statements in his own words, which will sound more natural. They also will be easier to remember in the actual situation.

Once the patient has developed statements for each situation in the hierarchy, he should rehearse them, in order from bottom to top, with the clinician, who will portray the other individual in the situation. The clinician should respond as the other person might to the patient's statements. Because it is important that the patient initially experience success in developing the statement, the clinician should not challenge the patient with difficult reports in situations low in the hierarchy. As the patient becomes comfortable developing assertive statements, the clinician can begin to offer more challenging responses. As the patient rehearses each situation, the clinician should inquire how comfortable he feels. The rehearsal should be stopped if the patient indicates that he still feels uncomfortable. At this point, the clinician should determine whether the statement the patient created should be revised or if the patient would benefit from muscle relaxation training to reduce the stress reaction.

*Step 6: Use an Assertive Statement in Each Actual Stressful Situation.* In the final step of assertiveness training, the patient attempts to use the statements in the actual situations. This should be tried first in the situation that is least stressful for the patient. The patient should agree to try the first statement and then contact the clinician by telephone before proceeding with the next. This contact ensures that the patient does not move too rapidly through the hierarchy and encounter a situation that he cannot handle. It also enables the clinician to plan with the patient how to handle unexpected problems that develop in the first try and to schedule an additional practice session, if necessary.

## Referring the Patient for Psychological Counseling

Some patients who present with symptoms of stress reactions have concomitant psychological problems. These patients should not be accepted into treatment for stress management. Instead, they should be referred to a psychologist for assessment and possibly treatment. Often it is not until the clinician has initiated a discussion of the details of the patient's problems that the need for referral becomes apparent. However, if at any point the clinician determines that the patient has problems that are beyond the clinician's capability to manage, the patient should be referred.

The clinician should review each of the patient's problems and consider three basic questions. The first question is: Do the patient's symptoms appear to occur in response to a specific situation or are they "free floating?" If they are the latter, the patient should be referred for evaluation of anxiety. If the patient's symptoms do seem to occur in response to a specific situation, the clinician should consider the second and third questions.

The second question is: Do the patient's symptoms represent inappropriate behavioral, cognitive, or affective responses? In some cases the patient's stress reaction may represent an extreme reaction to a situation. These types of problems include the following:

1. The patient has mood swings, from stress reactions to depression.
2. The patient describes an unreasonable fear of an object, organism, or place (i.e., a phobia).
3. The patient's stress perception includes a description of objects, organisms, and activities that other observers cannot verify (i.e., hallucinations or delusions).
4. The patient's stress reaction is extreme, given the nature of the stressor event.

If the clinician detects any of these problems, the patient should be referred for psychological evaluation.

The third question is: Does the patient use alcohol or drugs excessively to manage his stress reactions? The excessive use of alcohol and/or drugs to manage stress reactions is a poor prognostic sign. In most cases, such patients will not respond even to intensive interventions. Most of them will also reject the referral for psychological evaluation. The clinician should be open to any attempt by the patient to discuss the problem, but his goal should be only to provide consistent, firm encouragement that the patient seek psychological help.

## Case Illustration

Clinical application of the programs discussed in this chapter is illustrated in the following case, which shows how the clinician would use health behavioral counseling to help a patient identify and reduce a stress reaction associated with stressors in the patient's workplace. The case includes typical issues and problems encountered in the medical outpatient clinic.

### The Patient

The patient is a 41-year-old woman who works as a salesclerk in a large department store. She sought a medical evaluation from her physician because for the past 3 months she has increasingly experienced fatigue, nervousness, and acid indigestion. She is worried that she might have "something medically wrong." She inquired whether vitamin supplements might help her regain her energy. The patient is 5 feet, 6 inches tall and weighs 130 pounds. She does not smoke cigarettes.

### First Visit

The physician conducted a complete physical examination, with standard laboratory tests. No abnormal results were obtained. The physician concluded that the patient did not currently have an acute or chronic disease or condition. However, as he talked with the patient, she revealed that she had a very stressful job working (on a commission basis) in a department store. As she described her job, the woman visibly became more tense. The physician told her that she appeared to be experiencing stress reactions because of her job and suggested that she talk with another member of the clinic staff trained in health behavior counseling. He added that some of the physical symptoms the patient was experiencing might be due to the stress reactions. The patient agreed to see the clinician. The clinician implemented the 11 steps outlined in Table 2.

*Step 1: Identify the Problem.* The clinician interviewed the patient in some detail to determine whether or not she was experiencing a stress reaction. During the conversation it became apparent that the woman was not familiar with the concepts of stress reaction or stress management. She stated, "Everyone is stressed . . . it's part of business." The clinician explained how the human body reacts in response to a stressor, and that the physical symptoms of fatigue, nervousness, and acid indigestion could result from stressors at work.

*Step 2: Clarify the Goals of Treatment.* The clinician described the rationale for a stress management program and how the patient might be able to control her stress reactions. The clinician also said that while they would work as partners to help her achieve control, the responsibility for making the changes would be hers. He told her that the counseling would require several clinic visits and it would be some time before she could manage her stress reactions. The patient responded that she would like to eliminate these symptoms, and was willing to try the program.

*Step 3: Collect Information.* The clinician probed further about the patient's stress reactions. She reported that many demands were made upon her on the job that sometimes required immediate attention. She listed these as (1) taking care of customers, (2) supervising two other sales clerks, (3) managing inventory, and (4) displaying merchandise. She was proud of her work and did not view her responsibilities as unreasonable. She stated that she had felt more stressed recently because she was learning to use the store's new computer for inventory and sales. She recalled that she had felt increased pressure each time there was a major change in her job activities. Although she believed she would eventually master such new activities, during the initial weeks she always felt stressed.

The clinician asked the patient to keep a Daily Stress Record for the next week and note each occurrence of a stress reaction. A stress reaction was defined as feelings of pressure, nervousness, acid indigestion, or fatigue. The patient was also to give a brief description of her thoughts at the time of the reaction and to describe the situation. The patient agreed to return to see the clinician in 1 week to review the Daily Stress Record. The clinician wrote the assignment as a behavioral prescription for the patient (see Figure 5).

### Second Visit

The patient returned as scheduled for the follow-up visit in 1 week.

*Step 4: Develop a Behavioral Diagnosis.* The patient had recorded each day's stress reactions in the Daily Stress Record (see Figure 4). The clinician sum-

*Current Behavior: Experiences and stress reactions at work*

*The Antecedents*
Mid-afternoon.
2 or more customers waiting.
Display area needs to be changed.
Other salesclerk needs help.
Need to learn the new computerized system for sales and inventory.

*The Stress Reactions*

*Affective*
Sustained feelings of nervousness.

*Cognitive*
Concern that customers will leave or complain.

*Behavior*
Works as rapidly as possible to complete all tasks.

| Pos/ | |
| --- | --- |
| Neg | *The Consequences* |
| + | Completes all work herself so that it is done correctly. |
| + | Is relieved that no customers left or complained. |
| − | Is exhausted by end of work-shift. |
| − | Acid indigestion. |

Figure 6. Behavioral analysis for case illustration in stress management.

marized this information in a behavioral analysis that indicated the antecedents and consequences of each stressful situation (Figure 6).

The clinician used the behavioral analysis to identify the active factors that would comprise the behavioral diagnosis of this patient's problem. The clinician's diagnosis was that the patient was experiencing a stress reaction when she had to perform several tasks simultaneously; she felt that she must work rapidly and efficiently on all tasks to avoid criticism from her customers or her supervisor; she denied that this aspect of her job could be changed; recently, she has experienced a new stressor—learning to use a new computer system for management of inventory and sales; the patient does not possess an effective method for managing her stress reactions.

The clinician discussed this behavioral diagnosis with the patient, who agreed that it was an accurate description of how she viewed the situation.

*Step 5: Generate an Intervention Plan.* The clinician suggested that the patient would benefit from a muscle relaxation training program and explained that it would help her reduce the stress reactions she was experiencing. However, it would not solve her problem of performing several tasks simultaneously; it would only enable her to feel more comfortable. He then provided a brief overview of the muscle relaxation training program. The patient agreed to proceed with the program.

During the remainder of this session the clinician and the patient worked on the first four steps in the muscle relaxation training program. First, the clinician prepared the patient for the training by explaining each step in detail. Second, the clinician helped the patient create a hierarchy of stressful situations, using 10 levels. This list included each of the situations that the patient had identified in her Daily Stress Record, and two additional situations that she often encountered. Third, the clinician worked with the patient as she tried to imagine each situation. The patient was able to imagine these situations easily and to describe them in detail. Fourth, the patient learned the basic deep muscle relaxation procedure. The clinician decided to continue the muscle relaxation program at the next clinic visit. The patient agreed to practice the basic muscle relaxation procedure twice each day and to return for a follow-up clinic visit in 1 week.

## Third Visit

The patient returned for the scheduled clinic visit.

*Step 5 (continued): Generate an Intervention Plan.* The clinician taught the patient how to use systematic muscle scanning in place of the basic muscle relaxation procedure. He explained how to use focused breathing. The patient was able to use the techniques easily. She also practiced muscle relaxation while sitting in the office chair with her eyes open, as she listened to the clinician.

The clinician decided that the patient was ready to practice pairing the muscle relaxation with the imagined situations in her stress hierarchy. Beginning with the first level, the clinician guided the patient through each situation, to level 4. The patient signaled whenever her stress reaction began to increase markedly, and the clinician helped her cope with these feelings using the muscle relaxation procedure. The clinician suggested that the patient attempt to use the muscle relaxation in the actual level 1 and 2 situations over the next week.

*Step 6: Intervene.* The clinician cautioned the patient to use the muscle relaxation program only as they had practiced it. She agreed, and said that she would be able to use it for the first time on the next day. She would call the clinician if she had any problems with it. The clinician also requested that the patient use the Daily Stress Record to continue writing down her feelings and thoughts in situations that produced the stress reactions. The patient would return for a follow-up visit in 1 week.

*Fourth Visit*

The patient returned for the clinic visit, as scheduled.

*Step 7: Review the Patient's Progress.*   The clinician discussed the patient's successful use of muscle relaxation in the two minimally stressful situations in the past week. She expressed surprise at how much better she felt and said she was quite comfortable with the program.

*Step 8: Generate a Revised Intervention Plan.*   Because of the patient's initial success, the clinician decided that it would be appropriate for her to continue with the program as originally designed. He suggested that she use the muscle relaxation program for the next five situations in her hierarchy. The patient indicated that she did not think that this would be a problem. They practiced the situations and the patient appeared to be comfortable.

*Step 9: Reintervene.*   The patient agreed to use muscle relaxation in the actual situations over the next week. She also agreed to call the clinician if she had any problems. The patient would continue to keep the Daily Stress Record. A follow-up visit was scheduled for 1 week later.


*Fifth Visit*

The patient canceled the scheduled visit because she had to work overtime during a special sale. The patient returned for her next visit in 2 weeks.

*Step 7 (repeat): Review the Patient's Progress.*   The clinician reviewed the patient's progress. In the 2 weeks since the last visit the patient had successfully used muscle relaxation in the five situations (levels 3 through 7) in her hierarchy, as planned. She also said that she could not help but use muscle relaxation in the level 10 situation. She could not avoid the situation and had decided to see if she could control her stress reaction. She reported that she was able to use the technique and was quite pleased with herself. She was very optimistic about the remaining situations and did not foresee any problems.

*Step 8 (repeat): Generate a Revised Intervention Plan.*   No change was made in the program.

*Step 9 (repeat): Reintervene.*   The patient agreed to use muscle relaxation in the remaining three situations (levels 8 through 10) over the next week. She agreed to call the clinician after she used the technique in the level 10 situation. She would return for a final visit in 2 weeks.

*Sixth Visit*

The patient did not return for her next clinic visit until 1 month later. She apologized for missing the earlier appointment, but she had been feeling so good about herself and her ability to control her stress reactions that she did not feel it was urgent to return for the visit.

*Step 10: Develop a Maintenance Program.* The patient reported that she was no longer practicing her muscle relaxation. She was able to achieve a relaxed state within a few seconds using systematic muscle scanning and focused breathing. No maintenance program was needed.

*Step 11: Review the Behavior Change Process.* The patient did not anticipate any problems with the muscle relaxation program. Nevertheless, the clinician reviewed how she might use the muscle relaxation with other situations that were stressful. Together they listed each step that she had used in the current program. The clinician gave this list to the patient and indicated that if she detected any stress reaction that did not respond to the muscle relaxation program, she should contact him.

# 12. Referring Patients for Psychological Counseling

Health behavior counseling is a clinical approach designed for use with the wide variety of patients treated in the primary care setting. It functions like many other primary care activities in that it is the first line of evaluation and treatment before more advanced, time-consuming, or costly procedures are considered.

Many patients' problems can be managed successfully by the clinician using the health behavior counseling approach described in the previous chapters. As with any primary care activity, however, it is anticipated that some patients will have problems that require additional assessment or specialized treatment. These patients should be referred to a secondary care specialist. This chapter describes how the clinician can make a successful referral, one in which the patient values the counseling the clinician has provided and seeks additional help from a specialist.

## Referring a Patient

When patients' problems do not respond to health behavior counseling, the difficulty can usually be traced to one of three causes: (1) the clinician and the patient have not been able to develop a good rapport, (2) the problem requires a specialized intervention, or (3) the patient has other, substantial personal or psychological problems. In these cases, it is appropriate to refer the patient to a secondary care specialist specifically trained to treat such problems.

The indications of a lack of rapport between the patient and the clinician may be subtle. The clinician usually notices a continuing sense of uneasiness with the patient. The patient may appear reluctant to discuss his problems or seems distant. Other signs are missed visits and failure to complete agreed-upon homework assignments during the week. The clinician should recognize that not every patient will feel comfortable with him. Some patients feel more comfortable with certain therapists than others. If the clinician has worked with the patient to the best of his ability, he should not consider the lack of rapport a personal failure. Rather, he should use this as an opportunity to identify the typical characteristics of patients with whom he may have difficulty developing rapport in the future. Until the clinician learns how to work with such individuals, he should refer them to another clinician or therapist for treatment.

Patients whose difficulties have not been resolved after receiving health behavior counseling have more complex problems that require reassessment, or that may respond only to more powerful interventions. An example would be a patient who is experiencing stress reactions and who is not able to learn the deep muscle relaxation procedure. More advanced techniques may be necessary, such as biofeedback to teach the patient muscle relaxation or imagery training to help him develop a vivid, calming mental image. A therapist with advanced training and clinical experience may be able to help such patients achieve their desired behavior changes.

Patients who have personal or psychological problems that are affecting the health behavior change program complain of other priorities or of continuing emotional distress. They may display feelings that do not match the issues discussed (e.g., tearfulness, anxiety, sadness) or offer explanations for daily activities that do not seem plausible (e.g., a patient spending 2 days during the week with his parents without his spouse because he "wanted to see them"). An example is a patient with hypertension who needs to control her weight and sodium intake and who is having serious marital problems. She ignores the recommended dietary changes when she worries about her marriage. Other patients may display more typical symptoms of psychological problems, such as depressed affect or free-floating anxiety. Referral to a therapist to help patients manage these problems may be necessary.

The need to refer a patient to a therapist may become evident at any time during behavioral counseling. Some problems can clearly be identified during the initial session (e.g., bizarre or extremely emotional reactions). For other problems, the clinician must obtain sufficient information from the patient to develop a thorough understanding; this may occur only after several sessions. The clinician should resist the temptation to continue seeing the patient simply because of the time already invested in counseling. The patient would be better served by referral to a therapist, who should be provided a thorough description of the case by the clinician.

## The Clinician's Attitude

The most important factor influencing the success of a referral is the clinician's attitude. When a clinician recognizes that a patient needs to be referred because the behavior change program is not working, he may feel frustrated, disappointed, or angry. This combination of emotions is difficult to conceal from the patient, who is trying to gauge the clinician's true attitude toward his problem or understand why he is being referred to the therapist. The patient might misinterpret the clinician's feelings and think that the anger is directed toward him. The patient may believe that he has not performed as he "should have", or that the clinician no longer wants to see him as a patient. The patient may then not only not follow through with the referral, but also may not return for follow-up visits with the clinician. The clinician should be aware of his own reactions to the patient's continuing problems and their potential effect on the patient.

The appropriate attitude for the clinician to maintain when making a referral is similar to that recommended for conducting health behavior counseling. Convey care and concern for the patient's well-being, and be open and honest about the patient's problems, their attempts to resolve them, and the reasons for the referral. Information should be provided directly, without evasiveness or reluctance.

The clinician should view the referral as a positive step for the patient, and be comfortable with the counseling that has occurred and with the recommendation that the patient now may benefit from seeing a therapist with specialized skills. Even though the patient has not achieved the desired behavior changes, valuable information has been obtained that does benefit the patient. The data collected will contribute to the eventual understanding of the patient's problem, forming the foundation for later assessments and interventions. This attitude would be the same one the clinician might have in referring the patient to any secondary care specialist for evaluation and treatment.

### Discussing Referral with the Patient

Patients often are more willing to accept a referral, or even suggest it themselves, if they have been properly prepared. This preparation begins with a thorough review of the patient's problem. The clinician should initiate this discussion with the patient by acknowledging the patient's continuing discomfort and suffering. The clinician should be certain to acknowledge that the patient's problem and accompanying feelings are real, and are not simply "in the patient's head." The clinician's expression of understanding at this time is important.

Next, the clinician should summarize his understanding of the patient's problem, indicating the most likely behavioral diagnosis. He should review each of the strategies used to resolve the patient's problems and comment on why they did not help. The understanding that was achieved by attempting these solutions should be emphasized, rather than their failure to solve the problem. This information will be the basis of subsequent evaluations and interventions.

Finally, the clinician should tell the patient that he would like to have a therapist assess his problem. It is important at this point for the clinician to describe the need for additional assessment in order to improve understanding of the problem. As emphasized throughout behavioral counseling, the clinician and the patient are working as collaborators to understand and resolve the problem. The referral should convey the same attitude. The emphasis is on getting an assessment of the problem by a professional who possesses specialized training and clinical experience with these types of problems. This approach appropriately leaves open the issue of subsequent treatment since the problem has not been fully understood.

At this point, the clinician might wish to explain why he is recommending a particular therapist. A brief description of the therapist, the types of patients he works with, and the agency for which he works is sometimes helpful. However, regardless of the therapist's qualifications, the clinician should resist the temptation to assure the patient that his problems can be solved by the therapist. This determination is best left to the therapist.

It is most important that the patient leave the clinic session with a clear understanding of why the referral was made and a positive attitude toward the therapist to whom he has been referred, as well as toward the clinician. The patient should be provided with the opportunity to ask questions about the referral and the therapist. The patient should understand that, regardless of what he decides to do, he should feel free to contact the clinician for information or advice.

If the patient is properly prepared, the referral should go smoothly. In fact, the patient who is having psychological problems is usually relieved to hear that he may find some relief. However, patients who are not having psychological problems but who are having difficulty achieving desired behavior changes may become angry or embarrassed with the suggestion that they seek counseling from a therapist. They may say, "I do not need to see a shrink," or "You think it's all in my head," or "I am not crazy." Usually this reaction results from either a misunderstanding of the role of the therapist or a fear of being labeled a "psychiatric" patient. Often these reactions can be managed by reviewing the patient's problem, indicating the need for an improved understanding of it, and discussing the specialized skills of the therapist.

Most patients do not understand the range of problems that are treated by therapists. Although it is true that most therapists treat patients with serious psychological disturbances, individuals who have problems arising from daily living also are treated. Medical patients desiring help with difficult health behavior changes are often treated by therapists, but not as psychiatric patients. Explaining that the therapist's expertise is in understanding human behavior, including that of people who are not psychiatric patients, can be very reassuring.

The patient's concern about being labeled a "psychiatric" patient is a legitimate one in many employment and legal situations. Subjective decisions by others about an individual's abilities can be colored by their misinterpretation of medical or psychological information. This concern is difficult to manage, because most therapists treat psychiatric patients and are affiliated with a psychiatric clinic or a department of psychology or psychiatry. The best way to handle this is to identify a therapist who is affiliated with a medical clinic or department and who treats medical patients with similar problems. In this way all communication with the patient comes from a medical clinic rather than a psychiatric department or clinic. If this is not possible, the clinician might ask the therapist if he would be willing to see the patient in the clinician's medical clinic. In any case, the patient should be reassured that the information shared with the therapist is confidential and cannot be released to anyone without the patient's written permission or a court order. This includes the verbal or written release of information to the patient's employer, family, or physician.

Some patients are apprehensive about seeking treatment from a therapist because they do not know what to expect. They may have erroneous views of therapy based on fictional portrayals on television or in movies. The clinician can help relieve the patient's uneasiness by describing what the patient might expect from the therapist.

Although there is a wide variety of approaches in therapy, all therapists encourage their patients to discuss their problems freely. The patient's relationship with the therapist will become very much like the one with the clinician: open, frank, and honest. The sessions with the therapist should result in an enhanced understanding of the problem and, it is hoped, a solution.

Once the patient accepts the suggestion to see a therapist, the clinician should encourage him to contact the therapist himself. Although it may be easier for the clinician to arrange the meeting, most therapists prefer to talk directly with the patient, for several reasons. If the patient makes the contact, the therapist knows that the patient has made an active decision to seek help from the therapist and is not passively agreeing to the clinician's suggestion. This first contact will allow the therapist to assess the patient's level of distress. If the distress is great, the therapist might be able to arrange for an initial visit sooner than usual. Personal contact with the therapist also helps to reduce some of the patient's initial anxiety.

## What to Communicate to the Therapist

As with any referral to a secondary care specialist, the therapist's understanding of the patient's problem will be substantially improved by the clinician's timely communication of accurate information about the patient. The clinician should not hesitate to discuss his observations and thoughts about the patient's problems. This will help the therapist decide what the next step should be.

The therapist likes to receive several types of information from the clinician, and it is very important to clearly identify it as either (1) statements made by the patient, (2) the clinician's observations of the patient's behavior in the counseling sessions, or (3) opinions of the clinician. The therapist needs to separate the patient's statements from the clinician's direct observations and the clinician's opinions in order to form an accurate view of the patient's problems.

The clinician should succinctly tell the therapist (1) the patient's problem, (2) the objective data collected in the patient's self-record, (3) the specific strategies attempted to solve the problem, and (4) the specific reason for the referral. As a general guideline, it is better to describe what occurred as simply as possible and avoid using specialized terms or jargon. Unless the clinician and the therapist share a common understanding of such terms, misunderstandings can result.

## Continuing Contact with the Therapist

If the physician will continue to provide medical care for the patient, he should discuss the desirability of maintaining frequent contact with him. The patient is best served if the physician is regularly informed of the patient's progress in the health behavior change programs. Likewise, the physician needs to be informed of the patient's response to specific medications and of any changes in his medical complaints. The therapist should know if the patient's medication is changed or if the patient's medical condition changes. The desirability of attempting behavioral modification if the patient's medical condition changes also may need to be reassessed.

## What the Therapist Will Do

The therapist will attempt to develop a comprehensive view of how the patient's psychological and behavioral functioning contributes to the patient's current difficulties. The extent of this evaluation depends on the severity of the problem and the degree of psychological dysfunction suspected.

Initially, the therapist may take a broad approach in assessing the patient. Because the patient has already received some specific counseling and the behavior problem was not resolved, the therapist must determine whether or not other psychological problems are present and, if so, to what degree they affect the problem. To do this the therapist may wish to conduct a complete psychological assessment of the patient's cognitive functioning, psychological status, social interactions, medical and developmental history, and current symptoms and problems.

The therapist may use information about the patient's personality, intelligence, aptitude, current emotional state, relationships with others, or psychological functioning derived from various psychological tests. These tests may provide new insight about the patient or confirm perceptions that the psychologist has developed in discussions with the patient.

The therapist will ask the patient to discuss the problem in detail. Hearing the patient's explanation may confirm the therapist's understanding of the problem as obtained from the clinician or it may add new information. In some cases, the therapist may wish to talk with the patient's spouse or family to verify the patient's beliefs or reveal opinions and information the patient is not aware of.

The therapist also is careful to review the patient's understanding of his problem, and his thoughts about the strategies already attempted. The therapist needs to know what the patient believes have been the most effective as well as the least effective approaches. The clinician should not be concerned that the therapist will try to prove that the clinician was "wrong" or "incompetent." To the contrary, this review usually affirms that the initial strategies were reasonable, given the information known at the time.

Once the therapist develops a behavioral diagnosis of the problem, he can use a variety of intervention strategies that are compatible with the behavioral counseling approach. Most are drawn from behavior therapy and require advanced training to use them appropriately. Some of the more commonly used skills training programs are briefly described below.

## Autogenic Training

Autogenic training is designed to help a patient reduce the general level of tension experienced throughout the day when he is not being confronted with a stressor. The patient learns to adopt a passive attitude of internal calm, using positive, relaxing images and thoughts. Autogenic training might be used to help a patient who smokes and feels tense throughout the day to reduce the overall level of tension and therefore his smoking. Autogenic training is used to help patients whose tension leads to undesirable behavior such as not following an appropriate diet, overeating, smoking, anger reactions, stress reactions, and pain responses.

## Aversive Training

Aversive training is designed to help a patient stop a current behavior by repeatedly following it with an unpleasant event, usually a mild electric shock or nausea. An example would be to administer a mild electric shock to a patient each time he reaches to take a puff on a cigarette. Aversive training is used to help patients stop smoking, stop eating certain foods, and avoid alcohol or drugs.

## Biofeedback Training

Biofeedback training provides the patient with information about moment-to-moment changes in a particular involuntary somatic response. The information is usually presented quantitatively so that the patient knows the degree and the direction of change (e.g., a tone that varies in pitch, a needle gauge that indicates an amount, a digital display). The patient uses the information to achieve and maintain control over the targeted response. Biofeedback can be used to help patients achieve deep muscle relaxation, reduce pain, lessen headaches, and reduce blood pressure. The types of monitoring used in biofeedback training are

*Electromyograph* (EMG)—monitors microvoltage across large muscles, which reflects the level of muscle contraction (i.e., tension); electrodes are usually placed on the muscles of the forearm or forehead.

*Electroencephalograph* (EEG)—monitors alpha or theta brain waves, which reflect a "meditative" mental state; electrodes are usually placed on the scalp.

*Galvanic skin responses* (GSR)—monitors the degree of skin resistance when a very slight electric current is directed through the electrodes; a higher level of resistance is associated with increased emotional arousal; electrodes commonly are placed on the palm of the hand.

*Heartbeat feedback*—monitors the patient's heart rate, which reflects the level of autonomic arousal; electrodes are placed on the patient's chest or a stethoscope is used.

*Skin temperature*—monitors the temperature of the patient's skin, which reflects the amount of blood flow to a region; electrodes are placed on the hands or feet.

## Cognitive Restructuring

Cognitive restructuring is used to help a patient who has maladaptive or dysfunctional beliefs. These beliefs are self-defeating because they do not contribute to a resolution of the problem, and they create feelings of sadness, anxiety, or depression in the patient. The therapist identifies these beliefs, discusses their negative effect, and then instructs the patient how to detect and change them. The training involves developing appropriate dialogues, modeling, role playing, self-evaluation, and practice in problem situations. It is used with patients who are experiencing stress reactions, depression, and anger.

## Imagery Training

Imagery training helps the patient to create a vivid, absorbing image of a particular scene. The training usually draws on the patient's own experiences and employs all five senses. Imagery training is used to develop images for deep muscle relaxation, systematic desensitization, cognitive restructuring, and other cognitive interventions.

*Stress Inoculation Training*

Stress inoculation training teaches the patient how to anticipate, prepare for, and cope with stressful situations. The training involves (1) educating the patient about stressors and stress reactions, (2) helping the patient develop and rehearse a variety of potential behavioral and cognitive coping actions, and (3) guiding the patient in applying these coping actions in actual stressful situations. Stress inoculation training has been used with patients with problems of stress, anger, and pain.

## Locating a Therapist for Referrals

More and more therapists are specializing in treating nonpsychiatric medical patients who have psychological or health behavior problems. However, because the total number of these therapists is still relatively small, an appropriate therapist may be difficult to locate. The clinician may have to contact several institutions and clinics to find one.

In general, most therapists in this specialty are affiliated with a medical school, hospital, or clinic. In some institutions, formal programs or departments have been developed that are clearly identified as specializing in behavioral medicine or health psychology. Most often, however, the therapist is associated with a traditional department of medicine, psychiatry, family medicine, or pediatrics. In psychiatry, the therapist will be affiliated with either the consultation-liaison or psychology services. The therapist will see patients either in a general medical outpatient clinic or in a special clinic designated for the treatment of the psychological problems of medical patients (e.g., "Behavioral Medicine Clinic," "Pain Clinic," "Biofeedback Clinic"). Interns in psychology and residents in psychiatry often treat patients in these clinics at a reduced fee.

Another good source of therapists with specialized training in this area is a university or college. Programs in behavioral medicine have been developed in both psychology departments and counseling psychology departments. Faculty members frequently treat patients in a psychology clinic, counseling clinic, or privately. In addition, doctoral students specializing in behavioral medicine may be available to treat patients at a reduced fee.

Ideally, the clinician should identify an appropriate therapist before he needs to make a referral. The clinician should first contact the therapist by telephone and describe the types of patients that he might refer. If the therapist is interested in treating these patients, the clinician should ask about the type of therapy he provides. Some therapists treat only certain types of medical patients (e.g., those with diabetes, neurological problems, cancer, or cardiovascular disease) or specialize in particular treatments (e.g., biofeedback, hypnosis). The clinician should also determine how the referral should be made, and whether or not the therapist is willing to see the patient at the clinician's office.

It is also appropriate at this time to determine whether the therapist is willing to work closely with the clinician and/or with the patient's physician in the therapy. The clinician should express his expectations about this collaboration before the patient is referred. Most therapists are very willing to discuss these issues and to reach a mutually satisfactory arrangement.

Most importantly, the clinician should determine from this conversation if he will be comfortable referring patients to the therapist. The clinician should understand the therapist's basic therapeutic orientation, and how together they would integrate the patient's treatment for medical and health-behavior behavior problems. With this type of planned collaboration between clinicians in medicine and psychology, the patient with persistent health behavior change problems can be treated effectively.

# Appendix

### DAILY MEDICATION RECORD

Name _____

Date of clinic visit _____ Day: _____

Prescription:

   Medication: _____ Amount: _____

   Time dose is taken: Dose #1 _____ am / pm   Dose #2 _____ am / pm

                   Dose #3 _____ am / pm   Dose #4 _____ am / pm

| Date | Day | Time | Dose #1 | Time | Dose #2 | Time | Dose #3 | Time | Dose #4 |
|------|-----|------|---------|------|---------|------|---------|------|---------|
| — | — | — | O | — | O | — | O | — | O |
| — | — | — | O | — | O | — | O | — | O |
| — | — | — | O | — | O | — | O | — | O |
| — | — | — | O | — | O | — | O | — | O |
| — | — | — | O | — | O | — | O | — | O |
| — | — | — | O | — | O | — | O | — | O |
| — | — | — | O | — | O | — | O | — | O |

Comments:

## DAILY FOOD RECORD

Today's Date _____

| Time<br>Location<br>Other | Food | Amount |
| --- | --- | --- |
| | | |

## WEEKLY RECORD OF PHYSICAL ACTIVITY

| Date | Time | Activity | Duration | Distance | Pulse | Comments |
|------|------|----------|----------|----------|-------|----------|

# PERSONAL CONTRACT

Activity: _____

Level of Performance: _____

_____

_____

Consequences

If I follow the routine for _____ as outlined above, then I will provide myself with the small reward of:

_____

As further encouragement to follow the routine, if I do not do so, then I promise to:

_____

_____
Signature

_____
Date

# DAILY STRESS RECORD

Today's Date _____

| Time | Location | People | Feelings | Thoughts | Results |
|------|----------|--------|----------|----------|---------|

# DAILY SMOKING LOG

Day: _____

| U/C* | Time | Location | Importance rating (0–10) | Reason** |
|------|------|----------|--------------------------|----------|
| ____ | ____ | _____ | _____ | _____ |
| ____ | ____ | _____ | _____ | _____ |
| ____ | ____ | _____ | _____ | _____ |
| ____ | ____ | _____ | _____ | _____ |
| ____ | ____ | _____ | _____ | _____ |
| ____ | ____ | _____ | _____ | _____ |
| ____ | ____ | _____ | _____ | _____ |
| ____ | ____ | _____ | _____ | _____ |
| ____ | ____ | _____ | _____ | _____ |
| ____ | ____ | _____ | _____ | _____ |
| ____ | ____ | _____ | _____ | _____ |
| ____ | ____ | _____ | _____ | _____ |
| ____ | ____ | _____ | _____ | _____ |
| ____ | ____ | _____ | _____ | _____ |
| ____ | ____ | _____ | _____ | _____ |
| ____ | ____ | _____ | _____ | _____ |
| ____ | ____ | _____ | _____ | _____ |
| ____ | ____ | _____ | _____ | _____ |

*U = Urge
C = Cigarette

**Reasons:
1 = To handle something
2 = Physical craving
3 = To accentuate pleasure
4 = To reduce tension
5 = As a habit
6 = As stimulation
7 = Other (describe)

# Index